FACING
HUMAN
SUFFERING

WITHDRAWN

FACING

HUMAN

SUFFERING

PSYCHOLOGY AND
PSYCHOTHERAPY
AS MORAL
ENGAGEMENT

RONALD B. MILLER

AMERICAN PSYCHOLOGICAL ASSOCIATION
Washington, DC

Published by
American Psychological Association
750 First Street, NE
Washington, DC 20002
www.apa.org

To order
APA Order Department
P.O. Box 92984
Washington, DC 20090-2984
Tel: (800) 374-2721; Direct: (202) 336-5510
Fax: (202) 336-5502; TDD/TTY: (202) 336-6123
Online: www.apa.org/books/
E-mail: order@apa.org

In the U.K., Europe, Africa, and the Middle East, copies may be ordered from
American Psychological Association
3 Henrietta Street
Covent Garden, London
WC2E 8LU England

Typeset in Goudy by Page Grafx, Inc., St. Simons Island, GA

Printer: United Book Press, Inc., Baltimore, MD
Cover Designer: Naylor Design, Washington, DC
Technical/Production Editor: Rosemary Moulton

The opinions and statements published are the responsibility of the authors, and such opinions and statements do not necessarily represent the policies of the American Psychological Association.

Library of Congress Cataloging-in-Publication Data
Miller, Ronald B., 1948–
    Facing human suffering: psychology and psychotherapy as moral engagement /
    Ronald B. Miller.
        p. cm.
    Includes bibliographical references and index.
    ISBN 1-59147-109-5 (alk. paper)
        1. Psychotherapy—Philosophy. 2. Psychotherapy—Moral and ethical aspects.
    3. Suffering—Moral and ethical aspects. 4. Ethics. 5. Psychology—Moral and ethical
    aspects. I. Title.

RC437.5.M55 2004
616.89′14′01—dc22

                                                                    2004000156

British Library Cataloguing-in-Publication Data
A CIP record is available from the British Library.

Printed in the United States of America
First Edition

For Albert H. and Ruth S. Miller

CONTENTS

PREFACE

For three decades, my professional work as a clinical psychologist has revolved around four kinds of activities: the practice of clinical psychology, particularly psychotherapy; teaching in the psychology department of a liberal arts college (Saint Michael's College); directing a two-year master's degree program in clinical psychology (also at Saint Michael's); and writing about the philosophical problems of clinical psychology. In many ways, my work on the last task (philosophy) was a direct response to the tensions that were produced by actively pursuing the first three. When I first joined the psychology department at Saint Michael's College, it was a four-person department, and as with all departments of that size, everyone taught the introductory psychology course, as well as at least one other course outside their own specialty. So after seven years of being a full-time clinical practitioner, I had the unique experience of continuing to practice part time while teaching undergraduates introductory and developmental psychology, as well as more clinical courses such as personality theories, abnormal psychology, and theories of psychotherapy.

Most clinical psychologists view the scientist–practitioner schism in the field as one focused on the graduate training of professional psychologists, or perhaps on the kind of clinical practice ultimately engaged in by professionals. Although this is of course an accurate perception, it is also an incomplete one. As a result of my own career path, I have reluctantly come to the view that this schism permeates psychology from the first day that a student takes the typical Introduction to Psychology course and continues right on through the standard undergraduate psychology curriculum. The reason this is so little noticed is that practitioners like myself who have an appreciation of the power and depth of clinical knowledge, and who are therefore in a position to appreciate the one-sided view of psychology that is generally presented to undergraduates interested in psychology, rarely become full-time undergraduate faculty. The fact that, despite student objections, scientific psychology is presented to undergraduates as the unchallenged knowledge base of clinical psychology, although not entirely unknown to clinical practitioners, seems to fall well beyond the horizon of most clinicians. They probably recognize from their own career path that the study of undergraduate (and, unfortunately, sometimes even graduate) scientific psychology was a hurdle to clear rather than the foundation of their clinical understanding, but they are so relieved to have this period of their education behind them that they would rather not think about its implications.

This is a book about the dissociation between what students want to learn from studying psychology (practical–personal help with life's problems), what scientific psychologists claim they are teaching (psychology as a science and scientifically derived applied clinical psychology), and what is really being taught in most academic psychology departments (scientific psychology and a demoralizing *pseudoscientific* clinical knowledge). This dissociation leaves a path of intellectual malaise and dissatisfaction in its wake, from disillusioned students and ill-prepared graduate students entering their first internships to faculty "experts" who find their intellectual process of knowing more and more about less and less increasingly empty and depressing. All of these individuals are suffering in psychology at least in part because psychology has lost sight of suffering itself, and with it the moral ground from which the discipline emerged in the mid-19th century. We have forgotten that our primary raison d'être, going back to the time of the ancient Greek philosophers Socrates, Plato, and Aristotle, is to try to alleviate the emotional pain and suffering of human existence. I would submit that our ultimate purpose, whether we like it or not, is to help people find a way to come to terms with personal suffering and make a life for themselves that they can regard as worth living. It is a difficult but honorable vocation and one we can be proud of doing.

In these times when scientific thought is venerated, if not worshipped, it would appear anachronistic to claim that psychology, or at least clinical psychology, is more the practice of *phronesis* (practical wisdom) than science. Perhaps worse is that such a claim would seem absurdly impolitic, if not just uninformed or wrongheaded. Yet this is exactly the task I have set for myself, demonstrating both in my teaching and in this book that clinical psychology is largely about being morally engaged with the personal suffering of other human beings, who themselves have suffered in the absence of certain kinds of moral relationships in their own lives. Clinical knowledge is the moral knowledge that is evolving within our culture concerning the moral dilemmas of human relationships and survival in the postmodern world. This is not, some will be surprised to learn, an entirely novel assertion. In fact, a number of authors have reached the similar conclusion that all the health care professions, not just clinical psychology, are built on practical wisdom.

Most critiques of contemporary scientific approaches to clinical psychology are built on the European philosophical traditions of phenomenology and hermeneutics. These have much to offer, but the approach I take here is to mine the riches of common sense and the unanalyzed notion of *knowing people well* in everyday life that is taken for granted by both logical positivist and hermeneutic approaches to science. In this way, my approach resembles more that of the philosopher Stephen Toulmin than it does the Europeans Husserl or Heidegger. This has the distinct advantage of being closer to the everyday experience of students coming into the field and to clinical or professional psychologists who may be dissatisfied with the contemporary split between scientists and practitioners but who are unfamiliar with European philosophy.

I approach the moral engagement of clinical psychology in this book by examining four topics: the concept of suffering, the analysis of the concept of knowing people well in everyday life, the nature of clinical knowledge, and the narrative clinical case study as a vehicle uniquely suited for the scholarly communication of morally engaged clinical knowledge. However, this is not the order of topics that I researched for this book. I began with the conviction that the concept of clinical knowledge was insufficiently understood and appreciated in academic clinical (and general) psychology. As I attempted to explicate the meaning of clinical knowledge, it began to become clear to me that "good clinical work" was, in part, about "doing good," not as a slang expression for performing a task well but in the sense of making at least one corner of the world a better place and helping clients to have a chance of participating in the "Good Life." Here my background in moral and political philosophy became very pertinent, as I had studied Aristotle's concept of *phronesis* many years earlier and had rediscovered it as a framework for understanding clinical work. As often happens in such situations, I discovered in the literature and at various American Psychological Association (APA) meetings that several other psychologists and philosophers were at about the same time beginning to see the relevance of practical wisdom to the knowledge of clinical practice.

My study of clinical knowledge also brought me to the subject of narrative case studies, for it was there that I turned for one source of examples of what I considered true knowledge that had profoundly improved my own ability to practice psychotherapy. As I compared these case studies with scientific studies on similar topics (e.g., the treatment of depression, borderline conditions, or schizophrenia), it became clear to me that the case study not only used a different epistemology (manner of establishing true knowledge) but also often conveyed a subtle but profoundly important different moral perspective on the clinical situation. Because the case study was written in narrative form, it used the language of the culture to describe the problems being addressed, often in the client's own words. True theoretical and technical jargon could also permeate a case study, but in the descriptive sections of presenting problems, life history, family background, and so on, one often saw terms such as *betrayal, cheating, lying, broken vows, abandonment,* and *abusiveness,* which conveyed not only emotional pain but also moral transgressions. In reading cases, it became clear that in addition to there being an implicit or explicit moral dimension to the problems that bring clients to seek help, the clinicians' interventions have such a dimension as well. Readers of a case would note not only the clinical theory or technique but also the kindness, compassion, disinterest, or even rejection in the therapist's style or language. Cases stripped of this moral language and perspective would appear dull, lifeless, mechanical, and, more important, lacking in clinical import. They did not communicate how to be a better clinician. Thus I became convinced that the devaluation of case study research in the period of 1960 to 2000 in academic clinical psychology (and related mental health professions) was part and parcel of the demoralization of the discipline and that any attempt to understand the moral dimension of clinical practice would have to include an effort to rehabilitate the case study method of scholarly communication and research in psychology.

This volume also marks the first publication of information concerning the establishment of the Saint Michael's College Clinical Case Study Collection at Durrick Library and includes the bibliographic citations for over 350 published case studies and 125 casebooks that have been screened for inclusion. This will be, I hope, a first step in realizing Bromley's (1986) vision of a case law tradition in clinical psychology.

For me personally, this book documents a 10-year journey of trying to understand the concept of clinical knowledge and its relationship to moral and scientific knowledge. It was a journey interrupted, but fortuitously so, by the opportunity to act as the consulting and associate editor for the history and philosophy of psychology in the eight-volume *Encyclopedia of Psychology,* published by APA and Oxford University Press, under the direction of Alan Kazdin (2000). I had the opportunity to read, review, and in many instances discuss with over 30 of the leading historians and philosophers of psychology in the English-speaking world the articles they had written as contributors to this area of the encyclopedia.

This journey also has led me into correspondence and conversation with a number of distinguished psychologists and philosophers, many of whom pioneered the study of the topics discussed in these pages. Extensive and very helpful correspondence concerning clinical knowledge with Paul Meehl, and somewhat less extensive but still very helpful communications with David Bakan, Barbara Held, Murray Levine, Donald Peterson, Stephen Toulmin, Thomas Szasz, and the late Norman Care were all a great benefit to me, although I know each of them would take issue with some or even many of the conclusions I have reached. Ongoing conversations on the relationship of philosophy to clinical psychology, and more specifically moral to clinical knowledge, with two other major contributors to our field, Joseph F.

Rychlak and Alvin Mahrer, have over the years been a source of great personal and intellectual encouragement for which I am deeply appreciative.

On the subject of case studies in psychology, conversations and correspondence with the panelists on the 1999 APA invited symposium "Case Study Standards and the Knowledge Base of Professional Psychology" were intellectually invigorating and supportive. I extend my thanks to Lisa Hoshmand; Dan Fishman; Donald Spence; David Edwards, who traveled from South Africa; and D. B. Bromley, who came from England; the discussion was further enriched by the exchanges and comments we shared on each other's papers, including mine (R. B. Miller, 1999). Many of these discussions carried forward long after the symposium. Ultimately, Dan Fishman and I coauthored a joint proposal (Fishman & Miller, 1999) for the creation of a case study journal and on-line database that may yet reach fruition. Dan has generously shared with me his enormous command of the research process—both quantitative and qualitative. He has consented to my publishing as portions of chapter 6 those sections of the journal proposal that I authored. Additional portions of chapter 6 are drawn from R. B. Miller (1999). Portions of chapter 3 appeared in "Scientific vs. Clinical-Based Knowledge in Psychology: A Concealed Moral Conflict," published in the *American Journal of Psychotherapy* (R. B. Miller, 2001), and portions of chapter 5 appeared in "Epistemology and Psychotherapy Data: The Unspeakable, Unbearable, Horrible Truth," published in *Clinical Psychology: Science and Practice* (R. B. Miller, 1998).

Saint Michael's College supported this publication in a number of critical ways. In addition to the opportunities cited above in teaching and graduate administration, I am appreciative of a sabbatical leave in 1992 that produced much of chapter 5, and another in 1999 that resulted in solid portions of chapters 3 and 6. Through a Faculty Development Grant in 2000, the college made possible the purchase of the copyright clearances on the first 300 cases of the clinical case study archive. College librarians Mark McAteer, Robert Bouchard-Hall, and Kathy Godlewski were extremely helpful in the design and cataloguing of the collection.

As director of the graduate program in clinical psychology for over 18 years, I have had the opportunity to test my ideas about the role of clinical knowledge, moral engagement, and the case study in the process of training clinical psychologists, particularly in the crucible of the graduate Theories of Psychotherapy seminar and on case study thesis committees. Students in my undergraduate senior seminars on the Clinical Case Study Method helped me digest, apply, and critique Bromley's (1986) seminal work. Students in my senior seminar, Systems of Psychotherapy, provided detailed feedback on the first three chapters of this book.

A number of graduate students participated in the development of the case study collection by searching for, reading, and rating the quality of narrative cases. These include, in chronological order, Tanya Rexford, Vivianna

Gentile, Michele Goodman, Leila McVeigh, Andrea O'Neil, Mark Vail, Jason Fechter, Michael Hendery, Lisa Toburen, and J. P. Hayden. They all figured critically in one portion or another of the project and were particularly generous of their time and enthusiasm for the project. Caterina Eppolito began as a graduate student in our program interested in narrative aspects of play therapy and came back as an instructor for our case study thesis seminar and coordinator for the continuing development of the case study collection. She supervised the case study culling process with many of the graduate students listed previously.

Tara Arcury, the administrative assistant to the graduate program in clinical psychology, brought her considerable organizational skills, enthusiastic support, and critical reader's eye to our department at a crucial time in the preparation of this book. She not only kept the graduate program running on a daily basis without a hitch, permitting me more time to concentrate on completing this task, but she also helped in innumerable ways prepare the final manuscript for publication.

Four professionals in the field remain to be recognized for their contribution to this project. First and foremost, I acknowledge the contribution of my partner in work and life, Naomi P. Shapiro, whose inspired and dedicated work as a psychotherapist specializing in play therapy, school consultation, and child advocacy has always amazed and impressed me. Her work has served as an inspiring exemplar and model of what it means to do good by doing clinical work and to possess clinical knowledge, and I have shamelessly plagiarized from her experience as a clinician to write this book. Naomi has always been the first person I turn to for feedback on my writing, and she enthusiastically reviewed the first draft of every chapter in this book. Her love, humor, insight, magical imagination, and patience have sustained me as we have both worked to make a life together with our wonderful children, Ari and Maya. They are the lights of our lives and have generously demonstrated their love and support during the periods when I was immersed in this writing project.

Second, I am indebted to my colleague and friend of 18 years in the psychology department, Jeffrey Adams, who despite his excellent training as an empirically oriented social psychologist has always been interested in discussing the nature of psychology and the moral and epistemological issues of our field. Our conversations on the nature of psychology and its moral dimension have gone on for so many iterations over the years that at times it is impossible to say which ideas are whose. We usually start our discussions of clinical knowledge or cognitive illusions at opposite ends of the spectrum but end up somewhere close to agreement. Many of the arguments put forward in this volume were hammered out in discussions with Jeff, and while, of course, all failings remain my responsibility, it must be said that at least some of the successes are due to his careful logical analysis. Perhaps more important has been the hope that this dialogue with him has given me the belief that the schism between scientists and practitioners can indeed be bridged in a climate of open-mindedness, mutual respect, and persistence.

Two other psychologists whom I have encountered over the years have also served as exemplars of the meaning of clinical knowledge. The first is Bertram Karon, whom I first knew through his writings and later through his visits to Saint Michael's with his wife, Mary, during which he taught summer classes and offered workshops for our graduate students over a period of 15 years. For me, his psychotherapeutic work with patients thought by others to be "untreatable schizophrenics" epitomizes clinical knowledge that is both bold and innovative and yet presented in a manner that invites consensual validation by a community of learners. One of Bert's students, the late C. Sam Dietzel, was my first clinical supervisor, mentor, and a good friend who taught psychotherapy to several generations of students at both the University of Vermont counseling center and the Saint Michael's College graduate program in clinical psychology. Sam was in every fiber of his being a brilliant clinician committed to doing good in the world by doing good clinical work.

This is my second book and third major publishing project with APA Books. Hearing from colleagues and friends countless stories over the years of capricious editors and assassin reviewers, and having had in other settings similar experiences myself, I have braced myself each time I have undertaken one of these projects for the ultimate intrusion of harsh reality. Surely the sound advice, fair treatment, and enthusiasm that I have come to expect from the editorial staff at APA Books would sooner or later prove to be an illusion. But alas, it never has. It is real, and people like Gary VandenBos, Julia Frank-McNeil, and Judy Nemes make APA Books a rare oasis of sanity for the psychologist or academic facing the corporate world of publishing. I am also indebted to the two anonymous reviewers who read the book in its entirety and offered very focused and useful suggestions, and to Stephen Behnke of the APA Ethics Office, who raised a number of interesting questions on the section of chapter 6 concerning the ethics of publishing case studies. I particularly want to thank Mary Lynn Skutley, who has consistently been an advocate for this book despite the controversial character of its message and the delays in its completion.

My parents, Albert H. and Ruth S. Miller, to whom this book is dedicated, have been generous in their encouragement and support of the career path that has led me to this project. As members of a generation that lived in the shadow of the Great Depression, World War II, and the Holocaust, philosophical treatises can seem a luxury of life. In many ways, of course they are, and I am indebted to the hard work and perseverance that my parents have demonstrated throughout their lives for the opportunity to indulge in this luxury. As I examine the bedrock assumptions that I bring to this work, I see in bold relief the life experience and religious values they imparted to their children and grandchildren.

FACING
HUMAN
SUFFERING

1

AMERICAN PSYCHOLOGICAL
DISSOCIATION

Students and others who become interested in the study of psychology typically do so because of personal concerns or problems in their life. They are confused or troubled by some aspect of their own inner experience or behavior or that of someone close to them. They arrive at the doorstep of psychology brimming with questions about the meaning of their dreams, the influence of the mind on illness, why someone would kill him- or herself, how to be less depressed, how to stop a loved one from abusing drugs or alcohol, or how to recover from having been the victim of child physical or sexual abuse, and so forth. These are the same sort of concerns that, with an added sense of urgency, bring clients to clinical psychologists and other mental health providers. In either case, psychology is viewed by almost everyone outside of academia as a therapeutic, pragmatic, problem-solving profession and discipline. Today's aspiring psychologists share this pragmatic bent with the first person to be appointed professor of psychology in the United States, William James (1892/1983a), who wrote the following:

> We live surrounded by an enormous body of persons who are most definitely interested in the control of states of mind, and incessantly craving for a sort of psychological science which will teach them to *act*. What

every educator, every jail-warden, every doctor, every clergyman, every asylum-superintendent asks of psychology is practical rules. (p. 272)

James (1899/1962) expressed the same sentiment a little more broadly a few years later:

> I wish in the following hour to take certain psychological doctrines and show their practical applications to mental hygiene—to the hygiene of our American life more particularly. Our people, especially in academic circles, are turning towards psychology nowadays with great expectations; and if psychology is to justify them, it must be by showing fruits in the pedagogic and therapeutic lines. (p. 238)

Although these questions may have brought students to the literature or classroom of academic psychology, they might equally as well have been brought to the doorstep of a number of other academic, professional, or intellectual traditions, many of which were nonexistent in James's day. Within academe they might turn to courses in the undergraduate departments of sociology, anthropology, human development, nursing, social work, education (counseling), nutrition, and perhaps even philosophy or religion. At the graduate level, in addition to courses offered at a higher level in these same departments, specialized courses in departments of psychiatry, mental health, and alcohol and drug or rehabilitation counseling would also be an option. Outside of the academy participation in or study of a spiritual or religious healing or meditative tradition, a new age, or pop/self-help psychology, astrology, psychic healing and spiritualism, or even consultation with a personal trainer, might all be avenues explored in search of answers. Much as we, as academic psychologists, and many of our colleagues in these other fields would like to believe that our own specialized approach is unique and recognizably distinct from all the others, to the uninitiated this is just not the case. As Sarason, Levine, Goldenberg, Cherline, and Bennett (1966) aptly noted, the field of mental health is permeated by a kind of professional preciousness wherein each discipline believes that it is the only one really helping patients or clients and that, even worse, the others are probably harming them. This could certainly be easily extended to the non-mental health professions, disciplines, or traditions mentioned above. There is a competitiveness for the "hearts and minds" of those seeking comfort for their suffering that suggests that, despite our claims of preciousness, we know we are all attempting to serve a similar function, albeit in very different ways. The manner in which people seeking answers move easily back and forth across these various alternatives, and frequently find it difficult to distinguish psychiatrist from psychologist, psychotherapist from counselor or pastor, social worker from family therapist, and self-help from academic psychology, also suggests that our claims of difference are not all that persuasive.

Psychologists do not know very much about how people decide how to label or tag their experience of distress or decide that their life has become problematic and requires assistance from a specific type of helper. It seems reasonable to join with the social constructionists on this point and to assert that social processes (Gergen, 1985, 1991) must play an important role in this self-definitional act. One's culture or subculture defines for one a picture of how life ought to be, what optimal and less than optimal functioning is, and what should be done if one is not up to par. The questions and problems of life brought by the eager student to psychology unfortunately do not come presorted with only one tag on each problem telling what sort of problem it is and where to go to find solutions and answers. It is more likely that one begins with only a generic sense that something is not right. People recognize that they are feeling, thinking, or acting in ways that are painful or confused and that something needs to change. In other words, individuals know that they are suffering, that something very unpleasant or even destructive is happening in their lives, but do not necessarily know exactly what that something is, or what a productive solution would look like.

In a pluralistic society, part of our task is to choose a way to conceptualize and understand what is happening to us, so that we can begin to find answers. This preliminary stage in one's understanding—where one decides that one has a problem and *what the problem is*—turns out to be absolutely pivotal in determining what sort of help one will find. For different disciplines, traditions, and professions interpret the "presenting problems" that people bring to them in vastly different ways, and this may result in vastly different kinds of help being offered (some of which may not even feel like help to those seeking it). Does the problem as conceptualized dictate a major upheaval in one's life or just a bit of tinkering with some of the finer points? The literature or tradition to which an individual turns for help amidst the confusing array of possibilities, of which academic psychology is one and professional psychology a related but distinct other, would appear to be influenced by a number of factors. The observations of choices made, or suggestions given, by family or significant others, cultural mores and expectations communicated by word of mouth or the media, recommendations of trusted professionals in related professions (e.g., educators, family doctors and nurses, hairdressers), and input from acquaintances who are known to have had similar problems are probably all important. In this pluralistic society, these various sources of information about how to think about one's difficulties, and what to do about them, are likely to be somewhat inconsistent or even contradictory, although in different ways for different individuals.

Help, to be accepted, must be offered within the frame of reference or worldview of the individual seeking that help. If in fact that worldview itself figures in the configuration of the problem, as it most often does, then there is a fundamental paradox inherent in this process of human problem solving in the realm of personal life problems. If one does not question at least some of the basic assumptions and perceptions that an individual in trouble holds dear, one cannot be of much help to that individual. Yet, if one questions those assumptions and perceptions, one risks becoming incomprehensible, and therefore useless, to the very person one is seeking to aid.

How does academic psychology fare when it encounters the presuppositions of a discipline? Judging by the popularity of the introductory psychology course on college campuses (usually the most heavily enrolled introductory course in the liberal arts), and the number of students majoring in psychology (often one of the top three or four majors at most colleges and universities), one would think that all is well. Data on the meteoric increase since World War II (WWII) in the number of graduate students studying psychology, and the number of licensed doctoral practitioners in psychology, suggest a similar optimistic assessment. The numbers point to an undeniable success both within the academy and in the world of professional practice. Furthermore, because the path to professional practice passes through the academy, one would think that the success is a single unified story of the rise of "psychology" in the 20th century. The conceptual and theoretical parameters of such a unified psychology have been sought and debated by many luminaries in the field. One thing on which all can agree is that such unification is still far from having been achieved. Yet the myth of such a unified discipline–profession is a powerful weapon in securing a place at the table for those engaged in that disciplinary self-definition when it comes to institutional supports for research, teaching, or practice opportunities. One of the central propositions of this book is the belief that the price paid by students, practitioners, clients—and, in many cases, even academic faculty—in maintaining this myth of a unified psychology has been too great, and we are better served now by an open airing of the differences (differences that I ultimately argue are essentially moral or value differences) that sometimes bitterly divide us. At present, these critical and important differences are often swept under the rug, out of public view, to be settled by professional and academic disputations and politics.

If, rather than looking at psychology's "commercial" success in academia and in the health care marketplace, one examines the match or fit between the conceptual framework that academic psychology offers its student initiates or interested readers and the conceptual framework and presuppositions that these students and readers bring to psychology, one finds a kind of disconnection. One encounters within mainstream higher education psychology departments an almost universal mantra, that psychology is a science and that it solves problems by putting potential solutions to the test with scientific research methods. For a variety of reasons that I explore later (see chap. 4, this volume), the academic discipline of psychology in the English-speaking world has since the 1920s held dear a set of scientific presuppositions about the nature of psychological problems and solutions. Psychology (founded as a discipline only in the late 1880s) was to become an extension of the physical sciences of biology and chemistry, with mathematical formulations of psychological processes, laboratory experimentation as the preferred mode of research, and all concepts tied directly to overt behavioral phenomena. Central to this view was the belief that psychology must sever its historical roots in speculative theology and philosophy that provided deductive proofs of psychological principles that could not be challenged by their actual pragmatic consequences on people's lives. A scientific approach to theoretical questions would be matched by a technological approach to the practical problems of living. We would model ourselves after physiology as a basic science, and medicine as a profession. Given the astounding success of technology and medicine in reshaping life in the 20th century, this seemed like a good and safe bet. If science could allow humankind to overcome the force of gravity and fly around the earth, then certainly it could allow people to overcome the forces within themselves that trouble or confuse.

In their recent biologically oriented introductory psychology textbook, Gazzaniga and Heatherton (2003) initiated the student to the concept of psychology as a science in the following manner:

> In 1843, John Stuart Mill published System of Logic, in which he declared that psychology should leave the realm of speculation and philosophy and become a science of observation and experiment. Indeed, he defined psychology as the "science of the elementary laws of the mind" and argued that only through the methods of science would the processes of the mind be understood. (p. 18)

Similarly, Myers (1998) wrote in his popular introductory psychology textbook:

> As a science psychology aims to sift opinions and evaluate ideas with careful observation and rigorous analysis. In its quest to describe and explain nature (human nature included), psychological science welcomes hunches and plausible sounding theories. And it puts them to the test. If a theory works—if the data support its predictions—so much the better for it. If the predictions fail, the theory gets rejected or revised. (p. 4)

For many students and readers, however, who approach psychology with only partially articulated questions, and only a partially articulated idea of what sort of answers might work, this exclusively scientific framework often comes as a great shock. Often, such students have been brought to the study of psychology not only by their personal difficulties but also by use of their own personal learning in overcoming or helping someone dear to them overcome a particular problem or trauma. They may believe they have a knack or talent for being helpful to others because people are always thanking them for having been such good listeners. They are wondering whether their experience is unique or can be generalized to helping others. In addition, they may have a prior familiarity with some aspect of pop psychology and related literature in the spiritual counseling realm. This pop or self-help psychology they have been reading may well have been intriguing or helpful to them. Further, they assume that the word *psychology* has a relatively constant meaning in our culture and that consequently a course titled "Introduction to Psychology" will connect nicely to their favorite self-help book. They do not realize that in the popular culture, and even to some extent in the professional world, the *field* of psychology is much broader than the academic discipline will allow, if by *field* one means a topical area or subject area of interest, and by *discipline* what is typically taught in mainstream undergraduate departments. (In some cases, academic psychology taught in education, human development, psychiatry, social work, counseling, rehabilitation, and art and recreation therapies courses may fall closer to the popular conception than the psychology department's own attempts at self-definition.)

At the same time, the new student arrives at the introductory course having lived in a culture imbued with the importance of science, scientific research, and the benefits of technology that is seen as a direct outgrowth of the scientific method. Science has a prestige and scientists an élan that is hard to beat. Especially as this scientific approach is linked to modern medicine as a healing art that has benefited from becoming imbued with the scientific method, and the prospects of better and more effective pharmaceutical drugs for everything from male impotence to cancer treatments, our students arrive at the first psychology course prepared to endorse the wisdom of a scientific approach, even if they themselves have little interest in becoming scientists themselves.

In essence, many, if not most, new students encounter academic psychology having already come to believe as common sense at least two somewhat contradictory propositions: (a) Psychology can be helpful in furthering their ability to cope with the personal problems that are a part of the texture of everyday life and about which they already have some familiary and perhaps not a little understanding, and (b) there is a science of psychology about which they know little or nothing but which they will have to learn to really know the best, the most powerful and effective, ways of solving these problems. At first, most students do not see that these two propositions are contradictory; in fact, the discipline itself systematically fosters the belief that its scientific conceptual framework is or will ultimately be a superior instrument for solving the personal difficulties of life than the everyday commonsense understanding of these problems that people bring with them from their life experiences. In other words, the discipline presumes that one can, or will ultimately be able to, move back and forth between the scientific and the everyday conceptual framework without a loss of information, meaning, or impact. Consequently, the instruction from scientific psychology to the novitiate to discard all of one's commonsense prescientific understanding of psychological problems, unless that understanding has been independently validated by scientific research, is offered with the implicit promise that doing so will produce better answers to the original problems that brought the student to psychology. What students gradually come to realize, or at least react to with boredom or anger in their courses, is that academic psychology cannot deliver on this promise. Instead, in classic entrepreneurial style, academic psychology has engaged in a kind of "bait and switch" shell game, by redefining the agonizing interpersonal problems of living that the student brings to psychology into simple matters of deficient performance, productivity, efficiency, satisfaction, and other culturally endorsed goals or "goods" and then offering solutions to these redefined problems.

This process of problem redefinition is a very subtle one that can be seen more clearly by contrasting academic and popular psychology. These eager learners are received in very different ways in academic versus popular psychology. In popular psychology they are met by a vast array of self-help books, some quite intellectually substantial and well conceived (and of course some not) that suggest possible answers to these questions or solutions to problems. However, in academic psychology the novice is met with a very different kind of literature, with a very different message. The reader is required to forgo learning (what are disparaged as) "quick and easy" answers to these complex real-life problems and take the more arduous but ultimately (one is assured) more rewarding path of studying the science of psychology. Pop psychology's ready answers are disparaged as superficial and faddish, merely representing the opinions and biases of its authors. It is pointed out that the advice given the reader in such books frequently conflicts, and that although some of these ideas may be good ones, others are potentially harmful, and one has no way to separate the wheat from the chaff. It is suggested that the only way to find answers that are really solid, "objective," or "valid" is by following the scientific method. Unfortunately, the reader is warned, reading science is more difficult than reading pop psychology. Science progresses by methodical, incremental, logical steps. One has to start with very basic, general, and abstract principles and gradually build toward an understanding of practical everyday problems. It is argued (with a very one-sided version of the history of science and technology) that the sciences of physics, chemistry, and biology each evolved over several hundred years before they were able to give birth to technologies that could make a substantial contribution to solving everyday problems. Psychology students must be patient and support the development of psychological science, even if their own lives are not substantially improved. They are making a noble sacrifice for humanity and civilizations of the future! Anything less would be shortsighted, childish, and irrational, standing in the way of humanity's progress.

Even students who express a desire to go into applied areas of clinical and counseling psychology are given the same message, but with a surprising twist. Their scientist–professors tell these students that this study of scientific psychology is also an absolutely necessary preparation for learning to be a professional counselor or therapist. So it seems that scientific psychology will have the answers to life's problems not in several hundred years, but in the several years between a particular undergraduate student's choosing a major and that student's matriculation into graduate training to become a counselor or therapist. The truth is that it is necessary to have scientific training in psychology to be accepted into most mainstream graduate programs in clinical or professional psychology. However, the necessity is one created by academicians committed to the scientific model, not a necessity of the logic of clinical knowledge. Learning the skills of a counselor or therapist is dependent on a knowledge of scientific psychology only in the sense that scientific knowledge is one of several kinds of knowledge that provide a background for developing clinical skills and knowledge. Other components include a knowledge of the local community and culture in which one's clients work and live; self-knowledge; everyday knowledge of human beings and individual differences; knowing how to develop rapport, build trust, and confront difficult issues with another person; moral principles; and a sense of the historical forces at play during the client's lifetime.

Academic psychology is highly ambivalent about its relationship to counseling, psychodiagnosis, psychotherapy, and consulting. On the one hand, academicians thrive on the high enrollments in their courses that students' interest in these topics brings, and on the other hand, they are not really interested in these problems, preferring more abstract scientific questions about general laws of behavior or explanatory principles. The compromise they look for is one in which scientific principles are presented and then their potential application to real-life problems is suggested. Most textbooks for general, developmental, and abnormal psychology are now written in this manner. Experimentally derived applications may not really solve problems in a manner that can be systematically applied in the culture, but that is not really necessary, for they suffice to suggest that gradual progress is being made toward the ultimate goal of a technology of human behavior. Often, nonexperimentally derived clinical or consulting concepts or methods (such as listening skills, group dynamics, support groups, attachment processes, and interpretation of defense mechanisms) are misrepresented as derived from the findings of experimental research to bolster the appearance that experimental psychology has *discovered practical knowledge*.

This tension between practical and scientific psychology that begins with the student of pop psychology being shocked and dismayed by large portions of the content of the Introduction to Psychology course continues unabated through the typical student's disappointment with the experimental emphasis in the psychology major. Neither does it end with college graduation, for students wishing to pursue graduate study in clinical areas of psychology are confronted by the dominance of the Boulder model of scientist–practitioner training at most of the major universities in the United States and Canada (Belar & Perry, 1992). This becomes more than just an intellectual dissatisfaction as one experiences near panic entering the first practicum or internship experience with at least a dim awareness of how poorly academic psychology coursework has prepared one for the actual work of helping people with the sorts of problems one had originally declared a psychology major to learn how to solve.

Since the appearance of the professional schools of psychology granting the PsyD degree in the 1970s and 1980s, this is less true than it was when the Boulder model of professional training in psychology reigned supreme (Bourg, Bent, McHolland, & Stricker, 1989). Yet, there are still over 100 Boulder model programs training clinical psychologists, and the undergraduate psychology major has remained largely unchanged since WWII. This sense of disconnection between the psychology department curriculum and knowing how to assist clinical populations remains unfortunately pertinent even to the graduates of Boulder model training programs who pursue careers as practitioners rather than as teacher–researchers. (It should be noted that most graduates of Boulder model programs, because of the necessities of the psychology job market, are employed after receiving their doctorates in applied practice settings.)

THE HISTORY OF CLINICAL AND ACADEMIC DISSOCIATION

Institutions, because of their historical development, often contain such internal conflict and discontinuities, and academic clinical psychology is no exception. History helps to explain what logic alone cannot comprehend. Under the exigencies of WWII, thousands of psychologists were drafted into caregiving roles, despite their scientific interests. Some of them liked this change and the status it brought them as "junior psychiatrists" in the medical corps. They discovered, too, that the therapeutic relationship, which was clearly a psychological or psychosocial process, not a medical one per se, could be helpful even in serious cases of combat psychosis and that the work was exciting and challenging. The Veterans Administration (VA) needed immediate help with the returning psychiatric casualties and wanted to ensure a supply of psychologists for its hospitals. Given the success of academic or research psychologists in adapting to this new role, it seemed logical to offer psychology departments funds for training a new generation of psychologists for clinical work (Herman, 1995). Despite the basic antipathy felt within academia for such applied nonscientific work, the funding was too appealing for most universities to pass up. Although one would never ask the fox to raise the orphaned chicks in the henhouse, that is pretty much what the VA did when it asked the research community to train the next generation of clinical psychologists.

The American Psychological Association (APA) entered into the fray by undertaking to specify what this new graduate training should look like (Committee on Training in Clinical Psychology, 1948). The Boulder Conference and subsequent report (Raimy, 1950) set the standard for graduate education in clinical psychology that prevailed for 25 years and still has a strong hold on the most prestigious psychology departments in the United States. Making a virtue of necessity, it argues that research training is the best preparation for professional practice, because all good problem solving is a form of scientific thinking, and clinical methods are in need of much improvement. Any responsible practitioner ought to be constantly looking for opportunities to advance the field's knowledge in service of its patients. Actual clinical training would take place in hospitals and clinics outside of the university. The model's shaky rationale would be saved by the fact that experienced clinicians in the clinical settings would do the actual clinical training, and students would learn on the job, just as their predecessors had done in the military. The universities would get funds and students for their basic science courses in psychology—and, more important, research and teaching assistants to further their primary interest of research productivity. In this arranged marriage of clinical training to research departments the extended families of the betrothed (university graduate schools and the VA) benefited greatly; the actual partners (faculty, supervisors, students) were somewhat less fortunate.

To survive in such a crazy system one had to dissociate. Initially, there was little attempt to integrate the two experiences. Doctoral dissertations focused on purely experimental topics of learning, memory, perception, and so forth. Over time, this ostensibly improved as clinical students chose clinical research topics. The learning, memory, or perceptions of mental patients, counseling clients, personality types, and so forth, were studied, and then eventually etiology, diagnosis, and the treatment of various disorders itself became the focus of research. However, because of the prior commitment of the profession of psychology to rigorous scientific methodology, internal validity (design of the study) always took precedence over external validity (applicability to the real clinical world of practice).

Students found themselves studying research on schizophrenia thought processes, family background variables, or treatment outcomes, yet without any sense of how to be helpful to such a person. One could know the research cold and be still unprepared for even the briefest useful interaction with such a person. Conversely, one could develop a skillful approach to such clients, and be highly effective in talking and working with them, and still have not a clue how to predict the outcomes of the research studies. One just could not integrate the clinical and academic experience. One had to be one person at the clinic and another in the classroom and laboratory.

Worse yet was the obvious disdain that one's academic and clinical supervisors had generally for one another. The researchers saw the clinicians as modern-day witch doctors or shaman, using suggestion and prestige factors to manipulate client attitudes. The clinicians saw the researchers as ivory tower academicians unable to get their hands dirty in the real world and studying problems so cut off from the clinical reality faced daily by their brethren as to be nearly useless. Each thought the other to be doing more harm than good. The burden of this conflicted and dissociative experience ultimately produced strong cries of protest from PhD practitioners who, once free of their departments, were able to articulate what had been so difficult in their training experience (Peterson, 1985). Out of this frustration emerged the professional school movement a generation later, but not before tens of thousands of psychologists had been trained under the Boulder model.

This number is insignificant, however, compared with the millions of undergraduate psychology students who have been diverted from studying and experiencing a psychology literature or learning process that might address their deeply held desire to better understand themselves and others close to them. Worse yet, they are told no such literature exists in psychology, and they are instead instilled with a disdain for anything unscientific while learning a science that is largely devoid of useful information, though feigning that it is. By promoting a scientific approach to problems that are practical, contextual, highly complex, and multidimensional (social, psychological, moral, political, historical, spiritual, biological, cultural, economic, etc.) psychology has done incalculable harm by promoting pseudoscientific solutions to complex human problems. Students leave psychology further mystified and further away from understanding themselves better. Even worse for the success of the discipline and profession of psychology is that students leave the discipline prematurely, taking their interest in practical psychological problems to other departments, disciplines, or outside of the academy entirely and into the popular culture. Critical as the profession is of pop psychology, the New Age self-help literature, and other "unscientific" or "superficial" approaches to psychological phenomena, one would think that we would be doing all we could to keep the students who come so eagerly to psychology within our house. Most of these students abandon the discipline without ever having been exposed to the considerable serious, critical, scholarly literature that has emerged out of the world of clinical practice and other qualitative, narrative, or philosophical traditions within psychology. These alternative scholarly traditions have been marginalized by the dominant ideology of empiricism and biological determinism and reductionism within academic psychology. A student might leave the major after three or four courses, or even complete a psychology major at most colleges and universities today, without studying or even knowing about the existence of contemporary active programs of psychological investigation in areas such as phenomenological–existential psychology, psychoanalysis, humanistic psychology, qualitative research methods, case study methods, and nonmedical approaches to severe mental disorder.

Psychology textbooks typically present the student in general, abnormal, developmental, personality, counseling or psychotherapy, and clinical psychology with an array of different models or schools of thought. After noting that before the late 19th century, problems that are now considered psychological were understood as evidence of moral or spiritual conflict (e.g., possession by evil spirits, the devil, or moral weakness of the will leading to sin), the biological, psychodynamic, humanistic, cognitive–behavioral, and family systems theories are presented as alternative conceptual systems for viewing psychology and interpersonal problems. This gives the appearance of an open, even-handed, and inclusive approach to what everyone knows is a complex and mysterious subject: the nature and problems of the human mind, behavior, and relationships. However, the chapter on theories is soon followed by a chapter on the scientific method that is maintained as the best and most unbiased method of discerning the truth in psychology. Once this is accomplished, only those portions of the theories previously presented that are accessible to, and have been the object of, systematic scientific investigation are carried forward and applied throughout the text, leaving mostly biological and cognitive–behavioral theoretical frameworks as the focus of the remaining 90% of the textbook. Because the scientific worldview is so dominant in our culture, this is accomplished usually without raising any question or concern in the reader's mind.

Comer's (1998) abnormal psychology textbook is representative of scores of others in this regard. He argued that we need scientific research in abnormal and clinical psychology because theories and treatments developed out of clinical practice have often been rejected by subsequent generations of practitioners:

> These errors underscore the importance of sound research in abnormal psychology. Theories and treatment procedures that seem reasonable and effective in individual instances may prove disastrous when they are applied to large numbers of people or situations. Only by testing a theory or technique on representative groups of subjects can its accuracy or utility be determined. . . . Clinical researchers subject the ideas of clinical theorists and the techniques of clinical practitioners to systematic testing. *Research is the key to accuracy and progress in all fields of study and it is particularly important in abnormal psychology, because inaccurate beliefs can cause enormous suffering* [italics added]. (p. 30)

Any questioning of the scientific method as the preferred procedure for psychological investigations results in the accusation that one is inviting mysticism, irrationalism, or dogma into the discussion. In most academic quarters in psychology today, questioning the scientific method signals the death knell to a scholarly discussion. As I discuss later in this volume, there are many other forms of serious intellectual investigation of subject matter that do not fit the mold of the scientific method as portrayed in psychology, and these have been used by philosophers, psychologists, psychotherapists, and feminists since the birth of psychology in the late 1800s. Rejecting the scientific method as the only acceptable means for resolving competing truth claims in psychology need not result in any of the afore mentioned debacles—mysticism, irrationalism, or dogmatism—but it will result in one being systematically ignored and marginalized in psychology's textbooks. In fact, the blind faith in the scientific method as the primary means of investigating the *practical personal problems of living* is itself a form of dogmatic belief bordering on the irrational and mystical.

The irrationality that results from hewing to the mantra of the virtue of scientific methodology in clinical psychology is well illustrated by an example from Comer's (1998) abnormal psychology textbook. Having decried the suffering caused by the use of unscientific clinical techniques, Comer cited the psychosurgical technique of lobotomy as a case in point. One could not agree more that this is a clinical technique that should never have been used. It is the most barbaric in a litany of grotesque psychiatric interventions that have been presented to the public as having been scientifically researched and developed (R. Whitaker, 2002). Yet Comer failed to note that lobotomy, when first introduced in the 1930s, was considered supported by the best medical science of its day. Its originator, Moritz, was awarded the Nobel Prize in medicine, to this day the only "discovery" in clinical psychology or psychiatry to "warrant" that honor. In fact, as Comer presented a scientific approach to schizophrenia and other disorders in his textbook, he systematically deemphasized the extent to which subsequent generations of scientific researchers in psychiatry and clinical psychology discredit the scientific findings of the previous generation, in much the same manner in which he observed clinicians do. Of course, in so doing, Comer is reflecting the scientific ethos of the discipline, demonstrating the "best practices" of academic psychology.

CONFRONTING CLINICAL REALITY

When one finally leaves the classroom as a psychology graduate student and begins working in a practicum or internship as a psychologist in training one enters what I like to call *clinical reality*. In the clinical realm, the practical problems that brought the student to psychology are, at long last, at center stage, and the difficulty of relying on general, abstract theories or principles of learning, memory, perception, or neuroscience in responding to the demands of the clinical situation is apparent. Applying the research from personality, social, developmental, and abnormal psychology is only slightly less problematic. Which principles should be applied to this situation, right here, right now, in front of me? Should all the relevant empirical literature be considered, or is there some way to determine which laws of behavior are most likely to be useful? Perhaps I should skip directly to empirically derived treatment protocols and apply the relevant one. But my depressed client, who seems to fit the protocol, is also an American Indian, active in the civil rights movement for Native Americans. Does that change the applicability of the protocol, considering none of the research participants had that sort of family background? Should I not, as a scientist–practitioner, test the treatment on a similar patient population before "experimenting" on my client? The problems are endless, as one would expect when an inappropriate model is being used.

This clinical reality is often fraught with conflict and uncertainty for the student who must face the full range and intensity of human misery and suffering that may be well beyond her or his personal life experience. These problems in living are distinguished from the many run-of-the-mill daily problems by the intense emotions that are accompanying them. Many are personal and practical problems that involve life-and-death consequences: love and hate, jealousy and envy, betrayal and disappointment, attachment and loss, abandonment and death, family disintegration, sexual longings and infidelity, rage and despair, fear and trembling, and pain and suffering of all kinds.

Lucky is the student not thrown into a personal if not professional identity conflict. Do I really *know how* to be of help to these people? Do I *want* to help *these* people and be exposed to this side of human existence? How do I deal with all the other mental health, health care, human service, and perhaps even educational professionals who are asserting their authority over, or offering help to, my clients? What will my supervisor, colleagues, and teachers think of me and what I am doing with these clients? Will I ever make it in this profession and be successful? Can I survive in a field in which there are so many demands for my services and so little resources supporting me in delivering them?

In these questions, the suffering of the psychologist in training merges with the suffering of the clients. How much can I do for their suffering before I begin to suffer beyond my own tolerance? This merging of the subject and object of study (my suffering, their suffering, our suffering) takes us back to the new student's concerns that brought him or her to psychology initially. Mainstream academic and clinical psychology's response to this crisis of confidence is always the same: Learn scientific psychology, practice scientifically, and do scientific (research) to build more scientific knowledge for the future.

Practitioners often respond differently, suggesting that psychologists must understand and come to terms with their own human struggles and personal problems to understand and help their clients. They must understand and appreciate both their own and their clients' humanity. This humanity must be faced and accepted to move and change. Human beings have used their intellectual, social, emotional, and spiritual resources to do this for thousands of years, long before the advent of modern science, and they can continue to do so in the present without being tied to the scientific method.

And so the great scientist versus practitioner divide in professional psychology continues today unabated (Trierweiler & Stricker, 1998), as does the division more generally between pop psychology and academic psychology over the meaning of the term *psychology*. The unending, and largely unenlightening, discussions of this problem from the two camps are more reminiscent of warring religious sects than a true intellectual disagreement or debate. Theoretical and professional preciousness abound, and self-serving rationalizations have come to replace careful argument and reasoning (R. B. Miller, 1982). Yet the discipline prospers and grows. It is successful despite, or maybe because of, this dissociation that allows it to both effectively address the human problems of living and claim simultaneously that it is a rigorous scientific discipline like physics, chemistry, or biology.

THE MORAL DIMENSION OF CLINICAL REALITY

One might choose to simply observe these processes as further evidence of the absurdity of self-important intellectuals and academics and their students were it not for one critical feature of the picture: the welfare of the unsuspecting consumer of psychological services. These individuals, experiencing intense human suffering, responding to our assertions of competence to offer them help, show up at our doorsteps, and we incur an obligation to them. This obligation is rarely discussed, and it may variously be interpreted, but I assert that it ought to be an obligation to do everything humanly possible to see to it that their suffering is addressed and their lives made more tolerable. Although this may mean referring them elsewhere for help, it never means doing less than one might to help while they are in our personal care. For me this has always meant to define the practice of psychology broadly to include the mental health literature outside of psychology (e.g., psychiatry, psychoanalysis, psychotherapy, and social work), and literature outside of the formal mental health literature entirely, for example, philosophy, theology, and anthropology. It means looking for answers that have been proffered for situations that have not been extensively researched scientifically and carefully critiquing established scientific conclusions and research by testing such findings in my own work. Pragmatic, carefully thought out trial-and-error problem solving (Schon, 1987) with strategies that carry less risk than doing nothing and allowing the status quo to prevail is a further responsibility, regardless of whether empirically validated protocols exist for a problem. The interests of the individual client or family take precedence over the profession's self-important claims to scientific purity.

Although there was no stronger advocate for a scientific psychology, with its pragmatic implications, than William James, he understood the difference between general laws of behavior and practical application. In his famous talks to teachers, James (1892/1983b) commented on the pragmatic impact of a science of psychology on the practice of teaching. Many readers will be surprised given his claims on behalf of psychology as a natural science:

> I say moreover that you make a great, a very great mistake, if you think that psychology, being the science of the mind's laws, is something from which you can deduce definite programmes and schemes and methods of instruction for immediate school room use. Psychology is a science, and teaching is an art; *and sciences never generate arts directly out of themselves. An intermediary inventive mind must make the application, by using its originality* [italics added]. . . . A science only lays down lines within which the rules of the art must fall, laws which the follower of the art must not transgress; but what particular thing he shall positively do within those lines is left exclusively to his own genius. One genius will do his work well and succeed in one way, whilst another succeeds as well quite differently; yet neither will transgress the lines. (pp. 14–16)

The report authored by APA's Committee on Training in Clinical Psychology (1948), titled "Recommended Graduate Training Program in Clinical Psychology," served as APA's contribution to the development of the initial Boulder model of scientist–practitioner training. It strongly urged undergraduate preparation in the humanities in addition to the sciences as necessary for future clinical psychologists. Furthermore, the report listed 15 personal attributes that were essential in the "right sort of person to become a psychology trainee." Of these, 8 were clearly moral criteria: (a) regard for the integrity of others, (b) tolerance, (c) ability to develop warm relationships, (d) responsibility, (e) cooperativeness and tactfulness, (f) personal integrity and self-control, (g) discriminating sense of values, and (h) breadth of cultural background—"an educated man." The other attributes identify aspects of intellectual functioning. The report seems to reflect James's awareness that although a scientific psychology was needed to counter the abstract metaphysical philosophy of mind of the late 19th century, there was also a limit to what one can expect the sciences to do in preparing psychologists to be practitioners.

The addition of moral character traits to the list of prerequisites for admission into a doctoral program in clinical psychology seems odd today. One would expect today that if anything were to be added to the usual psychology course prerequisites, it would be courses in neuroscience and psychopharmacology, not moral character. What could the committee members' rationale possibly have been? These moral characteristics are necessary in practitioners because the practical problems of life that are brought to psychologists are moral problems—problems of what to do, how to act, how to treat others, or how one is being treated by others. The questions that are brought for answers to the psychologist's or psychotherapist's consultation room have to do with the difficult choices and decisions of life and the emotional concomitants and sequelae of those decisions: Should I stay in or leave this family, job, relationship, country, and so forth? How do I balance commitments and interests between work and family, family and friends, religious values and material success, and so forth? Should I take risks and pursue my dreams or play it safe and be secure? Someone has injured me, and I want to retaliate; is that acceptable? Is life worth the pain of living, or should I just give up and pack it in? How do I stop feeling guilty about every little mistake I make or feel less ashamed of my family or my ethnic roots? Each person has to find a way to make a life for him- or herself within the framework of the conditions into which one is born. Moral and ethical dilemmas are the core of that struggle and of the clinical problems psychologists study and in which they intervene.

Moral and ethical dilemmas are not just internal struggles but interpersonal ones as well. Family therapists and school and employee assistance consultants know all too well the scenario in which the person referred because of his or her emotional fragility (anxiety, depression, irritability) may only be "the identified patient" and that other, often more powerful members of the social system (e.g., parents, teachers, employers) are behaving in ways that are in the very least insensitive, or at the worst, traumatizing or even victimizing, the identified patient. The morality play enters a new act in which the psychologist or mental health consultant must consider the risk of confronting these more powerful members of the system about their part in the problem or whether to simply treat the individual referred for his or her "disorder." Of course, the feminist writers (e.g., Caplan, 1995; Chesler, 1972) were among the first to identify this kind of moral choice being made by physicians and therapists in the treatment of women depressed by their second-class citizenship in their marriage or society as a whole. They correctly pointed out the iatrogenic damage done when those who are supposed to be helping only add further to the client's difficulties by labeling their feelings as disordered rather than addressing the environmental and social conditions to which those strong emotions are simply just a human response.

For thousands of years prior to the late 1800s, these moral struggles gave rise to philosophical and religious responses. People looked to their teachers, gurus, and pastors for guidance and understanding. What counted as wisdom in a given tradition was the response to such problems and questions. Even today, when students and clients bring these issues to psychotherapists they typically use the language of ethics and morality to describe their problems (Margolis, 1966). They speak of guilt, shame, agonizing choices, injury and harm done to them by the treachery or insensitivity of others, impulses they are struggling to control, and so forth. They are experiencing moral confusion, injury, and pain, and to offer assistance without addressing those moral issues qua moral issues is to not address the client's concerns. No matter what mental health practitioners do or say, they have entered the moral sphere.

There is another sense in which the practice of psychology and psychotherapy is a moral enterprise. The obligation to, as James (1892/1983b) said, use one's genius, creativity, and powers of reason on behalf of one's students or clients to teach or reveal something to them is essentially a moral obligation. It is moral because it requires a concern for the other and not just oneself. Psychotherapy or mental health services are supposed to be for the psychological benefit of the client. The professional's gratification is to be limited to, as the Freudians first proposed, remuneration and a sense of satisfaction in a job well done. To choose this path over self-indulgence or self-interest in the therapeutic interaction is not always simple or straightforward, for it requires self-awareness and honesty in the psychotherapist and an ability to perceive moral dilemmas and choices. Such perceptiveness is not common in the discipline, and training in it is largely limited to a discussion of the APA Ethics Code (American Psychological Association, 2002) that only scratches the surface of the moral issues in psychotherapy and mental health work. The moral direction of one's clients' lives, and the moral direction of the therapy one practices and researches, is the great unspoken psychological conflict of our time.

The Claim of a Value-Free Science and Practice

The assertion of moral obligations as central to the practice of psychology runs afoul of one of the few propositions in the field on which both scientists and practitioners tend to agree: It is taken as an article of faith that both science and practice must be kept free of moral value judgments. It is a *shibboleth* of both mainstream science and clinical knowledge-based practice that psychological diagnosis and treatment methods are technical and not ethical procedures. Principles of practice, therapeutic techniques, and scientific findings are seen as neither explicitly nor implicitly moral in content but rather available to be used for good or ill by practitioners of any moral persuasion. The moral views and judgments of the scientists and practitioners are seen to have no part in the formulation of the theory and research or in their application to clinical work. Being judgmental is seen as a sophomoric mistake of beginning counselors and therapists. The prohibition against judgmentalism is one of the few generally agreed-on clinical maxims across the many theoretical perspectives on psychotherapy. It is a cardinal tenet of traditional natural science that scientific claims are neutral as to their moral implications and that any scientific truth can be used for good or evil and thus in itself is neither.

Ironic as it may be, it is this one area of agreement (on the moral neutrality of their work) that is the major obstacle preventing a meaningful or constructive dialogue from emerging across the scientist–practitioner divide. This claim to moral neutrality is based on a misunderstanding of the nature of moral and ethical principles. I argue here that both scientific research and clinical practice are, in essential and fundamental ways, expressions of moral and ethical principles and positions. Furthermore, science-based and clinical knowledge-based practices are based on fundamentally competing implicit moral principles. These denied moral conflicts appear in our discourse wrapped in the more accepted mantel of theoretical or empirical disputes. Yet, because moral arguments cannot be reduced to entirely empirical or theoretical questions about how human beings do in fact behave or act, but also involve questions as to how human beings ought to behave or act, such discussions are fruitless and leave all parties frustrated and doubting the other's rationality.

It is not the goal of this book to turn the clock back to the time when psychological problems were understood only as moral problems or when "treatment" consisted of moral lectures, preaching on the wages of sin, and the threat of communal ostracism. My goal, however, is to encourage a re-examination of the meaning of moral conflict for theories of clinical practice, whether such theories are based on scientific research or clinical knowledge. If psychological principles of practice are, as I believe, inherently and inevitably a form of moral principles, this will not require psychologists to be heavy-handed and morally judgmental or shaming of those who are suffering. Moral discussion and engagement must not be confused with the imposition of an arbitrary morality by representatives of authoritarian institutions. One might even consider modern psychotherapy as a societal attempt, although a concealed one, to develop a new method for dealing with intractable moral problems that were not handled by the existing institutions (e.g., family, church, schools) that had responsibility for moral education and problem solving. In fact, an explicitly moral approach to psychological problems of the kind I describe below would hold out the hope for an even more humane and respectful approach to human suffering than is possible in the current demoralized U.S. mental health system.

One might think that the existence of professional codes of ethics, like that of APA, indicates acceptance by the profession of the importance of moral principles in psychology. However, professional ethics are held to provide an ethical or moral framework for the practice of whatever scientific or clinical theory is endorsed by the practitioner. These ethical principles are seen as external to the psychological principles themselves and are not seen as offering alternative diagnostic or therapeutic conceptualizations or techniques. Paradoxically, because the ethical principles of the profession are not seen as derived from psychological principles or scholarship, their justification is found in the deliberative processes, committee work, policy debates and, ultimately, votes by the membership the professional organizations that sponsor the codes (e.g., APA). Of course, the personal ethics of the members of these organizations will affect the participation in such discussions and voting, and this is taken as an acceptable place for the intrusion of personal ethics into professional practice. In large organizations such as APA, which has more than 100,000 members and affiliates, it is obvious that deliberations over and determinations of ethical judgments and principles will also be affected by the politics of the organization and its bureaucracy, as well it should. The point is simply that this is a very different methodology than that used within the discipline for settling questions considered about the substance or subject matter of psychology itself. One does not leave to the committee work and deliberations of the professional organizations the decision as to whether, for example, depression is a function of learned helplessness or whether schizophrenia is related to cerebral atrophy.

Although professional ethics only scratch the surface of the ethical aspects of psychology, they do serve the purpose of logically opening the door to the discussion of how ethics and moral judgments play a part in professional practice, for if psychologists' personal and collective ethical beliefs have some impact on how they are to practice (e.g., no dual relationships, confidentiality, work for the welfare of the client), then it is not inconceivable that other clinical rules may have an unacknowledged ethical component as well. Some clinical maxims that are likely candidates as carrying implicit moral principles include the following: listen empathically, be genuine, show positive regard, encourage free associations, reinforce appropriate behavior, maintain therapeutic abstinence, remove irrational ideas, reduce family enmeshment, or medicate hyperactive children.

The Meaning of Moral and Ethical

I use the terms *moral* and *ethical* interchangeably, as is customary in philosophy. The basic feature of being moral or ethical is a concern with how one ought to live—how does one define and create the "good life?" The moral sphere is concerned with differentiating the ultimate meaning of right and wrong, good and evil, rights and responsibilities, and freedom and oppression. Rachels (1993) noted that although there is in moral philosophy no universal agreement on the nature of morality, most would agree that the minimum conception of morality is that "morality is, at the very least, to guide one's conduct by reason—that is, to do what there are the best reasons for doing—while giving equal weight to the interests of each individual who will be affected by one's conduct" (p. 13).

Moral discourse is therefore about moral principles or decisions and the reasons for them. Although the exact nature of moral or ethical reasoning remains highly problematic and controversial in moral philosophy, Aristotle's view of ethics as practical wisdom is increasingly seen as relevant to a contemporary understanding of morality. The logician Hilary Putnam (1978) wrote the following:

> I think that Aristotle was profoundly right in holding that ethics is concerned with how to live and with human happiness, and also profoundly right in holding that this sort of *knowledge* ("practical knowledge") is different from theoretical knowledge. A view of knowledge that acknowledges that the sphere of knowledge is wider than the sphere of science

seems to me a cultural necessity if we are to arrive at a sane and human view of ourselves *or* of science. (p. 5)

Critical to Aristotle's view is the distinction between scientific or theoretical knowledge and ethical knowledge, which he calls *phronesis*: "practical wisdom." Practical wisdom requires that one not simply know that it would be good to do something but that one actually do something good in a specific situation. Practical knowledge also requires that one know how to perceive or recognize the particular features of a real-world, real-time problem in such a manner as to permit action to be taken. In other words, one can see that there is a moral problem, and one can see what needs to be done to address it. In the absence of this moral knowledge there can be a kind of "moral blindness" to the events confronting one (Nussbaum, 1990).

Practical wisdom is very different from holding a theoretical view, or believing a moral principle, as to what the essential features of a generic kind of problem are, or what should be done to solve it. One might hold such a view and still not recognize or know how to solve the problem if one were to find oneself faced with it in one's daily life. Aristotle further recognized that practical wisdom cannot be held to as high a standard of certitude as theoretical or scientific knowledge. It must always be provisional and revisable because of the uniqueness and individuality of the problems, as compared with the general and abstract propositions of theory and science.

The Moral Sphere and Suffering

Martha Nussbaum (1994), in her role as classicist–philosopher, reminded us that philosophy was not created as a sterile, abstract, intellectual exercise but as an active, forceful attempt to cope with the *suffering of life*. The ancient Greeks struggled with the following sorts of questions: Is there relief from the pain and suffering of life? What must a person do to find peace and happiness? Is there a spiritual realm that offers us respite from the demands of the material existence of our bodies, and how can we know for sure the answers to our questions and not be misled by false gods and beliefs?

As these intellectual struggles yielded satisfying answers, various philosophers set up their own "schools" to instruct others in their philosophy of life. These schools often functioned as therapeutic communities in which students not only engaged in philosophical reflection but also adopted an entire lifestyle or way of living that differentiated oneself from the rest of the local community. Philosophy was a commitment to a way of life, to different patterns of behaviors and relationships. Instruction in these communities also varied from traditional classlike settings with lectures and or dialogue, to experiential learning exercises where one developed insight into oneself and the community:

The Hellenistic philosophical schools in Greece and Rome—Epicureans, Skeptics, and Stoics—all conceived of philosophy as a way of addressing the most painful problems of human life. They saw the philosopher as a compassionate physician whose arts could heal may pervasive types of human suffering. They practiced philosophy not as a detached intellectual technique dedicated to the display of cleverness but as an immersed and worldly art of grappling with human misery. (Nussbaum, 1994, p. 3)

Nussbaum's (1994) assertion of the centrality of ethics in philosophy is echoed in continental philosophy in the work of Levinas (1989). Writing in the phenomenological–existential tradition of Husserl and Heidegger, Levinas has suggested that the primary encounter that we have as humans is not between Being and non-Being but between our own Being and the Being of the "Other." Recognizing the existence of other beings, we are drawn immediately into the sense of responsibility or caring for the Other—the ethical and moral dimension of living.

Moral concern expressed abstractly in philosophical–theological explorations of the nature of the "good life" is not, as a set of goals we strive for, about finding out what is the case but rather what ought to be the case. It is concerned with reducing human suffering and maximizing human well-being or flourishing. The definition of *moral concern* offered here is a far cry from the use of the term in contemporary culture, where moral issues are thought to be restricted to religious prohibitions or injunctions against "sex, drugs, and rock 'n' roll." The term *moral* is associated with people in authority telling younger or less powerful individuals how to live and threatening damnation if they are not listened to. In reaction against this kind of moral authoritarianism, U.S. popular culture has become extremely relativistic on moral matters. It is presumed that morality is personal and private and that each person has to decide what is moral for her- or himself. No one is entitled to sit in judgment on the morality of another person's actions. Moral views are seen as a matter of taste, personal bias, or feelings. Even carefully worded inquiries asking for a reasonable justification of a moral position frequently trigger an angry reply or stony silence. As one might expect with something so personal and private, morality is little discussed, perhaps as unspoken in our day as sexuality was in Freud's. It is disturbing to note that the view of morality within the mental health professions seems more closely aligned with popular culture than with moral philosophy.

By reducing moral views to simple biases and prejudices, scientific psychology is able to easily dismiss the relevance of moral issues to psychological investigation. After all, the point of science is to eliminate superstitious and prejudicial beliefs and biases and replace them with objective scientific truth. In this way, the scientific worldview in psychology both dissociates itself from moral issues as not relevant to a theoretical account of natural phenomena (the way the world is) and at the same time (either implicitly or explicitly) asserts that it can replace moral theory because such theory is part of the biased, prejudicial view of the world that science is here to eradicate.

Although some have found the distinction overdrawn, the noted Cambridge philosopher G. E. Moore's (1903) famous description of the "naturalistic fallacy" seems to the point here. An account of the world as it is can never be a complete argument for an account of the world as it ought to be. One cannot logically derive an "ought" from an "is." To argue that human beings ought to behave a certain way (e.g., should nurture their children and not beat them, should be faithful to their spouses and not lie to them, should choose work that it is meaningful and not only materially rewarding) always requires a statement of a moral principle in addition to a naturalistic description of behavioral patterns. In the above examples, the terms *nurture*, *faithful*, and *meaningful* have both descriptive and moral evaluative content. All three ultimately depend for their meaning on *valuing* the making and keeping of commitments to other people or ourselves.

This distinction between descriptive and evaluative propositions, although abstract and philosophical, is of central importance to understanding the dissociation in American psychology between scientific and practical knowledge. To the extent that a proposition in psychology is truly an empirical one, it is devoid of moral content and cannot by itself dictate anything about practice. To the extent that supposedly scientific propositions claim to, in themselves, speak to practical issues, such propositions are pseudoscientific and already have had evaluative moral content implicitly embedded in their concepts and premises. Scientific claims about clinical practice are therefore either logically incomplete (lacking an explicit moral principle) or are pseudoscientific moral claims masquerading as objective scientific fact. In chapter 3, I explore the manner in which moral claims are embedded in theories of psychotherapy.

DEFINING *SUFFERING*

As one explores the intersection of moral and clinical issues, the concept of suffering is a recurrent, yet unanalyzed, theme. As Nussbaum (1994) eloquently noted, the point of moral philosophy was to reduce human suffering. Psychology evolved as a discipline out of philosophy, and although psychology as a discipline eschewed making moral claims in any overt sense, it also took as one of its central tasks the application of psychology to human problems that can only be described as various forms of human suffering (e.g. melancholia, panic states, substance abuse, or posttraumatic stress disorder). Yet suffering as a construct or concept does not exist in clinical or abnormal psychology. I could find only one serious discussion of suffering proper in the psychological literature: a book by the philosophical psychologist–psychoanalyst David Bakan (1968), *Disease, Pain and Suffering: Toward a Psychology of Suffering*. Szasz (1957/1988) and Mahrer (1978) have developed psychological analyses of the related concept of "pain" that will also prove helpful in developing the concept of suffering. The substance of Bakan's contribution is taken up later, but for now the important point is that with the exception of a later volume by Bakan on child abuse and infanticide (Bakan, 1971), the psychology of suffering toward which he was aiming has not emerged. This is particularly striking considering that if one were to ask most clinical psychologists and students of clinical or abnormal psychology what the point is of studying psychology, they would probably say something about wanting to be able help others who are suffering to lead happier lives. Yet, if one looks in the mainstream textbooks of abnormal and clinical psychology (or psychiatry for that matter) of the last 25 years, terms such as *suffering, anguish, sorrow, misery*, and even *emotional pain* hardly ever appear. In their place has arisen the vocabulary of illnesses and disorders enshrined in the *Diagnostic and Statistical Manual of Mental Disorders* of the American Psychiatric Association (*DSM–IV*; 1994) and adopted by the fields of abnormal and clinical psychology (although not without dissent). As emotional pain and suffering, and the agonizing moral choices, personal betrayals, and injuries that occasion them, are redefined as disorders of the person produced by the brain, psyche, or environment, the meaning of human suffering is fundamentally altered, and the act of altering it is almost magically concealed. This medicalization of such a universal and fundamental aspect of human experience, and the creation of a mental health industry as the new culturally authorized stewards of these illnesses, might well be one of the most profound changes in human consciousness wrought in the 20th century.

The psychiatrist and medical anthropologist Arthur Kleinman (1988) made a set of distinctions in his cross-cultural work that every graduate student in the mental health professions should be required to learn as a mantra. Kleinman distinguished *illness, disease*, and *sickness*, and he did so in a manner that pays particular attention to the concept of suffering and ultimately to its moral content.

> By invoking the term *illness* I mean to conjure up the innately human experience of symptoms and suffering. Illness refers to how the sick person and the members of the family or wider social network perceive, live with, and respond to symptoms and disability. . . . Local cultural orientations (the patterned ways that we have learned to think about and act in our life worlds and that replicate the social structure of those worlds) organize or conventional common sense about how to understand and treat illness; thus we can say of illness experience is that it is always culturally shaped. (pp. 3–5)

This is contrasted with *disease*:

Disease however is what practitioners create in the recasting of illness in terms of theories of disorder. Disease is what practitioners have been trained to see through the theoretical lenses of their particular form of practice. That is to say, the practitioner reconfigures the patient's and family's illness problems as narrow technical issues; disease problems. . . . In the narrow biological terms of the biomedical model, this means that disease is reconfigured only as an alteration in biological structure or functioning. (pp. 5–6)

Finally, Kleinman (1988) defined *sickness*:

To complete the picture, I shall introduce a third term, sickness, and define it as the understanding of a disorder in its generic sense across a population in relation to macro social (economic, political, and institutional) forces. . . . Not just researchers but patients, families, and healers, too, may extrapolate from illness to sickness, adding another wrinkle to the experience of disorder, seeing it as a reflection of political oppression, economic deprivation, and other social sources of human misery. (p. 6)

Kleinman (1988) used a study of patient narratives (case studies) to demonstrate that particularly in the case of chronic illnesses, the biomedical model systematically prevents the practitioner from taking seriously the patient's experience of suffering and the interpersonal and social precipitants and consequences of that suffering. He carefully documented what most of us know from our own experience as patients of biomedically trained physicians, that the patient's illness may be aggravated by successful, technically correct, treatment of his or her specific diseases. The result is more, not less, human pain, suffering, and misery.

Kleinman's (1988) analysis suggests a possible explanation for why the language of emotional pain and suffering has all but vanished from the landscape of abnormal and clinical psychology (and other mental health disciplines). As we have adopted the biological model in academic psychology, through physiological psychology, behavioral genetics, and neuroscience, and the medical model in professional psychology, through the adherence to the *DSM–IV*, increased use of psychotropic medications, and empirically validated treatments, we have systematically excluded the consideration of client–patient's suffering. The *DSM–IV* tells us that we "suffer from mental disorders" (American Psychiatric Association, 1994), but that is as close as the *DSM–IV* gets to the concept of suffering. It talks of distress, disturbance, disorder, suicidal and homicidal ideas, and a whole catalogue of symptoms that indicate that a person is indeed suffering, but not of the suffering itself. Do we suffer from mental disorders as the *DSM–IV* defines, or has our suffering come to be defined as mental disorders and colonized by the mental health professions as their special province of expertise? The patient's suffering is redefined as or seen as equivalent to "nothing but" the symptoms and diagnoses of the *DSM–IV*. Clinical psychology has emulated psychiatry so well that it has equally succeeded in abandoning its clients to their suffering.

In the analysis presented here, the everyday sense of the term *suffering* has been taken for granted. Given the theoretically contentious implications of this analysis, it makes sense to attempt to use the common or everyday, ordinary, pretheoretical language as a means of bridging theoretical divides, as Goldfried (1995) suggested. Perhaps we can take some reassurance as to the importance of this concept from the experience of the medical profession, which labeled as *pathology* the study of the nature and causes of diseases; the word's origins are the Greek words *pathos* ("suffering"), and *logic* ("to give an account of"; pathos + logic = to give an account or logic of suffering).

The basic meaning of the term *suffering* in *The Compact Edition of the Oxford English Dictionary* (1971) is "the bearing or undergoing of pain, distress, or tribulation." The root word, *suffer*, has a rich meaning universe:

1. To undergo, endure:
   1. trans. To have (something painful, distressing, or injurious) inflicted or imposed upon one; to submit to with pain, distress, grief
   a. pain, death, punishment, judgment, hardship, distress, grief, sorrow, care.
   b. Wrong, injury, loss, shame, disgrace
   2. To go or pass through, be subjected to, undergo, experience (now usually something evil or painful) (p. 3141)

One sees immediately that the sense of physical pain, harm, or death is the first or most common meaning but that it is quickly followed by reference to emotional pain, loss, difficult experiences, and the pain of having been injured or injuring others *in interpersonal relationships*. This is important to note, because in the biomedical model the patient's suffering is translated into physical pain, and that pain is then treated in terms of its physiological components or cause, and so the meaning of *suffering* is reduced from a multidimensional to a unidimensional construct. Unless the concept of pain includes the emotional pain of guilt, shame, jealousy, vengeance, humiliation, terror, and insecurity, and so forth, it is a great linguistic and personal disservice to patients to treat their suffering as simply "pain."

THE HISTORY OF SCIENCE, PSYCHOLOGY, AND MORALITY

The movement from the practical problems of suffering, with all of their moral implications, to theoretical explanations of psychological disturbances as diseases (i.e., as naturalistic, amoral entities or processes) is so familiar to us that we rarely even notice that such a transformation has occurred. This demoralization of psychology is part and parcel of a much broader movement in U.S. culture—the hegemony of the natural sciences and technology. Science has become our secular religion, and scientific experts are our priests, science's representatives on this earth, wielding power and authority. We put our faith in science to bring us salvation, calm our fears, and protect us from suffering. Although one would be very foolish to deny the tremendous power and impact of science and technology in our culture, and one risks being dismissed as heretical if one questions the faith in science that has permeated both the culture and the academy, this is exactly what is necessary to move psychology beyond the destructive schisms of the past 50 years. A scientific worldview, or *Weltanschauung*, is a necessary component of the knowledge base of clinical, abnormal, and professional psychology, but it is far from a sufficient knowledge base. It must be complemented by an understanding of people in their social and historical context, and this includes the moral framework of their lives. This latter understanding is often so context dependent and idiosyncratic to a particular life or family history as to make the application of scientific principles itself a highly creative art (Manicus & Secord, 1983).

This of course flies in the face of most of what we teach students in academic psychology programs about the relationship between research and practice or practical problem solving. It would be much easier and simpler if the mainstream view that good practice flows from good science were true, but alas, it is not. To understand this, it is necessary to step back from our current veneration and worship of science as a cultural icon and examine the history and philosophy of science. Those who have led the way in questioning the hegemony of science in psychology (e.g. Polkinghorne, 1983; Woolfolk & Richardson, 1984) have done so from the perspective of continental phenomenological, critical, or hermeneutic philosophy. Their critique, although most insightful, begins from premises so foreign to American psychology as to create a gulf between the reader and the subject matter. The work of the eminent historian and philosopher of science Stephen Toulmin (e.g., 1963, 1972, 1990) reaches very similar conclusions but begins squarely from within the natural science position and worldview familiar to all of us. He is similar in this regard to Polanyi (1962), an eminent natural scientist in Great Britain, who from his own scientific work discovered that the mainstream account of the scientific method as primarily an empirical process of observation and discovery was seriously flawed.

Toulmin's position, to which I return in chapter 4, is that the natural sciences—in particular, the scientific method—became the source of *authority for definitive answers* to all important questions in our culture as an outgrowth of historical changes that began with the Enlightenment. The logical positivist view of science of the 1920s–1930s that provided the philosophical justification for this supreme authority for most of the 20th century was a direct descendent of Enlightenment thinking and still serves as the justification for research methods in psychology in most mainstream textbooks in psychology. It has been under withering attack in philosophy for 50 years. Toulmin uses the careful logical analysis of Anglo-American philosophy to show that some of its most cherished assumptions about science are highly suspect.

Toulmin shows that the reasoned humanism of the Renaissance (ca. 1450–1600) was replaced by a dogmatic commitment to Rationality (he capitalizes the term to indicate its status as a dogma) in what came to be known as the Enlightenment. This Rationality, far from being an emphasis on the use of human reason to solve problems, was an attempt to create an alternative to Christian faith based on a naturalistic worldview. The search for timeless universal laws of nature was guided by a need to offer an alternative to the universal truths of the Church that had organized European life for 1,000 years and were, in the wake of the Thirty Years War (1618–1648), discredited. Natural science was the ideology of the secular authorities seeking to replace the civil authority of the Church as nation–states emerged in Europe. Scientific work that provided this sort of ideology and increased the power of those who ruled was supported and encouraged. On this account there is little difference between the support of technology and the support of science. Both are supported financially and through recognition in direct proportion to how well they contribute to the central government's authority, control, and power over the populace. Science does not exist in a vacuum or split off from the historical, religious, social, economic, or political forces at work in a society, thus the title of Toulmin's (1990) book, *Cosmopolis*.

The Greeks sought to organize their political life in accordance with how they perceived the cosmos to be organized. The natural world and the state should function as one. Toulmin believes that this is a reversible formula and that we attempt to organize our view of nature in ways that reflect how we view the proper order of society. Contemporary science favors the search for universal laws of nature rather than more individual, local, time-dependent, practical solutions to everyday problems, because the latter would lead to a much more decentralized and egalitarian worldview, thus threatening the very institutions and power structures in the society that are funding the growth of science.

The mainstream view of science and the scientific method was maintained dogmatically in psychology and among logical positivists in philosophy throughout the first half of the 20th century; at the very same time the oldest science, physics, was discovering phenomena in quantum physics and relativity theory that brought into question both our basic understanding of the matter that forms the basis of material reality and the existence of a material reality known independently of the observer (Pribram, 1986). The denial of such a self-evident contradiction is suggestive of powerful ideological forces at work within the scientific community.

Toulmin is particularly cognizant of the impact of these historical forces on the emergence of psychology as a science. To see this clearly, we need to return to the beginning of the modern history of science in the Thirty Years War. Although the Church was gravely wounded by the bloodletting between Catholics and Protestants, and the general population disillusioned with the benefits of Christianity if the outcome was to be such inhuman slaughter, the Church and various national churches still had considerable power and authority. In the aftermath of the war, the Church accepted a reduction in its civil authority in exchange for preservation of its spiritual–theological authority and, with that spiritual authority, a strong voice in matters of personal if not public morality. The immortal soul was its province, and "free will" dictated that the laws of nature could not replace Church law and morality as the primary influence on human action and behavior.

The new Rationality as developed in the work of the French philosopher Descartes excluded the human mind and spirit from the world of natural causes, thus avoiding direct confrontation with Church authority. Reason, not natural forces or processes, governed human action. The Church would maintain its authority over the life of the spirit and define our relationship to the hereafter. It gave up its right to authority over the interpretation and control of the natural world (science and civil government). Although Toulmin (1990) does not explicitly make this point, it is no wonder then that *psychology* (a word formed from combining Greek words meaning "to give an account of the spirit, mind, soul") would not easily emerge as a "science." For it to do so, it would have to fly in the face of this arrangement and threaten the truce between the Church, civil authority, and science.

Another consequence of this arrangement that Toulmin (1990) does note is that emotion was open to study only if it were conceived as a purely instinctive naturalistic response of the body to certain stimuli. During the Enlightenment, the humanism of the Renaissance was rejected and with it the tolerant and accepting view of human emotions as essential and valuable aspects of one's experience of the world. Human emotion was set off from both rationality and spirituality as evidence of the impact of primitive animalistic instincts on human behavior (referring to angry, violent, or sexually lustful feelings). Acceptable human emotions, such as love, caring, and compassion, were imbued with a theological interpretation as evidence of the spirit of the almighty and excluded from scientific theorizing as well. That undesirable emotions were explained both as naturalistic phenomena and as evidence of evil in a theological context suggests something of the powerful need to exclude human emotions from the realm of social acceptability.

In the Renaissance, everything that was human was interesting and worthy of exploration. Human emotions, conflicts, foibles, eccentricities, and the like were part and parcel of what it meant to be a human being. It was reasonable to expect human beings to be emotional in certain contexts and circumstances and that emotional responses would vary from person to person and situation to situation. Without the need for universal laws of explanation, or behavioral standardization across the population, emotional phenomena were just one critical component of what it meant to be human. What could be so threatening about love, jealousy, caring, sexual intimacy, anger, and resentment? Toulmin (1990) proposed an original, if controversial, theory to explain this. He maintained that sexual love as an intense romantic experience threatened the exclusivity of the aristocracy. If members of the royal families could fall in love and want to marry commoners, then the ability of the aristocracy to limit access to privileges based on hereditary rights would be threatened by constant breaches with each new generation. Over time, the aristocracy would weaken and be broken—by love and sex. Regardless of whether one accepts this explanation, it still remains true that the emotional components of human experience that had been accepted, even extolled, during the Renaissance were during the Enlightenment considered either the proper subject of theological teachings or the expressions of biological instinct. It is little wonder, then, that psychology as it emerged as a protonatural science in the late 1800s made little attempt to account for the role of emotions in human behavior.

Even psychoanalysis has had an ambivalent relationship with human emotions. On the one hand, Freud's theory is centrally concerned with the emotional basis of psychiatric disorders, namely in the form of understanding anxiety (irrational fears). On the other hand, this emotion (anxiety) is tied to the libidinal instincts, in keeping with the Enlightenment tradition of relegating nonspiritual discussions of emotion to the expression of biological or animalistic irrational forces. To this day, psychoanalysis debates the explanatory status of emotions. Are emotions important psychological phenomena in their own right, or are they merely derivatives of unconscious drive and conflicts? Not until the rise of the aptly named humanistic psychology of the 1960s did American psychology, for a brief period, study emotions as independent legitimate subject matter. Both before and after this period, human emotions have been accounted for in terms of cognitive, biological, or social explanations, but not as phenomena in their own right. The division of labor among the Church, the emerging civil authorities, and science, and the resulting dogma of rationality, left a lasting legacy here as well. The intensely emotional, intimate, personal relationships of lovers and family members were seen as the province of the Church's morality, outside the bounds of science. To become a science, and to exist at all as an independent discipline, psychology would have to avoid at all costs tackling these problems. To do otherwise would risk antagonizing both the powerful social forces of the Church, the political power of the ruling classes and the state, and the growing domain of natural science in the academy. I explore further the history and philosophy of science in chapter 4.

CLINICAL KNOWLEDGE

Toulmin's work validates an intellectual interest in and study of the local, time-bound, practical, and orally communicated knowledge. That sounds made to order for the study of clinical interactions and psychotherapy. It also invites a consideration of the emotional and the moral aspects of human experience as accessible to human reason, although not necessarily *rationality* (the Enlightenment's term for theory-driven natural science). This is the perfect framework for capturing what has been so elusive and opaque to analysis heretofore: clinical knowledge. During the decades of debate about the relationship of science to practice, scientific knowledge has always been presented in formal terms as meeting certain criteria, whereas clinical knowledge has been referred to as though it were an uncomplicated, obvious, simple, or commonsense term. Often it is subsumed under clinical hunches, bias, intuition, and so forth. Other times it is referred to as *clinical wisdom, expertise,* or *art.* It is assumed to be critical to therapeutic success; the outgrowth of clinical experience; but basically a mysterious, elusive, almost mystical process. Although it may not be possible to completely account for the phenomena of clinical knowledge (Yalom, 1989, pp. 180–186), surely we can do better than this hodgepodge of contradictory meanings.

Many have recognized that clinical knowledge is an extension of our everyday knowledge of how to interact with other people in our culture (Bugental, 1987; Fromm-Reichmann, 1950; Malan, 1979). Long before a person becomes a psychologist, he or she learns or develops ways of interpreting what people are up to, what they mean by what they say and do, and even how to be helpful with problems that others are having. Most of the time, these methods are effective, or one would be likely to perish. Our cognitive errors in person perception are recognizable only against a background of accurate person perception. Those who have failed to develop these rudimentary interpersonal skills are poor candidates for clinical training, for training as a psychologist begins where these everyday skills leave off. As Jonsen and Toulmin (1988) observed, clinical knowledge is a form of moral knowledge, practical wisdom, and our observations, judgments, and decisions about clinical matters take place in a moral framework. Many of these problems are not encountered in the daily lives of clinicians before they work in clinical contexts, and so the moral discernment and decision making require new learning. Also, clinical technique, tact, diplomacy, and so forth, are actions taken in the world: skills. Moral engagement is not simply the promulgation of moral principles but effective moral action. Clinical knowledge is not just propositional knowledge but "how-to" knowledge. As Toulmin wrote, the oral tradition of rhetoric requires an evaluation of not just the argument (as in written logic) but of its impact on the audience. Are they changed or moved by the argument? If science is the logic of psychology, clinical practice is the rhetoric. Rhetoric has of course been devalued in the modern era, and Toulmin thinks this is to our disadvantage.

Unlike the scientific approach that emphasizes causal explanation, universal principles, and predictability, clinical approaches (e.g., humanistic and psychodynamic) are more likely to emphasize understanding the particular circumstances and history of an individual life. Despite claims by logical positivists to the contrary, understanding is not seen as a special case of causal explanation. Understanding is more descriptive than explanatory theory, and it requires problem solving and deciphering camouflaged communication and finding the missing pieces of puzzles. Causal analysis, although not to be completely ruled out, is much less important to the clinical task than in science.

When a puzzle, problem, or mystery is solved, one is able to finally make sense of what has been heretofore incomprehensible. The connection between a puzzle and its missing pieces is not causal, but rather meaningful. The missing piece allows one to make sense out of the puzzle, to see what it represents, or symbolizes. The missing piece communicates meaning in the context of the whole puzzle. One can see what the meaning is for the creator of the puzzle. This is an intellectual and analytical process, but it is not a scientific one. Solving such a puzzle or problem is not unscientific but rather extrascientific; it requires both scientific knowledge and something more—understanding of a specific problem and its possible solutions.

Clinical knowledge requires that one go beyond the reductionism, materialism, and empiricism of the scientific model as well. Materialism is replaced by a realism that recognizes the reality and power of subjective experience as well as the reality and power of the body. Empiricism is broadened to its original meaning, "to be guided by experience," which is taken here to mean something like the subjective inner experience that is inaccessible to objective study. This inner experience can be studied descriptively or phenomenologically. Finally, material and efficient causation is supplemented by formal and particularly final causation (Rychlak, 1981). Human action or behavior is seen as purposeful and meaningful rather than simply functional. Our behavior is governed not only by causal forces in the universe of nature (whether biological or psychosocial) but also by the human capacity to choose—by freedom and responsibility for one's actions (Martin & Sugarman, 2000). Clinical work just does not get out of the gate unless one assumes that the client has the capacity for responsible decision making. One sees this even in the discussions of the most deterministic medical-model clinicians who see suffering as diseases to be treated by specific biochemical interventions. Treatment failures are often accounted for in terms of the patients' refusal to cooperate.

The clinical approach also challenges the mainstream models on the question of how one validates knowledge claims made about human problems in living. Although observation with one's senses (empirical knowledge) is of course a part of how one comes to know about these problems and what to do about them, it is far from the whole story. So much of our suffering goes on within our consciousness obscured from view by the rest of the world, and that which is observable is often masked or camouflaged, that empirical observation is often of little value. Instead, we need to use a combination of self-examination and exploration and develop ways of relating to others that allow these masks and diversions to be dropped, what Martin Buber (1958) called the *I–Thou relationship* and what Rogers (1960) called *accurate empathy*. The exploration of the intersubjective world—exploring another's consciousness with one's own consciousness is both an interpersonal and somewhat intuitive way of knowing, what the psychoanalyst Theodore Reik (1948) called "listening with the third ear." One comes to know a person in this way, through authentic encounter with his or her being, not by applying general laws of behavior to him or her. Generalizations emerge from the experience by virtue of working with many clients and sharing observations with colleagues in the same community of practice.

However, what we come to know in clinical work is not primarily empirical generalizations or causal explanations; rather, we come to learn the topography of consciousness, the meaning that individual human beings assign to their experience of empirical and inner reality, and the inferences, connections, interpretations, purposes, and plans that result from these initial meanings. We learn about the different purposes to which people put their lives, how these purposes are carried forward by different strategies of interaction with others, and how to connect seemingly purposeless behavior to these concealed purposes. This was in many ways the schema that Freud (1920/1966) put forward as the basis of psychoanalysis, although he often complicated it greatly with his meta-psychological theories. Yes, there are causal forces in our lives: sexual drives; emotional pressures from frustration, anxiety, or pleasure seeking; temperament, with which we are no doubt born; societal pressures to conform to this or that behavioral standard; family dynamics in which we are enmeshed. These may be important factors in a life history, but they are *never the most important factor*, although some would prefer that they were. The most important element in a life story is ultimately what we make of these factors and forces—*what we do with them, not what they do to us*. The human being is seen as actor, creator, and doer rather than as passive observer or conduit of external forces. Like the sculptor who must work with the piece of rock that is available, one fashions one's life, or chooses not to and remains an ill-defined weighted object. I explore clinical knowledge further in chapter 5.

CASE STUDY RESEARCH

The Judeo–Christian heritage from which this concept of choice—or, as it was called in earlier times, *free will*—has been derived also provided an epistemological answer as to how to find the truth on such matters, on how we would know the right thing to do, the right choice to make, the good in life to pursue. The method is *casuistry*, a case-by-case analysis of moral conflicts and dilemmas. Here, guiding principles such as the Ten

Commandments are applied to real-life circumstances with all their complexity, and an attempt is made to specify the best resolution of the conflict. Jonsen and Toulmin (1988) argued persuasively that all medical decision making—and, I infer, all psychotherapeutic decision making—is really a form of casuistry where the ethical principles are either concealed or expressed indirectly through medical–professional rules of practice (e.g., in a terminal cancer patient with intractable pain, allow doses of painkillers to increase into the range where death may result).

It is no wonder, then, that despite the strong movement toward empirically validated scientific principles, clinical practitioners have long relied on the case study as a central means of professional training and communication (Bromley, 1986; Fishman, 1999; Hoshmand, 1992; R. B. Miller, 1999). Of course, the prohibition of mixing moral judgment with professional judgment has precluded many of these authors from addressing directly the moral issues implicit in their cases. Nevertheless, as Kleinman (1988) noted, it is only in the rich narrative possible in a case study that the clinical reality of human suffering and healing can be captured. The case study can describe the context, the meaning of the problem to all those affected by the client's problem or illness, and the practical obstacles and resources available for its solution. The case study can capture the internal process of the helper and at least some of the internal process of the client. It can speak to thoughts, feelings, ambivalences, confusion, and trial and error in ways that traditional research reports cannot.

Students and trainees find case reports or studies to be an intriguing and enlivening component of their learning. It builds their confidence in approaching clients, for they feel they have a template to put up against their own experience for guidance. Well-written case studies read more like history or literature than they do technical scientific reports, and thus they are accessible to a much broader segment of the population, and with a gain rather than a loss in effectiveness because the case studies actually convey what the future clinician must think about. Practical judgment is the basis of clinical knowledge and is clearly distinct from scientific knowledge in that it is particular, moral (prescriptive), and practical, whereas science is universal, abstract, and descriptive. There is conceptual moral knowledge in being able to articulate what should be done, and practical know-how or skill in being able to actually do it. The result is a human interaction or action that makes the world a morally better place for human beings to live.

If the argument of this book—that clinical knowledge is a form of moral knowledge—is correct, then psychologists cannot build a knowledge base for clinical psychology on the kind of demoralized empirical research studies on which they have come to rely. We need the contextualized characterizations of clinical reality that only a case study approach can provide. At the same time, case study methods have been underdeveloped, if not downright ignored, for the past 50 years in clinical psychology, and a morally engaged clinical psychology is conceivable only if one can also envision a way to develop the case study method in such a manner as to permit the growth of professional knowledge and scholarship. In chapter 6, I explore the case study as the basic building block of knowledge in clinical psychology.

The following illustrates the power of even a brief case study to communicate morally situated clinical knowledge.

"Worms": A Case Study (Karon & VandenBos, 1981)

Karon and VandenBos (1981) discussed the case of a 7-year-old boy who was referred for a psychological evaluation before being admitted for hospitalization with an incipient psychosis. The boy complained that worms were crawling under his skin and he was desperately washing himself to rid himself of the worms. The child's pediatrician had diagnosed the boy as "psychotic" and recommended hospitalization. As was customary for this practice community, he was referred for a "psychological evaluation" prior to admission. Initially, the interview focused on the symptoms and tended to confirm the psychiatric evaluation (an irrational delusional belief), until VandenBos shifted the discussion with an open-ended question: "Tell me about what else is going on in your life . . . ?" This produced a serious of revelations that included the boy's fears about his parents' bitter divorce battle, their violent outbursts in front of the children, and a visit to the pediatrician (who had made the initial referral) in which the boy had been treated for "nervousness" and had been told that when one feels nervous it can feel like there are "little worms crawling under the skin." This allowed VandenBos to explain to the boy that grown-ups sometimes talk in funny ways, and the "little worms" that he was concerned about were not at all like the worms in the grass that need to be kept moist lest they die. Although he remained troubled by his parents' divorce, the boy's supposed "delusional state" was immediately resolved. Although a biochemical intervention had not yet been initiated, one can well expect that had he been hospitalized that would have been standard treatment, and the side effects of treating such a boy with major tranquillizers would have been likely to increase his sense of panic and his persecutory talk.

Here we have a clear example of a morally engaged clinician. It is always easier to support one's professional colleagues in their judgments than to radically disagree, especially if one is a psychologist and the colleague a physician. The psychologist's self-interest had to take a backseat to the client's needs. The child's best interests are clearly put ahead of massaging the egos of the adults involved. The child is respected as a rational being trying to make sense of his world, and his seeming irrationality turns out to be directly related to a clumsy adult communication. He was frightened by events in his life and frightened further by the doctor who was supposed to know how to make him feel better. The parents are invited to be moral agents, putting the well-being of their children ahead of their own need to vent rage. Had the child been labeled as psychotic and institutionalized, perhaps (we do not know this for sure from the case report) the parents might have been initially grateful and pleased to have one fewer child to worry about on a day-to-day basis in the midst of their divorce drama. Whether they would have been so sanguine once they saw that their child was now categorized as schizophrenic, and that the diagnosis meant to the health care establishment a lifetime of severe disability and treatment with major tranquilizers, it is hard to know. VandenBos took a risk on moral as well as clinical grounds, and as a result this 11-year-old boy had a chance for a life with dignity and self-respect. The medical approach that was under way would have allowed both the parents and the physician to disavow their own part in the boy's suffering, and he might have been labeled for life as psychotic (which to the medical community and, probably the parents, meant a presumably organic or genetically transmitted condition).

A case such as this is typical of the moral dilemmas that clinical practice presents to practitioners who are aware that they operate in the moral realm. In the ensuing chapters, I examine the nature of human suffering and the moral challenge it presents, the nature of morality and its relationship to scientific theories of psychology, and the nature of clinical versus scientific knowledge. Finally, I examine the case study method for clinical investigation as a vehicle for communicating clinical knowledge that is morally sensitive and clinically accurate.

2

SUFFERING IN PSYCHOLOGY

In clinical psychology, psychiatry, and the other mental health professions the amelioration of the suffering experienced by clients has been replaced by—and, I would argue, reduced to—a concern with eliminating what are construed as the symptoms or manifestations of mental disorders, disabilities, diseases, and dysfunctions. The client's agony, misery, or sorrow is viewed as a mere epiphenomenon to be replaced by a description of a clinical syndrome that is presumably more easily defined, measured, and scientifically explained as the consequence of some technical design flaw in the person's nervous system, cognitive processes, or learning environment that is amenable to change. Lost in the translation is the meaning to the person of the injury, harm, or loss incurred; the role of other individuals who contributed to or who are affected by the injury, harm, or loss; and any sense of the moral consequences or ethical impact of the same. As the biomedical model has taken hold in psychiatry and clinical psychology through neurophysiology, sociobiology, and behavioral genetics, the everyday illnesses expressed in the language of suffering have been replaced, as Kleinman (1988) noted, by diseases expressed in terms of causal forces and biochemical mechanisms and processes. Of course, at the molecular level the concept of suffering has no place: Only persons can suffer, not cells or the nucleic material in cells. Treating people as though they were nothing more than a collection of cellular mechanisms has become an unfortunate consequence of high-tech and high-cost medicine. It is this step of reducing people to simply the mechanistic processes that have been identified as associated with the illness that produces the patient's sense of dehumanization and leaves us with the all-too-common phenomenon in which the patient's disease is "effectively" treated but his or her suffering continues unabated, or perhaps even worsened. No doubt the increasing popularity of holistic and alternative medical therapies arises from this sense of being treated like an object, or as if one's own view of one's illness is irrelevant to the treating physician. Of course, there are fortunately some contemporary physicians who, like Siegel (1986) and Sacks (1987), have discovered that they can do both—pay attention to the person and the disease. Still, in the era of industrialized medicine, health maintenance organizations, and managed care, it is the experience of many if not most patients that such physicians have become the noted exceptions, not the rule.

Lest one be misled into considering this merely a semantic issue, or that focusing on suffering is the arbitrary selection of a prescientific term for essentially the same phenomena, one would do well to heed the writings of Janet and Paul Gotkin (1975/1991), leaders in the psychiatric survivors movement. Janet Gotkin described the moment when, after 10 years of psychiatric treatment by callous psychotherapists, hundreds of electroconvulsive shock therapies, and high doses of thorazine and other psychotropic medications, she achieved on her own the realization that would change her life, restore her self-respect, and allow her to take control of her own life and move it in a positive direction:

> I watched the Seine as it flowed and flowed.
> "For eons, since there have been human beings," I thought, "there has been this river. There has been this pool of suffering." It was as if a light came into the darkness that was in me at that instant.
> "There has been this despair," I whispered. "That is part of our condition, to feel despair. . . . Women and men have looked down into the pit that is themselves and that is life and questioned the meaning and mourned the futility of it all. No amounts of Thorazine will ever make this feeling go away.
> In the blackest pit of desolation, I felt that I had found myself, for the first time in my life.
> That blinding, searing, revelatory instant changed my life forever. A horror landscape of ten years was lightning bright; after a decade of brainwashing and mystification, I finally had the answers to a million questions that had plagued me, and Paul and my parents. The answer, as I said it, tentatively, quietly, at first, was so simple it was ludicrous. I knew why I could get well so easily (after an overdose induced coma); I had never been sick in the first place. Not in any medical sense. Certainly I

had all the trappings of what was called mental illness, but that is what they were, superficial trappings. (pp. 376–379)

As I noted in chapter 1, Kleinman is not the only mental health practitioner to take note of the importance of the everyday conception of suffering in effecting a shift away from the disease or biomedical model. For example, Mosher and Burti (1988/1994), advocating for a psychosocial approach to the severely mentally ill treated in community mental health centers, offered the following definition:

> Psychopathology is a form of human discomfort and suffering that, ideally, can be alleviated by professional help. But unfortunately, this process almost always imposes a psychiatric label, a diagnosis. . . . *In our work we are primarily concerned with needs; we prefer to consider symptoms as communications about unmet needs that may be recognized and met, rather than expressions of hypothetical, underlying, pathological process, whose classification results in little advantage to the patient.* [italics added] . . . A need is the lack of something experienced as essential to the purposes of life. It expresses itself as suffering. If the person is aware of the existence of a way to stop the suffering, the need expresses itself as a desire. (Jervis, 1975, as cited in Mosher & Burti, 1988/1994, pp. 19–20)

Even Kramer's (1993) best-selling tribute to Prozac as a new wonder drug that allows us to see the biological basis of the self and various personality traits alludes to the relevance of human suffering to the moral questions raised by the widespread use of Prozac for "cosmetic psychopharmacology." After his first patient showed the "mood brightening" (as opposed to antidepressant) effects of Prozac, Kramer wondered if he should be using a drug to treat what is not a clinical disorder but a style of personality:

> I was torn simultaneously by a sense that the medication was too far-reaching in its effects and a sense that my discomfort was arbitrary and aesthetic rather than doctorly. I wondered how the drug might influence my profession's definition of illness and its understanding of ordinary suffering. (p. 20)

Even after discussing approvingly and at length the speculative neuroscience concepts that might explain this mood-brightening effect, and giving many clinical examples of its seemingly miraculous effects, Kramer is still worried at the end of the book about the ethical and moral implications of using the drug. He used the fiction of Walker Percy to explore the issue further: "Better even more than the ethicists who responded directly to Prozac, Percy both depicts and personifies the objection to a technological attenuation of ordinary suffering" (Kramer, 1993, p. 275).

From the other side of the drug use in psychiatry spectrum, the psychiatric critic and reformer Breggin (1991) also frequently characterizes patients' problems in terms of human suffering and misery as he works to be of help without falling into the conceptual limits of the disease model. He characterizes the helping relationship in terms of one's empathy for the suffering of those around others.

> The heart of being helpful—the creation of healing presence and healing aura—draws heavily on empathy. If we feel empathic toward other human beings, we will feel motivated to respond in a positive healing fashion to their individual *suffering* [italics added]. . . . Only through a willingness and desire to do so can we remain in touch with the *pain and suffering* [italics added] around us, from our closest family members and friends to humanity itself. (p. 124)
>
> Healing presence is a journey and a process, not an accomplished fact. It requires patience with ourselves and with other people. Pain and frustration accompany the effort, as they do whatever whenever we fully involve ourselves in life. Healing presence acknowledges that *suffering* [italics added] and feelings of hopelessness are a part of living. (p. 10)

Breggin (1991) notes that although symptom suppression is common in modern medicine, it is counterproductive in helping people experiencing emotional pain and suffering:

> In the arena of emotional problems, it is even more important to avoid suppressing pain. Attempts to suppress painful feelings can do more harm than good. These attempts give the wrong impression to clients—that their *suffering* [italics added] is the problem, rather than a signal of their problems. Intense emotions should be viewed as indicators that something important is going on rather than as symptoms to be eradicated. (p. 33)

Breggin (1991) also finds the concept of suffering useful in discussing the impact that the exposure to other people's suffering has on therapists and human being in general.

> Probably every human being at times feels somewhat overwhelmed by the amount of *suffering* [italics added] in the world. All human beings have to make decisions about how to respond to *suffering* [italics added] and how to allocate their energies. . . . Induced *emotional suffering* [italics added], with its associated feelings of helplessness and overwhelm, is a powerful force in human life. It causes us to justify withdrawing from others. It makes us want to close our eyes to the plight of others. It shuts us off from our capacity to love and to care. It is a major psychological force causing us to turn away from *the suffering* [italics added] of others. (pp. 42–43)

The work of Kleinman, the Gotkins, Mosher and Burti, and Breggin identifies suffering as both a central feature of psychiatric and psychological problems and as systematically ignored in both the theory and practice of modern psychiatry and clinical psychology. Although all of these authors use the concept of suffering in their work as a primitive, unanalyzed, commonsense term, with the exception of Breggin they do not explore the theoretical implications of redefining the emotional pain of human suffering as some form of physical or cognitive disorder or disease.

The implications are truly horrific. Here we have a highly regarded cultural icon—modern scientific medicine—absorbing a massive amount of the society's financial resources and making physicians the most highly paid and respected professionals in our society, presumably because of the service they provide to their patients. Yet the patients' levels of pain, suffering, and misery are of no real theoretical concern and therefore are often worsened by the treatment provided. This sounds much more like a terrifying paranoid delusional system than a sober analysis of the social dynamic of a modern profession. Awful as this may be, it seems even more inconceivable that psychiatry and the mental health professions could have participated in such a system. When as a physician one is facing, for example, cancerous tumors, failing heart muscles, oozing abscesses, or paralyzed or gangrenous limbs, it seems understandable that the patient's pain and suffering might be seen as secondary to the physiological problems that must be solved. However, in psychiatry, psychology, and the other mental health professions it is usually the case that all the patient brings to the practitioner for treatment is emotional pain, suffering, and misery. For example, patients who have experienced abandonment, loss, or other traumas, and who feel terror, humiliation, isolation, hopelessness, and so forth, can only be said to be seeking alleviation for their suffering. To offer treatments based on theoretical models that exclude the consideration of the patient's suffering as the critical outcome criteria seems the height of absurdity, perhaps even dishonesty. Even more incomprehensible is how such a system of "care" could have survived and prospered. It is striking to note that a number of other theoretical models of psychotherapy have deemphasized the role of suffering as well. Many of the cognitive–behavioral approaches to individual therapy, and the strategic or pragmatic approaches to family therapy, share the goal of making therapy thoroughly objective and scientific, if not biological, and in so doing have sought theoretical constructs that lend themselves to behavioral and objective measures. Whether this was motivated by theoretical reasons or simply to rival medicine's scientific trappings is hard to say, but the end result is the same. Suffering is not a topic of discussion in clinical psychology. What possible purpose could be served by such an arrangement?

DENIAL OF PAIN AND SUFFERING

Perhaps the most inexplicable aspect of the above account is that clients would seek help for their suffering but then accept help that does not address that suffering. At a rational level this makes no sense, but at an emotional level there is a logic operating (a psycho-logic). Nearly all theoretical models in abnormal and clinical psychology have accepted some version of Freud's phenomena of defense mechanisms—particularly repression and denial—even if they reject Freud's theory of the childhood determinants of unconscious processes (Fisher & Greenberg, 1985). As human beings, we attempt to reduce the conscious experience of pain and suffering, even to the point of losing consciousness altogether in the face of excruciating pain. We want both to deal, and not to deal, with our suffering. We want to talk about the hurt, the loss, the betrayal, and the personal injury that have precipitated the suffering. We want to understand it better, in part so we can avoid it in the future and so that our lives can make sense to us again. Yet human suffering involves the unspeakable, unbearable, horrible experiences of life. It often defies verbal expression (Scarry, 1985) and can be expressed only through facial expressions, cries and groans, contortions of the body and face, or a breakdown in bodily functions. Our own suffering is forgotten and avoided whenever possible. We are both drawn to and repulsed by others' suffering, and ultimately we want to deny it as well. Treatments of suffering that avoid suffering altogether are therefore somewhat attractive to patients caught in their own ambivalence. If such strategies offered permanent solutions to suffering, we would all probably opt for them. Also a factor, no doubt, is the general low level of expectation of true help that most people have today in seeking health care services and, more generally, in seeking professional services in society as a whole. As R. Whitaker (2002) exhaustively documented, patients with the most severe psychiatric problems have historically received treatments that increase rather than decrease their long-term suffering. The poor in particular have suffered in this regard.

This begins to explain the consumer's role in seeking treatments that do not take suffering seriously, but what about the psychology's willingness to adopt models of explanation that leave suffering virtually out of the equation? To some extent, mental health practitioners are affected by a patient's suffering in the same way the patient is: They do not want to feel it. It is painful for most people to observe another human being suffering. The practitioner's defense mechanisms operate parallel to the patient's. Were it not for the fact that it is exactly this suffering for which the patient is asking help, one could thoroughly empathize with the practitioner's position here. Yet we know from the experience of psychotherapy training that helping professionals can and do learn to overcome their own resistances to the patient's pain. Indeed, Freud (Breuer & Freud, 1895/1982) once quipped that the goal of psychoanalysis was "to turn neurotic suffering into ordinary human misery." This means, of course, that the analyst has to be prepared to reveal to the patient the ordinary human misery he or she has sought to avoid through the development of the symptoms. So we know that practitioners can learn to attend to patients' suffering. Why is it that systems of care and institutionally supported theories cannot?

For an answer to this question we need to look to what Kleinman (1988) referred to as the dimension of *sickness*. Although he did not develop this notion as fully as the concepts of *illness* and *disease*, his analysis is suggestive of an explanation for the problem before us. When suffering is explored it often takes on a frankly moral character. Even more so in psychiatric than in purely medical contexts the patient's suffering is inherently bound up in his or her interpersonal and social context. Abandonment, betrayal, conflict, manipulation, and exploitation in personal, social, and economic relationships are common patient themes. These concerns throw the therapeutic relationship into the moral maelstrom of injustice, abuse, dishonesty, and, in some cases, clearly illegal activities (R. B. Miller, 1998). To address these problems may mean finding ways to protect patients from the torture others in fact are wishing to inflict on them, or it may mean affirming their sense of moral injury and supporting them in their efforts to seek restitution. In either case, the purpose is to deal with their sense that the world had become for them a place devoid of goodness and filled with forebodings of evil. There is no way to engage with that problem in a purely de-moralized manner. Kleinman argued that a consideration of suffering requires a moral dimension to treatment, and it is lacking in the biomedical viewpoint. Breggin (1997) reached a similar conclusion. (Neither Kleinman nor Breggin, however, took up the question addressed below as to why the moral point of view is excluded from the scientific enterprise.)

Pain and suffering encountered in these contexts take on yet another level of denial and repression: the perpetrator's denial of injury to others. This is dramatically seen in the literary critic and philosopher Elaine Scarry's (1985) monumental work *The Body in Pain*, in which she wrote about the most extreme form of interpersonally inflicted pain and suffering—that found in political torture and warfare. In considering the psychological or personal experience of intense physical pain and suffering, she wrote that

> one of its most frightening aspects is its resistance to objectification. Though indisputably real to the sufferer, it is, unless accompanied by visible body damage or a disease label, unreal to others. This profound ontological split is a doubling of pain's annihilating power: the lack of acknowledgment and recognition (which if present could act as a form of self-extension) becomes a second form of negation and rejection, the social equivalent of physical aversiveness. This terrifying dichotomy and doubling is itself redoubled, multiplied, and magnified in torture because instead of the person's pain being subjectively real but objectified and invisible to others, it is now hugely objectified, everywhere visible, as incontestably present in the external as in the internal world, *and yet it is simultaneously categorically denied* [italics added].

Fraudulent and merciless, this kind of power claims pain's attributes as its own and disclaims the pain itself. The act of disclaiming is as essential to the power as the act of claiming. It of course assists the torturer in practical ways. He first inflicts pain, then objectifies pain, then denies the pain, and only this final act of self-blinding permits the shift back to the first step, the inflicting of more pain, for to allow the reality of the other's suffering to enter his own consciousness would immediately compel him to stop the torture. (pp. 56–57)

The most fundamental power one can have over another human being is the power to inflict or remove physical pain and suffering. By examining the literature of practitioners and survivors of human torture, Scarry (1985) showed how the goal and experience of torture are to unmake the victims' worldview, to destroy the very purpose of their existence, their sense of a coherent self, and their ability to function in opposition to their persecutors. The goal is not just to punish them but also to undo their identity—how they have organized themselves in the search for safety and security in the world. Often this is done in conjunction with genocide as a means of unmaking a rival culture—to destroy the creations and way of life of a whole population.

Although Scarry's (1985) examples are drawn from the most extreme situations, the process she described fits well the context of the emotional pain and suffering patients bring to their psychologist or other therapists. Patients feel as though their world is coming apart, that they are losing their identity. Those who have participated with them in the interpersonal or social relationships that have precipitated their pain and suffering often deny there is even a problem to be addressed, that their own actions toward the client are reprehensible, or that the pain and suffering of the client are real. Clients are told that they are exaggerating, too sensitive, overreacting, and so forth. If their pain and suffering are from endemic socioeconomic conditions—poverty, discrimination, and so forth—what Kleinman (1988) called *sickness*, then the providers of care may stand in relation to the client in the same relative social position as those who have perpetrated against the client. The providers of care may, as individuals or as representatives of institutions in the society benefiting from the current socioeconomic conditions, routinely engage in the denial of pain and suffering in the class of individuals represented by the patient. In other words, providers may be unaware of the suffering of their patients because they have learned as a member of a privileged group in the society to discount that sort of suffering in virtually all members of their society. This is a moral position that may predate the professional's training or adoption of a theoretical model of disease. The privileged provider could not continue to exercise in his or her own society the privileges, authority, and power that he or she does and still remain aware of the kind of pain and suffering that results from the socioeconomic arrangements from which he or she benefits.

By avoiding the pain and suffering of the patient, and relegating them to an epiphenomenon, the biomedical and other scientific models in psychiatry and psychology offer a theoretical firewall against the intrusion of social, economic, political, and moral factors into the treatment room. Given the high cost in patient care dissatisfaction, one can only assume that at some level those who currently lead the mental health professions perceive the cost of acknowledging such factors in our treatment models would be even higher. Indeed, if one considers what has come to be called *structural violence* (Christie, Wagner, & Winter, 2001) as producing injury on a par with the kind of physical violence Scarry (1985) discussed, then the power structure of the society that the professions seek to serve and join would be very threatened by a full accounting of the contextualized pain and suffering of the populace. Unfortunately, rather than helping the client in this situation, the institution or practitioner "redoubles" the patient's suffering by denying its existence! Instead, the patient is diagnosed as personally defective in some manner (physiologically or psychologically). The moral, social, and political context of the suffering thus disappears from the theoretical and practical account of the problem.

Scarry (1985) considered the role of pain and suffering in not only the unmaking of the world in torture and warfare but also in the making of the world through creative imagination and productivity. Here the loss in conceptual and moral clout to psychology and psychiatry that is incurred by excluding the patient's suffering from the central conception of the clinical work may be even greater than the loss incurred in the characterization of the problem, for the pain is central not only to the problem but also to the solution. Scarry showed how the experience of intense pain is an indubitable reality for the sufferer that defies objectification, whereas imagination (the beginning of creativity and productivity) is the experience of a clear object totally lacking any claim to reality. One cannot articulate or verbalize pain except through metaphor, but many creations are, or at least begin as, pure verbalization. Pain and imagination seem to define the bookends of the mental realm.

> That pain and imagination are each other's missing intentional counterpart and that they together provide a framing identity of man-as-creator within which all other intimate perceptual, psychological, emotional, and somatic events occur, is perhaps most succinctly suggested by the fact that there is one piece of language used—in many different languages—at once as a near synonym for pain, and as a near synonym for created object; and that is the word "work."
>
> Work and its "work" (or work and its object, its artifact) are the names that are given to the phenomena of pain and the imagination as they begin to move from being a self-contained loop within the body to becoming the equivalent loop projected into the external world. It is through this movement into the world that the extreme privacy of the occurrence (both pain and imagining are invisible to anyone outside the boundaries of the person's body) begins to be sharable, that sentience becomes social and thus acquires its distinctly human form. (Scarry, 1985, pp. 169–170)

Work is associated not only with pain and suffering but also with creativity and satisfaction. Pain and suffering are frequently seen as the impetus to creativity, particularly in the arts, but Scarry (1985) is suggesting in this somewhat opaque passage that this connection is more pervasive. We work to rid ourselves of pain and suffering, whether by building a house to keep us from freezing or by creating a painting that expresses our grief. To be aware of our suffering is to be in touch with the wellspring of our creative abilities to improve our lives and communicate with our fellows. Work at its best is a voluntary, controlled suffering with a creative outcome—perhaps best exemplified in the labor of a mother giving birth to a wanted child.

How much more dangerous the biomedical and scientific models of mental health care appear in this context. Not only does this model exclude suffering in defining the nature of the problem requiring treatment, thus leaving the patient still isolated and alone with his or her suffering but, in excluding suffering from the treatment process, it cuts off the patient from the internal creative resources within him- or herself that would permit a true cure of the problem—the return to creative–productive living!

In her consideration of the relationship of pain to imagination, Scarry (1985) addressed directly the moral dimension of suffering that Kleinman (1988) identified as essential to an understanding of the meaning of illness:

> The imagination is not, as has often been wrongly suggested, amoral; though she (the imagination) is certainly indifferent to many subjects that have in one era or another been designated as "moral." . . . The realm of her labor is centrally bound up with the elementary moral distinction between hurting and not hurting. . . . The work of the imagination also overlaps with another interior human event that is usually articulated in a separate vocabulary, for it has become evident that at least at a certain moment in her life cycle, she is mixed up with (is in fact almost indistinguishable from) the phenomenon of compassion, and only differs from compassion in that in her maturer form she grows tired of the passivity of wishful thinking. (Scarry, 1985, p. 306)

Suffering, particularly the suffering that results from the intentional actions of other human beings—what Scarry (1985) referred to simply as *hurting*—is a social emotional phenomenon closely linked to our commonsense vision of evil or the immoral. To witness such suffering directly, or vicariously through hearing its retelling, can itself be traumatic and brings forth compassion for the victim and a wish to prevent the perpetrator from further acts of injury, if not to hold him or her accountable for past injuries. If the suffering of the victim is dealt with in a de-moralized manner, say as posttraumatic stress disorder or a paranoid psychosis, the problem is shifted to what is wrong with the patient rather than what is wrong with what happened to the patient. The moral sense of a wrong done to someone, evident in an account of suffering, has been exchanged for a functional sense of "wrong" (as in not working properly) as indicated by a diagnosis of mental disorder.

I have noted elsewhere (R. B. Miller, 2001) that a strict prohibition against psychologists making moral judgments has been one of the few points of agreement between researchers and clinical practitioners in the field of clinical psychology. Science and practice are almost universally conceptualized within the mainstream as morally neutral, technical activities. We like to say that like nuclear physics, psychology can be used for good or ill, and this is up to the policymakers, not the scientists and practitioners of psychology. Even Freud (1933/1965), who, as noted above, recognized the relationship between neurosis and human misery, maintained that psychoanalysis shared the "Weltanschauung of science." Across the board, leading 20th-century psychologists, from Skinner to Rogers and Maslow, sought a scientific basis for describing behavior in such a way that the "good" would emerge as a discovered natural phenomenon rather than as a chosen way of being. They joined Freud in thinking that their descriptions of "healthy," "actualized," "adaptive," "growth-oriented," or "species-preserving" behaviors or actions were value-free scientific discoveries. It seems as though one could not become a respected figure in American psychology unless one eschewed moral thinking and offered a naturalized ethics in its place. The theoretical and philosophical criticism of this position (of the value neutrality of applied psychology) has been devastating in its logic and consistency across a tremendous diversity of authors and perspectives (see chap. 3 for the detailed arguments). The concept and language of suffering alert one to the inherently moral nature of the problems for which psychology purports to be the answer. The failure to acknowledge the moral controversies implicit in the different theoretical models of treatment in psychiatry and clinical psychology represents a conceptual and logical lacuna that threatens the entire intellectual enterprise we call clinical psychology and psychiatry.

DSM–IV CASEBOOK AND
THE DENIAL OF SUFFERING

The *DSM–IV Casebook* (Spitzer, Gibbon, Skodol, Williams, & First, 1994) is a companion volume to the *Diagnostic and Statistical Manual of Mental Disorders* (*DSM–IV*; American Psychiatric Association, 1994). Brief case descriptions are given of actual clinical cases that are purported to match the various *DSM–IV* diagnostic criteria for specific disorders. The introduction to the volume states that the case studies have been edited to ensure that "all available information necessary for making a diagnosis has been included" (p. xi). Because a diagnosis is supposed to contain the essential information necessary to determine appropriate treatment, the absence of information would strongly suggest that the authors regard such information as peripheral or unimportant. The suffering of patients, particularly as reflected in their moral dilemmas and conflict, is starkly absent from these cases. As with the

DSM–IV itself, the pseudoscientific objective language of the descriptions directs the reader away from the experience of the patients and toward their disordered physiological and behavioral disabilities. What is missing from a case is always the hardest aspect of a critical analysis of a case formulation, because one tends to join in the worldview of authors and see phenomena through their eyes.

However, one case in which the conceptual absence of suffering from the case account is almost transparently obvious is the case of posttraumatic stress disorder titled "Eyewitness." A 39-year-old female television reporter has become disinterested in her work, irritable with her husband, and feeling numb and detached, after covering the prison execution of a murderer. She is having difficulty sleeping, nightmares, and flashbacks to the execution, where she observed, from a distance of about 10 feet, the throes of death.

It is, of course, risky to form clinical hypotheses for any given case with which one has had no direct experience of the patient. However, when one has worked in the field as a psychotherapist and teacher for many years, it is fair to make observations of the sorts of phenomena that might typically have accompanied such a clinical description but that have not been deemed relevant by the authors. In this particular case, the reader is also aided substantially by a discussion of social suffering by Kleinman and Kleinman (1997) in which the moral dilemmas faced by those who study and record the suffering of others have been explored. Kleinman discussed the work and eventual suicide of renowned war photographer and son of former President Jimmy Carter, Kevin Carter, who became tormented by images of the murdered political prisoners and starving children he had photographed.

Returning to the case report of the television reporter, one wonders but is not told what she thought and felt as she witnessed this death. Did she feel responsible, as a member of the society that was executing the prisoner, for his death? Did she feel her reporting had in some way contributed to either his conviction or sentencing? Perhaps the television network she worked for was advocating capital punishment. Face to face with his suffering, had she developed second thoughts about the morality of capital punishment? What meaning did she attribute to his suffering and death? Perhaps she has witnessed or fantasized the death of other people, and the execution reactivated the pain or guilty pleasure of those experiences.

Reporters, like the idealized behavioral researcher, are supposed to remain detached and objective in their reporting. How many other events like this has she covered, in which human suffering and the moral dilemmas it raises for all of us have been present but not acknowledged any more by her than by the psychiatrist interviewing her? One wonders, too, how the husband's proximity to these accounts of human suffering has affected him and whether theirs is a relationship in which the moral dilemmas of life are openly discussed. One tends to think not, because she is irritable with him, and the only treatment plan is couples therapy (although there may have been other marital issues not revealed).

The point of all these questions and musings is not that I can, given the case material presented, understand this case better than the clinician present, for surely that is impossible. Rather, the point is that when the experience of a clinical interview with a client is conceptualized by a morally engaged clinician, many additional relevant questions would need to be explored and answered before knowing what to do to be helpful. It is clear that none of these are covered in the case description offered even though it has been ostensibly edited to include all "necessary information to make a diagnosis." Technically speaking, because the DSM–IV diagnostic system is the product of a dissociated and demoralized theoretical model, the answers to these questions and musings are not necessary for a diagnosis to be made. Nevertheless, it is reasonable to imagine that an exploration of the human suffering in this case (the reporter's, the murderer's, and the victims of the murderer), and the concomitant moral conflict about rage, guilt, and responsibility experienced by the patient and the many other people associated with the case, might have been highly useful to a patient reporting such symptoms. As the case is written, one has no idea whether these issues were explored but proved unimportant or, as is more likely, were never explored at all. We do know from Kleinman's discussion of Kevin Carter that such issues can plague reporters and investigators as they struggle between their desire to get a story out in an effective manner and their survivor or bystander guilt. Was there a way to have gotten as good a picture or told as engaging a story, and to also have helped the victims more? Does my own suffering doing this work count for something, is it legitimate, or should I just make myself be objective and compassionless? Am I exploiting the pain of others for personal monetary or professional advancement? These are very tough moral questions, and to struggle with them alone within one's own heart and soul, bereft of human support, is to experience the social isolation of true suffering.

DSM–IV CASEBOOK CASE NO. 2: "THE WEALTHY WIDOW"

Lest one think that the case of the "Eyewitness" television reporter is an isolated example of de-moralization in the DSM–IV, consider the case of the "Wealthy Widow." This case illustrates how a disregard for suffering and overattention to the search for indications of individual disorder lead to a highly suspect moral and treatment outcome. A well-to-do 75-year-old widow of 6 months is brought by her three adult sons "against her will" and by use of "threats and intimidation" to a psychiatrist because they believe she is "senile." The basis for the assertion of senility is her behavior after the initial period of grieving. She decided to volunteer at a local hospital, and for the last 3 months she has been going out nightly to clubs and bars with the hospital staff. Although she does not drink, she enjoys their company and has recently announced her intent to marry a male nurse, age 25, with whom she is reported to be having a very active sexual relationship. She has also told her sons that she is planning to turn over her house and a large sum of money to her husband-to-be. Frequently, she sleeps only 3 or 4 hours at night and is spending $1,200 per week on shopping sprees and in support of her fiancé (a sum she can afford).

She has no prior history of psychological problems and displays no cognitive impairment in the interview. She is, however, furious to have been coerced into the psychiatric evaluation and resentful that her children do not realize that she is happy for the first time in her life—having always lived for her parents, husband, or children previously. She controls the interview and refuses to allow the psychiatrist to interrupt her with questions and also refuses any further psychological testing. She accuses her sons of "trying to commit her so they can get their hands on her money."

The diagnostic discussion suggests that although many a naïve reader might be drawn into thinking that the woman is right about her sons, she is really demonstrating symptoms of Bipolar I Disorder, Single Manic Episode, Moderate, Provisional (to rule out brain tumor or degenerative central nervous system disorder). The justification that is given for this diagnosis is that the patient is showing poor judgment in planning to turn over her house to someone she has only known for 3 months and that her irritable behavior, decreased need for sleep, expansive mood, and pressure of speech (in the interview) justify seeing this as a mood disorder. It is noted that it is most unusual for a bipolar disorder with manic features to make its first appearance at age 75, but that not withstanding, it is asserted to be a correct diagnosis.

If one considers this case history, limited as it is in information, from the perspective of human suffering, four concerns arise. First, there is the obvious suffering of a woman who has recently faced the loss of the person to whom she was married for many years. Such a loss often heightens one's sense of one's own mortality, of time wasted, opportunities passed by, and of the need to live life to the fullest with what little time one has left. One has to come to terms with the choices one has made and to accept the limits and limitations of life. In the immediate moment, she is also a person suffering with having been coerced to undergo a medical and psychiatric examination against her will, and she is enraged that her sons have done this to her. Not knowing the details of the case, one can only speculate from clinical experience what some of the parameters of this situation might be. First, is this typical of the lack of respect for autonomy in the relationships between the parents and (adult) children in the family, or of some other rupture in the mother's relationship to her sons that predates her recent romantic involvement? We know nothing of the mother's relationship with the father, or his with his sons, or if there are any daughters in the family.

The process of the father's death, and the sense of suffering experienced by family members in that process, also is unexplored. We do know that the mother feels as though she has never been allowed to live for her own happiness until now and that she has been giving to everyone else throughout her entire life. Her sons' coercing a psychiatric evaluation on the basis of their lack of approval for her sex life and how she was disposing of her wealth could be interpreted as confirmation of her statement that no one in the family ever put her needs first.

Second, one must question why a psychiatrist in the private sector (one can assume from the patient's social status that this is the most likely setting for the interview) would agree to see, against her own will, a patient who was clearly not psychotic. Because this would have been clear very early in the evaluation interview, one wonders why it was not terminated immediately and the patient offered a voluntary interview to discuss her family's predicament at another time. This also communicates a lack of respect for her personal autonomy, or at the very least viewing the sons as the client whose wishes are being satisfied. Again, this would tend to confirm the mother's sense that authorities, and men in particular, are dismissive of her needs.

Third, one wonders about the extent to which ageism has entered into the diagnosis. Were a 30- or 40-year-old woman to "carry on" with a 25-year-old man, one would think it exciting and romantic. Because the patient is 75 years old, there is an implicit assumption that she should not be that lively and sexually active, especially with a man that young. One can only speculate what a 75-year-old psychiatrist interviewing her would have thought—perhaps something along the lines of "Good for you, old girl!" Of course, it is possible that her 25-year-old fiancé is a gold digger and that she is being set up for a very hard fall that will only compound her sense of loss at the death of her husband. What if, though, her account is realistic, and this is the first time in her life she feels genuinely loved and cared for, that her marriage was empty and her husband unfaithful? She is at an age when life is full of loss, illness, and disability. We do not know exactly how wealthy she is and whether, despite her recent plans, and how well her sons are provided for in her will. Neither do we know anything about her fiancé except his occupation (male nurse) and his age. If it were to turn out that he was a very decent human being, caring and principled, and that her gifts to him were truly gifts that he has discouraged her from making, no doubt the decision to diagnose her with a major mental illness would be entirely suspect. She is struggling with the moral choices presented by the end of life, as is her psychiatric evaluator. She is seen as disordered because moral choices of the patient and the psychiatrist conflict or, put another way, the psychiatrist cannot appreciate or empathize with the moral choices of the "Wealthy Widow."

This brings us to the fourth area of concern: whether the clinical judgment is implicitly based on a moral judgment that widowed older women (or perhaps older women in general) should not behave this way. What if the patient were a 75-year-old widower taking up with a 25-year-old beauty queen? It seems the newspapers carry at least one such story per year. "Octogenarian Discovers the Fountain of Youth," the headlines would read.

It seems likely that the "Wealthy Widow" would have had every reason to be morally outraged at both her sons and the psychiatrist for forcing her to undergo an involuntary psychiatric evaluation. The diagnosis of a rather severe mental disorder provides a way of discounting her view and protecting the sons who can now question their mother's competency to change her will and of protecting the psychiatrist from the consequences of violating her civil rights. Her anger at being involuntarily evaluated could only have become geometrically greater as she sensed the implicit pathologizing of her behavior in the psychiatrist's questions. One can only imagine how further enraged and devastated she felt at hearing the diagnosis. Of course, once the diagnosis is made, any rage at being treated in this way could now be interpreted by the psychiatrist, her sons, and a potential judge evaluating her competency to manage her own affairs or change her will as further evidence of her instability and mental disorder. To whatever extent, if her affair with the 25-year-old nurse was indeed a distorted expression of the suffering in her life, and not the exciting if improbable romance that she experiences it to be, then the actions of the sons and psychiatry profession have made her suffering immeasurably worse. She will have less freedom to live the remaining years of her life as she sees fit and is more isolated from her sons, and the rest of society, as an identified "bipolar–manic type." Freud (1915/1959) once observed that falling in love was a nearly universal form of psychotic behavior because the judgment of the beloved's virtues and vices was usually, if not always, greatly distorted. One can certainly question the wisdom of the wealthy widow's choice of partner, as one often questions such things in other people. Given the divorce rate of 50% in the general population, one would probably prove right in such questioning half the time. This will not mean that half the time people in love have a serious mental disorder, even though half the time people in love make unwise choices.

A PSYCHOLOGY OF SUFFERING

From the preceding discussion it is clear that suffering is a critical dimension of human experience, one that has the capacity to either trigger creative imagination and problem solving or massive denial. It is closely linked to our experience of morality both in our raw experience that intentional injury of others is the essence of doing wrong in the world and the experience of compassion that can provoke moral action in the care of others who have been injured. Denial of suffering is then often tantamount to denying the evil in the world and denying its victims any restitution or comfort.

One does not have to dig very deep into Western or Eastern intellectual history to recognize that the topic of suffering, although little attended to in the psychological literature, has a very long tradition of examination in the philosophical and theological literature and artistic expression in the arts. From the Book of Job, to the Eightfold Path of Enlightenment of the Buddha, the message of the Gospels, or the philosophy of Stoicism, human beings have struggled to come terms with, or even vanquish, the ubiquity of suffering from human existence.

This is most clearly seen in the tenets of Buddhism. Conze (1959) wrote the following:

> In its origins and intention, a doctrine of salvation, Buddhism has always been marked by its intensely practical attitudes. Speculation on matters irrelevant to salvation is discouraged. Suffering is the basic fact of life. (pp. 15–16)
>
> In Buddhism suffering is understood as operating in both obvious and concealed ways. The universality of suffering does not immediately stand out as a self-evident fact. . . . There is much obvious suffering in the world. A great deal of it, however[,] is concealed, and can be perceived only by the wise. Obvious suffering is recognized by the unpleasant and painful feelings which are associated with it, and by reactions of avoidance and hate. Concealed suffering lies in what seems pleasant, but is ill beneath. (pp. 45–46)

Buddhism strives to teach us to move beyond wanting pleasure from sensory and bodily experience to avoid the suffering that inevitably results when such wants and needs go unfulfilled. As people, we must detach ourselves from our bodies and the cycle of birth, illness, decay and death to be free of suffering. Those Western, frequently Jungian, psychotherapists who attempt to incorporate Buddhist philosophies into their work, although outside the mainstream of clinical psychology, do, to their credit, face human suffering directly (e.g., Brazier, 1995; Epstein, 1995; Young-Eisendrath, 2000; Young-Eisendrath & Muramato, 2002).

Although the Judeo–Christian heritage is not as severe in its rejection of the body, neither is it entirely free of such thinking. Suffering is construed as only first a matter of the body, but more importantly also as a matter of the soul that can surmount the limitations of the body and at times even heal it. In Jewish theology, suffering is a sign of sin, evil, or immoral conduct. To cause suffering in others is a sin, and it is a great virtue (*mitzvah*) to relieve the suffering of another by offering comfort, food, or lodging, to a stranger, the poor, or the ill. Those who have sinned against their fellow men and women or against the Lord can expect to suffer the consequences from the Lord's judgment, unless they sincerely repent and pray for forgiveness. The cultural historian Amato (1990) wrote the following:

> The Jews of the Old Testament considered that God was singularly interested in their own well-being: God suffers Israel's tribulations. When

given a choice between the more pure theological desire to emphasize the transcendental nature of God and the desire to have a God who is more concrete and directly interested in human affairs and suffering, Jewish thinkers traditionally preferred a personal God, a God who rewarded, punished, and tested them. (p. 44)

One of the ways the New Testament offers proof that Jesus is the Messiah is by virtue of his capacity to heal those suffering from physical and spiritual ills. The suffering of Jesus on the cross, and of his disciples for being faithful to his teachings, are seen as marks of his devotion to humanity rather than as punishment for sins. Suffering takes on the meaning of martyrdom in Christian and later Jewish theology (after the destruction of the Second Temple). This is in the context of defending the faith against violent attacks from other societies (principally the Romans in ancient times, later others). Amato (1990) wrote the following:

Christianity spoke of suffering as the classical world did not. For Christians suffering is never meaningless. There is the suffering that people bring upon themselves by their self-abuse; suffering that comes from the first sin; suffering by which people test and educate each other; and finally truly redemptive suffering, the innocent and saving suffering of the prophet, messiah, or believer, which renews God's promise to his people. (p. 44)

These great world religions are centrally focused on understanding the pervasiveness of suffering and offering followers a means of reducing, or at least accepting, the suffering in their lives. The existence of suffering is often associated with evil and sin, and the lessening of suffering is seen as the goal and purpose of morality. In other words, the basis and justification of ethical or moral guidelines seem to be the pragmatic claim that human suffering is reduced by adherence to their principles. Once adopted, Judeo–Christian ethical principles are not open to individual pragmatic calculations as to how to reduce individual suffering but are universally required as obedience to the Lord's will and religious dogma. What appears to have begun as pragmatic amelioration of suffering became a practice of faith and obligation. Such acts of faith may also, paradoxically, be acts of sacrifice in which the faithful choose to suffer for a higher good (to reduce the suffering of humanity, or their own personal salvation in the hereafter).

The theologian Dorothy Soelle's (1975) widely read monograph on human suffering is perhaps the best single work on the subject in any discipline available today. She wrote "without Christian presuppositions" and attempts to create a dialogue between a scientific view of suffering (which she defines as the social, economic, and psychological viewpoints) and Christian theology. She is equally opposed to the theological position that invites or extols suffering as a proof of one's faith, which she labels "Christian masochism," and to a restriction of the discussion to exclusively scientific language: "The methodological prohibition against using theological–symbolic language in our day appears to be a demand for one-dimensional thinking" (p. 8). She begins her book with two basic questions:

(1) What are the causes of suffering and how can these conditions be eliminated?
(2) What is the meaning of suffering and under what conditions can it make us more human? (p. 5)

Soelle (1975) intriguingly contrasts suffering not with happiness but with "apathy": The "ideal of life free from suffering, the illusion of painlessness, destroys people's ability to feel anything" (p. 4). She observes that in the West we have been taught as individuals to deal with personal suffering through "illusion, minimization, suppression, and apathy, and this stands in our way of trying to understand suffering as a social or academic problem to be investigated" (p. 4). For Soelle, what distinguishes suffering from other states of being is the character of *affliction*, a term that she borrows from the writing of Simone Weil (1951): Extreme suffering or affliction always has three components: (a) physical, (b) psychological, and (c) social.

> Suffering . . . threatens every dimension of life: time to await what is promised, freedom of movement and opportunity for development, vital association with others, food and health and living space as one's share of the Promised Land. This kind of suffering has social dimensions—isolation, loneliness, ostracism—as well as physical.
>
> The structure of this context justifies our speaking of "suffering" thus going beyond the scientific diagnosis "pain."
>
> The word suffering expresses first the duration and intensity of a pain and then the multi-dimensionality that roots the suffering in the physical and social sphere. (Soelle, 1975, pp. 13–16)

This is rarely understood in the psychological literature, where the diagnoses that stand for human suffering are seen as essentially individual phenomena. There is a kind of physical, social, and ultimately moral (e.g., "I deserve this pain") isolation in human suffering that is to be distinguished from how we live when we are not suffering. We feel alienated and alone—outside the pale of the community. We feel not only the pain or hurt but also isolation from humanity. This perhaps explains the widespread appeal and success of the relatively simple community intervention of developing support groups for those who have experienced trauma and, more specifically, why it is so important to have the opportunity to tell one's story to others who will listen. The telling reintegrates the individual into the community. For Soelle (1975), this definition of suffering carries with it a moral imperative. We must extend ourselves to those who are suffering, for only we can end the isolation they experience. Although their suffering is, in one sense, theirs alone, it is not something they can end by themselves. We must offer support in the community. This is an innovative conceptualization not commonly understood in modern society. We who are witnesses to the suffering of others must make a choice: We must choose whether to be there for them or allow their isolation to continue—yet another way in which thinking about suffering qua suffering (rather than disease) requires that one engage the moral realm. Provocative also is Soelle's observation about apathy. The acknowledgment of suffering brings with it moral commitments, and the denial and avoidance of all suffering creates apathy and a loss of moral direction.

The South African Truth and Reconciliation Commission hearings on the crimes of apartheid are a moving illustration of this process (de la Rey, 2001). Victims of brutal beatings and disappearances accepted amnesty for the guilty in return for a full accounting of the crimes by the perpetrators, who publicly acknowledged their responsibility and culpability. Here the critical importance of being allowed to bear witness to the pain and suffering one has endured or witnessed others endure is dramatically illustrated. The community's acknowledgment and acceptance of this testimony was seen as a necessary step in healing the community from the divisions of apartheid.

Amato's (1990) work, cited earlier, is a comprehensive social history of Western religious, moral, cultural, and political views of suffering. He, too, emphasized the centrality that suffering plays in claims of moral wrongdoing, victimization, and our sense of injustice. He agrees as well with Soelle (1975) that suffering, unlike pain, is a totalizing experience. Pains can be focal, specifiable, and numerous. Suffering is a characterization of an entire state of being and is clearly linked to the forces of the environment, particularly the actions of other persons. Although Amato put this analysis of suffering to a very different use than did Soelle—he calls into question the manner in which various minorities and disenfranchised political groups in the West use their suffering as tantamount to an entitlement for reparations—his basic observations on the centrality of social and moral concerns to human suffering are supportive of her position.

Bakan (1968, 1971), as noted in chapter 1, is the only psychologist who has directly addressed the topic of suffering. He approached suffering through the concepts of disease, pain and death, using a psychological interpretation of the Book of Job as a point of departure. Having identified disease and pain as indications of a failure of the integrated, life-enhancing, purposive, organismic (physiological and psychological) functioning of the individual, Bakan analyzed suffering in terms of the requirement that we must make painful choices regarding life and death. We must choose not only how to live but also, as parents, who shall live (or live well). We do this knowing that we cannot choose ultimately whether we ourselves are to die. He suggests that the Book of Job calls into question the prevailing Jewish theology of the time (perhaps 600 B.C.) that indicated that good living was rewarded by the Lord and evil punished. The Book of Job illustrates, according to Bakan, that because death is the most painful psychological reality, and no matter how good we are we still shall die, suffering is inevitable as a part of life. He believes that our suffering is magnified by experiencing ourselves as responsible for the lives of our children, which might include the responsibility of infanticide, as in the story of Abraham and Isaac. He places the act of infanticide in the context of the choices facing parents in biblical times, when extreme scarcity and famine were not uncommon. Under such conditions, the parent might be faced with choosing between risking her or his immediate survival by allowing the child to live, or infanticide and preserving her or his own tangible individual life. It is the choice of making sacrifices for one's children and making sacrifices of one's children. However, the existential dilemma is intensified because it is not just a choice of between self-interest and the welfare of the child, because the parent has a strong self-interest in seeing the child live as evidence of her or his own immortality. However one chooses, there is pain and suffering. We suffer because there is death and because of the choices that the avoidance of death forces on us. These choices are, of course, the very subject matter of ethical and moral principles that deal with balancing one's own self-interest and the interests of others in the community and setting priorities for one's own life.

It has to be said at this point that Bakan's work, falling as it does under the rubric of existential psychology and philosophy, can be seen to be of a piece with the existential literature that dates back to at least the philosophers Kierkegaard, Sartre, and Camus and, more recently, the psychotherapists R. D. Laing (1965), Rollo May (1969), Alvin Mahrer (1978, 2002), and Irvin Yalom (1981, 1989). In a sense there has been a psychology of suffering, even if it has not been labeled as such. It is central to a major school of psychotherapy, although one that has been largely discounted by mainstream psychology as a fad of the 1960s.

In this regard, one should take note of earlier psychological analyses of the related but more narrow concept of pain. Szasz (1957/1988) (prior to his monumental work, *The Myth of Mental Illness*, published in 1960) conducted a careful conceptual and psychological analysis of the concept of pain. Although the analysis used the methods of philosophical behaviorism (finding the meaning of a proposition functionally, through its use in the world, rather than simply through semantic description), it was also clearly humanistic in that it emphasized the social communicative properties of the patient's assertions of pain without accepting the psychoanalytic metapsychology that Freud had used to explain hysteria and other perplexing pseudophysiological problems. Szasz interpreted such pains as communicating a need for care, or for relief from social demands and expectations that would otherwise be pressed on the individual. Such forms of indirect social communication are required for people whose social position or status does not permit them to expect a positive response to more direct requests for help.

Mahrer (1978), in his comprehensive theory of experiential/humanistic psychology and psychiatry, rejected the mainstream view of mental health and illness, psychoanalytic neuroses, and biological explanations of disorders (e.g., schizophrenia or depression). Instead, he offered an analysis of "bad feelings" and "painful behaviors" in a phenomenological account of the experience of

> being in pieces, fractionated, incomplete, disjointed; being torn apart inside, with one's parts at war and in turmoil; anxiety, threat, tension, dread, fear; helplessness, smallness, pawnness; shame, guilt, self-punishment, reparation, alienation, aloneness; meaninglessness, hollowness, depression, gloom; bodily pain and distress; hostility and anger. (p. 394)

Although the concept and experience of suffering are notably absent, Mahrer's agenda is certainly consonant with the thrust of the argument put forth here, namely, to examine the meaning of the experience of suffering itself.

Mahrer (1978) sees bad feelings and painful behaviors as resulting from a failure to integrate or fully accept all aspects of one's own experience, including potential experiences currently outside of one's awareness. When there are these "disintegrative relationships between potentials," we are prone to act in the world in a manner that creates the very experience we have disowned (as in psychoanalytic projection), or seek out experiences that confirm our worst fears, and then see our problems as environmental rather than internal. Mahrer, therefore, sees bad feelings and painful behavior as matters of personal responsibility and choice and as influenced, but not controlled, by the actions of others. Mahrer adopts an existential ethic, although he does not identify it as such. We have a moral responsibility to first come to terms with our own experience, not to change the environmental conditions that impinge on us. In fact, he sees all attempts to place pain and bad feelings "out there" in the environment, and then to try to change that environment, as ultimately counterproductive and likely to produce even more pain.

This more individual ethic may result from having focused on feelings and pain rather than the concept of suffering, which, as we have seen, is more totalistic as an experience and carries with it a sense of alienation from, or betrayal by, the social community. On the other hand, Mahrer's concern with individual responsibility and self-determination clearly places his theory in the moral realm, because he argues that the world would be a better place if we all attended to our own pain and stopped trying to engineer social and cultural changes that control the behavior of others.

The reasons given for discounting humanistic approaches to psychology usually have been that these approaches are too "soft," lacking in objective, empirical validation for their methods—or lacking in methods that can even be empirically specified. This—the assertion that existential propositions constitute unreliable and invalid knowledge—is essentially an epistemological critique. Using Toulmin's (1990, 2000) analysis (see chap. 4) from the history of science, we can make another more radical interpretation: Existential psychotherapy has been rejected from mainstream psychology because it introduces human suffering (and other intense emotions) into psychology, and this also implicitly introduces types of moral claims that are incompatible with the assertion of moral neutrality of the modern scientific paradigm.

SOME TENTATIVE CONCLUSIONS ABOUT THE PSYCHOLOGY OF SUFFERING

Drawing on the philosophical, theological, and existential literature on human suffering, as well as on observations that are available to any member of contemporary society, the following propositions concerning human suffering seem warranted.

1. Suffering is a totalizing, consuming experience blending physical conditions, psychological experiences, and the rupture of social connections.
2. Suffering is an inherent ubiquitous phenomenon of human life linked to mortality and the awareness of death.
3. Although some suffering seems inherent, not all seems inevitable or necessary. At times, we can prevent or lessen human suffering. The desire to heal suffering seems to be part of human compassion that in fact does address the sense of isolation and alienation in suffering. The Judeo–Christian moral response of compassion is healing—therapeutic.
4. Much of preventable suffering appears to come from destructive human relationships and even may be deliberately inflicted to punish or in an attempt to manipulate the behavior of others.
5. Deliberate injuring of others for the most part evokes an almost reflexive moral response of condemnation or opposition from those injured and from witnesses to the injury. It defines what we mean by experiencing evil in the world. There is both a perception and judgment that are conjoined in this experience, particularly for those with prior moral categories of thought.
6. Real suffering may at times be a necessary concomitant to productive work, creativity, personal insight, physical accomplishment, and so forth and is therefore sought after.
7. In a religious context, this productive aspect of suffering might be called *sacrifice* and may lead to martyrdom. Here suffering is actual proof of one's holiness or blessedness.

Masochism as a route to special spiritual status may be overlooked in a clinical context that is insensitive to moral issues. Extreme self-deprivation, harsh self-criticism, deliberate self-punishment, and, more obviously, deliberate self-injury are ways of inducing suffering in oneself. Indeed, such states of self-induced suffering are seen by many as the prototypical examples of mental illness or disorder. Yet we have come to know that these are often learned phenomena, or at least responses to environments that encourage such self-induced suffering, and that such environmental encouragement may be quite distant in time or place from when the suffering occurs—in other words, it may be easy to miss the external environmental factors and focus on what seems senseless.

8. Many religious traditions also view suffering as a divine punishment for immoral living. Individuals may be encouraged to self-punish as a means of preventing divine punishment.

9. It seems that suffering is distributed across the population in a manner inexplicable to the human mind, without rhyme or reason. One can never explain fully why one person has to face so much suffering in his or her life while a second person appears to sail through life relatively unscathed. Our basic sense of the unfairness of life seems closely related to witnessing these disparities. Alternatively, this seemingly senseless suffering is seen by some as a call to faith, to accept our limited power to control our fate, and to submit to a higher power.

10. Because pain and suffering are not, as Scarry (1985) wrote, "objectifiable" and resist verbal expression, they are not only easily denied but also easily feigned. It is possible to err in either direction, responding compassionately to the feigned suffering or denying the existence of the real. Suffering, and our response to it, is fully embedded in a network of moral dilemma decisions, those of others and ourselves. These are very difficult, and there is no guarantee that we will always make the right ones. Many times the right decision is indeterminate, and honest well-intentioned individuals will disagree as to the proper course of action.

Even when we know that a person's suffering is genuine, we may not be able to respond helpfully because of limited resources. In prioritizing services it is likely that we will give preference to those who have been most egregiously injured in terms of our sense of moral outrage and not just in terms of their overt symptom picture. This is yet another way in which moral concerns infiltrate the clinical realm.

11. There are, no doubt, a number of somewhat separate sources of human suffering. Those most often mentioned include natural disasters, disease and physical injury, war and civil strife, family conflict and schisms, personal betrayals and abandonment in love and friendship, economic hardship and insecurity, and victimization by criminal activity (assault, robbery, rape, etc.). There has been a tendency in the social sciences to study the conditions that contribute to suffering in place of suffering itself. We must understand the physical and social context that has precipitated a person's suffering to understand his or her suffering. The meaning that the person attaches to these circumstances cannot be ascertained without also exploring the context; however, the context or circumstances are not the meaning. This is where the investigation becomes the psychology of suffering. At the level of meaning, although suffering will be unique to each individual it seems there is also a universal sense of suffering. This is perhaps why it is possible to be of help to others who are suffering through life circumstances one has not ever encountered. One may not have ever lived through a nuclear accident, kidnapping and torture, or airline crash the way a particular client has, but one has known suffering.

12. The social political uses or function of suffering, although alluded to in Item 4, bear particular mention. States and governments use their power to define and inflict suffering as a means of control of the populace (Scarry, 1985). The powers that be generally deny such a blatantly destructive motive, often furthering this denial by asserting that the victims are merely feigning their suffering to manipulate public opinion or were guilty of even greater outrages themselves. A recent newspaper editorial on the Arab–Israeli conflict captures the deliberate use of suffering in manipulating others' behavior. A *Burlington Free Press* editorial ("Take a Stand," 2001), urging the Bush administration to take a more proactive approach to peace in the Middle East, concluded as follows:

> Yet, unless the United States backs some kind of a formula, and pressures both sides to respond to it, there is little chance of stopping the escalation of conflict. More tank fire, more mortars, more murders and soon, perhaps, missiles "what we have to look forward to" one senior Israeli diplomat said, "is each side testing the other's ability to suffer." (p. A10)

Others in the political arena might claim that the middle-class benefits by discovering or revealing suffering because they are the likely recipients of bureaucratic jobs or professional careers (such as psychology) aimed at lessening the suffering of those identified. Alternatively, faced with an inability to address the needs of a suffering individual, group, or population, we may as a *polis* choose to ignore their needs rather than identify and then not be able to meet them. Again, Scarry's (1985) work on the mystification of torture and injury in warfare is relevant.

MAKING THE MORAL EXPLICIT IN PSYCHOTHERAPY

In treating cases in which individuals have endured political torture, disappearances, and ethnic cleansing, attending to the patients' suffering brings the moral dimension of psychotherapy into bold relief. Someone who has been successfully targeted as the object of deliberately inflicted pain or emotional suffering experiences not only his or her existential vulnerability to the slings and arrows of outrageous fortune but also a sense of the dissolution of the moral order of the universe itself: "Why would someone deliberately do this to me?"

Although the moral injury is not often as blatant as in these cases, most clients have a history of being emotionally injured or hurt by the actions of other human beings whom they had at one time trusted, relied on, or loved. Often, too, they have a history of injuring others or themselves. Because mental health practitioners de-moralize these problems with *DSM–IV* diagnoses or some other kind of psychological formulations, the moral content or context of the symptoms is frequently obscured from view. The therapeutic relationship functions as a kind of psychological restitution for the harm done. Someone, who for the client represents a respected member of a profession and is seen as a gatekeeper of health and normality (i.e., goodness and blamelessness), hears and accepts the legitimacy of his or her story and acknowledges the wrong or harm done to him or her. Even if the perpetrators will not acknowledge the harm they have caused, a respected member of the community (the professional therapist) has done so. Clients often experience this as a critical therapeutic element—that someone else whom they respect knows and can say "That should not have happened to you; it is not your fault, you did not deserve it."

Here the moral dimension to psychotherapy is central to the therapeutic task itself. It is about making the world "right" again, restoring or perhaps initiating the client's faith in humanity, and we cannot leave consideration of the moral aspects of psychotherapy to a secondary reflection on "professional ethics." When we talk about instilling hope in a client, this is what the hope is for—a world that is safe to live in. As Kleinman (1988) indicated, the moral dimension of clinical work is revealed by paying attention to the patient's *narrative of his or her suffering*. Psychologists do not have to impose a moral framework on their clients' life stories; rather, they report and respond to the moral concerns that the clients themselves raise. To do otherwise, out of fear of becoming morally judgmental, would be to ignore the concerns clients bring to them for help. When clients talk about being betrayed, lied to, cheated on, abandoned, manipulated, physically abused, and so forth, they are discussing the ways in which they feel they have been "wronged" or "unfairly" treated. This is the language of moral concern. Psychotherapists are generally prepared to consider the emotional consequences of such interpersonal situations—the sadness, anger, anxiety, jealousy, shame and guilt that result. However, anxiety, shame and guilt are not just emotions—they involve moral perceptions and judgments, and part of the psychologist's job is to decide whether this is anxiety, shame, or guilt that is warranted by the client's own actions or the displaced moral condemnation felt toward others. The therapist makes a moral judgment as he or she decides how to respond to the client's anxiety, guilt, or shame.

As Erikson (1963) so ably pointed out in his developmental theory, healthy development requires some shame and guilt. If the shame and guilt are proportionate to clients' own misdeeds, psychologists will want to work with them on how to avoid doing such things in the future and how they might make restitution to others. If the shame and guilt are not proportionate to the clients' own deeds, but reflect the condemnation they might *rightly* feel toward the perpetrator, then psychologists work on (a) validating the clients' own sense that an injustice has been done to them; (b) how they might prevent, if at all possible, being victimized in the future; and (c) perhaps pursue some acknowledgment of guilt and or restitution from the perpetrator. There is a kind of moral as well as emotional sensitivity that is required to make these sorts of judgments. This usually is presented as a diagnostic problem, distinguishing neurotic from appropriate guilt. However, appropriate guilt is a moral construct first and only secondarily a psychological phenomena.

Psychotherapists need to be not only sensitive to their clients' moral dilemmas but also prepared to recognize that the psychological resolution of their anxiety or conflict depends as much on finding a good moral solution as it does on managing the symptoms of anxiety or depression. These moral judgments are currently being made as "clinical judgments," which of course they are, but these are the least examined and often the most difficult of the many kinds of clinical judgments psychotherapists make. Of course, it has not helped that most training programs in psychotherapy deny the moral content of psychotherapy theories and train students to avoid making any (explicit) value judgments about their client's lifestyles. This is very confusing to clients, who often profusely thank their therapists for giving them a sense of direction or telling them that they are in the right or not at fault, only to have the therapists become uncomfortable with having the moral aspect of their work acknowledged and appreciated. Therapists may even at such a juncture directly deny to their clients that they made such judgments (that they recognize as of the prohibited moral kind), saying, "Well, I didn't really say that. What I said was that I could tell that *you* didn't really think it was your fault." Or, "Well, you found that direction for yourself, I just helped you see that that was what you wanted." This is not incorrect, but it is only half true, and it is confusing to clients and detracts from a legitimate need they have that the therapist can fill: to have the moral order of their universe righted.

To believe that other human beings will be able to harm one, and that one has no recourse and no defense against such actions, is a truly terrifying and demoralizing worldview. One cannot live with such a state of affairs without suffering greatly—or, as we have come to say suffering great psychological damage. As Milton Erickson (1992, p. 219) wrote about physical pain, what makes pain become unbearable is knowing that it hurt yesterday, it hurts today, and inevitably it will hurt tomorrow, and the next day, and the day after that. Without those beliefs, pain is much more tolerable. There is *moral pain*, and its relief comes from finding oneself back in a moral relationship in which one's own needs are taken seriously and respected. Once this has happened in the therapeutic relationship it is possible to imagine it happening with other human beings in a less structured and protected environment. A moral conceptualization of the therapeutic task, rather than being countertherapeutic, is absolutely essential to what we normally consider a good outcome. Good clinical work involves doing good in the clinical relationship.

POSSIBLE OBJECTIONS AND REJOINDERS

1. Some may think this a surreptitious promotion of humanistic psychology rather than an even-handed investigation of the role of suffering in psychotherapy. It is true that the method of philosophical analysis has phenomenological elements, and so the approach to the topic might be seen as existential–phenomenological. It is also true that humanistic approaches to psychotherapy have generally been more open to considering the moral dimension of therapy than most other approaches. My goal has been to try to understand the role of human suffering and moral judgment in how we think about the psychotherapeutic process. I have followed the threads of the analysis wherever they took me, and they took me to some humanistic sounding places. Of course, there is nothing in this analysis of suffering that requires us to stop there, and although the present analysis would call into question the biomedical model,

it does not prevent one from considering both the moral and the biological aspects of the suffering; in fact, Soelle's (1975) theological model would insist that we do exactly that. If the patient is hemorrhaging from an immoral assault, one has to stop the bleeding and stabilize the patient before undertaking to apprehend and bring to justice the assailant or address the trauma and the patient's sense of despair at having been so victimized. Thus, an attention to the full meaning of suffering does not prevent us from addressing all facets of an individual's problems, so long as those facets do not require a denial of the moral realm.

2. Some other objections, mentioned earlier, include identifying moral concern with moral judgmentalism or moralizing or doing moral philosophy educational tutorials with the client. This is such a common misconception and objection to the line of argument presented here that it might be expressed by representatives of almost any approach to psychotherapy except the more frankly political feminist or radical therapists, who eagerly acknowledge the moral and political implications of psychotherapy.

   Many of the approaches used when making difficult interpretations or confrontations in therapy are applicable here as an answer to this objection. Moral dialogue can be respectful, compassionate, and genuine without involving moralizing, "guilt tripping," or holier-than-thou pronouncements. Horney (1939/1966) was one of the first to show that this could be done in the same Socratic style used when confronting other difficult topics, for example, defenses or unconscious conflicts. One can approach the moral directly, as in, for example, "I wonder if you have thought about the moral implications of this action?" or indirectly, by raising a moral concern without labeling it as such: "When you talk that way about hurting people, I become very frightened for you and the people you wish to hurt."

3. For cognitive–behavioral or biomedical theorists fully wedded to the moral neutrality of their work as scientists, there is no room for moral discourse or human suffering in their conceptualization of their work. They hope moral issues will be settled naturalistically by the data showing which behaviors lead to survival of the species (although one might ask in which geological epoch the data will be taken as conclusive). Furthermore, they maintain that the concept of suffering is too subjective to enter into a scientific formulation. Although there are certainly many practitioners who still subscribe to such views, perhaps the biomedical is being replaced by a

biopsychosocial theory of psychiatry Engel (1980) and the cognitive–behavioral approach by more integrative approaches such as Wachtel (1972) or Lazarus (1995) where emotional suffering need not be excluded from the diagnostic formulation. Nevertheless, not all models are equally accepting of human suffering and moral discourse in psychotherapy, and we can only hope for a fruitful discussion with these groups about the nature of science and morality that might prepare the way for such a discussion (see chaps. 3 and 4 for more on how to approach these discussions).

4. Criticism of the conceptualization of suffering offered here might also come from the opposite end of the therapeutic spectrum. Those more mystical approaches that blend Jungian or Eastern philosophy and religion with psychotherapy might argue that I have tied suffering and morality too closely to the psychotherapeutic relationship and not sufficiently considered the healing of suffering and the moral authority that comes from the spiritual rather than the interpersonal realm. Because I take suffering seriously, any clinical intervention that comforts or heals those who are suffering is, to me, valuable. No doubt in the thousands of years of human experience in the East and West there were many spiritual or philosophical practices developed that were proved helpful. Prayer, meditation, belief in a higher power, forgiveness, penances, and even sacrifices are likely candidates in this regard. I am not entirely unsympathetic with this criticism, but I must leave that intriguing dimension for others more qualified in these spiritual traditions.

5. If moral values influence the practice of psychotherapy, and there is not moral consensus among clinicians about the "good life," will not our divisiveness be increased or made inevitable? Currently, psychologists are, as a profession, at something akin to what Piaget (1952) called the *sensorimotor* phase of development concerning moral awareness. We are acting on moral issues with only the dimmest understanding and ability to verbalize our strategies or positions. Once we do this we will find that some of our differences are only semantic, or simply due to an incomplete analysis of the moral foundations upon which we work. There are many overlapping values even among very different moral traditions—respect for life, family, friendship, purposeful living, peace of mind, and so forth. No doubt we will also discover approaches to psychotherapy that are based on quite different moral values that cannot be fully reconciled. Here we will have to rely on the philosophical education that

will come from reading and studying moral philosophy (see chap. 7 for suggestions). One cannot help but emerge from such a study aware of the tremendous difficulty in achieving certainty about matters of moral right and wrong and with a certain humility about one's own positions and tolerance of others' views. In some very small percentage of situations our differences may rise to the level where we cannot tolerate each other's practices. Then, just as now, we will have political or legal avenues in which to pursue our moral differences. Unlike when this happens in the present, philosophically sophisticated psychotherapists taking such a route would have arrived at clearly demarcated moral positions. Before entering the legislative arena, their moral reasons and arguments for those positions would be developed in such a manner that the public or courts would have a clear sense of the nature of the choice being put before them. Neither the courts nor the legislatures are unfamiliar with the moral dimension in human suffering or with the dilemmas of having to make moral decisions on the basis of limited and incomplete information. Although they deal with suffering on a macrolevel, it is the business of psychology and psychotherapy to deal with the moral problems of suffering on the microlevel of individuals, families, and institutions, particularly where these problems do not rise quite to the level of severity (as in murder, rape, and assault) or the problems of evidentiary proof or restitution make the use of the political or legal system cumbersome or impractical.

It is fortunate that in a reasonably free and democratic society, individuals, families, and local and private organizations have the responsibility to define the meaning of the "good life" in their own terms so long as they do not jeopardize the rights of others to do the same. As Erich Fromm (1941) noted 60 years ago, this freedom is both highly sought after and terrifying to actually have. Most of us struggle throughout our lives to find what the "good life" will mean for us in the context of our family, friends, neighborhoods, and subculture. Psychotherapy can be an invaluable assistance in this process, provided the therapist is prepared for understanding the moral dimension in human suffering.

3

THE MORAL CONTENT OF THEORIES OF CLINICAL PRACTICE

The claim that clinical practice is a morally neutral enterprise has been challenged, although not effectively, almost since the inception of psychotherapy in the late 1800s. Beginning with the first exile from Freud's inner circle, Alfred Adler, a steady stream of independent thinkers in psychoanalysis, psychotherapy, psychiatry, and clinical psychology—including Karen Horney; Frieda Fromm-Reichman; Thomas Szasz; Rollo May; Perry London; and, more recently, Richard Chessick, Hans Strupp, Joseph Rychlak, and Allen Bergin—have attempted to dislodge this *idée fixee*. In his comprehensive and well-reasoned review of this extensive literature Tjeltveit (1999) wrote the following:

> Because psychotherapy is an inextricably ethical endeavor—not simply the technical application of scientific findings, not simply a medical treatment to reduce psychological distress, and not simply a journey of personal growth—we need to re-examine those understandings of therapy that are based upon the assumption that therapy is either value-free or inconsequentially value laden. (p. 231)

If one looks historically at the discipline of academic clinical psychology, one need look no further than Lightner Witmer for confirmation of the moral concerns intrinsic to our work. In the inaugural issue of his journal celebrating the establishment of the new profession of clinical psychology, Witmer (1907/1996) described two groups of children who had been served at his clinic at the University of Pennsylvania: "These children had made themselves conspicuous because of an inability to progress in schoolwork as rapidly as other children, or because of *moral defects, which rendered them difficult to manage under ordinary discipline*" [italics added] (p. 248).

Witmer (1907/1996) referred back to his 1896 address to the American Psychological Association in which he first outlined "a scheme for practical work in psychology." There he made a similar claim as to what will constitute this new practical psychology, mentioning moral problems in two of the four points:

1. The investigation of the phenomena of mental development in school children, as manifested more particularly in mental and *moral retardation* [italics added], by means of the statistical and clinical methods. . . .

4. The training of students for a new profession—that of the psychological expert, who should find his career in connection with the school system, through the examination and treatment of mentally and *morally retarded children* [italics added], or in connection with the practice of medicine. (p. 249)

There is a strong pull for the contemporary reader to find the term *morally retarded* old-fashioned and seek to replace it with the more modern-sounding *behaviorally disordered* or *emotionally disturbed*. This is done in the belief that the meaning has not been significantly altered and the semantic change harmless. Unfortunately, this small step and many more like it are the process by which clinical psychology became de-moralized (and perhaps also demoralized in the era of managed care), because the clinical terms *behavior disorder* and *emotional disturbance* do not direct one to consider, the way the term *morally retarded* (for all its harshness) does, the moral context of the child's life. From the moral point of view, instead of looking for something wrong with the child, one first looks to see who is responsible for the care of this child—who is morally engaged with this child's welfare, health, and education. The moral values and stance of not only the family but also the school and the neighborhood community become relevant. The moral point of view invites one to understand the world as the child sees it and how it might make sense to him to act in ways that others, or even he himself, regards as immoral. The moral is inextricably the interpersonal; it is about balancing a concern for oneself with a concern for other human beings. This is what it meant in Witmer's time, and this is what it means in our own. It has not changed, but clinical psychology and psychiatry have. These disciplines, despite the admonitions of leading members of their own professions, philosophers, historians, and sociologists, continue to attempt to work in a de-moralized theoretical and professional framework. Because these critiques are often done at a rather high level of theoretical abstraction (see Richardson, Guignon, & Fowers, 1999; Sadler, 1997; Slife, 2000; Woolfolk, 1998 for excellent examples), perhaps what is needed is a demonstration at the level of clinical practice how moral issues affect the ends and means of doing psychotherapy or clinical interventions. Throughout this chapter I examine the implicit or explicit moral content of the primary theoretical models of clinical practice, namely, the biological or medical, psychodynamic, cognitive–behavioral, humanistic, and family therapy models.

REEXAMINING THE "EYEWITNESS" FROM A MORAL POINT OF VIEW

By way of illustration of what is meant by psychotherapy as inextricably concerned with values and moral judgment, it might prove helpful to reexamine the case of the "Eyewitness," from the *DSM–IV Casebook* (Spitzer et al., 1994) and discussed in chapter 2, from the perspective of a morally engaged clinical psychologist. To review briefly the facts of the case: A 39-year-old female television news reporter recently covered (and witnessed) the execution of a murderer whose story she had been following for a number of years. She is seen by an employee assistance program (EAP) psychiatrist because she has lost interest in her work, feels detached and depersonalized, and is irritable with her husband. She is given a diagnosis of posttraumatic stress disorder (PTSD) and referred for marital counseling. In chapter 2, I observed that this is a case where human suffering figures centrally in the case and yet is never discussed or even mentioned.

Although on the basis of such a brief case vignette no one can say for sure what moral concerns might have troubled this particular individual, it is possible to examine the case from the moral point of view. It would be reasonable to suppose that a morally engaged reporter who is an eyewitness to the execution of a murderer would be in a position to both perceive and ponder any or all of the at least six difficult moral problems that follow: (a) Was the prisoner's conviction for murder fair and just? (b) Was the death sentence arrived at fairly? (c) Should the death penalty be used in U.S. society? (d) Is the television coverage being provided by the Eyewitness of this event good for the community? (e) If the Eyewitness believes that the answer to any of these questions is no, what are her moral responsibilities under the circumstances? Should she, for example, express her disapproval to her employers, to the courts or political authorities, during her broadcasts? What if her employers have "spun" the story for their own political reasons? Then she is faced with the excruciating moral dilemma of choosing between keeping her job, which she has probably worked very hard over many years to obtain, and expressing her moral outrage at the way this trial, sentencing, or execution has been conducted or reported. (f) This last dilemma raises yet another moral complexity: In addition to whatever conflict she may feel about risking her job for her moral principles, she must consider as well the impact that her unemployment might have on her husband. What duty does she have to him to keep her paycheck coming into the household, and how do her views on the moral adequacy of the criminal justice system, this trial, and execution, mesh with his? Have their discussions of this set of issues, or lack thereof, brought them closer as partners in life or driven a wedge between them? It would not be surprising, given the moral opaqueness and relativism rampant in our society today, that neither partner would know how to approach the sorting out of moral differences in the marriage.

Again, there is no way to know in the case reported if any of these moral concerns are present, although there is some indication from the write-up that it may not be far off base to suggest that this is likely. As Scarry (1985) observed, to witness the intentional physical harming of human life is the basis for our most straightforward recognition of the presence of evil in the world. Although little meaningful context is provided for understanding this case from the moral point of view, the Eyewitness is reported to have said, "Once you see someone die, you don't forget what it looks like." Thus, it does not seem farfetched at all to imagine her horror at witnessing, close up, the deliberate taking of a human life, and the death throes of the prisoner, and that she might reasonably be thought that to be feeling conflict or guilt over the news coverage she provided over the several years before the execution. The write-up indicates too that she has tried to stay objective as a reporter and keep her own emotional responses in check. This detachment is now exaggerated and feels depersonalizing and unwanted. Many emotions are what philosophers have started referring to as *moralized emotions*, because emotions such as shame, guilt, envy, and resentment carry a cognitive content that is decidedly moral. Perhaps the emotions she is trying to keep in check are of this sort.

The clinician interviewing the Eyewitness must be cognizant that suffering is often at least in part a moral problem and that suffering can be ameliorated by articulating and clarifying the problems in dialogue with other persons concerned about the same issues and then by deciding how to solve them. If these problems have not been tackled before by an individual, then the moral problems can feel overwhelming and disorienting. However, clarifying the client's moral dilemmas is only half of the process of moral engagement in psychotherapy. The other half has to do with the moral values that the psychologist brings to this task, and these usually are dictated by the psychologist's theoretical approach to psychotherapy (medical, cognitive–behavioral, humanistic, family therapy, psychodynamic, etc.), his or her personal value system, or both.

One can wonder whether the psychiatrist working for the EAP affiliated with the TV station felt a moral dilemma in weighing the interests of the station and the interests of the patient. If the Eyewitness were angry with her employer for the way she was required to cover the story, then the psychiatrist could choose to validate her feelings and encourage assertiveness in expressing them to the appropriate management individual, or the psychiatrist could choose to pathologize the anger as an inappropriate emotional response, a symptom of the PTSD. Once this initial moral question is resolved (who is the patient: the company or the individual?), the moral dimension of the therapist's work is only just beginning. A therapist who has been "listening to Prozac" with Kramer (1993) might see this PTSD as a kind of *forme frustes* of depression and offer a mood-elevating antidepressant (selective serotonin reuptake inhibitor [SSRI]). This would be justified, morally, on the grounds that she is experiencing unpleasant sensations of feeling detached from her own body, is irritable, is having difficulty sleeping, and is unmotivated to work. These are states of the body that are unpleasant, and life is much better without them; ergo, prescribe an SSRI. If she reacts to the medication by feeling better, taking life less seriously, and with fewer moral compunctions about the death penalty, or the media's responsibility in society, that is of little concern. Perhaps, Kramer speculated, some people who have strong social consciences are simply people who have tried to make a virtue out of masked depression, and now that we can treat their depression with SSRIs society can dispense with their heavy moral criticism of its institutions (Kramer, 1993, pp. 291–295). The goal that these psychiatrists and clinicians set for their patients is simply not to experience intense unpleasant sensations and feelings, regardless of the circumstances or conditions in which they live. Feeling them is "bad"; not feeling them is "good."

Of course, an existential–phenomenological therapist would take great issue with this medical approach. Anxiety about death and the moral quandaries it creates for human beings is the essence of what therapy is about; through it, one discovers the meaning of free will, responsibility, and autonomy, and ultimately one is forced to choose or find meaning in one's life. Depersonalization, anger, depressed feelings at work, and anxiety at recalling the execution would all be seen as an indication of a great moral–psychological struggle being waged within this woman's soul or psyche. Her job, and that of the therapist, is to see to it that this struggle is worked through to resolution and not abandoned out of fear and trepidation. This search for meaning and purpose in life, particularly in a person approaching midlife, may mean questioning her job satisfaction, career choice, the adequacy of her marriage, and her life priorities in general. An existential–phenomenological therapist may encourage as well the exploration of the transpersonal or spiritual elements of the crisis, perhaps in terms of the meaning of mortality, and the possibility of the continuity of consciousness in life and after death. For those completely immersed in the secular scientific worldview of our society, it has become uncomfortable to talk about strong feelings related to an afterlife, continued emotional connection to those who are deceased, and the felt sense that this life cannot be all there is to existence. Even in mainstream religious contexts, the power of the secular view is seen in the frequent attempts to reconcile religious views with scientific theories and rationalize religious beliefs and feelings, and the avoidance of intense emotionality when discussing these topics. How could intelligent life this complex, and this capable of creative symbolic, abstract, and nearly unbounded expression, be linked to such finite, brittle, and limited physical substances as our mortal bodies? These are the sorts of existential issues and values the Eyewitness might be seen as bringing or revealing to an existential psychotherapist.

A contemporary psychodynamic, object relations, or family systems therapist would view the PTSD symptoms of the Eyewitness in terms of what they indicate about the quality of interpersonal relationships in this woman's life. Had she become attached to this prisoner in covering the story for several years, and how does she interpret his loss? Losses earlier in her life might be explored by the psychodynamic therapist, whereas the family therapist would focus on her present relationships with her spouse and family of origin. Has she been feeling similarly overwhelmed and impotent to effect change at home or in the family? How do her relationships with the people at the television station reflect those family relationships, and can the communication patterns and boundaries be redesigned to work better for her? The assumption is, of course, that she will be better once her relationships are better. The concept of good or healthy relationships has many moral value judgments packed into it. When psychologists promote mutually respectful, open, supportive relationships, they do so from a moral position. When a psychotherapist "diagnoses" a relationship as aggressive, manipulative, exploitative, and destructive, there are both moral and descriptive contents to those terms; one is saying both that certain patterns of behavior are taking place and that they are wrong, and it may be impossible to separate the observation from the judgment.

A cognitive–behavioral therapist would be concerned about the Eyewitness's unpleasant sensations, her avoidance of work, and her expressions of irritability with her husband. Symptoms of anxiety will be approached by, for example, desensitizing her to images of the execution. If this does not reduce her irritability or avoidance, then those symptoms will be attacked directly by challenging her irrational ideas about her adequacy as a reporter or spouse and by instructing her in assertiveness so that her anger can be expressed in a more acceptable fashion. As in the medical model, the basic framework of her life will not be challenged, and the goal will be to restore her to the level of functioning she had prior to witnessing the execution (which is assumed to be better for her than her current state).

The case vignette indicates that the Eyewitness was sent by the EAP psychiatrist to a marital counselor. No justification is given, so one does not know if that reflects a conscious moral decision to put a priority on intimate relationships as the ultimate good in this person's life. Such a decision would certainly require the patient's consent, and it should be an informed one, based on understanding the moral issues at stake and the approach various therapies take to those moral issues. Perhaps instead the client would want to emphasize the individual existential or personal growth opportunities presented by the situation, or, conversely, she might want to focus primarily on not losing her job. In either case, the marital counseling misses the mark completely. It is entirely possible that the therapist's orientation to the moral realm will conflict with the client's and that what the client wants help accomplishing is not something the therapist finds morally acceptable. Of course, if the decision to offer marital therapy is presented as a purely technical, scientific, professional exercise of expertise, then no such discussion will take place with the client, who will have been further de-moralized by the process.

I was once consulted for psychotherapy by a gentleman who had been engaging in a series of extramarital affairs over a period of 10 years. One of his goals was to learn how to manage his lover and his wife in order to permit the affair to continue and escape detection. He felt more fearful than guilty, and he was clear in desiring therapy that would reduce both anxiety and guilt. More specifically, he was seeking relief from symptoms of sleeplessness, feelings of panic (at being detected), poor concentration, and excessive reliance on alcohol as a relaxant. He requested medication or some relaxation techniques to help him stay sharp and focused and not get caught. Should a psychologist offer to help with such a request? Those committed to a medical or cognitive–behavioral model might certainly agree without running afoul of the implicit moral values in their theory. (This says nothing about whether their *personal* morality might prohibit cooperation in such a professional relationship.)

A family therapist would be hard pressed to accept such a case, as the goal flies in the face of the implicit moral values of the theory. An existential–phenomenological therapist might agree to work with the client but only if the client understood that his moral choices might become a part of the therapy. Finally, it is difficult to say exactly how the psychodynamic approach would be likely to regard such a request for therapy. On the one hand, such a request might be regarded as simply a "presenting" problem and, like any neurotic expression of anxiety, likely to give way to other concerns once the therapy was under way. Thus, agreeing to start therapy with such a person without tackling the moral issue might be a strategic choice that would eventually lead to a change in moral priorities for the client. On the other hand, the request might be regarded as an indication that the person does not want the kind of therapy offered that focuses on self-exploration and improving the capacity to love and work—not to manipulate and dissemble. Such a client might then be asked whether he wants psychodynamic therapy or some other kind of behavioral consultation.

It can be seen from even as relatively simple a case of PTSD as presented in the "Eyewitness" vignette that moral issues are inextricably interwoven into the fabric of the case. One cannot clearly separate the moral from the clinical because, as the quotation from Lightner Witmer (1907/1996) demonstrated, the moral and the clinical are one and the same.

MORAL AGENCY AND CLINICAL PSYCHOLOGY

A student of psychology, or a psychologist, who has begun to recognize the moral concerns that are implicit in the practice of psychology often experiences a sense of confusion or disorientation at this point. Questions arise: What does it mean for a concern to be moral rather than just psychological? Cannot moral beliefs be studied scientifically, like any other attitude or belief, so that the right moral positions are determined with the scientific method? Are not all moral positions relative, so that if psychological practice is moral, that will mean that there are no right or wrong ways to practice? If moral concerns are an important aspect of psychological practice that has not been a part of one's education and training, how does one become an informed, morally engaged practitioner?

These questions can be seen as separating into three broad groups: (a) the nature of the moral point of view, (b) the relationship of moral concerns to the science of psychology, and (c) the application of moral theories and principles to clinical practice.

The Nature of the Moral Point of View: Moral Agency

The critical component of the moral point of view that is difficult for individuals in the mainstream of psychology to comprehend is the concept of a "moral agent." Rather than viewing human beings as simply a set of responses and behaviors that are determined by natural forces (physiological states, learning histories, genetically inherited traits, social forces, etc.), the moral point of view asserts that human beings are agents who actively pursue their various interests, goals, and purposes, not entirely passive objects that are manipulated and controlled by natural or external forces. Moral agents view themselves as responsible through the choices they make for their actions, behaviors, and responses to external forces. When their actions are destructive or hurtful to others, moral agents assume responsibility for the consequences of the decisions they make as well.

Viewing human beings as moral agents does not mean that one must ignore the basic physical, psychological, or social forces and processes at work that influence the decisions and choices that are made. The existence of irrational impulses, physiological drives, and interpersonal and social processes is not denied in this viewpoint. What is denied is that these forces completely determine human action. Human choices and decisions must be made in full cognizance of these forces, and at times these forces may negate the consequences of such an action by a human agent; however, even under such extreme circumstances the decision to act is still critical and meaningful as an expression of who one is as a person. The Czech playwright and statesman Havel (1990) observed during his imprisonment as a political prisoner under the Communists that hope for the future was critical for survival and that hope "is not the conviction that something will turn out well, but the certainty that something makes sense, regardless of how it turns out" (p. 181). Choosing what to believe in—one's values—is about as close as human beings can come to the experience of pure freedom. Even when one's choices are negated by circumstances and external (physical) forces, one preserves in the concept of oneself as a moral agent the critical feature of decision and choice that preserves both freedom and hope. Moral freedom, as the 18th-century German philosopher Kant (1781/1929) observed, is metaphysical: beyond the physical world of determinism. It does not deny the existence of natural forces; it transcends them through the powers of human thought.

As William James (1896/1966) pointed out more than 100 years ago, it is in the mental life that the limitations of a physical determinism can be seen most clearly. James pointed out that people who believe in their own powers of self-determination, and as a result take charge of their own lives and stop rationalizing all their mistakes, do in fact have different life outcomes than those who remain in the passive, deterministic, and fatalistic position.

> And often enough our faith beforehand in an uncertified *result is the only thing that makes the result come true.* Suppose, for instance, that you are climbing a mountain, and worked yourself into a position from which the only escape is by a terrible leap. Have faith that you can successfully make it, and your feet are nerved to its accomplishment. But mistrust yourself, and think of all the sweet things you have heard scientists say about *maybes* and you will hesitate so long that, at last, all unstrung and trembling, and launching yourself in a moment of despair, you roll in the abyss. In such a case (and it belongs to an enormous class) the part of wisdom as well of courage is to *believe what is in line of your needs*, for only by such belief is the need fulfilled. Refuse to believe, and you shall indeed be right, for you shall irretrievably perish. But believe, and again you shall be right, for you shall save yourself. You make one or the other of two possible universes true by your trust or mistrust,—both universes having been only maybes, in the particular, before you contributed your act. (p. 28)

This excerpt is from an essay in which James (1896/1966) took up the question of how one can justify to a suicidal and melancholic individual preoccupied with human suffering a faith in life over death. In his answer, he showed clearly that he understood the relationship between the assertion of free will and the existence of human morality:

> This life *is* worth living, we can say, *since it is what we make it, from the moral point of view;* and we are determined to make it from that point of view, so far as we have anything to do with it, a success. (p. 30)

For more than 30 years, Rychlak (Rychlak, 1969, 1981, 1994, 1997, 2002) has demonstrated through both philosophical argument and experimental demonstrations that human learning and information-processing studies can be viewed as establishing the role of freedom in human action. He calls this *logical-learning theory,* because the effects of the environmental stimuli are always filtered through the human capacity for negation of incoming stimuli. Before the stimulus "conditions" one's response, one makes a choice, conscious or unconscious, to accept or reject it. It is not that experimental data are unimportant in considering the sources of human action. Rather it is the interpretation of that data in a deterministic, mechanistic manner that distorts one's view of human agency.

Kant (1781/1929) used the term *antinomy of reason* to refer to the free-will versus determinism debate in philosophy. An *antinomy* is an apparent logical contradiction that does not result in one rejecting the truth of one side or the other. That humans are free moral agents and that they are a part of the natural world governed by scientific explanation are both propositions that we have good reasons to believe are true. They contradict one another (or seem to), and so logic demands that one must reject one of them. Yet one cannot reject either; thus, we have an antinomy of reason.

Psychotherapists frequently are confronted with practical examples of this antinomy in their daily work. Clients frequently seek help with problems where they feel they are out of their own control, behaving impulsively or compulsively. In fact, some of the most convinced determinists are people seeking help from a psychotherapist for addictive problems. Indeed, their life histories suggest many external forces that have influenced their lives and their addictive actions: problems in their families of origin, perhaps a parent with an addiction; rejections and disappointments; or a serious traumatic event that haunts them. Clinicians have much to contribute to this philosophical discussion, because it is impossible to be helpful to such clients if one adopts with them a strictly deterministic viewpoint about their behavior. All of the successful approaches with these problems depend on restoring a sense of personal responsibility as a means of ending the addiction. It is widely admitted that the most successful treatment for alcoholism known to date is Alcoholics Anonymous, which uses what I would call a *psycho–social–spiritual model* for recovering a sense of personal freedom and self-direction in life. To see clinical problems from the moral point of view does not require that one reject the study of external (physical, physiological, unconscious, or social) influences on behavior; it requires only that one not reject the idea that these forces act on a moral agent who then decides and chooses what to make of her or his life.

The Search for a Scientific Morality: Psychology's Utilitarian History

The view that moral concerns and controversies could be resolved by science was invented not by proponents of the Boulder model in the 1950s but by the 19th-century British philosophers who called themselves *Utilitarians*: Jeremy Bentham, James Mill, and John Stuart Mill, (Sabine, 1960). They argued that when faced with moral questions or dilemmas, one should evaluate the utility of various courses of action and always decide in favor that course of action that yields "the greatest happiness for the greatest number of people." With this formulation, John Stuart Mill claimed that the Utilitarians had paved the way for the creation of "moral sciences" that would develop calculi for deciding all questions of personal and public morality (Robinson, 1989). All that remained, now that the philosophers had done their work, was for the development of empirical methods for making such calculations—for measuring human happiness in the population (although see below for some of the philosophical objections to Mill's theory). Thus were born, in the early 20th century, at the London School of Economics, under the influence of the Fabians (MacKenzie & MacKenzie, 1977), the modern social science techniques of population surveys and other systematic methods for measuring social ills and social satisfaction.

Until very recently, histories of psychology, while acknowledging the philosophical origins of psychology in the 19th century, focused almost entirely on the questions in epistemology that gave birth to empirical studies of sensation, perception, memory, and learning, all of which directly pertained to questions about the nature and origins of human knowledge. What is deemphasized in these accounts, or missed altogether, is the relationship between the questions in moral philosophy in the 19th century and the development of empirical approaches to child development, personality, and abnormal psychology.

Systems of Morality

Moral theories have been propounded in moral philosophy to give human beings regarded as moral agents a theory or basis on which to make their moral choices and decisions. The central moral concept of concern to philosophers during the Socratic period in Greece was that of *character* and its role in human happiness and goodness. Character traits were described as either virtues or vices, and much effort went into describing the kinds of education, child training, and life experiences that built virtuous character and avoided the development of character excesses or deficiencies. The Socratic "golden mean" was a moral principle for use in guiding one's own behavior and in evaluating the character of others: Avoid extremes, and seek moderation in all things. Neither too much food nor too little is a good thing. The same is true for all human endeavors, whether it be exercise, alcohol, argument, affection, and so forth.

Character or virtue ethics can be contrasted with eudaimonistic ethical systems that define the Good in terms of promoting human well-being or happiness and deontological moral systems that define the Good in terms of a set of obligations and duties to be followed that emanate from a recognized authority, whether that be a spiritual or secular one. Utilitarianism is a eudaimonistic moral theory, whereas Judeo–Christian morality is an example of a deontological moral system in that it emphasizes the Ten Commandments given by the Lord to Moses on Mt. Sinai. Kant's (1781/1929) ethical theory attempts to extract from the Judeo–Christian heritage a logic or rational basis of moral authority. His fundamental moral principle is to will only those acts that one can will universally for all people—a logical distillation of the Golden Rule. It is a universalizability principle, that moral action must permit equal status for all participants in the moral framework. Derived from this was Kant's other famous moral dictum: To treat human beings always as ends in themselves and never as mere means to some other end. Kant thought that scientific principles of cause and effect were essential to the explanation of natural phenomena but that human beings, by virtue of their mental capacities, were capable of approaching a transcendental realm of pure thought that obeyed its own rules of explanation—logical and moral rules that were inherent in the human psyche and revealed through an analysis of the constant and unchanging aspects of human experience (the categories of thought: similarity and difference, enumeration, causality, space and time, good and evil).

Moral decisions based on Utilitarian principles are likely to conflict with those based on duty or obligation to obey moral laws. As I noted in the discussion of suffering in chapter 2, the justification for moral principles is often given in the Judeo–Christian heritage in terms of reducing human suffering and therefore is also implicitly eudaimonistic, even though the obligation of believers to follow the Ten Commandments and other rules and laws of observance is binding regardless of the immediate consequences and regardless of the pleasure or pain that results. One can imagine circumstances in which Utilitarianism would authorize the sacrifice of an individual for the benefit of the greater number in the community, whereas the Kantian or Judeo–Christian moral code would prohibit such sacrifice or devaluing of the worth of the individual. There are other circumstances in which the definition of happiness itself becomes problematic. For example, one might imagine that a sociopathic individual might report a great increase in personal happiness at having perpetrated a fraud, murder, or other violation of the Ten Commandments and attempt to argue that therefore his action was morally right or good. The definition of happiness must ultimately be based on some principle other than immediate satisfaction or personal emotional responses. From where is this principle for deciding on the meaning of real happiness to come, if not some rational or authoritative source outside the judgment of individual human beings? So it would appear that Utilitarianism gives way to some deontological theory of morality (Sterba, 1989). One must look for a basis for morality that, while not excluding human happiness as subjectively reported well-being (or the absence thereof), provides one with a means of including a true or deeper sense of lasting happiness as opposed to just immediate subjective pleasure and pain.

It is this very flaw in Utilitarian moral theory that limits the ability of a scientific psychology aimed at describing, assessing, and then explaining human pleasure and pain to serve as an effective arbiter or substitute for moral judgment in our culture. To the extent that Utilitarianism is an adequate moral philosophy, psychology can function as an applied science of human behavior directing people in their personal decision-making and clinical practices, for all applied and clinical questions are at least in part moral questions of how one should live one's life and find the "good Life." A theory devoid of moral content cannot begin to help one answer these kinds of questions. A morally neutral science cannot serve us, either. The only reason psychology has been able to pass itself off both as a science and as providing guidance on such matters is that it is the embodiment of Mill's (1840/1974) "moral science": Utilitarianism.

Utilitarianism is not without its advantages as a secular theory of ethics and morality. It is clearly tied to human judgment rather than a metaphysical or spiritual authority with which many would take issue. Second, it has a simplicity and intuitive appeal as it shifts the answer from what seems like an impossibly ambiguous and vague question—"What is goodness?"—to the answer to what seems like a much more straightforward and clear question: "What causes pleasure and pain?" Pleasure and pain appear initially to be phenomena closely linked to the physiology of the body (the gratification of motivational drives, avoidance of injury, etc.) and so, in essentially a single conceptual move (from "goodness" to "pleasure and pain"), one is presented with an account of morality as a naturalistic, scientific phenomenon. It is a brilliant philosophical gambit, and as both learning theory and psychoanalysis in the late 19th and early 20th centuries burgeoned as approaches to psychology, the mechanisms by which the pursuit of pleasure and the avoidance of pain influenced animal and human behavior only served to heighten the sense that this was the core of our very being and, by inference, the essence of living well or poorly.

The problem for psychology is however, that the history of philosophy is littered with brilliant gambits, each offering powerful insights, only to be superseded, as Hegel (1832/1969) pointed out, by some new antithesis or synthesis. One would be terribly shortsighted to either reject the insights of Utilitarianism or believe that it offers a complete account of the nature of moral goodness. In addition to its logical beauty, its social implications are largely ameliorative. It forces one to take account of the real impact of social policies and institutions on all persons who are affected and to count each person's pleasure or pain as of equal value. It is a democratic moral and political philosophy and recognizes the voices of suffering of the masses, not just the voices of the ruling elite. Considering that Utilitarianism was developed within 100 years of when the divine right of kings was still the governing ideology of most of Europe, this is a major contribution to the Western intellectual tradition.

Critics of the time were quick to point out the logical weaknesses in Utilitarianism, particularly the difficulty of creating a calculus of pain and pleasure once one leaves the simple realm of basic needs and looks to the "higher" pleasures (e.g., the arts or intellectual stimulation) and more complex pains (e.g., bittersweet attachments or the pain of vulnerability in love) of life. These could never be measured effectively across an entire population because there would be so much individual variability in how such activities were experienced. Yet if one insisted on measuring pleasure and pain, one would end up evaluating actions only for their crasser consequences, and this scientific morality would be shallow and hedonistic. John Stuart Mill acknowledged these criticisms (Sabine, 1960) and attempted to modify the theory so that it was still a viable logical account of the meaning of moral goodness; he cannot be held responsible for the actions of his followers who, ignoring these conceptual problems, attempted to empirically implement a "moral science" without sufficient attention to its obvious shortcomings.

Before leaving the topic of Utilitarianism in philosophy, it is important to note that some in philosophy have asserted that the search for moral truths (or principles that can be applied as universal guideposts to behavior) is futile. In general, this is called the position of *moral* or *ethical relativism*. On this view, moral principles are an expression of cultural, subcultural, or even individual subjective beliefs and customs. According to moral or ethical relativists, there is no way to judge these moral beliefs outside of the framework in which they originate, and so it is possible to have a sociology or psychology that explains how a group or individual learned or developed such moral positions, but this does not produce a moral evaluation of such beliefs. Moral principles are viewed as just another attitude or personality trait to be studied in social psychology, personality theories, anthropology, or sociology.

Moral relativism is a widely held view in contemporary America, both among the general population and among social scientists. It is linked as well to the modern development in philosophy in the early 20th century among the Anglo-American philosophers associated with logical positivism. Stevenson (1944) articulated a view of what he called *Emotivism* that held that moral values were simply the expression of strong emotional reactions, the verbal equivalent of grunts and groans or squeals of delight. Stevenson thought that as such emotive expressions, moral claims were largely devoid of cognitive content and therefore could not be true or false, right or wrong. They just were. Nothing more could be said about them. This obviously is an extreme form of moral relativism, since there could be a great variability in what emotions human beings felt in a given situation and no way to reconcile these feelings to reach a common one.

One can see in both moral relativism and emotivism an extension of Utilitarian thinking. In response to critics who said that the moral calculus would not work to define moral principles because of the variability in how humans experienced pain and pleasure, morality was redefined to accommodate this variability. If moral values are relative, then this is not a shortcoming of Utilitarianism, but a virtue. The results of applying Utilitarian thinking simply are seen as confirming the relativity of all moral values. Furthermore, if moral claims are simply the expression of almost reflexive emotional reactions to the environment, then the moral hedonic calculus that Mill envisioned would work, because higher pleasures and complex pains could be reduced to some straightforward sigh or groan.

Finally, if there really is no universal principle of moral goodness, and everything is relative to culture and context, then it is simply enough within any given culture to document how people react hedonically to various stimuli and that, by definition, will tell them how to behave. Research will help people anticipate where the pleasures of life reside, and they will then seek them out. Psychologists and social scientists are simply creating hedonic roadmaps for life. Here is a mountain of pleasure (go for it), and there, a valley of pain (watch out). If morals are simply natural or learned emotional responses, then psychology and the social sciences are the moral gurus of the modern era. It is a strange alchemy of naturalistic explanation and logical analysis. What is desirable is redefined as what is desired, and yet humans are still seen as requiring direction from experts to determine what they should desire. One would have thought that if this is such a naturalistic organic (and deterministic) process, we would inevitably and inexorably follow our emotional desires and always end up doing "good." We do not need an expert to tell us to eat when we are hungry or drink when we are thirsty, yet we seem to need experts to tell us whether our emotional reactions to leaving our children at day care, working 60-hour weeks, or using corporal punishment in the schools are valid indicators of what we should do.

Just as Utilitarianism had its critics in philosophy, so has Emotivism. In fact, social scientists and psychologists would be surprised by how little support there is for such a view among contemporary moral philosophers. Emotivism has been replaced by a view of morality as governed by reason (Baier, 1965; Hare, 1963; Nozick, 1981; Rawls, 1971) and, more recently, by a return to moral psychology in which the emotions are recognized as central to morality but now with emotions as having cognitive components as well as affective ones (Care, 2000). This parallels a renewed interest in the psychology of emotion within psychology itself and recognition that emotion and cognition are distinct but interactive components of experience (de Sousa, 1999; Nussbaum, 2001).

Psychology Attempts to Fill the Void

Psychology as it separated from philosophy in the early 20th century was eager nonetheless to adopt Mill's notion of a scientific approach to morality. The historian of psychology Leahey (1997) noted that once applied psychology became an active discipline and profession, it quickly took on the features of a secular religion: the gospel of scientism. Writing of the period just after the first world war, he observed the following:

> Science undermined religion; scientism bid to replace it. The Flaming Youth of the 1920's were the first generation of Americans to be raised in the urban, industrialized everywhere communities of twentieth-century life. Cut off from traditional religious values of the vanishing island communities, *they turned to modern science for instruction in morals and rules of behavior* [italics added]. Postwar psychology[,] no longer preoccupied with socially sterile introspection, was the obvious science to which to turn for guidance concerning living one's life and getting ahead in business and politics. (p. 368)

There is no question but that this trend has continued into the present, with the larger culture looking to psychology for answers on questions of child rearing, character (personality) development, and character problems (abnormal and clinical psychology). Psychologists have taken on these tasks for a culture that wishes to secularize moral issues and would like scientific certainty to replace the authoritative voice of religion, which held sway over moral matters in Western countries for the better part of two millennia. Mill's moral science calculus has unfortunately proved far more difficult to implement than it was to hypothesize. The difficulty of finding a consensus definition of human happiness that would result in the design of practical measures of human happiness that are useful across more than a rather narrow subset of the population has crippled the project. People of different moral backgrounds define happiness in radically different ways, and so there is no yardstick to hold up against reality to determine the most moral outcome of a set of options. Even our perception as to whether another human being is happy or unhappy is influenced by our moral judgment as to whether we believe they ought to be happy or unhappy. If we perceive a person as happy when we do not think she or he deserves to be, we probably would not describe the person as "happy" but rather as "manic" or "giddy." Similarly, if we perceive someone as unhappy but do not think they should be, we might say that person is "depressed." In this way, basic clinical judgments about a person's mental status can be influenced by our moral judgments concerning how we think people should behave. Deciding whether a parent is setting good limits versus punishing harshly and therefore "abusive" depends on one's moral beliefs about the inherent good or evil in human nature and one's moral values as to how spontaneous and autonomous children should be encouraged to be. Nussbaum (1990) noted that Aristotle and the ancient Greek philosophers were acutely aware of this problem. They noted that moral problems can be addressed only if there is a recognition or awareness in the first place that such a problem exists. This is not the case with many physical problems. If there is no water coming from the tap, we can all agree that there is a problem. But the observation that there is "no love" coming from a parent to a child depends on valuing a certain kind of emotional relationship. For one who does not believe that love (or structure, compassion, attunement, etc.) is required in such a relationship, there is nothing to note as missing.

Even if there were such a measure, using it to assess a population whose members realizes that their responses will have an impact on policy or their personal fortunes raises the issue of subject bias or measurement reactivity that makes the atomic physicist Heisenberg's "uncertainty principle" seem like a minor problem. Heisenberg (1958) noted that one could not know at the same time the position and speed of an electron, because the act of measuring one altered the other. In the case of human happiness, one has to choose between quantification and meaning. Any meaningful assessment of human happiness requires a narrative dialogue in a climate of trust and understanding. Otherwise, people will not share their intimate experiences of joy and happiness, or, on the other end of the continuum, sorrow and suffering (R. B. Miller, 1998). This means focusing on a small number of individuals (case studies) rather than large-scale sampling studies.

This of course would be entirely unwieldy in survey research, especially where many courses of action were being evaluated across a wide portion of the population. Quantitative survey instruments that involve brief structured interviews or that can be presented in written or electronic form are much more practical but are so superficial as to leave no doubt that something other than human happiness or suffering has been assessed. Yet it is this for which psychology and the social sciences have largely settled and what the public accepts to guide it in its decisions on whether children should be placed in day care, whether Ritalin helps children who do not pay attention to their schoolwork, or whether adults should take Prozac for their low self-esteem and inhibitions in the workplace.

Of course, we do not say that we are measuring human happiness anymore than we say we are treating human suffering. The outcome measures are of constructs such as self-esteem, attentive behavior, absenteeism from the job, or reading scores. The implicit moral judgments that one "should" pay attention in school and that children who pay attention are of "better" character than children who do not pay attention are so taken for granted as moral givens in our society that we do not regard it as necessary to explicitly state or defend them. One who questions such givens in a clinical or even casual social conversation is met by utter disbelief and not a little anger or consternation. "How can one question the value of paying attention in school?" "Everyone knows that paying attention to the teacher is what kids are supposed to do." The fact that we have a moral position that is so rarely questioned as to have become invisible to those who participate in it does not obviate the fact that it is a moral position and not a factual one. Even more interesting is the question of how our moral positions became so invisible. Perhaps it is because we have a consensus on what character traits we admire and wish to promote in our children, or perhaps it is just the opposite. We are so fractured and divided that we prefer not to notice when our values are coming into play. If we notice them, we will have to do something about them—defend them or attack the opponent's positions. Instead, we have become a morally mute nation, unable to speak about moral issues except under the guise of scientific controversy.

If one has any doubt at all about the extent to which in our culture we approach the moral dimensions of human character in a de-moralized manner one need look no further than the *Diagnostic and Statistical Manual of Mental Disorders* (DSM–IV; American Psychiatric Association, 1994). The entire Axis II, Personality Disorders, is descriptions not of symptoms of disorders but of lifelong patterns of thought, feeling, and behavior that are characterized as disordered. What the Greeks saw as character excesses or deficiencies to be molded by education and training we see as evidence of diseased or dysfunctional families or brain tissue. Personality disorders can be characterized as being *ego syntonic*, meaning that the individual regards the personality characteristics as unproblematic or even admirable, but the clinician is to judge them as disordered anyway. This is a rare kind of disease that the patient seeks not help with, and perhaps even enjoys, yet the physician is required to treat. Would it not be a whole lot more conceptually simple, and honest, to admit that psychiatry and psychology have taken on the responsibility of social control and the enforcement of moral standards of behavior in areas of intimate relationships and personal taste that are not amenable to criminal enforcement by the courts? We do not want to throw someone in jail for being self-absorbed, self-serving, and self-important (i.e., narcissistic personality disorder), but we do not want that person acting that way any longer, and we want someone (the therapist) to do something about it. Because the mental health professions do not diagnose people for a lack of moral rectitude, and because psychotherapy is not viewed as a moral undertaking but a technical application of scientific principles of human behavior, the project is quite doomed from the start. How can one change someone's moral character without ever discussing moral issues with him or her? One cannot, and so either the mental health professions really are not doing just technical interventions, or they are not truly addressing the narcissist's problem. Indeed, all of the *DSM–IV* diagnoses contain implicit moral evaluations concerning actions that are considered acceptable or unacceptable by the predominant moral values of the culture. With the personality disorders the mask is off, and the implicit moral judgment is barely disguised (Caplan, 1995; Kirk & Kutchins, 1992).

Scientific Theory Versus Practical Wisdom (Phronesis)

Faced with the overwhelming evidence that moral issues permeate clinical psychology, individuals on the scientific side of the scientist–practitioner schism in academic psychology often fall back on the following sort of argument. "Sure," they will say, "the uses of psychological knowledge are open to moral review, but the knowledge itself remains morally neutral. The study of the processes by which human beings develop problems or the techniques and processes by which they may be helped to overcome those problems are simply descriptive knowledge of the psychological forces in the universe." They claim that the although the goals of therapeutic work may be chosen on the basis of moral considerations, the methods or techniques (the means) are selected for their empirical or pragmatic consequences and are therefore morally neutral, or amoral. Moral neutrality is claimed not only for the techniques but also for any empirical research evaluating or developing those techniques. Scientifically oriented practitioners believe that one can separate the means from the ends and that research evaluating psychotherapy can thus be based on value-free measures of success or failure.

As I discussed briefly in chapter 1, Aristotle's (McKeon, 1941) notion that ethics is the province of phronesis is an important one in contemporary philosophy and should be in clinical psychology as well. Aristotle considered the relationship between means and ends in ethics, and his conclusions suggest an answer to those who would remove psychotherapeutic methods and the study of psychotherapeutic methods from the realm of the moral.

Aristotle was the father of logic, and the syllogism, including the following famous example:

a. It is good for all people to be respectful of others,
b. Socrates is a man; therefore,
c. It is good for Socrates to be respectful of others.

However, Aristotle noted in the *Nichomachean Ethics* (McKeon, 1941) that in this area of life reasoning follows a different format, which he called the practical syllogism. The practical syllogism has as its major premise a moral principle, as its minor premise a statement of fact, and as its conclusion a statement of an action to be performed, for example,

a. All men should be respectful of human life;
b. Socrates is a man; therefore;
c. Socrates should act in ways respectful of human life.

Aristotle was clear that the goal of ethics is not conceptual abstract knowledge but practical knowledge that produces the real-world results dictated by the practical syllogism. Only those who are capable of actually, in this instance, respecting human life can be said to possess practical wisdom. Jonsen and Toulmin (1988) argued convincingly that Aristotle's concept of *phronesis* is critical to an understanding of clinical knowledge in medicine and, I presume by extension, to all the clinical mental health disciplines.

> No professional enterprise today is closer to moral practice, or better exemplifies the special "practical" inquiries (about which Aristotle writes), than clinical medicine. Clinical practice, for a start, shares the emphasis on the certitude of direct experience that was for Aristotle a mark of the *practical* . . . clinical knowledge requires what Aristotle calls "prudence" or *phronesis*: practical wisdom in dealing with particular individuals, specific problems, and the details of particular actual situations. (pp. 36–37)

One particular feature of Aristotle's account of practical wisdom will prove central to the discussion of moral issues in psychotherapy, namely, that in the moral realm Aristotle holds that means have a special relationship to ends. He pointed out that in the practice of various crafts or skills, the means to an end may be a very different sort of action than the end itself. The carpenter may first have to engage in many acts that are, in and of themselves, destructive in order to arrive at a constructive or good end. However, in exercising moral judgment, and seeking the good for human beings, the actions (the means) that produce the good (the ends) are in themselves samples or components of the good.

The Aristotelian scholar Dahl (1984) noted the following:

> It has been standard practice since the time of Greenwood (1909) to distinguish two kinds of means in Aristotle's thought—external and internal (or constitutive) means. External means are causally instrumental in the production of ends. As such they are logically independent of their ends. Rubbing a person's body is an external means to warmth. Internal means, however, are not causally instrumental in the production of their ends, and they are not logically independent of their ends. In a sense they constitute their ends. They specify, "what it is" to act in accord with them. (p. 76)

Aristotle's analysis of phronesis shows logically that if the end or purpose of an action falls under moral purview, so does the action or means to that end. This can be seen if one looks at different theoretical approaches to therapy. Whatever the therapeutic goal, therapy consists of exposing the client to small, regular doses of that end. Medical treatment has the goal of altering a presumed biochemical imbalance. The treatment is regular doses of a biochemical substance. In existential therapy, the goal is increasing authentic experiencing of life, and the treatment is the weekly exposure to an authentic relationship. In rational–emotive and cognitive therapies the end is to produce rational thinking, and the treatment is weekly sessions in which irrational ideas are challenged. Finally, in family therapy, if the goal is increasing open and direct communication in the family, then the treatment consists of family sessions in which open and direct communication is prompted and encouraged. There are no techniques without moral commitments built in, and so research on techniques is never value free or morally neutral. In addition to whatever empirical question is under study, one is always also researching the impact or implications of holding a certain moral position in clinical psychology, and this is usually a moral position implicitly accepted by the researcher.

Jonsen and Toulmin (1988) made an additional logical point about phronesis that became central to moral reasoning for more than 500 years in Europe during the Middle Ages, namely, that problems of living must be contextualized and that ethical and moral decision making, although guided by broad principles, must be understood on a case-by-case basis—what moral theologians of the Middle Ages called *casuistry*. Here is where a society builds its moral and intellectual consensus—on the ground, so to speak, sorting out the pros and cons, consequences and implications of different courses of action. Practical wisdom is driven primarily not by the application of general principles but by real-world problem solving to determine the right thing to do. Jonsen and Toulmin observed that in problems of medical ethics, professionals can often reach an honest consensus on how to ethically handle a situation, even if they cannot agree on the principles that explain or account for their decisions. It is as though each individual has a practical moral sense that guides him or her and affirms or rejects various solutions even when he or she lacks an abstract moral principle to cover the situation. Phronesis, as a practical ethical concept, lends itself to case-by-case analysis of problems, which of course is the medium within which the clinician works, and suggests that the case study should be the primary research vehicle of the morally engaged clinician. (See chap. 6 for a discussion of the case study method of research.)

Practical wisdom has received much renewed attention from health care professionals looking for a way of remoralizing their disciplines (e.g., Hunter, 1996). It is important because it offers an alternative to scientific reasoning as a model for clinical reasoning. It is prescriptive rather than simply descriptive in that one of the premises in a practical reasoning argument is a moral principle ("One ought to keep one's promises," or "One ought to be compassionate to those who suffer").

As noted above, for Aristotle (Nussbaum, 1990) practical wisdom required the ability to *perceive* the moral question presented by a particular social context, and so one had to not only know moral principles but also see how to apply them to a given situation. Furthermore, the practical syllogism results in moral action, not just in a simple cognitive proposition stating what one ought to do (although that is possibly a part of doing it). Thus, practical wisdom is ideally suited to capturing the logic of professional practice, because it involves principles of action, an assessment of the situation that applies those principles, and action that brings about the desired end. Phronesis is results oriented: Good intentions are not enough, although they are usually preferable to bad ones.

Phronesis, or practical wisdom, once understood, makes moot the whole debate that has wrought havoc within the discipline of psychology between proponents of scientific- versus clinical-based knowledge. Knowing what to do in the world to bring about better states of affairs (such as clinical improvement in schizophrenia or depression) logically is a form of phronesis, not an extension of theoretical knowledge (Polkinghorne, 1999; Slife, 2000). Theoretical knowledge is not irrelevant, as Tjeltveit (1999) cogently argued, but it cannot possibly be sufficient to the task. Theories of how various physical or psychosocial circumstances or environmental conditions influence human action and decision making are useful and important (e.g., developmental sequences and critical tasks to be accomplished within those periods, cognitive biases and errors in reasoning, drug effects on the nervous system, and temperaments at birth). As moral beings, we are required to seek justice but also to show mercy. An appreciation of the circumstances that have influenced a person in becoming the person that he or she is necessary, if for no other reason than to be able to know when mercy is required.

Some Moral Interludes in the History of Psychotherapy

The emergence of psychotherapy as a practice and a profession owes a great deal to Sigmund Freud's development of psychoanalysis and his support of lay (nonmedically trained) psychoanalysts. Theodore Reik (1948) was the first person to receive a doctoral degree for the study of psychoanalysis, earning it from the University of Vienna in 1912. Freud was a mentor and advocate for Reik when his right to practice was challenged by legal authorities in Austria (Freud, 1926/1959). Although he had studied with some of the leading minds in psychology in the late 19th century, and was well schooled in both philosophy and the new experimental psychology, Freud found little in either that helped him in his practice of neurology, and he made no secret of his disdain for such an impractical psychology. In return, experimental and academic psychology has always been highly critical of Freud's theories and methodology while basking in the intense interest in psychology created by his writings. On one thing, however, experimental psychology and psychoanalysis agreed: Psychology was to be a science descriptive and explanatory of human moral judgment but not staking a moral position of its own. It was to be neutral on moral questions. It is interesting that Freud was the first person to translate John Stuart Mill's writings from English into German (Gay, 1988), and so he was most familiar with Utilitarianism and used the "pleasure" concept as a central feature in his psychology in the form of the *pleasure principle*, which states that all behavior of an organism is organized to increase the amount of pleasure and reduce the amount of pain. Like Mill, Freud sought to naturalize—and, in this case "medicalize"—morality by discussing guilt as "moral anxiety" and the conscience as the "superego."

Freud's inner circle included only a handful of aspiring analysts during the early 1900s. As is well known, Alfred Adler and Carl Jung were two of the leading members of the Vienna Psychoanalytic Society who broke with Freud and formed their own brands of psychotherapy. Adler called his approach *individual psychology*, and Jung named his *analytic psychology*, and each deemphasized the role of the Oedipal conflict and emphasized other sources of unconscious or childhood conflict. The rift between Freud and his followers involved far more than the nature of unconscious conflict. It also involved the "scientific" status of the whole enterprise.

Adler was a proponent of the *hermeneutic* approach to history and social science proposed by Dilthey (Warnke, 1987). He saw himself developing what he called "a secular religion" that would promote moral and socially responsible behavior in the population that was losing interest in the old religions (Ansbacher & Ansbacher, 1970). He was active as a member of social democratic political organizations, promoting a greater distribution of wealth and political power in Austrian society. In his writings it is clear that he saw his psychotherapeutic work and his psychological theory as going hand in hand with this political agenda. Feelings of inferiority and consequent strivings for superiority were all the product of how power was distributed in the family, schools, and society as a whole. Mental health was indicated by the degree of social interest one had in one's fellow human beings. Mental health was essentially defined as being a moral person in the Judeo–Christian sense of "being thy brother's keeper."

Jung grew up the son of a minister whose church duties drove him to suicide. Jung sought to find in psychology a religion without a church bureaucracy (Jung, 1963). His theory of Self provides a guide to spiritual development, sans spirit, and is very popular with people seeking a basis for pastoral counseling and integration of Eastern religions and psychology (Young-Eisendrath, 2000, Young-Eisendrath & Miramato, 2002). For Jung, analytic psychology was a means of finding direction and meaning in life. The culmination of psychological development is the integration of the Self where opposing forces and archetypes are reconciled, including the Shadow—the hidden and often malevolent side of the personality. It is a classic picture of the struggle of good and evil within an individual life, and Jung held no scientific pretensions about it. He had succeeded at what he had set out to do: establish a secular religion without a church bureaucracy.

Despite these clear indications from the early 1900s that the business of psychotherapy was in dealing with the moral conflicts and problems of life, especially for individuals for whom the organized religions of the day had lost their appeal, psychotherapy was predominantly associated in the public mind either with Freudian psychoanalysis or medicine (viz., psychiatry), both of which clung to the mantel of science in their attempt to gain respectability. Once behaviorism weighed in, with the promise of a technology of behavioral control in the 1920s, and the development of behavior modification, behavior therapy, and cognitive therapy in the 1960s and 1970s, the scientific metaphor was deeply entrenched in clinical psychology. When family therapy emerged in the same time period in psychiatry and social work (Satir, 1972), it too claimed scientific status by means of its association with general systems theory, a meta-theory integrating biology, physics, engineering, and information science.

Only the existential–phenomenological and humanistic approaches to therapy demurred. Even Carl Rogers (1955) and his students sought scientific respectability by trying to demonstrate empirically the process and effectiveness of his relationship-based client-centered psychotherapy. Rogers discussed moral concepts such as *unconditional positive regard* and genuineness as though they were purely psychological variables that could be studied in the laboratory. His efforts at peace building in South Africa between Blacks and Whites, and in the Soviet Union between American and Soviet citizens toward the end of the Cold War, showed clearly that he had a moral and political agenda to his work. His development of encounter groups, which were widely seen as one of the chief symbols of the counterculture, also had a clear moral purpose—to change the character of relationships in society in the direction of greater unconditional positive regard and openness (moral values, surely). It is probably the backlash in the 1980s and 1990s against the counterculture that signaled the demise of humanistic psychology much more than any criticism of the approach on psychological grounds. This seems generally true of psychotherapies—they come in and out of vogue with the mores and values of the culture, rather than because of scholarly critique.

This is true of the argument being put forward here concerning the moral nature of psychotherapy. In the 1960s, philosophers, beginning with Margolis (1966), identified psychotherapy as a moral enterprise. Szasz (1960/1974), Rychlak (1969), London (1964), and Chessick (1970/1987), among others, did the same in psychology and psychiatry, all of which I duly noted in my first publication on this subject in the early 1980s. No one to my knowledge has ever refuted the point, now generally accepted by all who examine the issue. Not refuted, the point is simply ignored by the *zeitgeist* of the times: Science is god, and it can solve all problems—even those that are not scientific problems.

One particularly salient and important chapter in this history of de-moralization came in 1980, when Bergin published his classic article critiquing the *secular humanist* values implicit in empirical research on psychotherapy and mental health in general and advocating for an empirical examination of the impact Christian values have on mental health. Bergin was, and remains, a leading authority on psychotherapy research, and so for him to have acknowledged the central role of moral and ethical values in how research on psychotherapy was conducted was a major breakthrough. That the *Journal of Consulting and Clinical Psychology*, the primary American Psychological Association-sponsored journal for the field of clinical psychology, published the article was potentially of even greater significance. This could have signaled the opening of an ongoing discourse within the field on the centrality of values in the work psychologists do. Instead, ignoring the obvious implications of the content of the article being published, the editors introduced the article with a terse statement that the article was being published along with several commentaries (essentially those defending secular humanism as a value system) but that no further articles on the topic would be published, because the journal was devoted to reporting empirical research. The editors were clearly afraid of being inundated with the return of decades of repressed moral argument. In fact, even a response by another leading psychotherapy researcher, Hans Strupp (1980), who served on the editorial board of the *Journal of Consulting and Clinical Psychology*, was not desirable and appeared in the divisional journal, *Psychotherapy: Theory, Research and Practice*. Strupp, relying on Szasz's 1965 analysis of the psychoanalytic relationship as a formal voluntary contract in which the first person (the therapist), for a fee, agrees to assist a second person (the patient) to realize his or her fullest possible human potential and freedom, showed the psychotherapeutic relationship to be deeply imbedded in the values not of the secular humanism of the 20th century but the values of classical humanism of the 16th century. The Renaissance humanists valued human life above all else and wished to see the full development of all aspects of creative expression for all human beings, regardless of their position in society. For Strupp, the values implicit in the therapeutic relationship are the values of the liberal democratic society: respect for all human beings, free expression of thought, social responsibility, and human compassion.

Strupp (1980) and Bergin's (1980) other critics were right in one sense: Not all modern psychotherapy was based on the hedonistic values that Bergin had ascribed to secular humanism. However, empiricist psychotherapy research, following the model that had developed from Utilitarian moral philosophy, very much embraced secular humanist values, and that was a discussion that the editors of a mainstream research journal either did not understand or did not want to see in the pages of their journal. It was a grand opportunity missed to explore the moral engagement of clinical psychology.

Contemporary Moral Positions in Western Culture

Of course, the de-moralization of psychology is part of the de-moralization of the wider U.S. culture that has received considerable attention in recent years (Bennett, 1995). To address the declining understanding of moral issues in our culture, there has been an increasing call for moral education in our schools (Bennett, 1995). A leading example of how this might be approached was an interdisciplinary seminar created for first-year students at Harvard University in the late 1980s. Hunter Lewis's (1990, 2000) book, *A Question of Values*, was a result of his work developing a curriculum for that seminar. In it, he attempts to show that the specific moral conflicts in our society over issues such as abortion, civil rights, drug use, capital punishment, and foreign intervention and war, are reducible to six fundamental moral positions that are held either singly or in some combination by members of society. In a sense, these are the bedrock reasons one gives when justifying one's more specific moral decisions and principles, the six distinct ways that one defines the "good." As moral agents, people require principles or guidelines in facing the choices and decisions that confront them in life.

The Good Is Defined by Authority

According to this moral position, a power outside the individual is granted the authority to decide right from wrong. This is usually a religious authority, but it may be a political authority or organization, or the weight of a cultural–historical tradition. This approach aligns closely with the deontological approach to ethics and morality discussed above. For the moral agent making decisions in everyday life, this simplified matters greatly. One simply must find out what the authorities say should be done, do it, and know that one has made the correct moral choice. So long as the authority retains its legitimacy, the moral agent has greatly reduced the uncertainty that many others feel in the moral realm.

This very legitimacy unfortunately becomes problematic if the agent has to justify her or his reasons for taking a particular course of action to someone else who does not accept the authoritative voice that the agent has heeded. Now the agent's task of justifying a particular decision has become the task of justifying the foundation of belief in the authority in question. This can be most clearly seen in the context of religious authority (although a similar argument could be constructed concerning the legitimacy of any authority that is offered as justification). "Why do action X?" has become "Why believe in or follow the teachings of this particular prophet or god?" The moral argument becomes a theological argument for the existence of a particular deity. Philosophical arguments of this sort often hinge on both reason and faith. On such matters we expect a great deal of variation in human judgment and have come to insist on freedom of worship and tolerance of differences as a safeguard against the kind of religious fanaticism and warfare that ravaged Europe during the Thirty Years War in the 17th century and rears its ugly head periodically in the modern era. In an atmosphere of tolerance and respect the exploration of differences in moral judgment by representatives of different religious faiths or theological beliefs can be an enlightening experience, as those who have done cross-cultural peace building have demonstrated (Diamond, 2001).

The Good Is Defined by Rationality

The individual looks to rational or logical thinking to discern the nature of the moral. Immutable self-evident truths are sought as justification for moral decisions. Kant's categorical imperative is the model for this approach to morality. By asking the moral agent to be reasonable and rational in making her or his decisions, we are invoking an ill-defined standard, but it does broadly delimit the sorts of justifications that will be permitted in moral decision making. Reason demands that one try to justify a moral position rather than simply assert that it is correct. Reasons that are given must be coherent—they must make sense and show a connection among expectable human goals, purposes, and desires. The agent's perceptions of the situation requiring the moral decision must also be reasonable and guided by an attempt to garner accurate information on which to make the decision. Estimates of likely outcomes and consequences also must be grounded in accurate information and reasonable predictions of likely scenarios. Rationality also requires with Kant's categorical imperative that one be consistent in one's moral decisions and avoid arbitrariness and unequal treatment of people in equal (similar) situations. It is likely that the meaning of rationality in ethics is derived in large part from contrasting it with what it is not—highly emotional responses that may be impulsive and poorly thought through. We seek to be measured, consistent, and systematic in considering our options.

One can see that this relatively dispassionate approach to ethics, when shared by all parties to a moral dispute, would be most conducive to collaborative problem solving. In a sense, rationality is practiced here, as the ultimate good, and the "good life" becomes the rational life. No other goal is as important as maintaining rational discourse, and so long as that remains the priority one can imagine a high degree of resolution of moral differences by moral argument. The problem, of course, comes when a participant in a moral dispute rejects rationality as the ultimate good and places passions more at the center of moral belief. There are times when, for at least some people, an action is felt at a profoundly deep level to be so wholly good or so horrifyingly evil that no reason can be given for such a belief other than that is what one believes or knows. If such *moral intuitions* (as Moore, 1903, called them) are challenged, there is no other response one can give except perhaps to say, "Put yourself in that situation and see if it doesn't feel awful (or wonderful as the case may be)!" The rational approach to the good shows us that at least some moral disagreements can be resolved by means of reasoned analysis and argument.

The Good Is Defined by Sensory Satisfaction

The individual seeks to surround her- or himself with sensual and sensory satisfaction, beauty, and novel stimulation. An artistic or poetic appreciation of the good is sought. This view comes close to being a purely eudaimonaic moral stance. Physical bodily pleasure is taken as the primary element of the good life. In that beauty as a physical characteristic, or sexual ecstasy as a physical act, may inspire art, sculpture, poetry, and so forth, and these artistic creations may capture and invoke these physical experiences, these higher pleasures are included as well but clearly in a derivative sense. The material body may provide a bridge to a more spiritual existence in this manner, but this is a far cry from the disembodied spirit of religious morality or the disembodied mind of Kantian transcendental rationality. Many would simply call such an approach *hedonistic*, and it certainly invokes images of self- and overindulgence of some elements of Ancient Greece and Rome.

Yet, we must also admit that in our own culture, this is in fact the sort of "good life" that is most frequently sought and a view to which many, if not most people, subscribe. (He who has the most toys wins!) A preoccupation with physical beauty, sexual attractiveness, luxurious housing, wine tasting, beer making, gourmet cooking, designer clothing, sport–utility vehicles, art collecting, and so forth seems to define the lifestyle we all aspire to emulate in the lifestyles of the rich and famous. As I mentioned in discussing Utilitarianism, moral systems that emphasize the physical aspects of pleasure lend themselves to some sort of hedonic calculus by which the ultimate value of things may be determined. Most of these "goods" can be assigned a monetary value and the material gain or loss in making various decisions calculated on a balance sheet. Economists do this all the time in their calculations of profits and loss, and so a moral balance sheet could easily be derived. As with the rationalists above, the hedonists will have a relatively easy time resolving among themselves moral differences, because they can review their balance sheets and determine where the calculations of utility vary. Differences that are found may be reconciled by an appeal to some kind of auditor.

The problem with the hedonist approach is quite apparent to people who are not comfortable with the materialism of the 21st century. Few would deny enjoying the material pleasures detailed above, but many would deny their centrality or adequacy in capturing the essence of what it means to be "good." There are just too many times in life that we see material success and satisfaction trumped by events in our interpersonal or familial environments. We experience a sense of satisfaction or loss that clearly takes precedence over the material world.

The Good Is Defined by Emotional Attachments

The individual seeks to maximize the experience of love and intimacy in all his or her decisions. Actions that promote these relationships are right and good. Here we have an ethical standard with much appeal to those in human services, for it asserts that human relatedness is the ultimate good in life and that all actions must be evaluated in terms of their impact on family, loved ones, and close friends. Although taken out of the theological and religious realm and placed squarely in a humanistic context, this standard certainly resonates with the concept of Christian love—agape—and with the Judeo–Christian emphasis on filial loyalty and love for one's parents and children. By stressing interdependency and connectedness (and, implicitly, the promotion of human life through the family), this standard serves to balance the self-absorption that may creep into attempts to live by the search for personal pleasure and sensual gratification and the cold and calculating rationality associated with the second standard.

The difficulty with this standard is that it places the potential for moral action somewhat outside of the control of the individual, who may have been born into circumstances impoverished of human love, support, and contact. Furthermore, all relationships, no matter how loving and caring, have their moments of despair, disappointment, and disillusionment, if only because of human mortality. We are imperfect beings, and jealousy, rivalries, and adverse circumstances may put a great strain on human relationships. There is no question that love, intimacy, human support, and feelings of belonging in a family are of great value in life. Yet there is certain circularity in justifying actions because they promote human connectedness. What are these connected people to do with their lives? Is it simply to seek out even more human relatedness, or are there other tasks in life worth pursuing for their own sake and not as a means to further human intimacy?

The Good Is Defined by Intuition

The individual seeks mystical experiences that provide an intuitive appreciation of what is good and right. Here we have what might have originally have given rise to the first standard, authority, but which exists also at the individual level or in groups that have not yet evolved into formal institutional authorities. Introspective, insightful phenomenological experience may give rise to a sense of "seeing the light," both figuratively and literally. In these intensely personal and emotional moments an individual feels as though he or she has had an interaction with the divine or some force for good in the world that shows him or her what direction to take with his or her life (Stace, 1960).

At a related but more logical level some philosophers, such as Moore (1903), have argued that the ultimate sense of what is good or evil in the universe comes to us from a "moral sense" that provides an intuitive sense of the worthy ends in life. One may experience these intuitions as a sense of what one must do, as opposed to as a sense of how to define the "good," but in either case the ultimate justification to be given is the assertion of an intuition that is taken as valid in its own right.

The intuitive approach to morality carries with it a certain liability when it comes to promoting the resolution of moral controversies. As with the appeal to authority, one has to now defend not what is good but one's trust in the mystical or intuitive itself. When individuals have had mystical experiences or intuitions that others have not experienced, there tends to be little that can be said unless an atmosphere of tolerance and openness to diverse viewpoints is present. Because most people have some experience of moments of insight or strong intuition, and often there is an underlying commonality in such experiences (the oneness of the universe, the power of love, etc.), this obstacle may not be as formidable as rationalists often claim. Our intuitions about the "good life" are probably quite similar, were we to pay attention to them rather than authority, reason, our senses, or our loyalty to others. When such intuitions diverge, one must rely on some other means of knowing and communicating about the "good" to bridge the moral schism that results.

The Good Is Defined by Scientific Experts

Here the individual relies on others to define the "good" on the basis of their specialized knowledge and technical expertise. The good must be tangible, measurable, orderly, predictable, and somewhat inaccessible to the ordinary person or nonspecialist. This last approach is a hybrid of the rationalist, sensory, and authoritative approaches to defining the "good" because, of course, science itself is a blend of reason and empirical data from the senses and in our society operates as a highly respected voice of authority. In most everyday discussions, the assertion that "science has shown" is enough to stifle any opposition. Of course, this is not the case among scientists, who know that science does not speak with a united voice on most subjects, and in fact the most likely scientific conclusion to any scientific report is that "more research is needed" to determine the exact nature of causal mechanisms.

Yet, as Leahey (1997) articulated in his history of psychology, the early 20th century saw the birth of a new religion: *scienticism*. Physicians, psychologists, sociologists, physiologists, economists, nutritionists, educational researchers, and a host of communications and information specialists all claimed expertise and knowledge relevant to solving the everyday interpersonal problems of living. Moral judgments associated with the old religious framework were to be replaced by scientifically proven strategies that "worked." Descriptive and inferential statistical calculations were performed on myriad personal and social variables, and the results were read like tea leaves for their moral implications. Statistical significance, which essentially means that a calculation is unlikely to be due to only random forces, was hawked to the public as though it really were a determination of social significance (although always with the appropriate disclaimers, like the side-effects warnings in small print on prescription drugs).

Like the rational approach to ethics and morality, this scientific/expert approach carried with it the promise of a deliberate and methodical system for resolving moral differences. Where the experts disagree, solutions are expected by conducting more scientific research on the problem in question. Because all experts had adopted the "scientific method" to become experts in the first place, they could be counted on to defer their moral judgment and passion until all the data were in. It is not surprising that, given the impossibility of the task of resolving normative and evaluative questions with factual description, this did not really work. Experts frustrated that their moral certainties were not accepted by other experts would question the validity of each other's data, methods, and integrity. The lack of scientific progress (Meehl, 1978), and the polemical nature of the discourse, suggested that the vaunted scientific method really was not doing its job. As it turns out, even in the physical sciences, personal beliefs, honesty, trust, and interpersonal and institutional rivalries are an integral part of the daily business of doing science (Mitroff, 1974).

As I discuss in chapter 4, the only real explanation for why our culture turned to science for answers in the moral realm has to do not with science but with the disillusionment with religion and the rise of secular nation states (Toulmin, 1990). Scientific experts may be sorely lacking in practical wisdom, but at least no one has as yet started any wars over scientific disputes. This unfortunately cannot be said for the major religions of the world. Professional expertise is by its very nature supposed to be calm, businesslike, and dispassionate. Righteous indignation just is not very professional. During times of great sectarian and totalitarian violence, the cool scientific expert offers a relief from moral positions and arguments that lead to violent confrontations and death. Under the circumstances, the implicit utilitarian message of scientific experts—that people should do what makes them happy, physically comfortable, and satisfied in terms of pleasure and immediate gratification—was a great relief to a populace weary of lofty moral ideals that required the ultimate sacrifice. The experts' advice was either so obviously superficial, irrelevant, or tentative as to prevent moral outrage among adherents and dissenters. We have scientific (psychological) experts giving us moral guidance not because their science allows them to know what we should be doing with our lives but because they cause so much less harm than their religious and political predecessors. Of course, for this moral disarmament to work effectively the scientific experts must be convinced of the truth of their message and the consumer assured that no better advice is available. These are two conditions that are rather easily met. In the presence of morally oppressive forces stifling individual freedom, self-exploration, and self-expression, scienticism as a moral system had a balancing effect within Western society. However, after nearly 100 years of this scienticism, and the continuing decline of moral authority and moral idealism in the culture, the pendulum has clearly swung in the other direction. We suffer now from a general de-moralization within the culture and the mental health professions. Once the solution, scienticism is now a central part of our problem.

Note that in justifying his position that science has become a moral value system in our society, Lewis (1990, 2000) cites as examples Freudian psychoanalysis, cognitive therapy, and behavior modification. He observed that far from being morally neutral intellectual and professional enterprises, forms of psychotherapy are, at least in part, forms of moral engagement. These six moral value orientations represent moral fault lines in our culture, and although there are certainly other ways to conceptualize the moral conflicts in our society, this is a useful one for examining the schisms in clinical psychology and psychotherapy.

THE MORAL POSITIONS
OF CLINICAL PSYCHOLOGY

It is helpful in examining theories of psychotherapy for implicit moral values to identify where within such theoretical constructions one might expect to find moral values embedded.

1. The definition of *mental health* or of psychiatric or psychological disorder is laden with either implicit or explicit moral values about how one ought to live and what constitutes the "good life." As a consequence, psychotherapists' diagnoses and treatment goals carry with them implicit moral commitments that certain ways of living, being, and relating are *good*, right, or virtuous, and others are not. When judging a person's need for treatment or readiness to terminate treatment, therapists are applying their moral judgment with their clinical judgment. This is true whether they like it or not and whether they use moral language or de-moralized language to describe what they do. They can call them "good" "healthy," or "adaptive," but unless they can define *healthy* or *adaptive* in some manner that is not ultimately evaluative, *healthy* and *adaptive* are just pseudonyms for *good*. No such objective criteria have ever been successfully put forward and defended.

2. The problems that people expect psychologists to help solve are usually framed by the person her- or himself in a moral

context. When clients present their conflicts, problems, difficulties, or confusions, they do so in the moral language of obligations, responsibilities, guilt, shame, respect, betrayal, and so forth. It is the clinician or researcher who de-moralizes the discussion. This is no mere semantic adjustment but a shift in conceptual frameworks with far-reaching consequences, which I explore below.

3. Clinical intervention or treatment involves a human interaction in which the therapist is required to make decisions on how to act for the betterment of the client or patient (as opposed to for the betterment of the therapist). This is, then, doubly moral for all human actions, and decisions are open to moral review (how ought one to act?), and the requirement that one act for the betterment of others is an embodiment of the Judeo–Christian maxim to love thy neighbor as thyself.

The above observations address the moral nature of practice, but researchers frequently exempt themselves from these considerations by claiming that their empirical methods are pure and unadulterated by moral commitments. They claim that they are simply evaluating whether certain means achieve certain ends and not what ends should ultimately be sought by clients or therapists. The discussion of practical knowledge above addressed this issue. To reiterate, if the ends are moral, so are the means. The means constitute the ends. This can be seen if one looks at different theoretical approaches to therapy. Whatever the therapeutic goal, the therapy consists of exposing the client to small regular doses of that end. Medical treatment has the goal of altering a presumed biochemical imbalance. The treatment is regular doses of a biochemical substance. In existential therapy, the goal is increasing authentic experiencing of life, and the treatment is the weekly exposure to an authentic relationship. In rational–emotive and cognitive therapies, the end is to produce rational thinking, and the treatment is weekly sessions in which irrational ideas are challenged. Finally, in family therapy, the goal is increasing open and direct communication in the family, and the treatment is family sessions in which open and direct communication is prompted and encouraged. There are no techniques without moral commitments built in, and so research on techniques is never value free or morally neutral. One is always researching the impact or implications of holding a certain moral position in psychology, and this is usually a moral position implicitly accepted by the researcher. Consequently, the outcome measures used in psychotherapy research will generally contain the same implicit values as the therapy being tested, accounting for the tautological nature of the conclusions drawn (were the values to be made explicit).

Identifying the Moral Commitments
in Science-Based Psychotherapy Practices

As indicated by writers such as Leahey (1997), Toulmin (1990), Bergin (1980), and Fishman (1999), in their historical, conceptual, and cultural analyses, scientific approaches to social problems are implicitly committed to certain moral values, that is, to a specific conception of the "good life," of how things ought to be, as well as the traditional mainstream commitment to describing things as they are. Of course, any particular scientific research program in context may have other basic value positions wedded to it by virtue of the personal moral beliefs of the investigators, or the institutional affiliations of the sponsoring organization, and so forth. This view of the social and moral interests inherent in all knowledge has been a central theme of the German philosopher Habermas (1971, 1973), following in the tradition of the Frankfurt School of philosophy that evolved out of Marx's critical social analysis of the concept of ideology. What follows, then, is a schematic characterization of the scientific value position in clinical psychology.

The scientific clinical psychologist places ultimate value on those aspects of human experience that are concrete, tangible, and material. Emotional, mystical, and the idiosyncratic or internalized sensory experiences of life are seen as of less importance. Submission to authority is little valued, unless it is a scientific authority. Rationality is valued, but as an end itself, not as a means of discovering moral principles. This is a view that, as noted above, is consistent with its origins in Mill's Utilitarianism, where the greatest happiness of the greatest number of people was to be quantifiably determined in a calculus of "the good." It is an approach that looks for tangible phenomena, universal principles, and group responses while leaving little room for the individual, idiosyncratic, and intangible goods of life.

In clinical psychology and psychotherapy there are two primary scientific approaches: (a) biological and (b) cognitive–behavioral. The biological, or disease model of psychopathology and treatment is more closely attuned to an ethic of sensory gratification being driven by a desire to reduce patient symptoms, which are largely complaints about the physiological concomitants of anxiety and depression: autonomic nervous system arousal, problems sleeping restfully and in eating, muscle tremors, spasms, pain, sexual dysfunction, physical addictions, and so forth. Like most medical professionals, the psychiatrist or disease-model psychologist hopes to give the patient relief from pain and an increase in physical well-being. Reports of bodily conditions figure heavily in diagnosis and treatment accounts.

This is such an accepted manner of thinking in our culture that one might easily miss that this approach is not only diagnosing and treating the physical dimension of life but also communicating a preference for addressing such phenomena as opposed to the myriad other kinds of phenomena in life (particularly intuitive, relational, or spiritual) that one might prefer to have help improving. On the one hand, one might ask, "What else should we expect from doctors but that they improve the conditions of our body?" Yet, in psychiatry and psychology, that begs the question whether it is in fact our bodies that we are asking help with, or, as Kleinman (1988) suggested, our suffering. By offering medication, electroconvulsive therapy, or psychosurgery, the clinician is giving priority to one realm of reality: the material, physical, sensory experience—both her or his own and that of the client. The therapist wants patients to have a different sensory experience in their bodies and to do so in a manner that provides sensory data to the therapist as feedback on the work done. The patient must feel better in ways that provide the kind of feedback that has value to the therapist: empirical data.

This analysis of values implicit in approaches to clinical practice reveals a feature of the scientist–practitioner split in psychology that is generally concealed from view or public discussion. The scientist's claim to superior knowledge via empiricism (i.e., knowledge from the senses) is usually seen in philosophy as an epistemological assertion as to the nature of knowledge and the criteria for truth. On the analysis offered here, it appears to be a moral claim as well, or perhaps instead. Perhaps the reason that the empiricism versus rationalism debate about the nature of knowledge has remained insoluble is that it is in fact an argument about how the world ought to be, not about how the world of knowledge is. Disagreements about ethics and morals are, as Levinas (1989) argued on different phenomenological grounds, first philosophy, the bedrock questions of our civilization. We do not need to find the criteria for true propositions to find out the truth in ethics; rather, we need to find to the real nature of goodness for human beings to know what is true for us. The "truth shall set us free," but not because we have to know the truth to find freedom, which is the most common understanding of the expression. Rather, that which set us free must be the truth. We find truth by finding what way of understanding the world leads to freedom and other moral goals. The moral is the warrant of true belief. Those perceptions of the world that conjoin or facilitate moral action are the accurate perceptions.

Cognitive–behavioral therapies are the second approach that relies on a scientific/expert model as an implicit moral system. These approaches put a premium on the client's overt observable behaviors and ability to productively function in one's social roles. Both the client and the therapist are expected to value order, structure, rationality, and predictability in life and in the therapy. These are more a blend of rational and scientific/expert values than sensory physical values, although those are present as well in emphasizing overt behavior, which is more clearly physical than, say, introspective experience would be. Productivity in society is also measured in physical terms—either actual product constructed or the monetary value of the same. To the extent that these objects are the product of one's labor with one's hands, they are an extension of one's physicality. Lewis (1990, 2000) did not have a category for valuing material objects above all else, as opposed to the sensory impact of products. The cognitive–behavioral approach invites consideration of whether identifying a seventh value system, where productivity and social appropriateness are paramount, might be useful.

Cognitive–behavioral theorists share with advocates of the disease model the strong commitment to empiricism as a means of validating their work. Cognitive–behavioral changes should be verifiable by means of the researchers' senses, but that data ought to pertain primarily to changes in the overt behavior of the client, not the client's sensory experience. There is a model of socially "appropriate" (i.e., conforming), reasonable, nonemotional behavior that is promoted as though it were universally desired, and objectively natural, and so is not ever justified as a moral position. Cognitive–behaviorists claim that it is just obvious and self-evident that children should pay attention, listen to their elders, do their schoolwork, and so forth, and that adults should be assertive, productive on the job, sexually orgasmic, and so forth. Attempts to justify these socially value-laden claims usually fall into a sociobiological framework that insist with foresight of geological epoch proportions that these are the behaviors that will lead to the survival of the species.

Scientific aspires to general laws of behavior both in a descriptive and a prescriptive sense; that is, it favors actions that maximize goals across groups or populations, and not necessarily any one individual in particular. By insisting on standardized treatment programs, empirical outcome measures, and replicability of findings, an implicit message is sent that the group's well-being is of more interest than the individual's well-being. As with the explanation of how Western culture could have come to trust its morals to scientists, the answer seems to lie more in the area of politics than epistemology. The affiliation of science and bureaucratic nation–states in the modern era would dictate that scientific experts of behavior be far more concerned with controlling the masses than with understanding the individual. The individuality of both the client and practitioner forms a practical limit to the degree to which these values can be realized in actual clinical practice, and this is certainly recognized by the research-consuming clinicians, if not by the researchers themselves. In some institutional settings, where there is little real interest in the individual potential of the clients, a scientist approach would be able to be consistently applied in which outcomes are reported not so much for individuals but for units of the institution, blocks, or entire institutions, in terms of readmissions, recidivism, and so forth. Empirical methods focusing on overt behavior are ideally suited to such social interventions in which the individual may not even be known well by the clinician, and indications that would come from a close working relationship are not available. The moral goal of addressing generic problems, or supporting social control and reducing the opportunity for social chaos, dictates the methodology, although this moral agenda is neither articulated nor defended. Instead, an epistemological defense is offered: Empirical knowledge is superior to intuitive or faulty subjective perceptions. We are told that science cannot be built on anecdotal evidence rather than that social control cannot be built on personal knowledge, nor need it be.

Implicit Moral Values in the Psychoanalytic Approach

As noted above, a number of psychoanalytic writers have directly considered the ethics and morals of psychoanalysis (Erikson, 1963; Strupp, 1980; Szasz, 1965). Although Freud himself did not believe that psychoanalysis had a moral position, he certainly expected analysts to be bound by conventional moral standards in, for example, handling transference and countertransference (Freud, 1915/1959). Freud's theory is a complex blend of physiological, social, and psychological, as well as uniquely psychoanalytic, theorizing. The theory has, like any scientific/expert system, an implicit moral value system that blends the sensory and rational models of moral thinking. Yet it places tremendous value on the intuitive in emphasizing the direction of behavior by unconscious influence and in the value placed on self-examination, introspection, and insight as a means of growth and change (Kirschner, 1996). The intuitive is ultimately made subservient to the rational—"Where Id was, there shall Ego be!" was one of Freud's pithy summaries of the psychoanalytic treatment process. Furthermore, the family triangle places such a central role in the theory via the Oedipus conflict that one would have to say that family connectedness is also a high priority for psychoanalytic theory. Freud pretty much rejected authority as a source of value, unless it was scientific authority, or himself. He demanded a loyalty from his followers that prevented them from challenging Freud's authority as the founder of psychoanalysis. So it might fairly be said that Freud at different times can be seen to be promoting all of six of the moral themes indentified earlier. The sensory (sensual) and rational (as befitting a scientist/expert) seem most prominent, with the mystical/intuitive and authoritative less instrumental but not entirely absent. Family connectedness and loyalty play a central but secondary role in Freud's own work, but in the neo-Freudian object relations theorists this is elevated ahead of rationality as a primary moral value. Freud's rationalism is important in another way, for it is associated with the Enlightenment, of which it is often said Freud was a great advocate. The humanism of the Renaissance and the extolling of human life, warts and all, is closely linked to his rationalism, as is his promotion of individual human existence. As with so many other aspects of Freudian theory, the complexity of its implicit moral values leads to both versatility and confusion.

Moral Principles Implicit in Humanistic Psychotherapies

The term *humanistic*, when applied to psychotherapies, covers a broader and more diverse span of approaches than is the case with other terms, such as *cognitive–behavioral* and *psychoanalytic*. Albert Ellis (1962) is frequently feted as a great humanist, as was Carl Rogers, yet two more dissimilar approaches to psychotherapy can hardly be found. Because some of the humanistic approaches, such as Ellis's rational–emotive therapy or Glasser's (1975) reality therapy, have a strong identification with rational or scientific/expert values, the focus here is on the more existential–phenomenological or experiential approaches (e.g., Laing, 1965; May, 1969; Rogers, 1960; Yalom, 1989), which have a moral basis clearly distinct from those approaches already discussed.

In these more existential–phenomenological approaches to psychotherapy one tends to see an explicit acknowledgment of the role of values in theories of psychotherapy. Because existentialism as a philosophy (Barrett, 1958) is clearly an ethical theory, related approaches to psychotherapy are explicitly moral in content. Humanists extol the human mind and value its complexity, conflict, pain, and suffering along with its joys, pleasures, and insights. Intuitive values are paramount, including the potentially mystical aspects of experience, which are described as consciousness expanding, enlightening, and transpersonally meaningful. Heightened sensory awareness is sought out both for its own pleasure and for its potential to stimulate aesthetic and altered states of consciousness.

Emotional awareness and intensity are sought as grounding experiences, not as distractions from rational thought. In fact, rational principles of ethics would be minimized, because overintellectualization is seen as a way of distancing oneself from the felt experience of the moment that may be revelatory. Authority and scientific values are also of little significance to this therapeutic approach, whereas human connectedness is of intermediary value. For some, like Buber (1958), the I–Thou relationship of human intimacy is the basis for and stepping stone to the experience of the divine. Rogers (1960) used this as a way of describing the therapeutic experience of empathy, unconditional positive regard, and authenticity. However, for most humanists, personal growth, self-actualization, and expanding personal consciousness are more important goals for therapy than promoting human connectedness. Freedom of the individual to direct and control his or her life is paramount, with human connectedness seen as a necessary step in the self-actualization process, not the sole end of therapy. Caring and supportive relationships are valued, but as much for the growth process they stimulate in the individual as for the experience of intimacy itself. However, this must be distinguished from the therapeutic work of some of the existential family therapists (e.g., Satir, 1972; C. A. Whitaker & Bumberry, 1988) in which it seems that growth and openness are paired effectively with connectedness and family loyalty, and one senses that both are of great importance and neither is only a means to an end.

This form of practice is often guided by a concern with the presence or absence of the intense but often ephemeral, idiosyncratic, even inexpressible emotional or sensory goods of life: love, joy, beauty, insight, and so forth. These are goods that often defy observation by impartial observers, electrical recording devices, or standardized measuring instruments. Such values may be highly individualistic and therefore very difficult to capture in a general statement of principles, and in fact they may defy verbalization at all. Yet for those to whom they are the ultimate good they give life meaning and purpose. When the basis for moral decision making contains such individualistic expressions of value that are largely internal, it becomes very difficult to find common ground among people who have differing moral views, unless they share a common mystical experience. This can certainly happen, but when it does not, then either a common bond of loyalty must be found as a joint basis for moral principles, or the humanists must end the dialogue. In the absence of a rational process for moral decisions, little can be done to bridge differences in moral intuitions.

Another quandary for the defenders of humanistic moral positions in clinical psychology comes when claims of a more general or universal character are made in support of such an approach. Some of clinical experience is concrete, observable, even universal, or at least psychologists make it so to communicate to others. How is this to be captured without losing the basic value position that places so much emphasis on individuality in the goals of life? In the final section of this chapter, I address the question of how to attempt to resolve these basic value differences.

Moral Positions Implicit in Family Therapies

There is, of course, a variety of approaches to family therapy, beginning with Adler's family education model (Ansbacher & Ansbacher, 1970), proposed in Vienna in the early 1900s. The focus here is on approaches to family therapy that are not an extension of a model already examined above (e.g., family–support and education associated with the medical model; behavioral family therapy, and psychodynamic couples therapy) This leaves us with the systems theory based approaches of writers such as Bowen (1978), G. Bateson (1971), and C. A. Whitaker and Bumberry (1988) and the strategic and structural models of the Mental Research Institute or Palo Alto group (Minuchin, 1974; Watzlawick, 1984). Some of these approaches are quite tied to a natural science worldview associated with general system theory (Bertalanffy, 1969), whereas others adopt a more social constructionist view of the family's reality. Nevertheless, one sees throughout this literature, either explicitly stated or implicitly assumed, that the importance of promoting a functioning family is a moral priority. In some cases they are almost a pure form of asserting that the "good life" we should all seek is one with a supportive but differentiated family. In some cases this is seen as launching a person into life, and so other values then supersede the family's importance; however, in other theories that emphasize the multigenerational family of parents, children, and grandparents, the family is the crucible of life itself. One needs a morally functioning family to have the "good life." This placing of supreme importance on the extended family is common in more traditional societies and can be logically extended to placing the well-being of one's community of extended relationships (kinship group or extended kinship group) into the position of the ultimate good. Once this step is taken in the moral argument, it becomes quite apparent that a relationship-based approach to defining the "good life" eventually must come into conflict with value systems that emphasize individual autonomy, personal development, and the mystical experience of the individual. In political theory this becomes the question of individual rights versus responsibilities and obligations to the group and eventually even the state (seen as the larger community). It is surprising to many in the clinical realm to discover how easily, when moral issues are not dissociated, a clinical issue, such as whether to recommend individual or family therapy, draws one into an age-old philosophical question at the heart of political theory: the individual versus group or the state.

Perhaps it is just that we live in a time where "family values" are a part of the public dialogue about the quality of life in our society, but it does seem that the psychological interventions must take account of the role of the family in clients' lives or risk becoming irrelevant to the client. Families have the potential to do such lasting good, or such horrible and indelible harm, to young children in their care that psychologists would be hard-pressed not to place enormous value on the quality of the love and attachment in a client's family relationships. There are certainly other goals or values toward which to direct clinical interventions, such as self-actualization, physical symptom relief, or productive work without which our lives are incomplete as well. Still, family loyalties and attachments must be considered an essential moral good in any systematic approach to alleviating human suffering in clinical contexts.

STEPS TOWARD A PSYCHOLOGY
OF MORAL ENGAGEMENT

As this view of the moral values implicit in the major schools of psychological practice shows, psychology is a morally divided profession that at the same time denies its moral functions and the implicit moral content in its theories, research methods, and practices. The first step, and one toward which I hope this volume makes some contribution, is to raise the awareness and ownership of the problem among the members of the mental health professions. Psychologists must acknowledge that the work they do, and the disagreements they have, are centrally, although not exclusively, in the moral realm. This in itself does not require them to change what they do, because assisting others in resolving the moral dilemmas and conflicts in their lives is part of what psychologists have always done, and often they do it well. Nevertheless, doing this moral work explicitly rather than implicitly will bring with it both risks and rewards. Moral conflicts are highly charged emotionally and, when approached directly, require great skill and tact to negotiate and resolve. Yet, unless such problems are addressed, there is no hope of truly resolving them. The existential literature (May, 1969; Yalom, 1981) is certainly a testament to the benefits for clients when therapists display this kind of moral perceptiveness and courage. To do this effectively, psychologists must educate themselves about the nature of morality, moral reasoning, and problem solving. This will give them the perspective they need for addressing more directly their clients' moral problems and the intellectual tools to tackle with reasoned argument the divisions within the profession. Toulmin (1990) recommended that we deal with these sorts of consequences of the hidden agenda of modernity by returning to the Renaissance values of reasonableness, tolerance of human diversity, and humility in the face of the imponderables of life.

In the end, psychologists must have clinical discussions about the values that guide their techniques. Where their fundamental values differ from those of colleagues, they may find some areas of intermediate values where they can agree and build consensus there. In many cases proponents of conflicting models of clinical practice disagree not in regard to the values to which they subscribe but in the priority assigned to those values.

IMPLICIT MORAL ISSUES
IN TREATING ACUTE ANXIETY:
AN ILLUSTRATION

Suppose an otherwise healthy adult client is suffering panic attacks, with chest pain, shortness of breath, perceptual distortions, and a fear of dying or losing one's mind. Practitioners who subscribe to the medical model will frequently be satisfied to reduce these symptoms with medication (perhaps one of the newer SSRIs) and consider the case successfully treated. A cognitive–behaviorist might set a similar goal for therapy (i.e., the reduction in physical symptoms) but might use a variety of structured interventions other than medication that will teach the client to cope with his or her anxiety with different responses to the initial sensations of anxiety that lead up to the panic. This may be simply a matter of means to a physical change, or it may represent a moral judgment by the therapist or client that it is wrong to rely on medications for a sense of security and that a person ought to learn to control by means of rational procedures his or her emotional and physiological reactions to the world. This value, however, is asserted as supplemental to the initial goal of eliminating the unpleasant physical sensations.

The existential–phenomenological, psychodynamic, and family systems therapists will in all likelihood also concur that the sensations of a panic attack are not an essential feature of the "good life"; however, there is a serious difference in how that panic will be understood. It will be seen as undesirable but at the same time as a valuable piece of information pointing to areas of the person's life where there are problems that are not being effectively faced and resolved. These three approaches will again disagree about what the most important unresolved problem areas that should be worked on in therapy (fear of mortality, fear of hostility toward loved ones during early childhood, or current family dynamics), and in so doing they may be simply asserting that they have a different technical approach to decreasing unpleasant sensations and increasing rational problem solving, or they may be asserting that they place intuitive or familial values ahead of rationality. Because the moral component has been largely ignored or denied in these disagreements, one often finds very tortured lines of reasoning used. For example, at times psychoanalysts have argued that behavioral interventions are unwise because they do not produce lasting change in symptoms (the old "symptom substitution" argument). At other times, their criticisms of symptom relief have been not that behavioral interventions do not work but that they do not work on the most important aspect of the person—it leaves the personality largely unchanged. Thus an opportunity to face demons of the past is ducked, and the client is robbed of a chance to be truly free of unnecessary (neurotic) limitations on his or her human potential. It would seem helpful to be able to agree on the value of reducing unpleasant physical sensations and then to consider the potential pitfalls of reducing immediate suffering at the expense of missing an opportunity to reduce long-term suffering. Expressed this way, it is clear that this is a decision that should not be made without consulting the client. It is a moral decision, not just a technical one. One feature of moral dilemmas is that one cannot always maximize all desired outcomes, and a choice between two relatively good or relatively bad outcomes must still be made. Under such circumstances, it is critical that the client be made aware that his or her request for a particular therapy will mean maximizing one valued life outcome and likely at the same time minimizing another element of the "good life." This discussion suggests as well that efforts to fashion an integrated approach to psychotherapy (e.g., psychodynamic with cognitive–behavioral therapy, family therapy with object relations therapy, or existential and family therapy) would be furthered by first making explicit the value positions and then working toward a moral integration as well as technical one, remaining cognizant of the moral tradeoffs in the previously conflicting models.

THE MORAL DIALOGUE IN CLINICAL PSYCHOLOGY

Moral dilemmas such as those detailed above abound in the field of mental health. Clients encounter agonizing moral dilemmas in leading their lives, and therapists in conducting their practices. Sometimes the clients and therapists have moral conflicts with one another within the therapeutic relationship itself, as in the case described earlier of the unfaithful husband wanting therapy to decrease his guilt and increase his chances of not being caught. Regardless of whether psychologists ultimately will be able to reach a moral consensus as a basis of practice within the mental health disciplines, the process of having reasoned discussions of heretofore-unspoken issues will do much to bridge the chasm among the various professions and theoretical orientations within the field. This is particularly true for the schism between science and clinical knowledge-based practitioners, where the moral differences are so deeply hidden as to cripple meaningful dialogue. A critical step in this process would be the development of a "truth in moral packaging" rule for the professions. Clinical practitioners and researchers alike should be required to examine, discover, and identify openly the moral value bases of their work. Consumers of research or clinical services need to know what values guide that work and the reasons those values have been endorsed by the professional. It may be, for example, that an individual whose values are what Lewis (1990, 2000) called *intuitive–mystical* would find it morally objectionable to receive clinical services guided by scientific–rational values. If so, such a person should be able to discuss this with a therapist at the beginning of their work together. Because of the contextualized nature of these issues, it may be that, despite these fundamental value differences, there is enough commonality on more intermediate moral issues (e.g., drug use, women's rights, sexual preference) for the work to proceed. With demystification of the moral aspects of clinical work, it should prove possible for clinicians to conduct such interviews without being morally judgmental or heavy-handed.

The same truth in moral packaging rule is needed for consumers or financiers of research. Knowing the value direction of the research might lead one to reject its conclusions, despite finding the methodology impeccable. Conversely, approving of the moral direction of a project might lead one to accept its conclusions despite an inadequate methodology. In either case, it would be important to distinguish the grounds for the acceptance or rejection of the research. In fact, I believe these sorts of responses to research are extremely prevalent, but psychologists simply have no conceptual framework for explaining these visceral reactions to each other's hard-won data sets. Under this proposal, such differences could be further explored at the moral level, and again in some cases the moral differences may not be as profound as first thought.

There is no doubt that in some cases the moral differences will be too great to resolve, and one group will find the other's work immoral. In a pluralistic society with freedom of speech, religion, and association, we have an honored tradition of tolerating great moral diversity. The same freedom of moral expression should be granted to practitioners of forms of psychotherapy as is granted to other groups in our society (political, educational, or religious). Except in the most extreme situations, our attitude toward therapies based on divergent moral principles should be one of vigorous discussion and debate but, ultimately, tolerance. However, as we do today in other aspects of moral differences in our society, if the moral differences become too great, the struggle must move to the legislative or legal level with an attempt to restrict certain forms of what are regarded as immoral practice. Realizing that this is being done on moral grounds, rather than simply because one form of therapy lacks "scientific data," will greatly clarify the ensuing political and legal discussions. Psychotherapy is inherently influenced by, and influencing, the moral character of society, and much of its importance stems from this feature. The mental health professions must embrace rather than deny this truth about their professional selves and work vigorously to expand the quality and level of the moral discourse in their work, both public and private.

4

PSYCHOLOGY
AND SCIENCE

Psychology is the science of behavior (Skinner, 1953; Watson, 1919). Psychology is the science of mind and behavior (G. A. Miller, 1956; G. A. Miller, Galanter, & Pribram, 1960). Psychology is the science of brain–behavior relationships (Gazzaniga & Heatherton, 2003). It seems over the last century that, quite paradoxically, psychologists have not been able to agree on what the basic subject matter of the discipline is, while at the same time being sure that it is nonetheless a science. Perhaps all would agree that the psychologists making such assertions have been expressing their intention, determination, and even dreams—that they would or could make psychology into a science—rather than describing the reality that psychology already was such a science.

Nonetheless, the claim that psychology is first and foremost a science is an explicit and unquestioned assumption among authors of textbooks in general psychology and in developmental, social, personality, experimental, and even abnormal and clinical psychology. This is not just a view expressed in the literature for the aspiring experimental psychologist but is promulgated to students wishing to enter applied and clinical areas of the profession as well. It is also a view that dominates in scientist–practitioner (Boulder model) graduate programs in clinical psychology and has its articulate and well-organized advocates in Section III of Division 12 (Society of Clinical Psychology) of the American Psychological Association (McFall, 2000). It is a view that has had a great appeal to policymakers seeking "accountability" for public health services and, since the *Daubert v. Merrill Dow Pharmaceuticals* (1993) decision of the U.S. Supreme Court regarding the nature of expert testimony, has permeated the legal system as well. Experts, including psychologists, must base their testimony on scientific evidence to be credible expert witnesses. It seems that except for the entertainment-oriented talk show psychologists, media attention to psychologists is almost always associated with the announcement of research findings on socially relevant topics or participation in court proceedings regarding the insanity defense, again as expert witnesses.

In this climate of popular opinion, or *zeitgeist*, the general reader and undergraduate student relatively new to the field also expect that psychology will be scientific while at the same time holding firmly to the belief that psychology must also be helpful with the serious personal problems of contemporary life. There is the implicit or explicit expectation that such an applied psychology—or, as Skinnerians called it, the *technology of human behavior*—will bring the benefits of the technological age to the human problems of living. Surely, it is thought, the intellectual and academic institutions that produced the manned space program, which put a man on the moon, or the Hubbel telescope traversing the universe, will find solutions to the mundane earthly problems of family conflict, social and racial prejudice, or suicidal and other violent behavior.

Nearly everyone in contemporary culture seems uneasy with the private, ephemeral, and highly subjective nature of most psychological phenomena. We cling, almost desperately, to the hope that objective scientific methods can bring order and predictability to the subjective domain as well. Science, we hope, will keep us as we study psychology from falling into the hazard of biases, prejudices, and misconceptions that can mar almost any attempt to understand the people around us. We are all too aware of how individuals may offer theories that are self-serving, self-excusing, or self-justifying and that essentially lead others to believe ideas about psychology that give their authors, rather than human beings as a whole, some advantage in the world. The content of psychology just seems so intimately connected to *our personal and social interests in the world* that we cannot imagine that a person's gender, sexual orientation, ethnicity, religion, social class, and so forth, would not influence his or her views on the psychology of gender, sexual orientation, race, religion, poverty, and so forth. We know that some constraints have to be put on this potential for personal or subjective bias, and science has come to be seen as the source of all objectivity in our culture, the great arbiter of truth. It is "science to the rescue," to sit as judge and jury on the great intellectual questions of our time.

The abstract science to which we all pay homage is thought of in our culture as a pure source of truth. We do not typically think that when science speaks that there is a fallible human being who is speaking for science, who may have succumbed to social or political bias or financial pressures in speaking for science as she or he has done. We believe that the discipline of the scientific method, including the requirement of experimental replication of findings and the norms of the scientific community, will reduce subjective biases and distortions to an insignificant level. We forget that without universities, think tanks, specific foundations, and industrial research facilities there would be few if any scientific findings, because contemporary, publishable, programmatic scientific research virtually requires the support of an institutional setting. These institutions often participate in almost invisible webs of other social, cultural, political, or commercial institutions that have agendas that are determined, or at least influenced by, the social and political agendas of their board members and mission statements. These research institutions generally require large sums of money to continue to do their work, and they aggressively publicize their efforts in the media and to various political and social organizations to obtain those funds. As science has evolved it has become increasingly expensive to participate in the "search for knowledge." In many areas of neuroscience and physiological psychology today, the outfitting of a technologically adequate laboratory necessary to make leading-edge discoveries or test controversial theories runs into the hundreds of thousands, if not millions, of dollars (for CAT scanners and positron-emission tomography equipment). Most psychological research in the United States today is funded through grants from the following federal government agencies: the National Institutes of Health, the National Institute of Education, and the Department of Defense. Although it is difficult to determine exactly how much is funded for psychological research in these budgets (as opposed to strictly physiological or educational projects), the National Institute of Mental Health research budget alone is $1.4 billion (Kobor, Silver, & Wurtz, 2002).

The moral and political philosopher MacIntyre (1984) made an important distinction between social practices and social institutions. Practices are rule-governed social activities wherein an individual develops skill and mastery in the context of a historical tradition of similar practices. Chess, baseball, nursing, psychotherapy, or physics are all practices. Practices, MacIntyre noted, are inherently ethical and moral undertakings. The rules limit one's pursuit of self-interest while engaging in the practice by defining cheating, and unsportsmanlike or unprofessional conduct, and by placing the importance of the practice itself above that of the individuals who are practitioners. There are generally a loyalty and camaraderie among the practitioners of any practice and a shared sense of common purpose in preserving and furthering the technical skills of the practice.

This is not the case with institutions that support the development of a practice, MacIntyre (1984) observed. Practices need institutions to support their development—professional societies, fund-raising organizations, and administrators to organize the various frameworks within which the practice is carried out. However, institutions serve a practice—but not all practices, only a particular one. Thus institutions representing different practices compete against one another for funding, space, publicity, and so forth. The institutions therefore operate primarily out of self-interest, defending their own social practice from the encroachment of related practices. Physicists may be noble in their dealing with other physicists, and therefore believe in the purity of basic physical science, but once these very same physicists begin working through various institutions for the advancement of their "pure" physics, they enter the institutional realm, where, like all other institutional representatives according to MacIntyre, they leave behind the purity of the "driven snow." Once the physicists must secure their funding in competition with the biologists, psychologists, engineers, or even representatives from the humanities, pure science becomes a mythical idealization. The idealization of "pure science" itself becomes fodder for the publicity mills of the institutions seeking financial or political advantage.

In spite of the obvious humanness of the practice of science, how, one wonders, did the institution of science in the West come to be regarded as offering certain, objective knowledge that was freed of the collective interests and biases of the professional scientists who conducted and interpreted the research? This is a question that many historians, sociologists, and philosophers of science have asked over the past 50 years (Kuhn, 1970; Polanyi, 1962; Toulmin, 1963, 1990), but their answers have been largely ignored in the mainstream textbooks of psychology, whether introductory or advanced, experimental or clinical (although Leahey, 1997, and Robinson, 1989, are exceptions). The answer will come as something of a shock to the reader who has been educated, encouraged, and some would say indoctrinated, to believe that scientists are simply highly disciplined, methodical, meticulous, and patient observers of nature, who *discover the facts* about the world and, in the process of culling these facts, finally, if they are lucky, discover principles or laws of nature that reveal how the world really works.

The answer will be disconcerting to the readers who have come to think of science as the supreme form of knowledge available to humankind and technology as the savior of Western civilization. Also troubled will be those who believe that the only rational choice available to an educated person today is that he or she places his or her faith in science. This is such a pervasive belief in our culture that sociologists and philosophers have dubbed this *scienticism*, the implacable faith that all problems of human existence permit of a scientific solution. This chapter is addressed primarily to readers who have, perhaps unknowingly, taken this leap of faith in science and who may not have ever examined closely the assumptions and presuppositions of that faith. What follows is an attempt to summarize for, and make accessible to, students or practitioners of psychology the implications of the contemporary thinking by philosophers and philosophically oriented psychologists on the philosophy of science (e.g., Bhaskar, 1994; Chessick, 1987; Harre, 1972; Howard, 1986; Kuhn, 1970; Manicus & Secord, 1983; Polkinghorne, 1983, 1988; Quine, 1980; Rorty, 1979; Rychlak, 1969; Toulmin, 1972, 1990, 2000). In this effort to synthesize, apply, and make accessible a complex and difficult literature that often is foreign to psychologists and other mental health practitioners, I have avoided lengthy lists of citations on points where I perceive an emerging consensus has developed as to either the mainstream understanding of the nature of science or the critique of that view. The specific focus of this chapter is to examine the implications of this literature for the question of how we understand *the nature of clinical mental health practice*—the self-understanding of the mental health professions and related academic disciplines.

THE MAGISTERIAL VIEW OF SCIENCE

The answer that has emerged to the question of how society came to glorify science is a rather straightforward one: We came to view science as magisterial because the institutions of science in Western society actively sought to be viewed in this manner. Like all other institutions in our society (e.g., political organizations, governments, churches), scientists and their organizations are actively self-promoting; self-aggrandizing; and seeking to garner authority, prestige, and status. We have come to worship science in much the same way as in other eras the populace came to worship the authority of their church, king, or political dictator.

One might think that this cannot be true, because the sciences are known for changing doctrine, revising theories, and making new discoveries. How can science be a form of orthodoxy based on faith? Do not the sciences seem the model of open-mindedness, encouraging self-criticism, testing ideas, and critical reflection? This is true of the content of science within certain limits (in reality, disciplines may develop social prohibitions against challenging particular leading authorities), the presuppositions of the scientific worldview, particularly its commitment to a naturalistic or materialist worldview and "the scientific method" as an infallible epistemology, remain constant and unquestioned within the practice of science itself. Still, it seems implausible that scientists alone could have engineered such a convincing mythology.

The historian and philosopher of science Toulmin (1990) provided an intriguing answer to this question. Toulmin (1990) showed how this magisterial view of science was promoted by the secular principalities and emerging national governments of Europe that sought to restore order and authority after the Thirty Years War (1618–1648) between Catholics and Protestants shattered faith in the Christian churches and Christianity itself. Toulmin (1990) showed that the rapid growth of science and modern philosophy during the Enlightenment was not the result of prosperity and a new intellectual vitality resulting from a reduced censorship of intellectual activity by the Church, as the end of the Middle Ages are usually characterized. That, in fact, is what the Renaissance represented approximately 100 years earlier. The Enlightenment was actually a time of great destruction and financial ruin leading to much intellectual and emotional insecurity and fear in Europe. The church hierarchies had in many ways lost their legitimacy in the eyes of the masses by having promulgated such a murderous war. But what could replace the security and dogma of the Christian faith that had given order, meaning, and comfort to personal and civic life? The oligarchies of Europe turned to the natural philosophers of the Enlightenment (e.g., Galileo, Newton, Leibnitz, and Descartes) to provide a sense of security or certainty through the dogma of Rationality (the term is capitalized to indicate that it differs from the everyday sense of rationality or reasonableness).

> The 17th century philosophers' "Quest for Certainty" was no mere proposal to construct abstract and timeless intellectual schemas, dreamed up as objects of pure, detached intellectual study. Instead it was a timely response to a specific historical challenge—the political, social, and theological crisis embodied in the Thirty Years' War. (Toulmin, 1990, p. 70)

The title of Toulmin's (1990) book, *Cosmopolis*, is taken from the ancient Greek notion that cultures should strive to shape the political order to match their understanding of the natural order of the universe. Toulmin (1990) argued that the converse is also true, that social and political leaders also seek to promote theories of the natural order (*cosmologies*) that justify the structure of the political order (the *polis*) already in existence. He pointed out how Newtonian physics is based on a blend of rationalist and theological assumptions concerning the inevitable mathematical ordering of the universe:

> In the three hundred years after 1660, the natural sciences did not march along a royal road, defined by a rational method. They moved in a zigzag, alternating the rationalist methods of Newton's mathematics and the empiricist methods of Bacon's naturalism. The triumph of Newtonian physics was, thus, a vote for theoretical cosmology, not for practical dividends and the ideas of Newtonian theory were shaped by a concern for the intellectual coherence with a respectable picture of God's material creation, as obeying Divine laws. . . . Using our understanding of nature to increase comfort, or to reduce pain, was secondary to the central spiritual goal of Science. Rejecting in both method and spirit

Bacon's vision of humanly fruitful science, Descartes and Newton set out to build mathematical structures, and looked to Science for theological, not technological dividends. (Toulmin, 1990, pp. 104–105)

Newton's physics produced a claim to certain and eternal knowledge of the nature of the physical forces that dominate the natural world and, as such, provided a sense of security about humankind's place in the universe that was independent of Christian theology but not inconsistent with it. This was a view that became "common sense" to the ruling elite in Great Britain and much of Europe. It served their social and political ends well, for it communicated the inherent order in the universe that should be duplicated in the political and social arrangements of human society.

After the catastrophic times from 1618 to 1655, a new and self-maintaining social order was gradually established. One thing helped the respectable oligarchy to take the lead in this reconstruction: this we shall see was the evolution of a new Comopolis, in which the divinely created order of Nature and the humanly created Order of society were once again seen as illuminating one another. (Toulmin, 1990, p. 98)

In a later chapter, Toulmin (1990) added the following:

The comprehensive system of ideas about nature and humanity that formed the scaffolding of Modernity was thus a social and political, as well as a scientific device: it was seen as conferring Divine legitimacy on the political order of the sovereign nation–state. In this respect, the world view of modern science—as it actually came into existence—on public support around 1700 for the legitimacy it apparently gave to the political system of nation–states as much as for its power to explain the motions of planets, or the rise and fall of the tides. (p. 128)

Toulmin (1990) made the intriguing point that the parallels between the social political system of order and the structure of nature captured in Newtonian physics extend even to the selection of the most basic concepts in the physical theory. In Newton's theory, matter, which is inert and powerless, is described as

physical mass, and is incapable of any spontaneous movement or action on its own. Energy and force must be applied to the mass for anything to move or change. This corresponded exactly with the dominant political theory of the Anglican Church of England that resisted any democratizing moves that would result in giving the masses of people more power to control their own actions and lives. Newton's choice of terms reflected favorably on the existing power structure of British society, suggesting that even in the heavens there are large bodies of inert substances, governed and controlled by a few very powerful forces (e.g. gravitational pull, motion, inertia). Theological arguments at the time reflected this concern with the religious Nonconformists rejecting Newton's physics with its implicit cosmology because of its implications for the polis. (Toulmin, 1990, pp. 120–121)

Although Toulmin (1990) did not deal extensively with the development of psychology and the social sciences in the late 1800s, one can extrapolate from his theory that for the few to rule the many, not only must the masses be seen as directionless but also the few must develop social and political structures that can direct and control the masses. It is hard to imagine that the needs of the modern nation–state to manage and control the social behavior of millions of individuals did not influence the development of a modern psychology that (a) emphasized overt behavior over inner experience; (b) favored the study of large groups of subjects and sought uniformities in behavior across the groups rather than individual uniqueness; (c) viewed the control of behavior as proof that the behavior was understood; (d) viewed human behavior as naturally and ultimately under the control of external forces (whether biological or social) rather than self-directed; and (e) viewed psychological propositions as morally neutral rather than as a form of moral legislation. Perhaps it is also no coincidence that research participants were called *subjects* for the first 100 years of psychology—a term with obvious political connotations of passivity and powerlessness.

A science of behavior that showed that human beings were not free, even when they thought they were, certainly invalidates or undermines political attempts to obtain civil freedom for the common man and woman in the modern bureaucratic nation–state. Why should we not (as B. F. Skinner, 1971, argued in *Beyond Freedom and Dignity*) jettison political notions of freedom and dignity if we are not really free anyway in the natural environment of human society? (In his later book, *Return to Reason*, Toulmin, 2000, was critical of Skinner's psychology, with its emphasis on prediction and control.) It was just this implication of Skinner's psychology that led Rogers to challenge the wisdom of developing a technology of behavior in their series of debates in the 1950s.

In the Enlightenment view of Rationality, laws of behavior (legislation) would emanate from the national government, or *polis* (to be enforced by military or police forces), that would reflect the laws of the universe, or *cosmos*, as discovered by natural scientists. Initially, there were no social sciences because the mind, which was presumed by Enlightenment thinkers from Descartes forward to govern behavior through the power of reason, was thought to be outside of the natural world and causal mechanisms. Perhaps because he feared the power that the Church still wielded against heretics, Descartes avoided pushing a mechanistic explanation of the mind, although he certainly hinted that such a theory might be plausible. The postmodern era has rejected Descartes's worldview of dualism (e.g., Rorty, 1979) and has been seeking to eliminate mind–body and other related dichotomies: objective–subjective and free will–causal determinism.

Only in the middle to late 1800s, some 250 years after the Treaty of Westphalia, which ended the Thirty Years War, did the social sciences and psychology emerge as scientific enterprises. Even then, these new disciplines were careful not to challenge religious authority on moral matters, claiming to be value neutral and capable of the same objectivity as the physical sciences. Of course, by this point in history the authority of orthodox religious institutions had been vastly diminished by the rise of urban and industrialized societies that decimated the familial communities of rural Europe. Although the Church was wounded, it was not entirely powerless, and the nascent fields of psychology, economics, sociology, anthropology, and political science were vulnerable if directly attacked, particularly at Church-supported institutions of higher education.

Nevertheless, these new disciplines, once they were up and running, joined in the modern agenda of the cosmopolis to strengthen the hand of the nation–states that supported their emergence. Their role was to describe, predict, and demonstrate how to control the "natural" patterns of behavior in the populace that were of interest to the rulers of these nation–states. In the history of psychology this typically is viewed as providing a scientific basis for legislation, or *social engineering*. Psychology and the social sciences provide a scientific foundation of information that enlightens legislation. According to Toulmin's (1990) view of science, one has to look at the flow of influence in the other direction: that those who are creating legislative laws of behavior (the political leaders of the society) have an interest in seeing that the science being practiced by psychology and the other social sciences supports the legislation that they want to write. The social and political powers that be want the "laws of behavior" generated by the scientists to facilitate the drafting and implementation of legislative laws (of behavior) that they will enforce. So theories and research that show that people "naturally" want or need to behave in the ways that legislators wish to require of the population for political, economic, or social purposes will be favored and encouraged. R. Whitaker's (2002) account of the role that social scientists played in the eugenics movement of the 1920s and 1930s in the United States, and Lifton's (1986) account of the role of medical and social sciences in support of racist policies in Nazi Germany before World War II (WWII) are excellent illustrations of this kind of subtle reversal of influence between these two kinds of "laws of behavior." Behavioral scientists would make a "naturalistic fact" out of a behavioral regularity required by those with political–economic power (the supposed physical superiority of the ruling class or Aryan race.)

Of course, in more recent times the involvement of science in government, and government in science, is pervasive. The U.S. government, as noted above, sponsors billions of dollars in psychology-related research every year, and policy questions are routinely referred to panels of scientific experts to find scientific answers to the social and political questions of our day (I present a more extensive discussion of the U.S. government's role in the development of modern psychology later in this chapter). The largesse of private philanthropic foundations, too, is often bestowed on scientists, suggesting that the wealthy and powerful members of the society outside of government also see their own vested interests in the promotion of the scientific worldview and scientific research.

The conduct of science is of course more than simply playing politics, for there are genuine philosophical and intellectual questions about nature and the physical universe that individuals explore out of curiosity, interest, or even a personal need to find answers. One must with MacIntyre (1984) recognize the practice of "pure" science as every bit as noble as the magisterial institutional science claims itself to be. This pure behavioral science is worthy of preservation and must be vigilantly protected from institutional encroachment and corruption, as with any other social practice. It exists in the creative and dedicated painstaking work of individuals working alone or with small groups of colleagues on highly abstract theories and problems. It exists within institutional settings as well but is always in tension with institutional political agendas that are likely to corrupt it.

There is no doubt that many of the leading psychologists and social scientists whose theories and research have, over the last century, been used to support the interests of the powerful in our society began their research with a serious intellectual commitment to the work they did and interpreted the extensive financial support that they received from the government or foundations as simply a tribute to the brilliance of their work rather than its political use. Others may have shared the political views of those in power and found the consilience between their views of nature and the needs of the nation–state fortuitous. Still others may have, over time, shifted their theoretical or research interests to bring them into line with the goals of various funding sources, perhaps fearing the consequences for their careers if they did otherwise.

At the most fundamental level, our commitment to a magisterial view of science may simply be a means of keeping religious views and institutions from recapturing the public's imagination. By emphasizing the scientific understanding and control of the natural order of the world, the public's enthusiasm for policies justified by reference to supernatural, mystical, and mysterious forces of the world is diminished. Given the trauma of the Thirty Years War, and the other religious conflicts that have been a scourge to humankind, this would appear to be no mean accomplishment when it succeeds. Yet as dangerous as the marriage of political power and religious authority proved to be for Europe in the 17th century, the marriage of the nation–state and modern science has proved cataclysmic.

Toulmin (1990) wrote of the Enlightenment's dogmatic commitment to the powers of Rationality as countering the Church's influence on many fronts, but only by abandoning the intellectual and religious tolerance of the

Renaissance. The Renaissance was a time when the integrity and diversity of human ways of being were all valued—reason, faith, emotion, passion, mind, and body were all acknowledged. In the Enlightenment, Rationality was elevated to a position of preeminence, and this has come down to us as a faith, a veneration, and an awe of science. Lurking always in the shadows of any argument concerning the legitimacy of this faith in science and scientific experts to decide the important questions of life is the haunting question "So, would you prefer that religion and religious institutions return to control our lives?" Toulmin (1990) rejected this dichotomous choice and suggested the human reason (not Rationality) as it functioned during the Renaissance is a third way:

> Our revised narratives of the stages of Modernity, indeed, embody implicitly a history of "modern" idea about rationality. For 16th-century humanists, the central demand was that all of our thought and conduct be *reasonable*. On the one hand, this meant developing modesty about one's capacities and self-awareness in ones' self-presentation; all the things that Stephen Greenblatt calls "Renaissance self-fashioning." On the other hand, it required toleration of social, cultural, and intellectual diversity. It was unreasonable to condemn out of hand people with institutions, customs, or ideas different from ours, as heretical, superstitious, or barbarous. Instead, we should recognize that our own practices may look no less strange to others, and withhold judgment until we can ask how far those others reached their positions by honest, discriminating, and critical reflection on their experience. . . . As we enter a fresh phase in the history of Modernity—seeking to humanize science and technology and re-appropriate the aims of practical philosophy—we need to recover the idea of rationality [reasonableness] that was current before Descartes. (pp. 199–200)

THE RECEIVED OR MAINSTREAM VIEW OF SCIENCE

Since the activities of the Vienna Circle of logical positivists in the 1920s and 1930s, the philosophical community has focused its efforts on the question of the nature of science and scientific reasoning. What emerged over time was a consensus view, which came to be called the *Covering Law* or *hypothetic–deductive* view of science (Hempel, 1963). This view was widely accepted in psychology through the influence of Bridgman (1928) and maintains that science begins with a rational conjecture (a proposed law) about the relationship between or among phenomena—for example, that water boils at 212°F. To support this theory, a specific hypothesis must be generated that can be tested. It must specify some actual states of affairs in the world that would demonstrate the law's validity in predicting various fact patterns. For example, one would specify placing a certain number of ounces of water into a glass beaker, using a gas to heat the beaker, measuring the temperature of the water at given time periods, and observing the water to boil. Should the water boil, one derives confidence in the theory, but because it is a universal principle, and one has not tested it in all possible contexts, one cannot say that the theory itself is confirmed. However, if the water does not boil, one has reason to reject the hypothesis and, depending on the confidence one has in the execution and design of the study, one might actually reject the law (Popper, 1959).

This conventional view of science, the received view, is actually built on several critical assumptions about the nature of reality and knowledge that are not subject to scientific experimentation but are rather the worldview that makes experimentation possible to conceptualize in the first place. These are summarized below:

1. *Naturalism/materialism*. Science gives a systematic account of the natural world—thus excluding the spiritual, mystical, non-material, supernatural, ephemeral, and anomalous. Science is about matter, objects in the real world, and nature in all its manifold expressions.

2. *Universality*. A systematic account seeks universal principles of explanation (laws) that apply in all time periods and places. The phenomena studied must be sufficiently powerful or forceful to control events across all contexts.

3. *Theories/facts*. Scientific theories state universal laws or principles of explanation that must be supported or disconfirmed by research that establishes factual data relevant to a research hypothesis. Although theories are subjective, intuitive, and creative products of the human mind, facts correspond to reality and provide an objective check on fallabilistic human reason.

4. *Causality/prediction*. Science seeks explanations that identify causal mechanisms at work in nature and lead to the ability to predict and control the natural phenomena under study. Science assumes that all natural events have natural causes.

5. *Probability*. Because of the complexity of nature, and perhaps because of either its lack of complete orderliness or the inability of the human mind to grasp that orderliness, science must settle at times for statements of greater or lesser probability of events rather than perfect predictability or control.

6. *Quantification*. Mathematical precision and elegance are the hallmark of modern scientific theory. The deductive, mathematical system of Newtonian physics is taken as the model for all science. All subjects studied must permit of measurement and quantification.

7. *Scientific method.* The scientific method of searching for, or creating, in nature or the laboratory, the opportunity to isolate and measure a specific phenomenon (called now an *independent variable*), and then isolating and measuring at least one other phenomenon (called now the *dependent variable*[s]), and determining whether changes in the first variable are associated with changes in the second variable or variables, is absolutely central to the practice of science. The elimination of extraneous factors by the use of controls is critical to this task.

8. *Reductionism.* Because nature is of a piece, and there is only one nature, then the laws of scientific explanation ought also to be capable of unification. This was generally regarded by the logical positivists to mean that the laws of the social sciences would be reducible to laws of psychology, the laws of psychology would be reducible to the laws of biology, the laws of biology would ultimately reduce to the laws of chemistry, and the laws of chemistry would reduce to the laws of physics. The universal laws of nature would truly be universal (the same for all phenomena), all encompassing, and reductionistic.

THE CRITIQUE OF
THE RECEIVED VIEW

I have found in teaching undergraduate and graduate courses over the past 20 years, whether in the introductory course or an advanced graduate seminar, that if one examines the presuppositions of science, rather than taking them for granted, as is usually done in psychology courses, that students are generally incredulous that anyone would have seriously thought that the problems that brought them (the students) to the study of psychology, would, or even could, be solved by means of a mainstream scientific approach. Common sense is not always right, but one risks a great deal by systematically ignoring it, especially, as in this case, when some of the best minds in the history and philosophy of science have reached the same conclusion.

The claims of Hard Science from which this section began—the search for abstract universal theories with timeless general laws, the demand for detached objectivity, and the insistence that investigations be value-free—are not (in Popper's phrase) "demarcation criteria" to separate truly scientific projects and disciplines from unscientific speculations: the Black from the White, or the Saved from the Damned. They serve only to define the Newtonian pole of this spectrum, while at the opposite pole we can find local, timely, and value-laden projects, each with its own methods, objectivity and organization. (Toulmin, 2000, pp. 82–83)

I now examine each of the seven presuppositions of science from the viewpoint of reason rather than Rationality.

Naturalism–Materialism

Of course, we live in the natural world, and we are a part of it. Life is material, but is it only material? Thousands of years of Western and Eastern philosophy have struggled with the tension between *materialism* and what is called *idealism*. This is not the idealism of youth who seek moral purity (although it is related indirectly to this phenomenon), but a more general view that our ideas, our consciousness, is a consciousness of both natural phenomena and nonnatural or ideational phenomena that are equally real to us. Some have even claimed that this ideational world is more real and important than the natural world. In fact, some of the early empiricists, such as Bishop Berkley (1685–1753), took the view that the data of our senses are important not because they provide a window into nature but simply because they are all that we have to go by and thus all we can know. Basically all knowledge is knowledge of sense data. It is obvious, then, that to be empirical does not necessarily mean to be a materialist, but in contemporary discussions empirical methods are assumed to provide a direct representation of reality. Realists, conversely, are generally those who accept the reality and importance of both realms of reality—the natural/material/objective physical world and the nonnatural/ideational/subjective world of mind and consciousness. Many of the philosophers of science who are critical of the received view identify themselves as *Critical Realists* (see Manicus & Secord, 1983, who summarized and synthesized the work of many contemporary philosophers of science who subscribe to this view).

For psychology students, not yet acculturated into the scienticism of the discipline, the question of whether the problems they are looking for psychology to solve fall into the natural realm is a troubling one. They cannot turn on a television or open a newsmagazine without being bombarded with advertising from drug companies telling them that all their problems are the result of a "biochemical imbalance in their brain." Even before the discipline indoctrinates them, the culture does! (What this says about the discipline I take up in a later section of this chapter.)

Nevertheless, when they consider the problems they have concerns about—troubling dreams and nightmares, conflicted feelings about loyalties and goals, pain over a death in the family or a romance that has ended badly for them, jealousy toward a sibling who can do no wrong in mom or dad's eyes, feeling devastated by a career-ending knee injury after having been a high school all-American athlete, and so forth—their reactions are quite different. Obviously, one has to have a body or a brain to experience these problems. If one were not part of the natural world, one could not play sports, make love, sleep and dream, and so forth. Although it is necessary or a precondition to be a part of nature to have these psychological problems in living, the problem is not in the body or nature per se; the problem is in the person. We experience the material world, nature, as distinct from the world of imagination, fantasy, hopes, dreams, goals, and purposes. This is what the phenomenological psychologists refer to as the *intentional realm*, where things are not just things but have a meaning that directs one away from the thing that carries the meaning toward something else. If I yell, "FIRE!" the physical sound created by my voice and my body movements used to communicate that sound are all physical, but if you are to survive the fire, you had better not respond by commenting on the unusual tonal qualities in my voice or by noting the decibel level of my production—you had better respond to the meaning: that there is a fire in the room and you better get out. Meaning has been the Achilles heel of the physicalist, materialist, naturalistic approach to psychology and the social sciences since the mid-1800s, as revealed in the work of F. D. E. Schleiermacher and William Dilthey (Warnke, 1987). The meaning, intention, goal, and purpose of any given behavior or brain state are very unlikely to ever be captured by a simply materialistic account of that behavior or brain state. All of the sophisticated philosophical arguments in support of this argument aside (Searles, 2003), it remains clear that, when put in this context, few students find it even plausible to view psychology as exclusively concerned with the natural world, as sciences are supposed to be. In fact, they see the problems that bring them to psychology as distinctly not about the natural world but about the interpersonal world of relationshipsand the intrapersonal world of feelings, intentions, hopes, goals, and dreams.

Universality

Universality is not very plausible in psychology, and the dearth of laws of behavior that have emerged and survived more than a few decades of examination is certainly acknowledged by the scientists themselves. They defend the principle on the grounds that psychology is a young science, and so psychologists have not yet gotten to a set of powerful universal principles— but give them time, and they will. However, it is hard to imagine any such set of universal laws that will be of much use to those interested in solving life's practical problems with psychology. As James (1892/1983b) warned, the general laws, if and when they emerge, will be only partially informative of what to do in the real world. As Toulmin (1990) pointed out, scientific Rationality eschewed addressing context-dependent practical problems of living. Problems that are unique to a particular locality and period and involve actually making a difference in the immediate situation are relegated to engineers and civil servants. Even in the material world, engineers must add their own engineering knowledge to scientific principles to solve real-world problems. The universal laws of physics do not ever suffice. This is logically determined by the structure of scientific laws that are developed by holding "all other things equal"—that is, by the critically important method of scientific research referred to as *controlling extraneous variables*.

In the real world, as Manicus and Secord (1983) ably demonstrated, all other things are never equal. In any real problem situation there are always a multitude of interacting phenomena or factors in addition to those that have been isolated in lawlike principles of science. These extraneous variables are not extraneous in the real world, they *are* the real world, and they must be considered and dealt with, or the application of the science will fail miserably. In fact, on the basis of the logic of science itself, one might question whether it is ever legitimate to apply a scientific principle in a specific context in which it has not already been systematically studied. Given the great lengths to which science goes to control the impact of extraneous variables to accurately measure the impact of one variable on another, once those extraneous variables are present in the real world, as they always are, the scientist must acknowledge that the actual impact of manipulating the independent variable in the real world is unknown! Under these circumstances, a mechanic who is very experienced in fixing a particular kind of engine failure might be more successful than a metals scientist applying the laws of metallurgy to the problem. (Of course, if the two could work together respectfully, that would probably be the best of both worlds, but then the difference in their social and economic positions would have to be bridged, and that is another story.)

To the student, it is quite intuitively obvious that each human being is quite unique, as are family backgrounds and life histories, and the problems they face, while not without some similarities, also remain unique. They are surprised and somewhat relieved to find that there are psychologists who believe that they can learn from studying life histories of others and that there may be more similarity than they realized in the problems human beings must face over the course of a lifetime. These heuristics (rules of thumb) are useful to learn, and helpful to apply, but they do not approach lawlike, scientific principles. It is good to know, for example, that most people respond well to some form of empathic listening when they are sharing a problem (Rogers, 1960). Yet there are people who do not respond well to it, and there are situations, such as crisis intervention or interviewing sociopathic individuals, in which it is generally not a good thing to consider doing at all, unless other issues have been dealt with first. Expressed in this way, psychological knowledge does contain general principles, but they resemble more moral than scientific principles. The highly regarded philosopher Davidson (1979) referred to these as *heteronomous* principles.

Theories–Facts

The distinction between a theory as a general or universal statement and a fact as a description of a specific sate of affairs in the world at a particular time and place is a relatively straightforward one. However, when the universal statement is not just an empirical generalization (e.g., "all the pencils in this drawer are yellow") but also a scientific principle, such as "depression is caused by insufficient norepinephrine in the caudate nucleus," the plot thickens. How one chooses to define *depression* is of critical importance to the facts one will find. One can define *depression* in strictly physiological terms (e.g., poor eating, sleeping, or motor movements), and this will significantly affect the "facts" one finds. If one sees depression as an interpersonal phenomenon and therefore insists that data must be collected that reflect the relationships the patients have with their significant others, including the life circumstances that have affected those relationships in the last six months to one year, then a very different picture of depression will emerge.

It is likely that a biologically oriented researcher might even reject interpersonal variables as insufficiently scientific (objective, measurable, etc.) to be studied at all, and so a true test of the competing explanations may not be possible. Philosophers of science call this *incommensurability*: Crucial tests across radically different theories of the facts may not be possible, because what counts as facts under one theory do not count as facts under the other. Thomas Kuhn (1970) was one of the first, and most recognized, of the historians and philosophers of science to draw attention to the indeterminacy of research paradigms vis à vis "the facts." Quine (1980) argued that facts and theories constitute one another and that one cannot always clearly differentiate a so-called fact from a so-called theory. Some concepts are more theoretical, and others more factual, in their meaning, but no conceptual or propositional expression of a fact is entirely independent of the theoretical propositions under which it was observed. Within a theory, one can specify what is to count as a fact and what is not, and sufficiently similar theories can share fact patterns quite well enough. However, when there are true clashes of paradigms—as, for example, in psychology, between the behaviorists and the humanists, or between the family systems theorists and the psychoanalysts—then resorting to empirical research to resolve the differences is an unproductive strategy.

Students entering the field often arrive with a very high regard for objective observation as the answer to controversial questions. However, they also seem to intuitively recognize when presented with four or five different models of development, personality, or psychotherapy that in some sense they each have something valuable to say and that to try to determine which one is right and which wrong seems like a hopeless task. Although I used to think this was a dodge to avoid doing the hard conceptual and critical thinking that theoretical comparisons require—and in some cases that might be just what it is—I now think this student response is again the wisdom of common sense. Presented with incommensurable paradigms, their initial response is that the task of looking for "the right" approach to psychotherapy was a futile endeavor. It makes more sense to look for the contexts in which one paradigm is successful and the other not, or for the particular way in which facts are construed by one paradigm or the other.

Charles Taylor (1973) argued that the social and clinical aspects of psychology are lacking in what he called *brute data*, in that the observations made by such psychologists are so laden with theoretical (and, I would add, moral) meaning that it is inconceivable that one could design effective tests among competing theories. This is so because the data required to disconfirm the theories would be so disparate as to make it impossible to compare the results of the studies. The differences are incommensurable—not permitting of measurement. Perhaps this is why in psychology the validity of the measures of phenomena is debated so assiduously in psychological research, sometimes more than the data themselves, for once the decision is made as to what to count as data had been made (on implicitly theoretical grounds), the outcome of the research, and the theory the data will support, is already partially determined.

Causality–Prediction

On the issue of causality, and the determination of causality by research methods that aim at prediction and control of variables, the applicability to psychology is more complex and controversial than with materialism or universality of principles for, as I discussed in chapter 3 under the topic of agency, we experience ourselves as both governed by forces outside our control (whether social or biological) and as having some ability to act as the cause of our own behavior. This is truly, as Kant (1781/1929) observed, an antinomy of reason. Humans have believed, with about equal fervor for thousands of years, two contradictory positions: (a) that people's actions are under the control of their own powers of reason and foresight and (b) that their actions are caused by forces over which they have little or no control.

Even the concept of causality itself is difficult to define. Rychlak (1968, 1981, 1994), following Aristotle, has identified four meanings of the concept of causality: (a) material, (b) efficient, (c) formal, and (d) final. *Material* and *efficient* correspond with scientific explanation; whereas *formal* and *final* are more consistent with how one explains one's own actions in terms of reasons for doing something. Material explanations explain events in terms of the substances that are present. If one says that depression is caused by a depletion of serotonin in the brain, one has cited a material cause. *Efficient* causation refers to an explanation that depends on showing how substances or forces interact in a dynamic sequence. So, if one says that Prozac works to lessen depression because it inhibits the reuptake of serotonin by the presynaptic membrane, one has given an efficient cause to explain the drugs success. *Formal* causes describe a pattern of events or characteristics that is not easily recognized and, when it is, one experiences a sense of understanding. To tell someone that his or her pattern of not sleeping, loss of appetite, poor concentration, irritation, and constipation means that he or she is "depressed" is to explain all the symptoms as caused by a common factor: depression. *Final* causality refers to giving an account of the purpose or ultimate goal of the subject of interest. If one says that a person's depression is caused by a need for attention, or a desire to withdraw from responsibilities in the world, one is giving a final-cause explanation.

So, even the concept of causality is itself ambiguous, and we cannot expect to resolve this thorny philosophical issue here. However, it is important to take note of the concept of final causation, for it provides an account of what it means to give reasons for behavior rather than material causes. When people give reasons for what they do they are giving the purpose, intention, goal, or meaning that the behavior represented for the person engaging in the behavior. Final causation views behavior, and implicitly brain states, as having a symbolic, and not just a physical, reality. The behavior means something to the person engaging in the behavior, the actor, and it may mean the same or something different to those interacting with the actor. Those meanings add to the physical reality a dimension that is critical to *understanding* the interpersonal or intrapersonal world of the individual. Reasons, rather than causes, point us to the importance of the *concept of understanding* in psychology and that understanding the meaning of behavior is not the same intellectual task as explaining the causes of the behavior, if explaining is taken to mean prediction and control.

Understanding is a somewhat amorphous concept, and the term is often used in psychology without clarification. It will be helpful to try to clarify it. *The Compact Edition of the Oxford English Dictionary* (1971) defines *understanding* as follows:

    I. (trans. v.) To comprehend, to apprehend the meaning or import of, to grasp the idea of;
      b. To be thoroughly acquainted or familiar with (an art, profession, etc.) to be able to practice or deal with properly;
      c. To apprehend clearly the character or nature of (a person); and
      d. To know one's place, or how to conduct oneself properly.
    II. To comprehend by knowing the meaning of the words employed; to be acquainted with (a language) to this extent;
      b. To grasp the meaning or purport of the words (or signs) used by (a person); and
      c. To understand each other—to be in agreement or collusion: to be confederates.

We can see here that understanding has three related but not identical components.

    1. There is a conceptual component, as in comprehending the meaning of an idea, or a linguistic communication.

2. There is a pragmatic component of expertise or know-how.
3. Relative to understanding other people, the term *understanding* further indicates both an awareness of another's true character or a closeness and collusion. This may be in the sense of two people "having an understanding"—an unspoken collusion to do something that others won't know about, or would not like if they did.

In addition, one can *be* understanding, as in supportive, helpful, and nurturing. It would seem that the latter two senses of understanding that exists *between people* are derivative of understanding *of what people mean by what they say and do*. Such mutual comprehension would lead to a sense of collusion or confederacy, although this collusion suggests that an additional element has been added: approval or support for those meanings that have been clarified or determined. In the third sense, this approval for the meaning extends to the person as a whole; to be understanding means to be supportive and empathic and nonjudgmental of what one is being told. At the same time, being understanding generally, although certainly not always, permits one to develop an understanding of another person—to see the world as that person sees it and to be able to make sense out of his or her actions—to see the point or the goal of his or her actions, and why he or she did not take, or perhaps see, any other route to the same end. It places the person's actions in the context of a choice, to do X rather than Y or Z, and explains to us why X was chosen in terms of the reasons X was seen as preferable to Y or Z.

Of course, it is not always others whom we do not understand, but sometimes ourselves as well. When we do not understand ourselves, we cannot see what sense there is in our own behaviors. It might be said that this was the whole point of psychoanalysis as Freud initially conceived it, to find the sense in what seemed senseless to the person him- or herself. Alfred Adler had a slightly different way of conceiving of the process that removed the material causation from the formula. He said that we lose track of, forget, perhaps even actively repress the goals we have set for ourselves, but this does not stop us from acting on them. They remain *our* goals, but we have disavowed them, and so our actions seem under the control of some outside force. Adler thought that as we reclaim our forgotten goals and choices, we are able to understand ourselves better and be more socially responsible with our actions.

When we understand a person, he or she makes sense to us; we can place his or her actions in a logical framework. A person with these goals, when faced with these circumstances and constraints, will choose Action X, because Action X has a greater likelihood of reaching Goal X than any of the alternative courses of action. To understand how this person has these goals in the first place, we must look at his or her life history, predominant emotional responses to their environment, likes and dislikes, joys and satisfactions, and so forth. We have to get to know the other person quite well (see chap. 5 for further discussion of knowing people well). Notice how different this is from predicting and controlling behavior. In fact, it is quite odd how attached we are to prediction and control in psychology, given that many acceptable sciences do not use this criteria. Evolutionary biology, to which many scientific psychologists are very committed, developed without any such experimental efforts. Geology, archeology, and astronomy are other examples, and history, although not a science, is a widely respected intellectual and scholarly field of research without any such scientific pretensions or requirements.

Discussions of prediction of behavior are always interesting with my students. Everyone wants to make the problematic people in their own lives become more predictable. They do not want any more rude awakenings from the people they care about changing directions in their lives and leaving others behind. A psychology that could help them predict such things is very much what they want. Equally, they would like to be able to control others more, so as not to feel so powerless. They would like to be able to get their old girlfriend to love them again, or their mother to stop smoking, or their father not to work so hard, and so forth. Yet at the same time, none of my students ever want *others* to become better able to predict and control their own (the students') behavior. Furthermore, when faced with a context in which they do not currently understand why they are doing something, they naturally look for self-understanding and do not think to approach their own lack of self-understanding as an inability to predict and control their own behavior. If they are unpredictable and out of control, they want to understand what is making them behave that way, and they are not looking for variables in their environment or psyche to be manipulated by someone else until a clear pattern of cause and effect is established. This asymmetry is important. It suggests that our desire for prediction and control of behavior comes from some source other than the desire to learn more about behavior. It has to do with interpersonal power or feelings of powerlessness. One can only imagine the devastating impact that this pervasive desire *not to become predictable and controlled* by others has on the results of all psychological experiments involving human participants.

During the 1950s and 1960s, Carl Rogers and B. F. Skinner held a series of debates about the future of psychology and behavior control (Wann, 1960). Rogers, the humanist, frequently observed that totalitarian antidemocratic forces in U.S. society might easily abuse Skinnerian learning theory for politically repressive ends. Perhaps Rogers knew and was not saying, but the problem was not that a psychology of prediction and control might be abused in this way. The problem was, and still is, that Skinnerian theory's widespread appeal in organizational, institutional, and governmental contexts was its very capacity to be used in this way. Of course, its proponents did not view this as abuse, but simply as bringing Rationality to the manner in which the society attempted to control the behavior of its members through policies and legislation. I discuss this further in the section on the U.S. government's support of psychological research.

Probability and Quantification

Students beginning the study of psychology are hopeful that it will give them certain and final answers to all of life's problems. It is a harsh lesson in reality when they learn that not only scientific but also clinically based theories and research cannot meet this expectation. The disappointment is not too difficult to overcome, if in fact one *has something of use to offer* in place of certainty and simplistic answers. In fact, it is not hard for any person to accept that life is uncertain, and unpredictable, and that the best one can do usually is to have knowledge that is more right than wrong. In other words, both clinicians and scientists have to learn to live with the uncertain nature of their knowledge in psychology. Lacking the lawlike principles of the natural sciences, psychologists have other intellectual resources at their disposal. They search for ways to engage in trial-and-error problem solving, looking for ways to minimize the negative effects of errors by testing the waters, taking small initial steps, looking for parallel situations where solutions have been found, and avoiding very risky trials unless all other attempted solutions have failed. This process of reflective practice (Argyris & Schon, 1974) is a well-documented approach in all the professions, and I take it up in chapter 5. Suffice it to say that this kind of reasoning is heuristic, probabilistic, and creatively divergent. Because of the complexity of real-life clinical situations, it is not always possible to determine in advance what all the possible outcomes might be, and so determining the probability of occurrence is impossible. In addition, even when the potential outcomes of concern have been specified, the actual universe of concern, or base rate in the population, may well be unknown. So the clinician is managing uncertainty in a broader sense than just probabilistic knowledge versus certain knowledge. Even when outcomes are specified and base rates in the population known, predicting clinical phenomena with statistical significance is a Herculean task because of the problem of low base rates. When base rates are low (say, under 5%), one can have a very high rate of success (in this instance, 95%) by always predicting that the clinical phenomena will not occur.

Furthermore, there is a serious question that has been raised by the humanists, phenomenologists, and even Freud since the beginning of experimental psychology that has been sidestepped in this discussion of uncertainty: whether the important phenomena in question can be effectively measured without so seriously distorting their reality as to make such measurement meaningless. This interacts closely with the question of prediction and control in two ways. First, prediction and control can be demonstrated only by quantifying phenomena (unless one has a perfect prediction equation, in which case the relationship is absolutely obvious). Second, the ability to quantify relevant phenomena is vastly improved when one is concerned with overt public behaviors (e.g., preferences for Coke or Pepsi, strategies for crowd control, or leadership styles). As soon as one goes to the kind of problems *that individuals bring to psychology* and not the problems *that institutions bring*, measurement becomes highly problematic. Subjective judgments of a subjective state made by the client–participant or the psychologist are extremely difficult, if not impossible, to standardize (no one has succeeded to date), and many would argue that it is unnecessary or wrongheaded to even try. What makes psychologists think that dreams, fantasies, goals, and intentions are the sorts of things that can be systematically measured to begin with? In my experience, the thought of doing so strikes most people (not indoctrinated into psychology) as implausible. An articulate minority in the field has taken the view that this is an area for only qualitative and narrative analysis (e.g., Hoshmand, 1992; Howard, 1991; Polkinghorne, 1988). Although measurement, which developed as a social practice, makes sense in the material realm, it does not make sense in the realm of the subjective–ideal–meaning.

The Scientific Method

In my 20 years as a psychology professor, only a small percentage of the students whom I have encountered would take a course on research methods in psychology without being required to do so. What should be even more disturbing to the discipline is that this percentage does not increase very much when one asks those who have completed such a course whether they believe that psychology students should be required to do so. Experimentalists interpret this reality as a sign of how intellectually challenging research methods and statistics are to understand. They believe the students are rejecting the work because it is too difficult.

The analysis provided here suggests another plausible interpretation, but one the scientists in psychology will find uncomfortable to consider. Perhaps the real reason students reject research methods in psychology is common sense. If they come into the research course believing with good reason, as most students do, that behavior is not strictly a material, observable phenomenon; not primarily caused by outside forces; that it cannot be meaningfully quantified; and furthermore, that understanding other people does not primarily come by means of prediction and control, then why in the world would they be motivated to learn the research methods currently taught? When they struggle through the research methods courses and come out on the other side battered, beaten, but still majoring in psychology, the discipline of academic psychology declares victory over the irrational, intuitive, error-prone, commonsense ways of thinking of the masses.

Yet one does not have to completely reject the scientific method, or at least components of it, to do justice to these students and their interests in a practical psychology. Anyone who comes to psychology to learn implicitly makes a commitment to exercise reason in the study of the subject matter. To the extent that the *scientific method* means careful and unbiased observation, the systematic examination of data for patterns of meaning and behavior, the avoidance of factual claims unsupported by evidence, and care in not drawing conclusions that go beyond the data and arguments presented, the scientific method is a necessary component of the discipline. To say this is not to say that the scientific method is the end-all and be-all of psychological investigation, for psychology may require other methods of analysis as well (e.g., introspection–free association, moral self-examination, intuition–insight concerning first principles, philosophical analysis, naturalistic observation, or hermeneutic understanding)—it is, however, to acknowledge a role for elements of the scientific method, or what Toulmin (1958) would simply call the *rules of argument*, or *informal logic*, in the teaching and learning of psychology.

The presuppositions of science are all closely linked, and it is obvious that if one is rejecting materialism, universality, the focus on and quantification of overt public behaviors, causality, and prediction and control, then the justification for the scientific method is almost completely eroded. This is often taken by defenders of the scientific model of psychology to mean that rationality is being replaced with a wild, free-for-all, snake-oil peddling hucksterism, where anyone can claim anything they want to about the mind and its powers, or their powers over the minds of others, and so forth. We are told that either we accept the complete naturalistic scientific model of psychology or we will quickly devolve into spiritualism, mysticism, or some vapid self-help commercialism.

This whole line of argument is a red herring, designed to detract our thinking away from the forms of reasonable inquiry and dialogue on matters of intellectual importance and interest that do not follow the scientific method. In a sense, the argument is correct, but not in the way it was intended. Because the Rationality (and with it this rigid notion of science) of the Enlightenment was a desperate leap of faith in the face of the declining legitimacy of Christianity, then to reject it would invite another faith (such as spiritualism or faith healing) to replace it. However, if one seeks to be guided not by Rationality in psychology but by reasonableness (Toulmin, 2000), no flight into another faith is necessary. Faith, reason, passion, empirical experience, logic, and practical know-how are all welcome to find a place in psychology's house.

There is much to learn about the human psyche and interpersonal relationships. Patiently conducted, careful observational studies; in-depth case studies based on a confidential and trusted relationship; correlational studies of public behaviors related to personal concerns (child abuse, divorce, sexual assault, crime, accidents), about which data are kept by civil authorities—all can play a part in that learning process. None of these methods necessarily are committed to prediction and control of the populace by those seeking power or to a strictly causal model of human behavior. Some require quantification; others do not.

Many experimentalists will be incensed by this list of acceptable research methods. What of the replicated findings that show that aggression is affected by modeling, that reinforcement influences rate of behaviors, that the fundamental attribution error or other cognitive errors are commonly observed? Is the use of the scientific method not empirically supported by its results? There are two answers to this. First, even a staunch supporter of empirical methods such as Meehl (1978) lamented the meager results in what he called "soft psychology" over its first century. (For Meehl, these are the areas that Taylor, 1973, referred to as lacking in "brute data.") However, in my view this lack of progress is overshadowed by the consideration that the research methods that are designed to "reveal" the regularities of nature may be in fact simply be creating the observed regularities by constraining the responses of participants in subtle ways and thus eliminating the individual variations and choices they would normally demonstrate in their responses to similar circumstances in the natural environment. In other words, there is a constant *demand characteristic* on what was called for 100 years *subjects* to subject themselves to the environment or other stimuli of interest to the experimenter and shift their own actions away from the kinds of self-direction in which they would normally engage. The experimental paradigm "reveals" laws of behavior more subtly, but essentially in the same manner as the patterns of automobile traffic reveal "laws of behavior" when people stop at stop signs or red lights. People respond predictably when others have made an effort to control them, and they have *chosen* to cooperate with that demand. Research shows the choices people make, not just the determination of behavior by causal forces beyond their control (see Rychlak, 1994).

In an experiment, the experimenter or experimental situation communicates directly or indirectly to the participants that it is important to attend or respond to certain stimuli, tasks, drugs, or people. People who do not respond in this way (pay attention, follow instructions, attempt the tasks, take the drugs) are seen as not cooperating in the experiment, and their data are thrown out, and often not even mentioned in the final report, because they did not cooperate in the role of participant (they were not good subjects to "the lord or lady"). Why do researchers not report these failed responses to the experimental situation as evidence that behavior is not determined by the environment? If a researcher explains ahead of time to a participant what a study is about (assuming there is no deception involved) and the participant does not show up for the experiment at the appointed time, should this not be the first bit of data one has on the power of the experimental situation to influence behavior in the predicted direction? Customarily, the response would be "of course not." Only if the participant actually showed up and submitted to the protocol would one think that the participants' behavior reflects on the experimental hypothesis. However, from the point of the view of the participant, a no-show *might* suggest that he or she does not think the hypothesis interesting, important, or worthy of his or her time. This, I would submit, is relevant to the hypothesis and does reflect on its validity. If we think of the famous Zimbardo prison study (Zimbardo, Haney, Banks, & Jaffe, 1974), but modified so that students participated only with full informed consent, probably few would volunteer, and this would say something about the hypothesis, which was that prison conditions invite brutality and submission to authority. By refusing to participate, the students would be saying, in effect, "I refuse" to place myself in a position where the environment would influence me to abuse other people. This both supports and disconfirms (remember Kant's [1781/1929] antimony of freedom) Zimbardo's hypothesis, for the power of the environment is acknowledged and then in the same breath resisted (Fromm, 1973). However, under current experimental norms, such refusals would not be reported, only the results from those who actually participated in the planned experimental conditions. Of course, the data sample is now obviously missing this group of participants who quit the study and who would have been most likely to resist the environmental pressures had they participated. Studying human action in highly contrived situations that invite passivity and the subjugation of one's own interests to those of the experimenter is an excellent way to study the degree to which human behavior can be manipulated and controlled by people in positions of power. Whether the knowledge gained in such contexts is generalizable to people and contexts that do not uniformly invite passivity and submission remains highly doubtful.

Reductionism

The scientific establishment—particularly, in recent years, geneticists, biochemists, psychopharmacologists, and the drug and medical technology industries—has done a powerful job of convincing all of society that everything we are or do is in our genes and will be ultimately correctible by science. Successful commercial psychopharmacology projects, such as the selective serotonin reuptake inhibitors, methelphenidate (Ritalin), and clozapine, were responsible for many billions of dollars in sales each year over the past decade (R. Whitaker, 2002); if one adds to this the illegal drug trade in the United States for mind-/mood-altering substances, one might conclude that just about everyone accepts the idea that their psychological problems are just a biochemical imbalance in their brains. At the least, the drug companies would like us to go down that road of faulty reasoning. Valenstein (1998) and Breggin (1991) have both articulated the problem with this line of reasoning. The fact that aspirin takes away the headache that was caused by getting hit by a baseball does not mean that one got the headache because there was too little aspirin in one's body at the time of the injury. Long before we even knew that there were neurotransmitters, millions of human beings depended on mood-/mind-altering substances to ease the pain of living. The pandemic use of drugs to alter mood and behavior does not prove that psychological problems are simply nothing more than physiological or biochemical disturbances.

Manicus and Secord (1983) articulated a clear alternative based on the work of several contemporary philosophers of science loosely associated with what is called a *critical realist* perspective. Their position is based on a hierarchical view of reality, from the relatively simple physical processes identified in Newtonian physics to the highly complex social phenomena of psychology and the other social sciences. Chemistry and biology fall in between. Each of the relatively simple levels will develop their own laws and principles that operate probabilistically and that set some general parameters for the phenomena at the higher levels of complexity.

The laws of physics limit the speed at which a human being can travel unassisted, the impact the human body will have if it is traveling at a given speed and encounters a brick wall, and so forth. The laws of chemistry will dictate what will happen to one's esophagus if one swallows a large quantity of concentrated carbolic acid, and the laws of physiology will dictate what will happen to one's body at puberty. Yet, at each level of new complexity, new laws are needed to explain the phenomena that exist at that level and that were nonexistent at the lower or simpler level. To explain why, for example, at shortly after puberty a particular youth would deliberately drive her or his new BMW at 100 mph into a brick wall, or choose to swallow carbolic acid, is not a question that the other sciences are equipped to answer, or even ask. So psychological explanations are logically required, and logically cannot be reduced to sentences using only the nonpsychological terms of biology, chemistry, or physics. This is referred to as the *emergent properties* argument. Gestalt psychologists made a similar point 100 years ago by arguing "the whole is greater than the sum of its parts."

Manicus and Secord (1983) also discussed the different kinds of explanation offered in the different sciences and argued that although physiological psychology; the study of psychophysics; and, possibly, some aspects of sensation, perception, and learning do lend themselves to causal analysis, the problems of developmental, social, personality, and abnormal–clinical psychology are biographical and do not lend themselves to causal analysis in the traditional sense. Thomas Szasz (personal communication, March 29, 1996) remarked that the reason he knew that mental illness was not a medical disease but a social stigmatization was that from his youth he observed in Hungary that people were brought to mental hospitals by people in the community who already had decided that they were mentally ill ("mad") before the patients ever saw a doctor. Furthermore, the doctors made the diagnosis on the bases of the reports of what the people had done in the community, their bizarre behavior, and not on the basis of a physical examination. All of the talk about brain disease was by inference from the behavior, and references to brain structures and processes hypothetically involved were just that—post hoc hypotheses that were rarely, if ever, tested. Medicalizing the process conceals the deprivation of civil rights that have taken place in the process and hides the intolerance of the community behind a medical protective "humanitarian" shield. Consequently, this kind of reductive materialism so common in psychology and psychiatry today not only is logically unsound but also leads to social policies and treatment of patients that are morally suspect.

Most people new to the study of psychology (and psychologists who have not studied philosophy) have a difficult time evaluating the concept of reductionism. It is difficult to try to think about all these disciplines, some of which one may never have studied, and try to see how they all do or do not fit together. When students do understand it, some see immediately that it requires an acceptance of materialism that they had already rejected in the beginning of the discussion. Others, oddly, do not object to reductionism nearly as strongly as they do to other features of the scientific worldview. I am at somewhat of a loss to explain this. Perhaps they welcome anything that simplifies the overwhelming complexity of trying to understand the world from so many different perspectives—physical, chemical, biological, psychological, sociological, and so forth. Perhaps, too, they think that, against all reasonable belief to the contrary, "wouldn't it be awfully nice if we could solve all our problems with a pill." The high rate of drug and alcohol abuse in the college-age population may mean that by challenging reductionism I am threatening their own rationalizations for their drug and alcohol consumption. "Mom's on Prozac, brother is on Ritalin, what's the harm if I snort a little coke? We are all just adjusting our brain chemistry a tad!"

I cannot fault them their logic, especially given the strong biochemical affinities among Prozac, Ritalin, and cocaine (see Breggin, 1991). However, critical realism does not require one to reject material reality, or to see relationships between different levels of reality, it requires only that one *not entirely* reduce the complex to the simple. It is possible that some *aspects* of the features of depression are physical, just as the injuries in an accident will be related to the angle and force of my body's impact on whatever substance I strike. Still, if I had not decided to jump out the window, or drive into the wall, the injuries would not have been caused by the wall or ground. I reject theoretical reductionism in that no description of the physiological condition of a person can entirely account for or describe the psychological condition of that person. It is a logical impossibility, and it follows that no psychological problem can ever be *just* a physiological one.

THE U.S. GOVERNMENT AND PSYCHOLOGY
AS AN ACADEMIC DISCIPLINE

It would seem that the received view of science in psychology is no more tenable than it has been in science as a whole. As in the sciences generally, this lack of logical or commonsense validity has not prevented it from holding sway over the entire academic discipline. Toulmin's (1990) explanation for this is the wedding of the power of the nation–states of Europe to the growing scientific and technological practices of the academy. If he is right, we ought to see this played out in the relationships among prominent psychologists, psychology departments, and the U.S. government and related nongovernmental organizations that influence public policy.

Those who doubt the implications for psychology of Toulmin's (1990) general theory that social political limitations are placed on scientific thinking would do well to examine Herman's (1995) historical research findings reported in *The Romance of American Psychology*. Herman documented in careful detail the extensive influence the needs and requirements of the U.S. government have had on shaping the research agenda of American psychology, specifically in terms of what questions are worthy of research and what methods of research are acceptable. The governmental influence was not a result of the government imposing its agenda on psychology in authoritarian fashion, but rather the result of leading psychologists seeking legitimacy, status, and financial backing for their research by shaping their research agenda to appeal to governmental policies and priorities. The growing status of applied and clinical psychology was directly related to successful efforts to convince the leaders of the military and intelligence communities in World War I (WWI) and WWII that psychologists could contribute to the successful conduct of major military operations. Whether in the development of testing procedures for the selection of personnel, the front-line treatment of the psychological trauma (*combat neuroses and psychoses*, as they were called then) of warfare, the selection of Office of Special Services (precursor to the CIA) agents, the psychological profiling of national temperaments or leaders of enemy nations for propaganda or planning purposes, or boosting morale among the troops, American psychologists and social scientists were determined to show their practical value to the nation.

> Psychology's political progress was founded, first and foremost, on the ever-present militarism of the war and post-war years. World War II had been generous to psychological experts. Because of it, they gained abundant training opportunities, professionally beneficial contacts, and a stockpile of theoretical leads to pursue when the fighting ended in 1945. They understood that helping win the war was their first obligation, but experts never hesitated to experiment in the laboratory of international military conflict with an eye toward enhancing their scientific standing and improving the effectiveness and marketability of their technological talents. (Herman, 1995, p. 305)

After the war, well into the 1960s, the vast majority of federally supported research in American university psychology departments came directly or indirectly from defense- or CIA-related budgets and went to research teams that were associated with individuals who had served in the war effort. Major components of counterinsurgency planning associated with the Vietnam War were developed by psychologists and other social scientists.

> Between 1945 and the mid-1960's, the U.S. military was, by far, the country's major institutional sponsor of psychological research, a living illustration of what socially minded experts could accomplish, especially with a "not too gentle rain of gold." . . . The military had more money than any other public institution during these years, and during the Korean War, the [Department of Defense] spent more on social and behavioral science than all other federal agencies combined. (Herman, 1995, p. 126)

Herman (1995) revealed that a 1965 behavioral science data analysis of North Vietnamese morale and social institutions was used within the government to justify the massive bombing of the North Vietnam that began that year. The RAND Corporation, a private think tank, conducted studies of Viet Cong Motivation and Morale (VCM&M) for the military at the insistence of Gen. Westmoreland, commander of U.S. forces in Vietnam. Tragically, these reports repeatedly indicated that the morale of the North Vietnamese was near the breaking point, and the "light at the end of the tunnel" was within sight. The failure of the prediction was "punished" by a doubling of the research contract for 1966.

> VCM&M was a classic example, during the Vietnam era, of the basic axiom about bureaucratic survival and expertise that policy-makers had learned during World War II: *government uses social science the way a drunk uses a lamp post, for support rather than light* [italics added; an observation originally attributed to the psychiatrist Alexander Leighton based upon his work with the army and the Japanese internment camps]. (Herman, 1995, p. 167)

Furthermore, a computer simulation of social and political processes in Chile in the early 1970s done by Abt Associates for the Department of Defense was used by planners to justify the assassination of Chile's left-wing President Allende. The analysis rightly predicted that the country would remain politically "stable" after his death. The Cold War was to see a growing use of psychological research.

The list of psychologists and other social scientists who did research and writing for the U.S. military reads like a who's who of American behavioral sciences—and includes some surprising names: social psychologists, psychoanalysts, and anthropologists, such as Gordon Allport, Erik Erikson, Margaret Mead, and Gregory Bateson, as well as experimentalist–quantitative researchers, such as Robert Yerkes, Samuel Stouffer, Rensis Likert, and Leonard Doob. What better illustration of Toulmin's (1990) thesis than the shaping of the American experimental and applied research agenda in psychology by the military and intelligence departments of the U.S. government?

The prestige and status that psychologists and other behavioral scientists gained from their military experience quickly carried over into domestic social programs of the federal government. Herman (1995) noted that federal expenditures on the "psychological sciences" increased from $38.2 million in 1960 to $158 million in 1967. Although the source of this spending shifted from the Department of Defense to the Department of Health, Education, and Welfare, the amount spent on defense-related topics never decreased (Herman, 1995 p. 172).

In this context, the prediction and control of human behavior, once articulated by Skinner as the sole purpose of American psychology, takes on a clearly augmented meaning. Are prediction and control the epistemological test of valid knowledge that Skinner claimed, or is it the test of the *utility to a bureaucratic organization within the nation–state* of the discipline of psychology as a whole? The government and military wanted to predict how various conscripts would respond to training programs, or how various enemy populations would respond to propaganda. It wanted to control the behavior of men under extremely stressful conditions, or the level of support among the civilian population for the war effort. In fact, the whole movement toward a quantifiable psychology that can estimate from samples what whole populations will do has an obvious relationship to the needs of the bureaucratic organizations that administer the nation–state. During the Cold War it was common for American psychologists to decry Soviet psychology as a sterile outgrowth of the narrow adoption, for political purposes, of Pavlovian conditioning as the fundamental model of human psychology. It was said that Pavlovian conditioning, based as it was on an animal model of learning a physiological response (salivation to the sound of a bell), fit nicely with dialectical materialism in Marxist philosophy that saw human existence entirely in physical terms. To American psychologists who had adopted Pavlovian conditioning as an important theory of learning, but not as *the* theory of learning, it was obvious that scientific theory had succumbed to political ideology. At the same time, Soviet psychiatry was condemned for allowing itself to become a pawn of political repression for its participation in the massive drugging of political dissidents. So although psychologists were all too aware that scientific and clinical psychiatry–psychology could become the tool of the bureaucratic nation–state in the Soviet Union, they never thought to consider how, through research and training grant funding patterns, this might be true in U.S. society as well.

Since the end of the Cold War in the 1980s, government funding of behavioral sciences research has shifted away from the Department of Defense to the National Institutes of Health and the National Institute of Education. The clear preference for research that allows for the prediction and control of various groups of people who are problematic to the orderly conduct of society remains in place, with an increasing interest in pharmacological rather than psychosocial control of disruptive, delinquent, and nonproductive behavior.

There is no avoiding the embedding of scientific theory and research in the social, economic, and political forces of our culture. There is no value-free, pure science to be had. Rather, we must be able to identify what moral and political values and interests we wish to be associated with such a psychology. As long as the sociopolitical commitments of a theory are hidden or concealed, we are in jeopardy of being manipulated or misled by it. It is part of the rhetoric of science that it is created by disinterested, objective professionals, who are merely seeking the truth with no axe to grind. Although there are certainly more or less egregious conflicts of interest that researchers might have, researchers with no interests other than pure knowledge are a fictitious creation of the dogma of Rationality. Mitroff (1974) showed that even NASA astrophysicists are influenced by a variety of nonrational factors (concerns for reputation, personal loyalties and relationships, and political loyalties within and across the several professions working on the project) when interpreting research *data on moon rocks* that bear on the question of the origins of the Earth's moon!

MORAL VALUES AND SCIENCE

I am not planning to end this analysis with recommendations for how to develop a science of psychology free of social, political, or moral influences but rather with those for how to create a science of psychology in which the interests and value commitments of various theories are identified and transparent. Students entering the discipline may then choose a form of psychology that is most aligned with their own moral values. The choice of a scientific outlook is already a moral choice, as I mentioned in my discussion in chapter 3 of Lewis's (1990, 2000) six fundamental value systems. The values of mainstream natural science can now be seen and outlined as advancing the values of the modern nation–state:

1. A materialism that emphasizes objective reality is sought, in part, because the modern nation–states are committed to economic materialism and deemphasize subjective emotional states that cannot be easily measured (e.g., suffering).
2. Universality and group data are sought, in part, to foster group conformity and social order.
3. Facts are preferred over theories in part because facts are public

ate disadvantage in gaining acceptance.

4. Prediction and control are sought in part to manage the public behavior of the populace and prevent civil unrest.

5. Quantification is sought in part to measure the degree of group conformity or control that has been achieved.

6. Causality and determinism are preferred forms of explanation in part to reduce the assertion of individual free choice against the state.

7. Reductionism is preferred in part because it allows one to minimize the social and psychological effects of the socioeconomic policies of the nation–state and explains all suffering as a natural phenomenon that occurs independent of any of the political actions of the state.

With this awareness of the social and political embeddedness of psychology's scientific ideology, it is possible to consider conceptualizing science and its relationship to psychology differently. For example, one might identify substantive areas of theory of psychology that strengthen the power of the nation–state's bureaucracy, as compared with other theories that strengthen the power of individuals to survive within, or even resist, the stranglehold of large-scale bureaucratic organizations. One might call these "state-sponsored," or "corporate-sponsored," versus "individual-sponsored" psychologies. There might also be "religiously sponsored" psychologies, or "liberal-" and "conservative-sponsored" psychologies.

THE CURRENT MEANING OF
A SCIENTIFIC CLINICAL PSYCHOLOGY

Even in the mainstream histories of psychology and clinical psychology (e.g., Chaplin & Krawiec, 1979) it is clearly stated that WWI gave a tremendous boost to psychology in terms of formalizing the use of intelligence testing on a massive scale and that the overwhelming number of psychiatric casualties of WWII was essentially the impetus for the development of the profession of clinical psychology as a major force on the health care landscape. Both in the military and through the efforts of the Veterans Administration (VA) after the war, psychologists were "drafted" into the role of psychotherapists, and this eventually carried over into civilian life as thousands of veterans and others entered the Boulder model clinical psychology doctoral training programs created in the postwar period and funded by the VA.

This history is generally presented as though the military and the VA discovered an independent existing science of psychology that could contribute to the national defense and wartime efforts of WWI and WWII. From the vantage point of Toulmin's (1990) analysis of the history of science and Herman's (1995) analysis of the history of American psychology, it is clear that there is more to this story. Psychology not only shaped the military with its recommendations on screening inductees or special services applicants, boosting morale among our own troops and undermining it in the civilian populations of our enemies, but psychology also *was extensively shaped into a science by the pressures and financial rewards of the military bureaucracy.* Psychologists became an auxiliary part of what President Eisenhower called the *military–industrial complex,* and their theories and methods were developed in the service of those sociopolitical and economic ends. This was an agenda in which the need to predict and control the behavior of large groups of people or entire populations was of life-and-death concern. Although individual differences were indeed important in this regard (finding the right person for the right job in the military), individual autonomy and development were not. Combat was an environment in which an individual was routinely expected to behave in a manner that put the well-being of the social group (their unit) ahead of his or her own individual well-being, even if it meant his or her life. Individual freedom, rights, self-direction, and so forth were just not psychological or moral issues on the radar screen. This is not meant to imply criticism of such military values. It is hard to imagine how else one would run a wartime military effort. However, it is not hard to imagine how else one would design the academic discipline and intellectual traditions of psychology. Caught in the grips of the bureaucratic needs and power of the modern nation–state, psychologists' collective imagination in this regard was severely constrained. Perfectly reasonable and well-articulated alternative scientific and clinical paradigms were repeatedly advocated from within and without psychology (Cahan & White, 1992), but a dialogue has never emerged, only splintering and schisms. At stake is probably the oldest and most central question in the political branch of moral philosophy: the rights of the individual versus the demands of obedience and loyalty from the social group or state. The debate between the advocates for a science-based practice and those who would base practice on clinical knowledge appears to be about epistemology, but as I argued in chapter 3, these are more accurately characterized as moral conflict about the goals of psychological work, not about the truth conditions of the claims psychologists make.

This shift to a focus on the moral foundation of the discipline of psychology is one of enormous import, for the history of psychology that most psychologists learned in graduate school emphasized the epistemological question of empiricism versus rationalism, and the ontological or metaphysical question of the mind–body problem, as the key 16th- and 17th-century philosophical debates that gave birth to an empirical psychology. This history was presented to students of psychology as though an empirical research psychology put an end to the debate between empiricists and rationalists in epistemology (the theory of knowledge) and between idealists and materialists in metaphysics (the theory of the nature of the nature of ultimate reality). They were taught that psychology evolved from these more primitive forms of investigation and established a philosophy-free zone of inquiry. The fact that eminent pioneers in psychology, such as Wilhelm Wundt and William James, never believed this and continued to write philosophical papers on psychology along with their empirical research and textbooks never seemed to merit much consideration. Also ignored in these histories were the continuing development of rationalist thought in Europe and the creation of a phenomenological approach to psychology that grew up alongside empirical psychology and continues uninterrupted as existential–phenomenological psychology (Churchill, 2000). What psychologists consider the independent discipline of empirical–experimental psychology is in reality nothing more than the continued development of an attempt to demonstrate the truth of an empiricist theory of knowledge. The predominant interest in cognitive psychology parallels exactly the empiricists' concern with showing that ideas were nothing more than associations of sensations (i.e., information processing). Experimental psychology is an elaborate and concentrated attempt to find evidence to support the empirical point of view, and the shortcomings of contemporary experimental psychology might be said to suggest the limitations of that viewpoint.

The same can be said of physiological psychology with regard to the mind–body problem. Physiological psychology is a sustained and elaborate attempt to find evidence to support a material theory of mind, one that reduces the mental to the physical as a solution to the mind–body problem. Phenomenological–existential psychology and other humanistic approaches to the mind may be seen as a sustained attempt to demonstrate the superiority of an idealist ontology (theory of the nature of being) or metaphysic that asserts the priority of mental experience or consciousness over physical substance.

What James (1907) knew was that in the end, these debates would be settled not by the data but by the totality of the persuasiveness of the arguments, which would include as a primary consideration the practical (pragmatic) consequences of psychological theories on the quality of life of the general populace. They, not the philosophers, theoreticians, or researchers, would decide the validity of psychological constructs on the streets, so to speak. Ultimately, what psychologists care about is what gave rise to all of the philosophical discussion to begin with: the question of how to live one's life so as to minimize the pain and suffering and maximize one's satisfaction and happiness in life. Behind the question about the nature of knowledge and truth (empiricism vs. rationalism) is the question of how one evaluates conflicting claims about the nature of the "good life." The reason we care so much about the mind–body problem (idealism vs. materialism) is not because the difference between mental and material phenomena is so intrinsically fascinating but because of the question of free will, which is central to accountability in ethics. If the mind is controlled by the body, and the body dictates one's actions, then strict moral responsibility, accountability, and punishment seem harsh, unfair, and unworkable.

Were psychology or the government to promote the sacrifice of the individual to the welfare of the state or national group on moral grounds, it would first of all raise objections from religious leaders who, although no longer as powerful as in the Middle Ages, are still a force to be reckoned. With such a direct moral pronouncement psychology would also risk the loss of social status as technical–scientific experts, because most people in Western democracies are aware of how important it is to resist the loss of personal liberty and rights and are suspicious of governmental efforts to convince them otherwise. With social scientists and psychologists running interference and pronouncing the military personnel selection and morale-boosting programs as scientific, individuals were more likely to go along with the bureaucratic agenda of the state without voicing or perhaps even registering their own moral objections to the loss of individual autonomy or freedom.

Although psychologists might rejoice in the contribution that psychology made to the defeat of Nazism in WWII, their enthusiasm for the role of modern science and medicine in the war effort must be greatly tempered by the results of Lifton's (1986, 2000) research, which is an examination of the manipulation of scientific and medical research and training during the Third Reich. Lifton showed clearly how the extermination programs of the concentration camps were presented as scientifically and medically necessary to purify the Aryan race from deadly racial pollutants (primarily Jews, gypsies, the mentally ill and retarded, the physically handicapped, etc.). The scientific experts were used as a device to mute criticism, conceal the real impact of the genocide program, and confound and mystify the populace. Lifton's research is a marvelous example of painstaking, meticulous, morally grounded, and even-handed narrative research in psychology–psychiatry carried out in the tradition of Erik Erikson (1963), Daniel Levinson (Levinson, Darrow, Klein, Levinson, & McKee, 1978), Robert White (1975), and Henry Murray (1938).

In approaching the scientist–practitioner schism in clinical psychology, one must avoid the false comparisons between some idealized characterization of one side with a more realistic view of the other. Participants in this divisive controversy on both sides have often fallen into the trap of such specious arguments. One must not, for example, compare an idealized unified natural science following a universal method of research with a realistic account of clinical observation and psychotherapy with all its shortcomings. Neither can one compare an idealized account of clinical practice without its cults of personality and hundreds of "theoretically" driven splinter groups with a realistic account of science influenced by institutional biases and interests. Instead, one must come to a realistic account of what science is capable of accomplishing in an effort to provide knowledge concerning the solution of the practical problems of human suffering. This modified but realistic approach can then be compared with what knowledge can be realistically generated in a clinical context. This would make for a fair and informative discussion.

We know first of all that it is impossible to reduce psychology to physiology or chemistry. Physiology will set some of the parameters for psychological intervention (people with brains deprived of oxygen or saturated with alcohol or cocaine or who have suffered massive trauma and injury do respond differently to psychological and social influences). However, general laws of biochemical mechanisms, and even general laws of behavior, being probabilistic and theoretical, will never provide a complete answer to the question presented by a clinical problem. Science, even clinical science, never provides more than a partial and very incomplete answer to a clinical problem, because (a) the clinical problem is about a specific contextualized psychosocial situation that is much more complex than the simplified laws address, (b) psychosocial problems contain emergent properties that are not directly derived from the sorts of variables studied in lower level sciences, and (c) psychosocial problems contain moral dilemmas that science prejudges by generally devaluing the importance of human freedom and individuality. This last point is crucial because, if the whole point of bringing a scientific viewpoint to clinical psychology is to assure that the psychological concerns that bring people to psychology must be brought under the curve of a prediction equation and *amenable to social control by others*, then the scientific viewpoint essentially cancels out the primary goal and function of many forms of psychotherapy—the encouragement of the individual's development as an autonomous person. (It is no wonder that biological and cognitive–behavioral approaches are able to provide the most scientific validation for their work. These are approaches that value control of variables in research and view the therapist as an expert who can control the symptoms of clients in the clinic, and so the research methodology of prediction and control is synchronous–congruent with the goals of the therapy.)

HUMAN SCIENCES: UNDERSTANDING HUMAN ACTIONS

Faced with the limitations that a mainstream natural science approach places on anyone trying to understand people and their problems, many scholars have urged the development of what has come to be called a *human sciences* approach (Giorgi, 1970; Howard, 1986; Polkinghorne, 1983). Undergraduates and even graduate students in mainstream programs are rarely even introduced to this substantial literature, which dates back to the 19th century (Cahan & White, 1992; Warnke, 1987). These philosophers, historians, and early social scientists saw that explanations of what human beings do rely on the process of human understanding that is fundamentally distinct from the explanatory processes used in the physical sciences.

One can see how different this "understanding" is from being able to give a causal explanation of another person's behavior, because one may comprehend another's character, or be a confederate, without having any ability to predict or control the other's behavior. Conversely, one might be able to effectively predict and control the behavior of another human being without feeling any sense of collusion or support for that person, or understanding of his or her motives. Meehl (1970) gave a wonderful example of an established heuristic used by the military: When faced with increased desertions, announce that all deserters will be shot on sight. Meehl claimed that one can confidently predict and control the rate of desertions after making such a statement to the troops, but one may not have any idea what makes it work, or why the men were deserting in the first place. Still, one might say that a general who does this "understands desertions" in that he or she does know how to "deal with properly" the problem.

Because psychologists are themselves the sort of phenomenon they are studying, they have certain potential advantages and disadvantages over the physical scientist attempting to unravel the mystery of, for example, nuclear bonds or DNA. The advantages are four: (a) Psychologists have the ability to introspect and self-observe to supplement their more objective observations of other human beings; (b) they may be able to enlist their "subjects" in a collaborative enterprise of understanding so that they reveal to psychologists what they do not understand; (c) psychologists can use their own powers of empathy to attempt to discern what the other is experiencing; and (d) by virtue of having lived as a human being, with other human beings, psychologists enter into the study of just about any topic in psychology with a certain level of commonsense knowledge about people and how they behave, and this may include for some people a sense of how to explore with others what psychologists do not understand in their behavior. This knowledge—some call it *folk psychology*—is not insignificant in its powers of discernment, but of course it is incomplete and imperfect. Collaboration, introspection, empathy, and commonsense folk psychology are all disparaged as subjective and unreliable sources of data in scientific psychology, and so typically students do not explore how their understanding of psychology might expand were they to use such methods.

It is true that psychologists' closeness to the participants they study, and their use of common sense, may leave them vulnerable to prejudices and biases in observing and interpreting the actions of others. This may interfere with the usefulness of introspection, empathy, and collaborative interviewing as research methods. Although experimentalists have worked hard to control the various biases that may creep into scientific research, there has been little recognition that serious efforts to control bias in the human sciences have been undertaken (R. Elliott, Fischer, & Rennie, 1999). It is true that researchers in the human sciences approach must also guard against the more unconscious biases that influence the meaning assigned to overt actions and situations. As one attempts to discern deeper layers of meaning, more emotionally charged material is present, and this is more likely to trigger defensiveness in an observer. Research can be tainted by many conscious, unconscious, and even deliberate attempts to mislead those who consume the research reports. A greater attention to the personal social, political, and economic interests served by various research agendas and programs is necessary among all researchers, whether mainstream or human sciences.

In fact, the critical-theory approach to science, which originated in Marx's philosophical materialism and has been continued by the Frankfurt School of social philosophy (Adorno, Frankel-Brunswick, Levinson, & Sanford, 1950; Habermas, 1971; Marcuse, 1964), asks us to pay close attention to the ends to which science is put, and it is suspicious of the hidden economic, class, or power agendas that drive research funding and programs. Toulmin's (1990) and Herman's (1995) analysis are certainly compatible with this approach, although neither is identified as a critical theorist per se. Prilleltensky (1994) wrote an excellent analysis of these problems consistent with the Frankfurt approach.

Investigators in the human sciences research patterns, structures, and explanations of behavior that focus on the meaning that various events, situations, and actions have to the individuals involved. The term *hermeneutics* has been borrowed from Talmudic and other biblical forms of scholarship to describe this approach to the human sciences. *Meaning, intention,* and *purpose* were all terms banned from behavioral psychology and are still only used in cognitive psychology in a mechanistic sense. These are, of course, concepts familiar to the free will-versus-determinism argument, because to know the meaning or intention of a behavior is to know not the cause of it in the *scientistic* sense but the *reason for the behavior in common sense.*

Meaning, as Rychlak (1988) has pointed out, is often complicated and ambiguous. Meaning can communicate ambivalence ("yes" and "no" at the same time). Meaning can be confused and mysterious, as when an individual does not understand her or his own behavior or why she or he did something. Meaning is not univocal; it does not always speak with one clear voice. Investigators in the human sciences value the process of investigation in psychology even when definitive answers cannot be found. The collaborative research process allows for the building of socially nurturing and rewarding relationships as part of the process, something unheard of in the scientific community, in which investigators are separated from participants to prevent contamination of the findings. Participants in the research may experience beneficial effects from having collaborated in the study regardless of the results. They may gain self-understanding, or a sense of empowerment, from having collaborated in the study. Research is not necessarily separated from life; it is a part of it.

The one area in mainstream psychology in which there was some limited room for an interpretive approach was in the study of personality, particularly in the research of Henry Murray at the Harvard Psychological Clinic in the 1930s–1950s. Murray attempted to integrate laboratory studies, objective and projective personality assessments, life history research, and clinical interviewing methods into a comprehensive assessment of human personality (Murray, 1938). He saw himself as an advocate for the more qualitative, interpretive, approaches and expressed the view that the natural science paradigm was both inappropriate as the primary approach to the study of personality and inexorably becoming predominant in the field. He pioneered the life history method in personology (White, 1964, 1975), and his use of a "diagnostic council," whose members each studied the individual in some format and then all read each others' reports and discussed them before the comprehensive assessment was written, provides a model for a consensus model of knowledge building. In this model, Murray anticipated by 30 years Habermas's (1971) or Rorty's (1979) notion of knowledge growing out of a community dialogue that takes place in a free and open context in which individuals are free to express their thoughts, revise their ideas, and reach a common understanding.

Carl Rogers also adopted the human sciences approach to understanding the nature of science in psychology, but this was quite late in his career, and the research for which he is known was an attempt to use traditional quantitative, experimental methods while trying to study very humanistic variables (empathy, unconditional positive regard, and authenticity or genuineness).

Various advocates of the case study method (Edwards, 1998; R. Elliott, 2002; Fishman, 1999; Hoshmand, 1992; R. B. Miller, 1992b; M. B. Shapiro, 1966) have also recognized the inherent limitations in the received view of scientific research, and I explore this in chapter 6. I should note here, however, that a substantial number of researchers in other applied fields, such as education and business, have anticipated this return to case study research in psychology, having realized the limitations of logical positivist-inspired research considerably earlier.

The human sciences approach to psychology (and the other social sciences) has had its adherents in anthropology (e.g., Geertz, 1973) and sociology (e.g., Berger & Luckman, 1966; Goffman, 1961) as well. *Narrative* or *qualitative* research usually refers to research done in this tradition. Because neither anthropologists nor sociologists study human social phenomena that permit an experimental approach (how does one bring a non-Western aboriginal tribe into a laboratory for study?), the dominance of the natural science research paradigm never could take hold as completely in these disciplines, although certainly many sociologists have contributed heavily to the agenda of the corporate nation–state through the development of survey research.

Within psychology, another branch of the human sciences approach is what is called *phenomenological* psychology, a theoretical framework based on the work of German philosopher Edmund Husserl (1859–1938) who, following in the tradition of German Idealism that evolved from the philosophy of Immanuel Kant (1724–1804) and G. W. F. Hegel (1770–1831), rejected empirical knowledge as the primary means of gaining knowledge of the world (Churchill, 2000). Husserl believed that we must set aside or "bracket" questions about the relationship between our ideas and the physical world and explore fully our own mental constructions and processes, which provide the interpretations and meaning for the sensory input we receive from outside of our bodies. His method of phenomenological description of experience, and philosophical reflection and analysis of experience, is called *phenomenology*. It leads to an introspective psychology that is descriptive and qualitative. Giorgi (1970) pioneered this approach in the United States and established a department of psychology along phenomenological lines at Duquesne University in Pittsburgh, Pennsylvania. His students have established departments along similar lines at West Georgia State University and the University of Dallas, and Giorgi himself has moved on to the Saybrook Institute in San Francisco (a doctoral degree granting institution committed to a human sciences approach to clinical and other forms of applied psychology). Play therapy pioneer Clark Moustakas (1994) advocated for a similar approach to human science research through his work at his own clinic and the Union Institute and University, in Cincinnati, Ohio, another well-established and respected nontraditional program in which one can do doctoral work in psychology from a human sciences perspective. More traditional doctoral programs that have a strong emphasis in philosophical psychology often focus on the theoretical basis of phenomenological and hermeneutic approaches to psychology; they include Brigham Young University in Utah, and York University in Toronto, Ontario, Canada. Membership in the American Psychological Association divisions that attract those most interested in the human science approach—Division 24 (Theoretical and Philosophical Psychology) and Division 32 (Humanistic Psychology)—each number more than 600 members, and Division 39 (Psychoanalysis) has several thousand members, although their interests are more likely to be in treatment than in psychoanalysis as a research method. Freud (1933/1965) indicated that he thought of psychoanalysis as both. As a research method, psychoanalysis is closely aligned to the phenomenological–hermeneutic approach, although Freud insisted that he was operating at all times as a natural scientist, observing patterns and theorizing about what would explain the phenomena in question. Ricoeur (1977) argued that psychoanalysis is both a natural and a hermeneutic science. Given that there are approximately 100,000 doctoral-level psychologists in the United States, these numbers are not overwhelmingly impressive. However, if one considers the disincentives that exist for anyone in American academic psychology to identify her- or himself as a psychoanalytic, humanistic, philosophical, or phenomenological psychologist it is really an astounding number. It is as if we had discovered that 2,000 graduates of West Point had become pacifists. We would think that was very significant if 2,000 of the best and the brightest of America's trained military officers decided they did not believe in the institution of warfare or the use of violence to resolve conflicts.

In American psychology today, there are thousands upon thousands of practicing psychologists who have been trained in the Boulder model of research in psychology who find experimental research of no relevance to their work (Strupp, 1981; Trierweiler & Stricker, 1998). They do not conduct research, and they do not even read research reports in the journals, even on topics that are ostensibly relevant to their clinical practice. They find it irrelevant. They may not have reached the point of thinking that it is the philosophy of research and science that is at fault, or that psychology is not only a science but also a form of moral engagement; however, they have decided that the current scientific approach to clinical psychology is not helpful to their work. Researchers have tried to come up with all kinds of explanations of this problem that blame the therapists for not reading the research (e.g., greed—reading research would take them away from their highly paid therapeutic activities—or intellectual laziness). Researchers have in recent years attempted to make their findings more relevant to practitioners by using actual clinical patients as participants in their studies. However, the philosophy of science that is offered in justification of the empirical research method, and the logic of the methods themselves, remains largely unchanged.

As the philosopher and historian of science T. S. Kuhn (1970) pointed out in the history of the natural sciences, paradigm shifts (when a science rejects its old conceptual framework and methods and adopts radically new ones) do not come primarily from people committed to the old paradigm changing their minds and adopting a new one. New paradigms emerge as new practitioners adopt a new paradigm and abandon the old one to the old scientists. In Europe, except for in Great Britain, the strength of phenomenological and hermeneutical approaches to philosophy and the high regard in which psychoanalysis was generally held meant that the dissociation and demoralization that accompanied the logical positivist-inspired hegemony of experimental psychology in the United States never really took hold. French psychology is particularly open-minded in this regard. For the student wondering whether to follow his or her inclination to explore these alternative approaches to psychology and psychological research, the awareness of the historical roots and renewed contemporary interest in the human sciences approach to psychology both here and in Europe is critical. It can go a long way in calming the fear that one is pursuing some flash-in-the-pan phenomenon, passing fad, or flaky fringe group (as these approaches are typically characterized by proponents of the received view of psychology as a natural science).

The mainstream or received view of science, and psychology as such a science, is fundamentally flawed and needs jettisoning. It is no wonder that so many have found the return on psychology's deep investment in it to be so meager (Fishman, 1999). It was ill conceived, although executed faithfully, with disastrous results. I say *disastrous*, rather than just *insignificant*, because this logical positivist model of research in psychology also meant a proclivity to adopt the medical model of psychological explanation in which human suffering was marginalized in the description of the patient's problems. It not only wasted effort but also prevented others who could help from being recognized as legitimate helpers. A cold, callous, essentially uncaring approach to treatment could masquerade as "humanitarianism" because science was being brought to the rescue to solve the patient's problems, and we all knew science was going to have the answers. Because the gift of science was so great, it was believed by some that treating a patient with a scientifically derived intervention was enough, and common human courtesy and respect in interaction with patients was thought to be superfluous and expendable. As part of the denial of human suffering (justified by the lack of public indicators of suffering as an essentially private event). The mainstream views of scientific clinical practice is a primary obstacle in the way of the development of a morally engaged clinical practice. We need to move on to a new model of knowledge creation in psychology.

It is incumbent on those who would continue to use such a destructive and outmoded model of science to conduct the business of psychology to justify their actions and choices. The devastating intellectual critique of the received view of science has not been answered by psychology's faithful, only ignored. Why do they present a reductionist, materialist, causal, quantitative, and methodologically constricted view of human psychology? The million new students who take Introduction to Psychology every year in the United States, the hundreds of thousands of psychology majors, and tens of thousands of graduate students in the field deserve much better. The students know this is true, and they have been trying to tell us but we, in our intellectual arrogance, are sure that we know better than they do what their problems are and what they need to help them.

5

CLINICAL KNOWLEDGE

One of the central features of the Boulder model of scientist–practitioner training in clinical psychology (that has been emulated in social work and psychiatry) is to assume that knowledge derived from clinical experience is inferior to scientific knowledge. Clinical theories were ultimately to be replaced by theories of human behavior that had scientific status, based on scientific research on clinical populations (McFall, 2000). Clinical experience was seen as inherently vulnerable to subjective biases, selective, and even self-serving at the same time as it was seen as indispensable to the training of clinical psychologists. The research that would replace it would be objective, controlled, quantitative, and experimental. In essence, this has become the standard for scholarly work in clinical psychology over the past 50 years, particularly in the academic literature of psychology, and in the 100 or more American Psychological Association approved training programs in clinical psychology that are committed to the Boulder model.

To many students entering the field, this comes as the greatest shock of all. It is somewhat understandable that general psychology, with its interest in sensation, perception, and brain–behavior relationships, would take on a scientific pose or stance. Although students may not be crazy about studying such part processes of the person, to do so has a certain commonsense appeal as a necessary prerequisite for studying more applied problems of the whole person. However, when the curriculum finally gets to these whole-person problems, and the textbooks and journal articles are still discussing processes and variables in an experimental paradigm of research, a certain incredulity, if not hostility, sets in. Some in the discipline may again choose to dismiss this reaction as a sign of immaturity or lack of intellectual hardiness, yet it is this same position that the eminent social and political philosopher Charles Taylor (1973) took in his discussion of "brute data" in psychology, and on which the whole human sciences approach to psychology is based. Perhaps the students' frustration with contemporary psychology is more than a little justified.

From the discussions of suffering, moral issues, and philosophy of science in psychology we have already begun to fashion a strong case against this view. We understand on the basis of those analyses that clinical knowledge and expertise will be a form of *phronesis*, or practical wisdom. Clinical work must be inspired by a vision of the "good life" and a desire to help others in their quest for such a life as well. The moral principles that emerge from reflection on the nature of the "good life" serve as major premises in the reasoning of practical wisdom. Understanding the suffering that may ensue when human beings do not perceive their lives or relationships as leading to good ends is also part of the knowledge base of clinical psychology. By engaging with the moral dimension of clinical practice psychologists enrich the meaning of clinical knowledge, but do not exhaust it. There is still an enormous need for a moralized and clinically relevant understanding of personality, psychopathology, and psychotherapeutic interventions and relationships that can come only from clinical experience and systematic and critical reflection on that experience. Moral engagement is a necessary but not sufficient component of clinical knowledge.

Given the previous discussion as to the nature of science and its relationship to clinical practice, it is clear that the clinical realm does not lend itself to truly scientific theorizing or research. Clinical practice is moral not only in theory but also in action. It is focused on pragmatics and the practical problem solving of everyday life. Descriptive scientific generalizations or explanatory theories set the stage or provide the backdrop for moral and clinical action—helping others in the world—and may eventually be modified and revised by the success or failure of those actions. The inherent flaw in the logic of the Boulder model—namely, how clinical knowledge could be logically derived from, or integrated with, scientific knowledge—was little discussed prior to the 1980s. Psychologists had thought they could apply scientific knowledge to practice the way one applies wallpaper to the surfaces of a room, just cut out the conclusions from a research study and paste them onto clinical reality. Would that it were so simple.

EARLY ATTEMPTS: ROGERS AND MEEHL

A review of the historical literature on the relationship between clinical and scientific knowledge finds very little discussion of the topic. It was recognized as a critical topic just after the Boulder conference by both of the most influential figures in the postwar boom in the profession of clinical psychology: Carl Rogers (1955) and Paul Meehl (1954). Each independently attempted to explicate clinical experience or knowledge in the hopes of bridging the growing schism in the field. It is intriguing to look back half a century and see individuals identified with such divergent traditions struggling with the same issue—how to integrate the knowledge gleaned from clinical practice with a scientific approach to clinical psychology. Rogers, the consummate humanistic psychologist but committed researcher, and Meehl, the logical positivist, quantitative Minnesota Multiphasic Personality Inventory researcher, and a practicing psychoanalyst, each finds something invaluable in both traditions. Yet each finds most of his colleagues choosing to reject one side of the polarity or the other, and each struggles to present a balanced view and to avoid defining their preferred position in an idealized way while offering a demonized view of the opposition. It is interesting that after their seminal works on this topic, each continued to publish on the problem throughout his career, although this work received little discussion in the literature (cf. Rogers, 1985; and Meehl, 1967, 1973b, 1983, 1997).

Carl Rogers's Epistemology

In his classic article "Persons or Science: A Philosophical Question" Rogers (1955) attempts to both lay out and resolve the central tension in his professional life. He is torn between what he knows about psychotherapy as a participant and what he is permitted to claim to know as a scientist. His scientific side will not accept as legitimate knowledge what his clinical side is telling him is true. Rogers (1955) noted that his initial approach to the other person is based on a desire to build a personal relationship, not a desire to diagnose, cure, or intellectually comprehend another person's life. The success of this relationship will depend on his ability to communicate to the client three aspects of himself: (a) his faith and confidence that change will take place, (b) his liking of the client, and (c) his understanding of the client's inner world. Rogers is quick to point out that this understanding is not strictly a cognitive process. A process of becoming unfolds if both therapist and client can overcome their fears about forming a relationship, even though Rogers does not "know" where it is going in the short term. Despite these noncognitive emotional, interpersonal—and, I would add, moral—elements, Rogers (1955) maintained that there are knowledge-building processes at work as well:

> Another way of looking at this process, this relationship, is that it is learning. But it is a strange type of learning. Almost never is the learning notable by its complexity, and at its deepest the learnings never seem to fit well into verbal symbols. Often the learnings take such simple forms as "I *am* different from the others"; "I do feel hatred for him"; "I am fearful of feeling dependent"; "I do feel sorry for myself." . . . But in spite of their seeming simplicity these learnings are vastly significant in some new way which is very difficult to define. (p. 248)
>
> Let us try still one more way of defining this type of learning, this time by describing what it is not. It is a type of learning that cannot be taught. The essence of it is the aspect of self-discovery. With "knowledge" as we are accustomed to think of it, one person can teach it to another, providing each has adequate motivation and ability. But in the significant learning which takes place in therapy, one person *cannot* teach another. The teaching would destroy the learning. (p. 249)

What Rogers knows about therapy from doing it is in part how to describe it as an experience. Phenomenological, subjective description is an important element. Rogers (1955) notes that his knowledge is not particularly cognitive, but laden with emotional, nonverbal, elements and that it involves discoveries of a very personal nature (self-knowledge) for both participants. Through multiple exposures to such experience, Rogers begins to see patterns developing. Some experiences seem more powerful than others in producing or signaling change, patterns and structure can be found in the process, and certain experiences (e.g., highly differentiated or abstract verbal–cognitive responses) are notable in their absence.

After considering the scientific objections to accepting the truth of these claims, Rogers (1955) struggles to reconcile his clinical knowledge with the requirements of scientific theory and method. In a solution that he admits is only tentative, he reinterprets scientific knowledge as a disciplined form of subjective truth. Its function is to keep us from fooling ourselves about what we know and clarifying those aspects of our phenomenological experience that remain unclear to us. Science has a place in psychotherapy only if it can help the therapist to extend the special cognitive–emotional–interpersonal knowledge gained from clinical experience. In later years, Rogers (1985) identified himself with those promoting a hermeneutic view of psychology and rejected scientific methodology as the best watchdog against subjective bias and distortion. He took the view that psychology was a human science and therefore could not depend on the methods of natural science for determining the validity of its claims. However, this does not fundamentally change his characterization of the knowledge that grows out of clinical experience that is the present focus of study.

Paul Meehl's Epistemology

Paul Meehl's work is generally, although incorrectly, perceived as antithetical to a trust in clinical experience. He is identified with demonstrating the advantages of actuarial over clinical prediction. His work is frequently cited as giving great impetus to research on clinical judgment that for the most part is highly critical of the reliability and validity of clinical diagnosis. Wiggins (1973) noted that the most interesting and valuable contribution that Meehl (1954) made in his classic *Clinical vs. Statistical Prediction* was not in reviewing the literature on empirical studies comparing the two forms of prediction but in his discussions of the nature of clinical judgment. Specifically, Meehl attempts a logical analysis or reconstruction of what clinicians do and how they think, what he calls *clinical activity*. He follows this with an analysis of clinical intuition—a special sort of clinical activity. Except for Meehl's own later writings on clinical judgment and the logic of the case study in psychoanalysis, one is hard-pressed to find reference to these important chapters in the literature on clinical judgment that ensued.

First, Meehl (1954) noted that there are two distinct but related questions: (a) What sort of data should be collected—clinical judgments or objective psychometric responses from the patient? and (b) should the data be processed by clinical judgment or by actuarial prediction equations? On the issue of data collection, Meehl (1954) noted that the clinician is able to "notice the unusual" in a clinical situation. No psychometric instrument can measure all the possible factors that might in an individual case play a part in the assessment, but a sensitive clinician can notice such an unusual event relatively easily. Against this must be weighed the propensity for error in human observation, recording, retention, and recall of such events (Meehl, 1954, p. 27). In this early work, Meehl (1954) appears to come down hard on the clinician as a data gatherer or observer of behavior. However, in several later articles he implied that such clinical observations are of considerable value.

> Well, what can the clinician do well? However well or badly he does certain things, he alone can do them, and therefore it is administratively justifiable to occupy his time with them. He can for instance observe and interview the patient, functions which are not eliminable by any kind of statistics. He can *be* a person himself with all that this means for the helping process. He can construct hypotheses and carry out research to test them. . . . I am extremely skeptical myself as to the predictive power of the available tests in the personality field. I have held for some years that life-history and "mental status" variables are probably superior to existing tests. (pp. 595–596)

Somewhat later, Meehl (1983) returned to the question of the validity of clinical knowledge:

More generally, a complicated and controversial topic deserving more discussion than the present context permits, we still do not have an adequate methodological formulation as to the evidentiary weight that ought rationally be accorded the "clinical experience" of seasoned practitioners when it is not yet corroborated by quantitative or experimental investigation that meets the usual scientific criteria for having formal "research status." (p. 363)

Meehl just is not sure what credibility to give to clinical knowledge. He seems to want to give it more credence than the "superskeptics" he describes in his 1954 book and less credence than might the unrestrained true-believer clinician. He also acknowledges that the existence of such useful clinical data raises a thorny epistemological problem for clinical psychology. However, Meehl's central concern is the problem of clinical prediction and not the validity of clinical data per se. Here he sides with actuarial methods, but with an important proviso: He does not believe that all clinical activity itself reduces to actuarial activity. Instead, he describes clinical activity as striving toward the "formation of a conception of the person." Here, like Rogers, Meehl is drawing attention to the process of understanding another person. In keeping with his psychoanalytic orientation, Meehl views this process of understanding more in cognitive than existential terms, but for both Rogers and Meehl a special form of knowledge emerges out of the treatment context.

In forming a conception of a person, Meehl (1954) points out that psychologists perform two activities that are not actuarial. First, they develop specific hypotheses about how general laws apply to a specific individual's behavior, and second, to do this, they must first see the relationship between the facts of the case and potential hypotheses. In other words, they see the potential meaning or pattern in the behavior. This is a creative process, and not a mechanical one.

What I am suggesting is that high-level clinical hypothesizing partakes to some degree of that kind of psychological process which is involved in the creation of scientific theory. It is from this point of view that one can do justice to the intuitive and nonrational element of clinical work without committing oneself to any unscientific heresy. (p. 65)

This creativity is often referred to as *clinical intuition*. Meehl was adamant that intuition need not be eliminated from clinical practice for practice to be more scientific. Psychologists can study the outcomes of their intuitive predictions, and perhaps even identify characteristics of individuals who are likely to have good intuitive abilities, even if they can never specify exactly what intuition is. The fact that they cannot utter abstract propositions (psychological principles) about this intuitive process does not prevent at least some clinicians from knowing what to do.

What I am saying is that even in the Utopian stage of clinical psychology, when we have sufficient methods of selecting clinicians and have made explicit all that can be made explicit about the psychological principles we use, at the moment of action in the clinical interview the appropriateness of the behavior will depend in part upon things learnable only by a multiplicity of concrete experiences and not by formal didactic exposition. . . . But that the existence of certain kinds of behavior and discrimination are the results of such an accumulation of experiences is precisely what most of us have in mind when we refer to the artistry of the individual who is clinically skilled. (Meehl, 1954, p. 82)

As with Rogers, Meehl points to a kind of knowledge that can be seen to operate in the clinical situation but that cannot be formally taught, because it involves acting on a kind of insight into the meaning of a behavior or experience that is not strictly a cognitive or propositional form of knowledge.

Finally, Meehl (1954) observed that the predictive hypotheses made in psychotherapy are unlike those made in prediction studies in two important ways. First they are often very useful even when they are wrong, because they move the therapeutic process along. They stimulate the client to understand him- or herself, and if only 1 in 10 hypothesis is helpful, the client still benefits. Second, the clinician must decide when to make a predictive hypothesis and what the likely alternatives are out of an unknown but presumably much larger set of possible hypotheses. To make an accurate prediction in such a context is surely much more difficult than predicting from a given set of outcomes (e.g., whether the diagnosis will be in one of four *Diagnostic and Statistical Manual of Mental Disorders* [e.g., American Psychiatric Association, 1994] categories). One has to see the problem as a something requiring explanation in the first place. Again, for Meehl, the most critical element of the cognitive activity of the clinician is that of noticing what is important in the first place (i.e., seeing what the problem is and a pattern or structure in the case that makes sense out of it). There must be a constant interplay between hypothesis formation and clinical observation in the clinical relationship.

In summary, Meehl's position is that typical forms of clinical judgment, such as diagnosis or predicting the outcome of treatment (prognosis), are inferior to actuarial predictions based on regression equations. However, Meehl recognizes that the clinician must be relied on to collect data in the interview, and although he recognizes the potential biases that may be introduced into the situation by the clinician, in balance he expresses trust in life history or mental status data that emerge from the clinical interview. Meehl further notes that in clinical treatment contexts the development of very specific hypotheses about the nature of a clinical problem (i.e., the meaning of a piece of behavior or its connection to other aspects of psychological functioning) is a critical function that only the clinician can perform and that these "predictions" are not to be discredited by his other observations on the limitations of clinical prediction (diagnosis and prognosis). Meehl has complained in writing on several occasions (e.g., 1973b, pp. xvi–xvii; 1997, p. 93) that he has been misinterpreted as being generally distrustful of or opposed to clinical practice as a whole. It is much fairer to say that Meehl would like to see as scientific a practice of clinical psychology as we have the scientific means to develop and, where scientific validation of knowledge claims is lacking, intellectual integrity requires that observations or assertions be presented in a provisional manner. Meehl is as opposed to substandard quality research in psychology as he is to overly ambitious knowledge claims from clinicians.

As with other philosophical articles in clinical psychology, this aspect of the work of both Rogers and Meehl has been largely ignored, whereas their research contributions in other areas (psychotherapy and psychopathology–psychological assessment, respectively) have received a great deal of attention. As members of a discipline, psychologists need to try to complete what they started: the development of an epistemology of practice. Today, the profession is still burdened by a view of clinical practice among practitioners that claims that clinical art, intuition, acumen, skill, wisdom, or knowledge is self-warranting. It is equally burdened by a scientific community that labels clinical knowledge as *bias*, *superstition*, *ideology*, *anecdotal*, *speculative*, or *mystical*.

CONTEMPORARY VIEWS ON THE LOGIC OF SCIENCE AND PRACTICE

Rogers and Meehl made very important contributions to psychologists' understanding of clinical knowledge and its relationship to science; however, they both recognized that their work was an attempt to open up an area of discussion and not the last word on the subject. Given how little discussion of this aspect of their work ensued, it is not surprising that the discipline is not much closer today to a comprehensive understanding of clinical knowledge than it was in the early 1950s. In the last decade of the 20th century, a number of writers attempted to revisit these epistemological issues (e.g., Hoshmand, 1992; Hoshmand & Polkinghorne, 1992; R. B. Miller, 1992a; Trierweiler & Stricker, 1998). These analyses relied on new thinking in the philosophy of science, particularly the social constructionist and hermeneutic movements that rethink the relationship between scientific and practical knowledge and argued for the contextual and individuality or specificity of clinical knowledge, or what Trierweiler and Stricker (1998) called *local-science*. Hoshmand and Polkinghorne (1992) provided a more radical approach, drawing on phenomenological and hermeneutic views of the subjectivity of the human sciences and the importance of understanding meaning in cases rather than providing causal analyses of outcomes.

Although both of these approaches have much to recommend them, and move the discussion forward appreciably from the position of McFall (2000), or from where Rogers (1955) and Meehl (1954) had left it, they both are derived from, or depend heavily on, revised philosophical or theoretical notions first of science and second of practice. My approach is complementary, for I attempt to understand clinical knowledge as an extension of everyday ways of knowing people and therefore ground the discussion in our intuitive and ordinary ways of thinking about the world. Ultimately, as I show later, the three analyses converge.

OUR EVERYDAY KNOWLEDGE OF PEOPLE

Most general psychology textbook authors, and virtually all social and personality psychology textbook authors, acknowledge that every human being who begins the study of academic psychology must, by virtue of her or his survival, already have a considerable understanding of people and their behavior. As I noted in chapter 1, this commonsense or folk psychology is approached in a very ambivalent fashion. The high interest in psychology as a field of study comes from this sense that one already knows something about the area and wants to know more. This may or may not be conjoined with the belief that because psychology is something already familiar and known, it will be an easy subject matter to study. Rather than trying to build on this storehouse and foundation of common sense knowledge of people, authors in psychology usually, in the first chapter of their texts, highlight the shortcomings of common sense as an argument for why the study of scientific psychology is necessary. Myers (1998), in his popular introductory psychology textbook, described commonsense and intuitive psychology as sometimes "untrustworthy" and that a scientific approach allows one to "sift reality from illusion taking us beyond the horizons of common sense and intuition" (p. 16).

This is really a self-destructive strategy. All scholarly knowledge is a "bootstrapping" operation. One has to start with some propositions that are axiomatic for the science, that are taken as givens, and do not need to be proved. As Rychlak (1968) showed, the presuppositions of scientific psychology are grounded in philosophical positions, and these philosophical positions must ultimately be justified by philosophical argument and common sense, not scientific research. So psychologists disparage common sense on the one hand, while subtly relying on it both for the demand for their courses and books and the conceptual foundation of the "scientific theories" that they then use to disparage common sense. The experimental psychologist can largely do this with impunity, for academic freedom permits one to narrow one's focus of study however one chooses, even if one chooses foolishly, and new candidates for the professorate are drawn from those generally accepting of this self-contradictory viewpoint.

However, the clinical psychologist is in a much more difficult position. Within academic clinical psychology one can choose the same path with almost the same disregard for its ultimate utility, but in the realm of clinical practice, where one has to talk to real people (not subjects, or research participants), program administrators, board members, and legislators, who themselves are immersed in a commonsense or folk psychology, it is not so simple. Unless one's scientific theories sell in Peoria, they are not of much use, as William James noted for slightly different reasons 100 years ago (1892/1983a). Academic psychologists often react to this problem as though it were merely one of translation—translating the scientific terms and theories into laymen's language.

This ignores the original purpose in creating the scientific language of psychology: to get away from the commonsense psychology, which was thought to be inexact and muddle headed. It cannot both be the case that the scientific language of psychology is superior to commonsense psychology in precision and clarity and be fully translatable back into a muddleheaded language of common sense. Another option is to adopt modern scientific medicine's strategy that one need not really talk to patients anyway, because the biomedical tests and examinations will tell one all one needs to know about the disease, and the patient's view is subjective and misleading. Although biologically based psychiatry might attempt to adopt such a risky strategy, the option is not very appealing to psychologists, who at the very least must have client cognitions, if not the whole range of social and emotional phenomena, with which to work.

The problem of translating scientific psychological language back into everyday psychological speech is an important theoretical stumbling block for psychologists committed to the Boulder model. Because it is irresolvable within the framework of conventional philosophy of science, trainees have to develop a dual system of understanding of clinical topics. In other words, the two kinds of knowledge, ostensibly about the same topic, have to be dissociated.

By virtue of being functioning human beings psychologists already have at least a rudimentary understanding of human psychology, human suffering, and what they might do to solve psychological problems and alleviate suffering. Indeed, many students are drawn to the profession of clinical or professional psychology for the very reason that they have already spent their lifetime listening to people's problems, being supportive and helpful (i.e., morally engaged). Students come to psychology with some understanding of stress, conflict, loss, abandonment, hope, and healing. How else could they even know that the field is a desirable one to study? Academic psychology encourages a dissociation of this knowledge from that which is learned from scientific research. In my own case, I worked in the profession for almost 20 years before it dawned on me that the clinical knowledge that was so difficult to integrate with scientific knowledge was an extension of the everyday knowledge of knowing people in daily life (R. B. Miller, 1992b). This discovery came as a result of attempting to defend the validity of clinical knowledge, particularly case study knowledge, from logical positivist attacks such as Grunbaum's (1984), who sets science up as the arbiter of truth in psychology. I was willing to concede that my clinical knowledge, which was useful in doing psychotherapy with a particular client, and which might be further enriched by work with that individual client, was not scientific in the ordinary sense of that word. It seemed to me that my clinical knowledge had improved over the years and that I had a better understanding of what troubled people, and how I could help them, than I had earlier in my training. It also seemed clear to me that there were other practitioners who did not understand things as well as I did, and others who surpassed me in their ability to understand and help. So, although it was not scientific, it clearly was not simply a matter of self-serving bias or commercial "puffing." This knowledge was *personal* (as it required me to expand my self-knowledge and self-understanding), *private* (as it related to matters that were often confidential and could not be revealed without divulging the identity of a client), *practical* (as it required not only abstract knowledge but, more important, know-how, or skill), highly specific to the individual requesting help, and yet communicable in both abstract and experiential ways. Some of it could be set down, not in universal laws but in heuristic rules of thumb. A negative instance, which would completely refute a general law, is expected in implementing a heuristic that is useful when it is simply more often right than wrong.

It was also clear to me that clinical knowledge was as much about the therapeutic relationship as it was about the client's problems or the technique of therapy. My knowledge was about how to relate to or *work with* people toward common goals, not work on people to fix them. My clinical knowledge had evolved in the same way other knowledge sets had evolved in the interpersonal realm. Over the years, like most members of the human species, I have learned how to relate to and understand people in a variety of contexts, for example, the ball field, the classroom, the ballroom, the stockroom of my father's store, summer camp as a camper and then as a counselor, the dormitory, debate society, philosophy club, antiwar rallies and meetings, and graduate school seminars. In each context, one gets to know the people with whom one must work and their expectations, abilities, limitations, and level of cooperativeness versus competitiveness. There is a process to this learning. It involves observation, finding peers who are trying to learn to survive in the same environment and helping each other out, finding slightly older peers who have already "made it" and finding out from them how they did it, and finding mentors from among the more senior members of the profession who will shepherd one through the minefields that lay ahead. Over time, one gets to know some of these people very well, and others only superficially. One not only gets to know people, one gets to know how to get to know people—in other words, a method for learning about other human beings, their lives, and how they will interact with one's own goals and aspirations.

Of course, in all of these contexts in which one is learning about understanding other people, the knowing-people task is seemingly secondary to learning some competency—playing baseball, mathematics, living on one's own, debating skills, and so forth. Consciously or unconsciously, these are also avenues for developing relationships. For some people, those probably not destined for a career in the practice of clinical psychology, these social opportunities are clearly secondary to the competency-building activities, whereas for other people the social component may take precedence over the task at hand. These are the people who go to school or work to socialize, and the task is of little or secondary importance.

It seems evident, then, that the learning of clinical skills or the development of clinical knowledge can be conceptualized as a continuation or augmentation of the everyday process of knowing people, particularly knowing people well. How else could it be that untrained people can offer each other help in difficult times? The movement in the 1960s and 1970s to develop programs to find paraprofessionals to work with underserved populations (Cowen, Gardner, & Zax, 1967) was based explicitly on the idea that such people could be found and, with minimal training, provide real mental health services. Indeed, it is the existence of these everyday helping skills in some members of the general population that, in my view, makes it difficult to show the benefits of training in counseling and psychotherapy in outcome research (Strupp, 1989). Rather than interpret such studies as showing the inadequacy of expertise in counseling and psychotherapy, these studies should be seen as documenting the existence of significant psychological know-how in everyday life.

Clinical theory needs to supplement and bolster the conceptual framework of everyday life, not try to replace it. Otherwise we risk jettisoning the hard-won interpersonal skills and understanding that have developed in our culture over thousands of years and that are captured in the vocabulary of our language for describing people, their character, and mental or emotional states.

THE LEGITIMACY OF COMMON SENSE IN PSYCHOLOGY

Since the work of Fritz Heider (1958), social psychologists have (somewhat ambivalently) acknowledged the critical centrality of naïve or commonsense psychology to the development of a scientific social psychology. This was reaffirmed by Harold Kelly (1992). In social psychology, common sense is taken to mean *what* we, as human beings, know about people's behavior from common sense before we ever study psychology. This study of common sense is very much like a conceptual analysis of the key concepts we use in ordinary language for thinking about each other's behavior and the use of these concepts in propositions about human behavior based on our everyday experience.

> These Common Sense psychology-generating intellectual and interactional activities occur under a wide variety of conditions. I would suggest that the most important ways those conditions vary are with respect to *level, familiarity, and personal involvement.* My hypothesis is that Common Sense psychology is most likely to be both extensive and valid when it refers to events that exist at a middle level (rather than a macro- or micro-level), that are familiar (rather than alien), and of which people are observers (rather than involved participants). . . . Most of subjective daily life is carried on at what I am here calling the middle level. . . . This is the level of planned, goal-directed activity), immediate and direct consequences, time-spans of minutes to days, and face-to-face interaction of small numbers of people. This level is the focus of attention in everyday life, and it provides information that permits conscious and deliberate processing. This also happens to be the level to which most social, motivation, and personality psychologists direct their attention. (Kelly, 1992, p. 6)

Bruner (1976, p. 185), too, noted that the existence of a workable commonsense psychology suggests the existence of a commonsense way of knowing, in other words, a process for discriminating true from false commonsense propositions. This is a point of view long held by personologists such as Allport (1937, p. 369) and Korchin (1976), in his classic textbook:

> Whether as psychologists or as laymen each of us each day engages in informal assessments. . . . Our judgments of others even in brief encounters are remarkably full and accurate. Often however, they are incomplete, distorted, and inaccurate. . . . We all know people who seem to have an uncanny understanding of the feelings and motives of others, who are in the German word "Menschenkenner," "people knowers." There are others incapable of understanding people, who are grossly insensitive to our needs and feelings. (pp. 144–156)

As I became more aware of the role of knowing people in everyday life in developing clinical knowledge, I became alert to other clinical theorists and writers making similar observations. Fromm-Reichmann (1950) wrote,

> Once the psychiatrist has carefully collected and mulled over the information obtained from the patient and from his own observations, *he*

should use his general life-experiences [italics added] and his professional experiences in evaluating the data. *Life experience should enable the psychiatrist to differentiate those aspects of the patients' communications which are characteristic of his educational and cultural background and those which are affected by his emotional difficulties* [italics added]. (p. 51)

Bugenthal (1987), in *The Art of the Psychotherapist*, wrote,

What the therapist must bring into action—in degrees which vary from patient to patient, even from session to session—is an appreciation for the patient's immediate experiencing, for the intentions implicit in his participation, for the ways he structures his own life, and for his accessibility at any given moment. *This is the normal sensitivity that all of us have in relating with others, but it is that normal sensitivity carried to a greater than normal acuity* [italics added]. (p. 11)

From a more research-oriented approach to clinical psychology, W. Russell Johnson (1981), in discussing interviewing skills, wrote,

Truly successful interviewers and psychotherapists are intelligent people who *rely on life experience, perceptiveness* [italics added], and general knowledge of theory to understand patients and clients rather than engaging in the academic exercise of fitting the patient or client to a particular theory. Real interviewing[,] like real psychotherapy[,] requires commitment and thinking, therefore it is infinitely more risky than academic exercising, and consequently more effective. (p. 85)

One of the clearest statements comes from the psychoanalyst and researcher David Malan (1979):

This leads at once to one of the most important qualities that psychotherapists should possess, which is *a knowledge of people, much of which may come not from any formal training or reading but simply from personal experience* [italics added]. (p. 3)

Haveliwala, Scheflin, and Ashcroft (1979) wrote,

Practicing mental health (work) involves staying human and using common sense. . . . Using common sense in the helping situation means using the *common knowledge open to anyone who has become an adult member of this society. This knowledge is the knowledge that has been tested and found practical* [italics added]. Applying common experience in therapy means remembering to be practical and not letting cherished professional doctrine or method become a dogmatic explanation for behavior and events. . . . Tactics are useful only when we use common sense to guide us in their use. (pp. v, xiv)

Perhaps the most surprising confirmation of the importance of our knowledge of people that comes to us through nondisciplinary channels is from the famous Shakow report (Committee on Training in Clinical

Psychology, 1948) that was the basis for the development of the Boulder model of training the scientist–practitioner. This report indicated the kind of undergraduate education and the kind of person required for proper training in psychology at the graduate level. In addition to the usually quoted sections on the importance of scientific preparation, it says,

> The ability to carry out effectively the combination of functions called for depends upon the clinical psychologist being *the right kind of person, a person who has a relevant informal experience background* [italics added] into which has been integrated the proper formal education, both undergraduate and graduate. . . . Since it is reasonable to expect the clinical psychologist be interested in people and a broad base of human contacts, he should have experiences, particularly in his college years . . . involving close relations with both ordinary and unusual persons in field, factory, institution, or laboratory. In addition to direct contact with people of various kinds he should have the indirect acquaintance with people that comes from immersion in great literature, because of the emphasis which such portrayals place on the molar aspects of behavior and the insights into human nature they give. (Committee on Training in Clinical Psychology, 1948, pp. 540–541)

Meehl (1997) also addressed the issue of commonsense knowledge in clinical psychology. (It is interesting that Meehl published this after having read an earlier draft of this chapter, although it is unclear whether that was the stimulus for the following observation.)

> Surely we can sometimes learn about facts and their relations without conducting controlled experiments or computing statistics? Yes! I am not a scientistic fanatic. I agree we know that the thunder occurs after the lightning, that a wine glass shatters when dropped on a tile floor, that if you regularly say cruel things to people, they will dislike you. But these commonsense, everyday observations about readily observable and closely connected physical events are not something it needs a PhD to discern, warranting a professional fee for technical knowledge. Humankind has also "learned" a large number of erroneous relations about black cats, and witches, and petroleum dowsers. A clear message of history is that the anecdotal method can deliver wheat or chaff, and it does not enable us to tell which is which. (pp. 93–94)

Although those in the professional-school movement have questioned the hegemony of science, and pointed to the importance of other ways of gaining knowledge (e.g. Trierweiler & Stricker, 1998), such as self-awareness, cultural understandings, and "local-science," the everyday concept of *knowing people* has not been explicated; neither has its importance to the development of clinical knowledge been sufficiently recognized. Because this is an implicit aspect of the conceptual framework in clinical psychology, it warrants careful philosophical analysis to tease out its meaning and implications for clinical knowledge. This is a task for which the ordinary language or analytical philosophy of Ryle (1949), Austin (1964), and, to some extent, the later Wittgenstein (1958) is particularly well suited (Urmson, 1956). Although such an analysis is never the last word on the significance or meaning of a concept, it is often the only place from which one can start.

KNOWING PEOPLE IN EVERYDAY LIFE: A CONCEPTUAL ANALYSIS

In everyday word usage one finds four senses of knowing people:

1. Simple acquaintance—"I know her."
2. Knowing information about people—"I know Professor Kant took his daily constitutional at 2:00 p.m."
3. Knowing how to handle people—"I know my customers; I can sell a lot of these widgets."
4. Knowing people well—"I know him, and he wouldn't do such a thing."

The first sense, knowledge by direct acquaintance, is straightforward. One knows a person if one has met them, been introduced, or has direct contact with that person. One can know a person in this sense without knowing much about him or her at all, except perhaps what he or she looks like. It is important nonetheless because such direct experience does permit the forming of impressions and the beginning of knowledge of another person that goes beyond what can be known simply by having information about another person.

This brings us to the second sense of knowing people: knowing about them. If I have read a biography of someone—for example, President Kennedy—I may know a good deal about him, although I obviously have not met him. What I know is information about him. This information will be based on observations of his behavior; reports of those who did know him, various documents and other records (video- and audiotapes), and the conclusions of various investigators relied on by the biographer. Research can supplement this type of knowing people. Particular importance will be placed on certain sources who knew the president well. Built into everyday language usage is recognition that there are degrees or depths of knowing. One says, for example, "I only know her a little," or "I know her extremely well." We notice when someone is hard or easy to get to know and that some individuals are better than others at getting to know people (e.g., individuals who are particularly sensitive or insensitive to others).

In everyday life, if one wants to know something about another person, the simplest thing to do is ask him or her. If one cannot do that, then the next best thing is to find people who know the individual well and ask them. Even if one can make direct inquiries, one may still wish to talk with such informants. However, to know or understand someone well may also require that a particular sort of moral relationship exists between two people. If there is a relationship of trust and compassion, then innermost thoughts, weaknesses, hopes and dreams for the future, fears and misgivings may be shared (Jourard's, 1964, notion of self-disclosure). Knowing someone well may involve virtue as well as information—honesty, courage, and fairness. Dishonesty and manipulation are central threats to the validity and depth of the information and the relationship. These threats are unique to this kind of knowing and require a different strategy than the threats to validity with which one customarily deals in evaluating information about one's world. In the natural sciences, concern may be raised about the honesty or trustworthiness of a researcher. However, in the human sciences one must also be concerned with whether the participants are telling the truth and whether they perceive the researcher as trustworthy.

Knowing someone well at an intimate level involves knowing how to as well as knowing that—knowing how to listen, affirm, take risks of self-disclosure, enjoy, and influence the other. It is an interpersonal process of caring as well as learning. It can fail when either the knower or the knowee is unwilling or unable to form a relationship. Knowing someone well often involves having an influence over the other's actions (the third sense of knowing people listed above). It is possible to combine simple acquaintance and knowing about people in such a way as to produce an understanding of how to influence, handle, or manage people, without knowing them well. Good managers, salespeople, and many sorts of human services workers might be said to really know how to work with one group or other of people, meaning that they know how to get them to do what they want them to do.

It is clear that knowing someone well may allow for prediction and control of the actions of another not only because of superior actuarial acumen but also because of the nature of the relationship—if I ask them to do something, they will do it for me. Predictability may also come from familiarity, having seen the individual in sufficiently similar situations to know how he or she will act. Knowing people well means having spent a great deal of time with them under many different conditions. This is what I have found in surveying students about what it is that makes them think they know someone well. They usually say something like "We spent so much time together, I know what she is thinking before she tells me." That is to say that knowing people well is both a more complete and a more powerful sense of knowing people than any of the others.

When one knows someone well, one is likely to also speak of "understanding" a person as much as knowing him or her. This is a concept I examined in chapter 4, and both knowing someone well and understanding someone carry the same duality of a cognitive element implying extensive information or comprehension of a person's actions and motives and an interpersonal element of closeness or intimacy that implies approval or support the person (if not of his or her actions). A critical aspect of getting to know someone well is negotiating the moral realm of coming to see one another as good people and knowing that we are perceived in this manner so that we need not fear moral censure or condemnation for our mistakes. Knowing people well loses any pretense of cold, hard objectivity and is ultimately and acceptably preferential in the sense that the people who know us well are prepared to give us the benefit of the doubt when things do not go well. They assume the best about us unless proven otherwise. Knowing people well is embedded in a moral engagement with everyday life.

ANECDOTAL DATA AND
THE LOGIC OF TESTIMONY

We can test how well we know someone by testing the relationship—creating opportunities to match words with deeds, by seeking out independent opinions from others in a position to know, or verbal confrontations with the person in question. Our own level of trust or comfort is often a guide to the validity of what we know about the other. Thus, one must know one's own feelings and judgments well to know others well. In addition to these interpersonal means of evaluating our knowledge of people, we also use the same rational processes to evaluate our knowledge of people that we use to evaluate any information or theory (Bernstein, 1983). We look for inconsistencies or conflicting descriptions of attributes or events, and corroborating material—records, documents, and so forth. We compare the accounts of different people who claim to know the person well. Coherence and cohesion in the life story or history are of critical importance. Are there holes in the story, or gaps of time that are unaccounted for that suggest that something important is missing? We look for structure, pattern, and meaning in the behavior of those around us, and we are more confident that we know something about another person when we find it. These rational methods are equally applicable to knowing people well or knowing about people. Scientific psychology sees this as a reliance on anecdotal data, which of course it is, but the scientists should be aware that it is a reliance they share.

As the Australian philosopher C. A. J. Coady (1992) observed, every time an experimental psychologist writes a research report in which anecdotal evidence has been assiduously avoided, he or she is generating anecdotal evidence in the actual written report itself (in other words, that the experiments were actually performed in a particular way and that certain data were obtained). Colleagues in the discipline must rely on this anecdotal report of a scientific observation if the report is to become an accepted part of the literature of the field. Even when researchers replicate a study, they rely on the anecdotal reports of the original experimenters for guidance in the execution of the study. The research report is itself an anecdotal report. Life as we live it would be next to impossible if anecdotal evidence were usually mistaken or invalid. At the same time, we learn quickly in life that not all anecdotal reports are to be trusted and that certain sources (e.g., jealous siblings), certain topics (who loves whom in fourth grade), or certain media (cereal commercials on television) are not as likely to yield valid information.

The epistemological status of anecdotal evidence concerning the lives of other persons has been largely ignored in contemporary philosophy as well. This may be changing with the attention being given to Coady's (1992) book *Testimony: A Philosophical Study*. Considering natural testimony as well as formal legal testimony, Coady (1992) examined in intricate detail the logic of our belief in what we tell one another about the world:

> It seems that testimony is very important in the formation of much that we normally regard as reasonable belief and that our reliance upon it is extensive. This reliance is not limited to the everyday or the merely practical . . . since highly developed theoretical activities are also marked by a reliance upon testimony. (p. 8)

Coady (1992) agreed with Thomas Reid, the 18th-century Scottish philosopher of common sense, that testimony is a primary (direct) source of knowledge and does not logically require corroboration from other sources (memory, the senses, other persons). Following Wittgenstein's (1958) and Davidson's (1984) analyses of language as fundamentally a social phenomena, rather than as a translation of private experience, Coady argued that our social life and common use of a language within a culture could not even get off the ground unless there were a basic veracity to most of what we say to one another (i.e., anecdotal reports). To speak to one another, we must trust each other's use of words, and it is impossible to have a common use of words in a community of liars!

In other words, the warrant for the basic reliance on testimony is logically embedded in the exercise of linguistic competence by a community of speakers. This warrant may be revoked in individual instances of testimony—it is defeasible, but the presumption is, and must be, that reliance on testimony is warranted. In proving that a particular piece of testimony is false we show how it differs from typical testimony, not how testimony per se is invalid. Asking someone to defend why he or she uses testimony (i.e., anecdotal evidence) to know about another person is like asking someone why he uses his eyes to know where he is going when he drives a car. In the event that a person misses a stop sign, the question is "Why weren't you looking where you were going?" not "Why were you looking with your eyes?" Similarly, if one is misled by a particular piece of anecdotal evidence, the proper question is "Why weren't you looking out for the weakness in that piece of evidence?" not "Why were you using anecdotal evidence at all?"

If we return to the question as to how psychologists validate their clients' claims to have experienced horrible events in their lives that they have concealed from the outside world, the answer is rather straightforward. As a form of natural testimony, there is a presumption that the claims are true. On the other hand, there is awareness that there are a number of warning signs that the claims might be false. Coady (1992) proposed that there are two basic criteria that people use in everyday life to evaluate the claims of testimony: (a) cohesion and (b) coherence. *Cohesion* concerns the internal consistency of the testimony with itself and with information from other sources (other witnesses, sources, etc.). *Coherence* has to do with how the testimony matches our preexisting understanding of the order and patterns in the universe—does it make sense given what else we believe to be true about the world?

Even a cursory study of the legal system shows that we are not limited to the choice between total acceptance or total rejection of all anecdotal data. The rules of evidence found in Western legal systems (e.g., Lilly, 1987) have evolved over hundreds of years, and although they are not perfect, they do offer at least one model of how testimonial disputes may be resolved without recourse to the "scientific method." The courts look to impartial persons (judge or jury) to resolve disputes regarding facts, have a preference for eye-witness over hearsay testimony, allow noncontested facts to be stipulated rather than proven, assign a burden of proof to those arguing that someone or something is at fault (so that there is a presumption of innocence or acceptable behavior), maintain a presumption that testimony against one's own self-interest is true, and so forth. Although these rules cannot be carried over into the evaluation of clinical data without considerable modification (who will be the judges?), the legal rules of evidence provide a model of the sort of structure that will probably required in psychology for evaluating much of what counts for clinical data. Ambiguous, incomplete, and concealed data are the norm in legal matters, and so the accumulated wisdom of the legal profession in this regard cannot help but be useful.

I have long puzzled at the difficulty I have experienced trying to show my otherwise-rational experimentally oriented colleagues why we ought to rely on the clinical observations of responsible clinicians. I believe Coady's (1992) analysis shows the problem. The defense of anecdotal evidence (testimony) has to be made at the meta-level of analysis, by discussing the logical presuppositions of language, rather than by talking in that language about the veracity of clients, therapists, or the accumulated clinical experiences that lends credibility to a particular observation. The latter are fine for defending any particular piece of anecdotal evidence; in fact, that is exactly how such evidence is validated. However, to defend anecdotal evidence as a whole one must move to the analysis of language itself, not the clinical data. It is there that the warrant for clinical knowledge as a whole is to be found. Much of what over the last hundred years has been called *clinical* wisdom, intuition, art, acumen, or insight is the facility psychologists develop in the handling of the testimony of their clients and colleagues—evaluating, integrating, organizing, and interpreting what people say about their lives and the lives of others, and, of course, what they will not say. However, this skill in using anecdotal evidence is not the justification for using this class of data in the first place. Clinicians are justified in using anecdotal data as a whole because it is a form of natural testimony, which is a presumptively valid means of gaining knowledge about the world. Professional skill in processing the testimony of clients and colleagues permits psychologists to use this source of information about the world to develop an understanding of people that goes beyond what is available to others through testimony in everyday life.

This is obviously a fallible process. Betrayals in friendships, romances, and business partnerships are often punctuated with cries of "But I thought I knew her so well," "I just can't believe the person I knew would do something like this," or "I guess I didn't really know you after all." Our knowledge of people in everyday life is far from exhaustive and perfect. Sociopathic personalities thrive on this human limitation. Note, too, that the failures of anecdotal knowledge reflect a breakdown in our moral rather than strictly cognitive perceptiveness. We misjudged how well a person should be trusted, his or her honesty or commitment to a relationship.

However, the failures should not be taken as the norm. We do know the difference between knowing someone well and knowing someone only superficially. We do know how to get to know someone better and how to judge how well that process is going. We can tell the difference between someone who is hard to get to know and someone who is relatively open. We form working models of each other's behavior and can notice when inconsistencies emerge, or the picture is incomplete, or just does not make sense. I think it is fair to say that this everyday indigenous methodology for validating how well we know each other is a robust one.

CLINICAL KNOWLEDGE: A CONCEPTUAL ANALYSIS

One way to approach the question of the nature of clinical knowledge is to ask "What is to be learned—what knowledge gained—from a clinical practicum or internship experience that could not be gained from reading, doing, and discussing basic quantitative or experimental research in general or clinical psychology (including the developmental, abnormal and personality subfields)?" The first answer that comes to mind is that in the clinical setting one experiences directly what has been described in words or numbers in the research literature. The British philosopher Bertrand Russell (1959) identified this as *knowledge by acquaintance* and noted that it is not exclusively a propositional form of knowledge; it is sensory and perceptual knowledge. In such situations it is common to hear trainees say, for example, "I knew a lot about paranoia before, but now that I've worked with someone who is paranoid, I really know what it is, and I really understand what all those words (in the textbook) mean." Of course, knowledge by acquaintance is important not only in the realm of psychopathology but also in every aspect of what might be called *clinical reality*. It is equally important to know what it is like, to experience directly different clinical settings, different treatment approaches, the interface of clinical service with educational institutions or the legal system, different kinds of supervision, turf battles with other mental health professionals, and so forth. Even if we were to assume that the literature of scientific psychology were a faithful (schematic) map of clinical reality (a questionable assumption for many), it is nevertheless evident that knowing a map well is very different than knowing well what has been mapped. For example, knowing well the map of a city is not interchangeable with knowing the city itself well.

To take this analogy a step further, maps often come with guidebooks of what to do in a given city. Knowing the best restaurants, museums, parks, scenic walks, and shops, and so forth, is very different from what one will know after actually having visited these places. Furthermore, if one does not know how to handle oneself in a new restaurant, or has little experience in museums or with scenic walks or pricey shops, one may gain nothing of actual use during one's visit from having first known what the guidebook said to do. Applied research in psychology (e.g., treatment manuals for empirically validated treatments) often attempts to similarly guide clinicians or the general populace with recommendations of how to handle various life problems or developmental crises. In the clinical practicum or internship, it is not enough to know about what the literature recommends be done in a given situation—one must also know how to do it.

In the clinical setting, the trainee gains knowledge by acquaintance and know-how. Ryle (1949, p. 32) pointed out that much of our so-called knowledge is not abstract propositions but actually knowing how to do something. This is certainly true in clinical practice. In fact, the term *knowledge* rarely occurs in the language of clinical discussions, but clinicians do talk a lot about colleagues who do, or do not, know what they are doing. We recognize different levels of expertise, skill, and competence in the work of clinicians with whom we come into contact. Note, too, that there is a knowledge by acquaintance factor built into know-how. Clinical know-how involves direct experience with clinical reality. One directly experiences the success or failure of various clinical techniques or interventions to produce predicted consequences. Trainees can be often heard to comment, for example, "I had read that active listening was effective in this kind of problem, but now I really know it works, because I did it and it worked."

Of course if we could only learn to be clinicians through knowledge by acquaintance, each of us would have to reinvent the profession. We also learn by observing the practices of others and from the descriptions and narrative accounts that experienced practitioners give of their practices. Knowledge by acquaintance and know-how do get converted into propositional knowledge of a descriptive and prescriptive kind. We highly value those individuals who can give sensitive and accurate phenomenological narrative descriptions of clinical settings, populations, interview processes, and intervention procedures and their outcomes. Clinical instructors and supervisors who can relate their own experiences orally, and clinical literature that does so in writing, are highly valued. We say that such individuals "really know what they are talking about" on a given clinical topic. One does not learn how to practice psychology just by doing, but also by hearing about what others have done before.

Equally important in this learning process is the sharing of clinical and supervisory experiences with fellow trainees at different stages of their training. One compares notes on what the direct experience of clinical practice is like—what it feels like to be in the interview with a disturbing schizophrenic, the supervisory style of a staff member, whether a case presentation made any sense at the last staff meeting, the utility of a particular article on depression, and so forth. In all of this communication about the experience of practice, one's own knowledge by acquaintance and developing know-how is and must be converted to propositional form. This communication serves to organize, synthesize, and integrate clinical experience. Being recognized as an expert clinician involves both knowing what to do, or know-how, and the ability to communicate that knowledge propositionally. Knowing-how and knowing-that (propositional knowledge) are interwoven, each augmenting the other.

The impression is often given among scientists that this sort of educational or training experience is essentially an indoctrination process, involving acceptance of an ideology on faith, rather than a rational process based on reason and evidence. Clinical training is seen as a socialization process in which one adopts the attitudes and values of one's mentors and leaders. Leaders are seen as gurus, demanding their loyal followers adopt unquestioningly a dogmatic set of therapeutic principles. Indeed, there is some truth to this characterization, in that clinical training, as any educational process, involves socialization and forms of influence that are not strictly logical and rational. It is sad that, in some instances, clinical training is primarily or exclusively such a process and devoid of the kinds of indigenous empirical and rational validity checks that might be used. One can find doctrinaire, controlling, and essentially closed-minded teachers and educational or training environments in any group one chooses to examine (including, of course, scientists).

However, what has been overlooked is that the clinical setting can, and in the better settings does, provide numerous checks on the reliability and validity of clinical data and that such data can be used to check the fallibility of many clinical hypotheses, especially hypotheses that relate to the clinical process itself and related outcomes. Where clinical case conferences, workshops, supervision, and courses are offered in a nonauthoritarian setting that encourages critical thinking, there are many opportunities for clinicians to compare notes, discover things they have missed in their own cases, try out a new theory to see if it makes sense out of an otherwise-puzzling case, or consider a radically different therapeutic strategy that makes sense to them. It is a very empirical (in the original sense of *empirical*, i.e., "guided by experience") and pragmatic process. In essence, the practitioner says, "Here is my experience of working in this sort of situation. What is yours?" Some of the most exhilarating moments in my career came when I shared with several fellow clinicians my frustration with using a particular clinical method that was highly touted in the literature but was not working at all, and I discovered it was not working for them either. This led us to then to reexamine our thinking and toward developing more effective practices.

Of course, these interactions with other clinicians do not always lead to new insights. Often the experience is one of hearing a case, theory, or method presented and finding that it does not match one's own experience well at all. One comes away thinking that the other person really does not know what he or she is talking about or doing. Discussions are held with others who heard or read the presentation to see what their reaction is, and we try to explain the differences. Is the clinician in question working with a population that is much different than the one with which we work? Has the clinician represented her or his work accurately or perhaps not reported case failures (maybe we can find someone who has worked directly with this clinician to find out)? Is there any reason to distrust the clinician's honesty? Perhaps there is a different value orientation than our own, and what is meant by a *good* outcome is very different from our own understanding of good. If we have not seen their method demonstrated, we think "I want to see this before I believe it."

All of this illustrates the kinds of checks clinicians do if they are serious about developing their expertise and knowledge. It can work remarkably well. There often develops out of these kinds of discussions a working consensus as to what works well, with whom, in the setting in question. Certain clinicians may be acknowledged as "masterful" and others as deficient, and here, too, there is often not much disagreement. Certain articles or books are regarded as very informative and useful, and others are not. In other words, agreement can often be reached as to what is true or useful and what is not. The clinical realm is not just the babble of voices it is often portrayed to be. Beneath the theoretical din, there are some harmonious chords and at times captivating melodies. (There are striking parallels here between this description of the validation of clinical knowledge and contemporary views on the nature of scientific validation reviewed by, e.g., Bernstein,1983, or Toulmin,

1990, which places more emphasis than traditionally was done on the social conditions that create scientific consensus. The analysis offered here has no doubt been influenced by such a view but is not logically dependent on them. It stands or falls on its own merits as a conceptual analysis of knowing people in a clinical context.)

Illustrative Examples of Clinical Knowledge

It is clear to me that the areas of clinical knowledge in which there is good agreement and a solid foundation for practice are the areas that we all take for granted. They are the parts of clinical practice that blend into our everyday ways of thinking about people and obtaining knowledge of people. Much of the agreement is in area of describing the behavior associated with various clinical syndromes. For example, the description of an obsessive–compulsive person's behavior, thoughts, and feelings in the interview itself, and how such a person responds to the typical questions in a psychosocial history interview, is pretty uniform across all theoretical orientations to personality and psychotherapy (as in Sullivan, 1954; MacKinnon & Michaels, 1971; or D. Shapiro, 1966). The agreement on descriptive phenomena has been ignored for two reasons: (a) Theoretical formulations on etiology or treatment methods are more valued in the profession, and (b) descriptive information is often enveloped in theoretical formulations and difficult to separate from it.

In addition, there is quite broad agreement on the importance and utility of a number of clinical skills or strategies. The following come readily to mind:

- the importance of listening skills and a nonjudgmental attitude in building rapport;
- the need to, whenever possible, gather a broad database on the client that we call the *psychosocial history*;
- that crisis intervention must be more directive and structured than other forms of psychotherapy;
- that persons struggling with violent impulses should be, where feasible, separated from their weapons and the substances they abuse;
- that it is not very useful to tell a person who is delusional that he or she is wrong in his or her beliefs;
- that psychotic reactions are more difficult to resolve than adjustment disorders;
- that, in general, it is helpful to examine the circumstances in a person's life at the time of the first appearance of his or her disturbing thoughts or feelings;
- that, in general, when dealing with a long-suppressed difficulty,

there will be considerable cathartic relief to a person in confiding his or her story to another trusted human being;

- that the problems of children must be understood in the context of their relationships with the significant adults in their lives;
- that it is important to determine a client's reasons for wanting psychological assistance, not all of which may be congruent with the psychologist's reasons for offering such assistance.

It would be a useful and interesting undertaking to compile across theoretical orientations this corpus of clinical knowledge shared by experienced clinicians and to organize and systematize its principles. Such work would also identify areas of disagreement, where the process of developing clinical knowledge outlined above is inadequate to the task and where systematic research is called for. For the purposes of this chapter, however, the critical point is simply that such principles of clinical knowledge, however comprehensive or narrow they turn out to be, do exist.

Knowing People Well and Clinical Knowledge

Clinical knowledge is an extension of commonsense psychology in that it uses the commonsense method of knowing people, in particular, knowing people well, as the vehicle for developing clinical knowledge. Intensive psychotherapy shares with everyday life many of the features of knowing people well. There is a personal relationship involving regular and repeated contact on a reliable basis. Cognitive information and emotional support are interwoven. An effort is made to form a coherent understanding of the other person's life. However, clinical knowledge is *not* just common sense because it applies this method to people most of us do not get to know very well in our everyday lives. Clinicians are experts at exercising the capacity of getting to know people, particularly with those who are difficult to get to know: people in crisis, those who are extremely resistant to being known, those who are overwhelmed or overwhelming. It is not a scientific research process by any means, but neither is it merely the development of biases and conjecture. Clinical knowledge is the knowledge generated in the social practice of clinical psychology by using and refining the commonsense manner or process of knowing people well from everyday life.

Unspeakable, Unbearable, Horrible Truth

People who are difficult to get to know often are that way for very good reason. They are concealing aspects of their lives that they believe it would be dangerous to reveal. The information they possess involves aspects of human relationships that are regarded as shameful and immoral, if not illegal (child physical and sexual abuse, illicit sexual affairs, deviant sexual interests, cheating and dishonesty in business, etc.) There is a qualitative difference between the content of the knowledge that is concealed regarding other people and knowledge that nature conceals in the natural sciences via mystery and complexity. Only in a relationship that contains certain moral features—trust, safety, respect, and confidentiality—can these critical features of human existence be revealed and discussed. A psychology that wishes to go beyond the surface of social pretense and masks must provide a methodology for exploring the taboo and forbidden aspects of human relationships (Faberow, 1963). Freud (1920/1966), writing in the *Introductory Lectures on Psycho-Analysis*, made the point that the data of clinical psychoanalysis—and, by implication, psychology—are vulnerable to this sort of distortion:

> The talk of which psycho-analytic treatment consists brooks no listener, it cannot be demonstrated (to the audience). A neurasthenic or hysterical patient can of course like any other, be introduced to students in a psychiatric lecture. He will give an account of his complaints and symptoms, but of nothing else. The information required by analysis will be given by him only on condition of his having a special emotional attachment to the doctor; he would become silent as soon as he observed a single witness to whom he felt indifferent. For this information concerns what is most intimate in his mental life, everything that, as a socially independent person, he must conceal from other people, and beyond, that, as a homogeneous personality, he will not admit to himself. (pp. 20–21)

Rollo May (1969) concurred in *Love and Will* and quoted H. S. Sullivan as expressing a similar position:

> But neither these psychologists in their laboratories nor those philosophers in their studies can ignore the fact we do get tremendously significant and often unique data from persons in therapy—data which are revealed only when human beings break down the customary pretenses, hypocrisies and defenses behind which we all hide in "normal" social discourse. There is also the curious situation that unless we are oriented towards helping the person, he will not, indeed in some ways cannot, reveal the significant data. Harry Stack Sullivan's remark on research in therapy is still as cogent as when he first made it: "Unless the interviews are designed to help the person, you'll get artifacts, not real data." (pp. 18–19)

Whether one wishes to join the more psychoanalytic observers in believing that all clinical problems have at their core such unspeakable elements, or whether one takes the more moderate position that many, if not most, do, it is clear that the clinical method of gaining knowledge in psychology is, for all its limitations, the only game in town. As with Heisenberg's

(1958) electrons, we are not free to measure clinical reality however we would wish. The reality dictates how it will become accessible to us. The problem of external validity is maximized in this domain. If one seeks interrater reliability on these sorts of clinical phenomena by introducing an independent observer, then external validity coefficients will fall to between 0 and −1.0. Without confidentiality, the information obtained in a clinical interview will either be random noise or will deliberately mislead one away from the truth.

The moral dimension of clinical reality—that it deals with some of the most morally abhorrent features of family and interpersonal dynamics—is a matter of great epistemological as well as clinical significance. These phenomena are not just concealed or hidden by virtue of their complexity, or the limits of our understanding, as with problems in understanding inanimate nature or cellular biology. These phenomena are hidden and concealed because they contain information that if revealed would cause people to be shamed in their communities, physically threatened, or prosecuted by the law. The personal safety, perhaps even the lives, of one's clients and their significant others, as well as professional ethics, requires that confidentiality be strictly maintained. The following case vignette illustrates this feature of clinical knowledge. The details of the clinical situation have been altered sufficiently to protect the identity of the client but still preserve the essential ingredients.

The Case of Mrs. M

Mrs. M is a 25-year-old college graduate, professional public service administrator, and mother of three children, referred by her physician for depression. She is the daughter of Italian immigrants and is married to a 30-year-old man of South American descent. She has been depressed for a period of 2 years coinciding with her husband's job change, which resulted in increased business travel away from the family. Her husband has recently moved out of the house, and over a period of the next 12 months, as she is attending weekly psychotherapy sessions, it emerges that he is having an affair with a much younger woman (their babysitter).

At this point, Mrs. M. becomes distraught, agitated, and actively contemplates murdering her husband. Despite the fact that she is entirely rational on all other matters in the conduct of her life, including a responsible administrative job, in therapy she continues to discuss her desire to kill her husband. Finally, in desperation, her therapist discusses with her the therapist's own experience working in a correctional center with people who had killed family members and how awful her life would be in jail. In the next session Mrs. M. makes a major shift away from homicidal ideation and explains that, before the discussion of the likelihood of her serving jail time, it had never occurred to her that she would be arrested for killing her husband. Surprised at her own failure to consider such an obvious feature of reality, she had puzzled over how this mental lapse may have occurred. "I wonder if the fact that my father was a hit man for the Mafia had anything to do with it? Did I ever tell you that was what my father did for a living?" she asked. The answer was that of course she had not. This information opened the door to considering her relationship with her father, which she had avoided in therapy to conceal his occupation and which proved critical in understanding many aspects of her problems in living (trusting men, panic attacks, dependency on her mother, etc.). There are not, perhaps, many cases in which the need to conceal the truth is so apparent as in this one, but as I review my caseload over the past 10 years it seems to me that many, if not most, have at least one critical component in which the notion of a dangerous horrible, unspeakable, unbearable truth applies. These are cases in which a critical feature of the clinical reality would remain unknown were it to be investigated using what is typically referred to as an *empirically rigorous* method. The clients simply would not risk the possibility that relative strangers presenting themselves as reputable researchers might, in some way, discover their identity or misuse the information in such a way as to put their life or those of their family members, their fortune or career, or their personal reputation or liberty in serious jeopardy.

The Pervasiveness of Dangerous Data

Although it is not my purpose here to marshal all the available evidence in support of the proposition of privileged clinical access to at least some crucial life history or mental status phenomena, I should note that there are a number of areas in the literature in which it is already acknowledged that clients suppress and conceal critical aspects of the clinical picture out of fear of the consequences of disclosure:

- the problem of family secrets in the family therapy literature (e.g., Imber-Black, 1993);
- failure of victims to disclose or report domestic violence, rape, child physical or sexual abuse, or other crimes perpetrated against them (e.g., M. Elliott, Browne, & Kilcoyne, 1995; Singer, 1988; Wetzel & Ross, 1983);
- the silence of victims of political terror and repression when they are still residing in areas controlled by the forces that terrorized them, and in severe cases (Holocaust survivors, prisoners of war, etc.) even after being removed from the dangerous environments (e.g., Fogelman, 1994; Suarez-Orozco, 1991).

In addition to these groups of potential clients, there are others who actively conceal the truth about their lives from their psychotherapist for fear of prosecution and incarceration. I have in mind here a wide variety of individuals likely to be seen in compulsory treatment contexts, for example, substance abusers who are dealers; perpetrators of child and domestic abuse; and criminal personalities. Here at least clinicians tend to have some idea that there are important data likely to be missing in formulating the clinical picture, although they may not know exactly what data are missing.

How does one evaluate the "truth" in clinical situations involving concealed and dangerous information? First, it is necessary to recognize two levels of testimony: (a) the therapist's account of the therapy process and of the client's life history and (b) the client's account of his or her history and life circumstances as reported to the therapist. The therapist must decide whether the testimony of the client is to be believed. The reader must decide whether the therapist's testimony is to be believed. This is not just a matter of assessing facts and logic, although those are involved, but also a matter of assessing the moral–emotional authenticity of the reports. Does the case vignette "ring true," does it resonate with our experience of human beings in our own world whom we have seen in the midst of such a moral crisis? We must also evaluate whether the therapist's reasoning about the case is sound and whether the basic theoretical framework in which the facts are reported and reasoning conducted is sufficiently clear and sufficiently sound as a theory to warrant accepting the vignette as a useful piece of clinical knowledge.

How one evaluates the validity of a case report is discussed in detail in chapter 6, but suffice it to say here that although it is not a simple process, it is not that different from many everyday contexts in which one knows confidential information about friends, family members, or oneself, and so neither is it an overwhelming difficult task to expect clinicians to perform reasonably well. Much of it comes down to a matter of trust—and trust is a matter of logic, judgment, and faith. The therapist must decide whether to trust the client, and the reader must decide whether to trust the therapist reporting the case. To the extent that these concealed truths pertain to areas of social existence outside the clinician's everyday experience, one relies on clinical supervision, training, and literature to assist in making these determinations. This is one of the reasons that the development of a robust clinical case study literature is so important to psychology.

There is no way that studying the experimental "scientific" literature of clinical psychology can be of assistance with this task, because the phenomena in question remain entirely concealed within that research paradigm. If such clinical principles work in ascertaining the probable truth in such highly charged and difficult clinical contexts, there is no reason to believe that the cohesion and coherence of client and psychotherapist testimony will not also be an acceptable method for ascertaining the probable truth in a wide variety of more mundane clinical contexts (e.g., symptomatology, response to interventions, and at least some etiological factors). In other words, the field of clinical psychology as a scholarly and scientific discipline would be epistemologically warranted in relying on so-called anecdotal data for a considerable portion of the knowledge base of the profession.

EPISTEMOLOGY OF PRACTICE

The hope of the individuals who created the Boulder model was that applied science was still science and that applications of science would be like deductions from a theorem or principle to a more narrow range of phenomena, requiring no basic change in theory or verification. In retrospect, this hope appears to have been mostly wishful thinking. Practical knowledge does not easily flow from scientific knowledge, and in fact, as Schon (1987) argued, it seems to have its own independent sources. Whatever content or direction it draws from science, it also grows out of the experience of practice itself—when that practice is subjected to reasoned examination. Schon (1987) observed that the entire modern system of higher education has failed to adequately understand practical knowledge, and he called for an epistemology of practice to be developed that rectifies this problem. Argyris and Schon (1974) detailed a similar schism between practitioners and academic scientists in all of the university-based professions: engineering, management, education, architecture, psychology, medicine, law, nursing, and so forth. In each field there is the tension between those who would train students by educating them in the basic scientific principles of an academic discipline thought to be relevant to practice and those who believe in training by the case method. In the case method, practitioners introduce students to the problems they will be expected to solve as professionals by sharing cases from their own or similar practitioners' experiences and helping the students to work their way through to solutions. In their analysis of this sort of practical knowledge, Argyris and Schon emphasized that the knowledge is in the action performed. They used Polanyi's (1962) notion of *tacit knowledge* as a central feature of their explanation. The practitioner knows more than he or she can say. Argyris and Schon also introduced the concept of *reflection-in-action* to explain how practitioners develop new knowledge in their profession. Schon (1987/1992) summarized this process in the following way:

> In the course of such a process, the performer "reflects" not only in the sense of thinking about the action he has undertaken and the result he has achieved, but in the more precise sense of turning his thought back on the knowing-in-action implicit in his action. He reflects "in action" in the sense that his thinking occurs within the boundaries of what I call an action-present—a stretch of time within which it is still possible to make a difference to the outcomes of action. (p. 58)

Schon (1987/1992) held that this reflection-in-action is the critical feature in an epistemology of practice. Although he has illustrated it with examples drawn from psychotherapy supervision and a seminar for graduate students in counseling and consulting psychology, it is offered as a first step in building an epistemology of practice, and a perfectly general one at that. In this epistemology, action (practice, skill, know-how, artistry) is in a dialectical relationship with propositional, conceptual knowledge; abstract knowledge; or theoretical knowledge. Our ideas about what we are doing and how to do it must both guide and be guided by our acting on the world. This is pragmatism to the second power, for not only are our ideas evaluated by whether they work but also our ideas are about our work and have meaning only in the context of the actions we perform. Another way of saying this is that theories of practice are a different category of knowledge than scientific theories that are intended to give an account of the nature of the world as it is. Theories of practice are the conceptual piece of a complex activity in which we work to change the world, to create a difference in our world. Because these theories include descriptions of the events, circumstances, and people that one encounters in the course of engaging in the practice, as well as account of relationships of these events, circumstances, and people to one another, it is easy to see why so many have mistakenly assumed that these are observational or explanatory propositions of the sort encountered in the natural sciences. However, the function served in professional knowledge by such accounts is as intermediary steps in the process of acting on the world in a very specific context, and they derive their validity from this function, not from their capacity to be independently evaluated as scientific propositions in a laboratory or experimental context, or even in a radically different practice context.

If we think about this in a setting other than clinical psychology, it may be easier to accept Schon's (1987/1992) point. Consider the heavyweight boxing champion Mohammed Ali (Remnick, 1996). He was a brilliant strategist, both in the ring and in reflecting on boxing matches before and after the match. In the match against Sonny Liston, he was determined to convince Liston that he was mentally unstable and therefore an easy mark. He hoped that this would lead Liston to fail to train properly for a long bout and that with Ali's youth and speed, he might wear the stronger champion down. These were important ideas, inferences, and observations about who Sonny Liston was as a man and what he might believe about Ali (then known as Cassius Clay). However, they had meaning and importance only in the context of Ali's physical abilities and boxing skills, which were deceptively easy to underrate if one was not in the ring with him. Once in the ring, Ali shocked Liston with how good a fighter he was, and only then did the "truth" of his own knowledge of Liston become confirmed. If one tries to separate Ali's beliefs about Liston from his sense of himself as a fighter and his skills in the ring, one is left with a shell of an argument to attempt to disprove.

Had Ali lost the fight, no one would have awarded him the heavyweight championship of the world by virtue of Ali having written a *Psychological Review* article on the theory of winning prize fights, and of course no one would have any interest in reading or evaluating the article, nor should they. It would be an irrelevancy. Having won the fight, Ali's observations about Liston's character, and about boxing strategies, are of some interest and worthy of our consideration. To submit Ali's observations or theories of boxing to scientific testing to determine their validity, however, would be the height of absurdity. Their test was in the ring, and no further testing is practically or logically necessary. We do, as the *Compact edition of the Oxford English Dictionary* (1971) noted, sometimes refer to a boxer as practicing "the science of boxing," but this is a mostly archaic use of the term to refer to boxers who are very methodical, clever, and highly skillful. In this sense, one might practice psychology "scientifically," but only this sense.

The distinction between propositional knowledge that forms a part of reflection-in-action and propositional knowledge that represents scientific observations or theory is a critical one. In the absence of such a distinction, an eager scientist who read and understood exactly Ali's boxing philosophy and mental and physical strategies might think her- or /himself ready to go a few rounds with the current champion. The typical psychology student studying scientific abnormal psychology in preparation for a career as a clinical practitioner is about as well prepared as this eager scientist would be for a heavyweight fight.

Both the major works on professional knowledge in psychology of the last decade, authored by Trierweiler and Stricker (1998) and Hoshmand (1992), have relied heavily on Schon's (1987) analysis of the epistemology of practice, and his notion of reflection-in-action, as a model of practitioner knowledge. Hoshmand (1992) integrated this view of practitioner knowledge with a postmodern view of science influenced by the narrative and hermeneutic approaches to human science (see chap. 4). If psychology as a science is to be a human science examining the meaning that people create and the reasons for their actions, then psychology becomes a practical "science" and the integration with professional knowledge is a seamless one. Schon (1987) advocated for training in case study research as the paradigm of research in professional practice.

For Trierweiler and Stricker (1998), the practitioner is cast as a "local-scientist" applying traditional scientific knowledge to specific contexts and unique situations through the powers of deduction and inference. They allowed that other forms of knowledge, such as self-knowledge, are critical components of a clinician's knowledge base, but anxious not to stray too far from the logical positivist mainstream, the authors pay far less attention to the epistemological status of these other forms of knowledge than to "local-science."

Although it is true that the practice of psychology shares epistemological features with the other professional practices studied by Schon (1987) that permit one to distinguish scientific from practical knowledge, it is argued here that the epistemology of knowing people well is also critical to an understanding of clinical or professional knowledge. Knowing people well has its own epistemological features, particularly concerning the confidentiality and privacy required as a result of the profound moral dilemmas that can emerge in the process and the heavy reliance on personal testimony as a basis for information and evidence. Just as clinical knowledge is a dialectical component of practice, knowing people well is a dialectical component of a relationship between two people, and it cannot be evaluated independently of that relationship. Sometimes one trusts a person's information because one trusts the person, and rather than this being a biased judgment, it is a reasonable or fair one. The moral framework of the relationship can at times provide the warrant for one's belief in various statements about the person or the relationship.

LIMITS OF CLINICAL KNOWLEDGE: THE BOUNDARY WITH SCIENCE

Clinical knowledge clearly exists and can be differentiated from clinical nonsense. It is closely linked to one's everyday knowledge of people and the means by which one comes to know and understand people well. It must be said, however, that there are many claims to clinical knowledge that are faulty and made without having been passed through the indigenous validating process discussed above. Furthermore, this indigenous methodology is not foolproof. It does not permit of great precision, and it is very bound by its context. What clinicians know best is the clinical situation or context and how it relates to various life histories. It is not a good basis for micro-, macro-, or statistical knowledge of human behavior. Clinical knowledge is of the *middle level* of behavior, to use Kelly's (1992) term, and the middle level of abnormal behavior at that. It is obviously poorly suited to many developmental questions, because a clinician's interactions with clients tend to be cross-sectional rather than longitudinal. (Direct clinical observation of such developmental phenomena is not very likely except in long-term work with children.) Clinical knowledge is extremely vulnerable to the destructive effects of an authoritarian learning or work environment—but then, what knowledge isn't?

Perhaps the greatest limitation is the lack of recognized standards in the profession for the presentation of clinical knowledge claims (although R. Elliott, Fisher, & Rennie, 1999, and R. B. Miller, 1999, are a start).

Theory and data are poorly differentiated, and methods of validating clinical claims are rarely specified. The profession needs to develop standards for the presentation of qualitative and narrative data similar to those that exist for quantitative data. I discuss these at length in chapter 6.

The most difficult remaining question is how to assess the limitations of clinical knowledge vis à vis scientific knowledge in psychology. What makes this so difficult, in part, is the problem of defining *science*, as discussed in chapter 4. As discussed there, traditional views that strictly separated objective empirical sciences from other forms of rational inquiry have come under close scrutiny and attack in the philosophy of science. Yet even under these new approaches to the philosophy of science differences remain. The most obvious difference between clinical knowledge and scientific knowledge is that clinical knowledge is primarily concerned with understanding individuals, and scientific knowledge is concerned with understanding universal principles or laws. This is the familiar and much-debated idiographic–nomothetic distinction in psychology (Holt, 1962).

Clinicians do, however, form generalizations about types of patients, and they do see patterns across individuals that constitute in part their clinical knowledge. In fact, although knowing people well always involves knowing each person individually, and each case has unique features that are critical, without the knowledge of clinical patterns and processes that are relatively constant across individuals there would be little clinical knowledge. The difference between clinical knowledge and scientific knowledge is not simply between general principles and individual understanding; rather, it seems to be more a matter of the role of moral values in clinical knowledge. The most powerful clinical generalizations are rules of what therapists should or should not do for clients and what clients should or should not do to better their own lives. The moral dimension is much more in the foreground than in scientific laws.

Do psychologists study individuals to find universal principles that explain how the world works, or do they study universal principles to help them in understanding individuals? The scientist does the former, and the clinician does the latter. There is a vast difference between studying an individual for the purpose of being helpful and studying an individual to abstract from his or her experience or behavior what that person shares in common with other people. The scientific theory must ignore the particular circumstances of the individual and assume "all other things being equal." Individual variations due to participants or circumstances are partialed out as random noise in the data. Science can ignore the uniqueness of the person or the life history, because its goal is not the description, understanding, or betterment of the individual but the advancement of an explanatory set of principles (scientific knowledge). In the long run, scientific knowledge presumably will reap rewards and benefits that will feed back to individual human lives and, with luck, to those very lives that were studied. But this is not the primary concern of science, and it may not even be a concern at all, of the scientist. Science, as ideally envisioned, is an end in itself. Scientists must be free to explore whatever intrigues them. Academic freedom protects the investigator from restrictions growing out of a concern that no immediate benefit will accrue to anyone from her or his work. No question is too small or too large if the scientist's creative imagination has been captured by it. Theories may be entertained on the basis of their novelty, beauty, and elegance as much as on the basis of their utility or moral relevance.

How different this is from the restrictions placed on the clinician. The universal scientific principles of use to the clinician must be very robust, not easily negated by individual situational circumstances, of clear relevance to the central life concerns of patients, and easily integrated with clinical knowledge of the individual case. (Of course, in experimental psychology Meehl, 1978, noted how rarely one finds such robust principles in the "soft" domains of personality, abnormal, social, and developmental psychology. Here auxiliary principles are always required on a pretty much ad hoc basis to explain the failure of the data to validate a hypothesized general principle.) Furthermore, general principles of use to the clinician must be expressed in a conceptual system that is compatible with the clinical knowledge that comes from knowing a particular client well. Scientific knowledge may extend or refine clinical knowledge as it is applied to clinical experience, but it cannot reject the basic commonsense framework out of which clinical knowledge grows.

This being said, I nonetheless do not doubt that scientific psychology is relevant and one important component in the development of clinical knowledge and the training of clinicians. As Meehl (1954) indicated, scientific psychology functions as one source of the hypotheses that the clinician uses to formulate an understanding of a person and which is then checked out by what I have called *knowing the patient well*. Bandura's (1986) social learning theory, Piaget's (1952) theory of cognitive development, Seyle's (1974) work on the "general adaptation syndrome," and more recent work on the fundamental attribution error and cognitive heuristics (Tversky & Kahneman, 1974) strike me as excellent candidates in this regard. This, of course, reverses the received view of the relationship between science and practice, where it is said that clinical work provides hypotheses for scientific research but is otherwise invalid as a basis for knowledge.

The possibility that scientific knowledge can assist the development of clinical knowledge suggests that these two forms of knowledge are logically of the same genus. They inform one another and may conflict with one another. How this can logically be possible is tricky to reconstruct, for much of clinical knowledge is prescriptive and, as observed above, very directly a form of moral concern and judgment.

Clinical knowledge as know-how is prescriptive action-oriented knowledge. It is about how, what, where, and when to do specific actions to accomplish certain ends or goal. It is also about what those ends or goals should be. There is a descriptive and explanatory understanding of human beings on which these judgments rely, but the know-how cannot be reduced to or derived from this descriptive knowledge base. The know-how is an additional knowledge system.

HOW CLINICAL KNOWLEDGE MIGHT INFORM PSYCHOLOGICAL RESEARCH

One must not approach the question of the limits of clinical knowledge without also realizing the limits of scientific knowledge in clinical psychology. There are many areas of scientific psychology that might gain from paying attention to the indigenous methodology of knowing people well in everyday life, specifically, the social, abnormal, developmental, and personality subfields. These are areas of psychology that often study the aspects of the human experience that people are reluctant to reveal. People experience shame, humiliation, and horror at discussing or revealing their part as victim or victimizer in a socially stigmatized interpersonal process. Clinicians frequently report (e.g., Karon & VandenBos, 1981) that in severe disorders such as schizophrenia, patients do not reveal the most important aspects of their life histories until they have been seen regularly for a considerable period of time. If one thinks of research as a process of knowing people well, this is not a surprising observation.

If one views human research in psychology as an extension of the ordinary ways of knowing people in everyday life, rather than a specialized procedure for extracting data from humans that is set apart from human existence, then there is a way of approaching research on sensitive issues that can do justice to them. This would require shifting some of the value commitments of the research community, for one has to make a commitment to care about and affirm those people who volunteer to be "subjects" to a much greater extent than we currently do. We have to befriend them to be given the information they so assiduously withhold from the world.

Of course, this is exactly what has been happening in the real world of clinical practice anyway, as clinicians have for the most part eschewed clinical research as a basis for practice and relied on clinical wisdom, lore, experience, and tradition for guidance. Acknowledging that at least some of this tradition is valid as a knowledge base for the profession, rather than rejecting it as anecdotal and unscientific (i.e., invalid), would produce potentially momentous changes for the discipline. Such an epistemological move could free up much of the energy that currently goes into feuding between researchers and practitioners and convert it to collaborative endeavors that would greatly improve the quality of both research and practice. Once this philosophical shift has taken place, there are a number of specific ways in which research in clinical psychology could augment clinical knowledge and practice:

1. Researchers might consider helping clinicians supplement or complement clinical knowledge rather than automatically replacing it. Furthermore, such research would not automatically be assumed to be for the purposes of confirming causal hypotheses but would instead be discovery oriented (Mahrer, 1988). Researchers might identify highly competent clinicians and approach them as expert knowledge systems to be explicated (after Shanteau, 1992) or assist such clinicians in organizing and systematizing the wealth of testimonial data they have accumulated through years of clinical experience. Busy clinicians often do not have the time or inclination to do this task, but they might be spurred on to do so by the researchers' interest in helping them extract, from their own experience, knowledge for the entire discipline.

2. Analyze historically important published case reports and theoretical clinical papers for areas of agreement or disagreement on specific topics (e.g., treatment of depression, crisis intervention with suicidal clients, or children with anxiety disorders) and then design studies to assist in resolving differences. Such studies would perhaps still rely on testimonial sorts of data, but it would be more systematically collected from clinicians. Alternatively, such research may involve more traditional observational, self-report, psychometric, or clinical rating procedures, depending on the clinicians' judgment that such data collection procedures are not unduly intrusive.

3. Bring experienced clinicians into the planning of research on all clinical questions (whether diagnostic, etiological, developmental, or therapeutic) to determine whether any nonclinical research approach has any likelihood of ascertaining the likely truth and to rule out the likelihood of concealed data being pivotal in the phenomena in question.

4. Relate clinical testimonial knowledge to areas outside the experiential domain of either the clinician or the client (e.g., physiological variables, social or historical forces or factors, developmental variables that may not be available to memory or that are outside the awareness of the child, exceedingly complex or subtle social phenomena in the social psychological sphere that clinicians or clients might otherwise miss [e.g., cognitive biases]). In some of these areas of research one of the key variables will be the testimonial knowledge of the therapist–client dyad, and the other variable will be a more

traditional quantitative one, whereas in other areas all the variables will be of a traditional sort. In any case, the moral and political values implicit in the research must be identified and clearly articulated by the researchers. As a society we are still paying the price for the pseudoscientific, politically inspired eugenics movement, sponsored by some of the biggest names in American "philanthropy" (R. Whitaker, 2002).

This is a reminder once again of the moral dimension of clinical knowledge. Erikson (1963, pp. 416–417) asserted that one cannot do psychoanalysis or understand a person psychoanalytically unless one has a concern for social justice. Caring is a necessary moral condition for knowing well in the human realm. A clinical psychology that is oriented to promoting individual freedom, growth, and creative personal living will be evaluated first and foremost as a moral endeavor. Clinicians or researchers who wish to develop technical skills because these are highly remunerated in the current political economy must consider the epistemological consequences of such a moral decision: They will never develop more than a mediocre ability to know people well. They may contribute to some kinds of what were referred to earlier as *state-* or *corporate-sponsored* clinical psychologies that aim to control the expression of certain emotions, actions, or thoughts of members of the society according to the political or economic needs of the state, bureaucracy, or corporation. They may know a great deal about people, but they are forever shut off from the knowledge that can come only from understanding and knowing people well.

6

DEMONSTRATING CLINICAL KNOWLEDGE IN THE CASE STUDY

To those uninitiated in the ways of psychological research methods, the term *case study* simply means a research report of any kind. It might be the account of psychotherapy with a single client or a complex study comparing several different treatments over hundreds of clients, following a carefully prescribed research protocol and filled with statistical measures on hundreds of clients. Of course, it may be a study not of psychotherapy at all but on any of the hundreds of psychological processes or variables that psychologists study in both humans or laboratory animals: brain imaging the frontal lobes of twins who do or do not share certain personality characteristics, the inheritability of maze-running intelligence in rats, mother–infant interactions that establish bonding and attachment, and so on. Technically, the term *case study* is reserved in psychology for reports on a specific individual or situation that has been in some way or another studied by a psychologist. It may be someone the psychologist has sought out to study because of his or her unique characteristics or unusual experiences, or it may be someone who has sought out the psychologist for professional services and whom the psychologist then decides to make a study of in addition to providing the requested service. Traditionally, there have been no formal standards applied to case study research, meaning that the researcher may use whatever means that are at her or his disposal under the circumstances. It may involve interviews with various individuals, public or private documents, health records, autobiographical or biographical writings, naturalistic observations, or even systematic measures or psychological tests. In traditional research methodology, case studies are presented as the most rudimentary and least systematic manner of studying a problem, justified only when other more rigorous methods that involve studying groups of subjects with similar characteristics are not feasible. In general, students are cautioned that no valid conclusions can be drawn from case studies because there is no control over the conditions encountered by the individual being studied and no way to guard against bias on the part of the individual doing the study (although several leading methodologists have pointed out that if naturally occurring circumstances are just right, it may be possible to assert causal conclusions from a case study; Campbell, 1975; Kazdin, 1981). These exceptional circumstances aside, the case study is seen to be useful only as a means of formulating hypotheses that might be tested by more formal methods of correlational or experimental research. As a result of this logical positivist inspired research philosophy, case studies fell into disrepute in American psychology after the 1950s. Even in abnormal psychology and psychotherapy journals, the case study, which had been the mainstay of psychological research, gradually disappeared and was replaced by correlational and experimental studies.

Those who follow pedagogical trends in psychology will note an apparent exception to this observation that began to emerge in the late 1980s. Publishers and authors of the mainstream abnormal psychology textbooks that had become essentially literature reviews of research on the etiology, assessment, and treatment of *Diagnostic and Statistical Manual of Mental Disorders* (e.g., American Psychiatric Association, 1994) diagnostic categories began reintroducing case examples into the body of the textbooks or in separately published ancillary "casebooks" for their pedagogical value with students. In other words, the field of abnormal psychology realized that what students wanted to read, could understand, and wanted to discuss in class were case studies of abnormal psychology. Once again, this was typically viewed by faculty as a sign of the intellectual weakness of students who needed to be entertained by "human interest" stories to sustain their attention and interest in the real stuff of psychology—the scientific research. This ignores the obvious alternative explanation that the case studies were fascinating to students because, unlike the empirical research that dealt with depersonalized causal variables, case studies presented information that students could actually use and that made sense to them in their lives.

In my own experience, I was stunned by the intensity of the enthusiasm I encountered in first-year graduate students who were helping me search the literature and evaluate the quality of published case studies. They indicated that for the first time they were able to understand how psychotherapy actually was done within the various theoretical models they had studied, not as a theory but as a real human interaction with another person. The students commented that many of the case studies were compelling reading and made the study of clinical psychology come alive for them. I saw a level of excitement and engagement in the learning process rare even among the best psychology graduate students.

I was initially taken aback by this student enthusiasm for clinical case studies, because I become interested in them from a more analytical, even philosophical perspective. During the decade of the 1990s, as I developed my notion of clinical knowledge as an extension of the everyday morally engaged process of knowing people well, I began to develop an interest in the case study. Once I had a clearer sense of what I meant by *clinical knowledge*, I realized that the primary means by which clinical knowledge could be communicated to others was by virtue of informal and formal case discussions, conferences, demonstrations, and written case reports. I then realized that the clinical theorists whose work I had most appreciated and found useful over the years of my own training and practice were those who integrated a great deal of case material into their writing and lecturing. These were clinicians from a variety of mental health professions who described their cases and work in pragmatic detail so that one could actually picture the people involved and how they related to one another in terms of what exactly they thought, felt, said, and did.

It then seemed obvious to me that if psychologists, as members of a discipline, were to develop clinical knowledge—a knowledge of how to understand and help people with the problems of human suffering—then the case study method would have to be resuscitated and improved to become one of the primary vehicles of scholarly endeavor in clinical psychology.

Of course, educated as I was in the logical positivist research tradition of clinical psychology in the 1970s, I knew that the case study had fallen on hard times as a legitimate research method. Nevertheless, I was determined to see what sort of cases had been published and what, if anything, had been written about the case study as a research method since the 1960s, when it had virtually vanished from view.

At first, this process began as a painstaking review of the abstracts of half a dozen clinical psychology or psychotherapy journals, and library catalogues for books on the case study method, from 1970 to the mid-1990s. After a year of this effort, during which I was assisted by several graduate research assistants, it was clear that my sense that few case studies were being published was clearly correct. Nevertheless, we discovered two things that would greatly expedite our efforts. First, we learned that a psychologist in England, D. B. Bromley (1986), had published a book, *The Case Study Method in Clinical Psychology and Related Disciplines*, in which he essentially argued for the very point I had come to understand: Case studies are the lifeblood of the profession and needed to be revived in the discipline. Second, we discovered with the help of the American Psychological Association's (APA's) PsycINFO staff that it was possible to efficiently search for *clinical case reports* in the database as a "TYPE" of publication. Ironically, "TYPE" of publication was aptly dubbed a "submerged field" in the abstract notation for a publication, and so searching for either *case-study* or *clinical case report* in the primary search box of PsycINFO did not bring up any of these studies except in the rare instance that those terms were actually written in the title or abstract itself. (Interestingly, the PsycINFO staff had reserved the term *case study* for studies of a nonclinical nature.)

The power of the computer age was never more evident in my experience. Now what had taken a year to do for half a dozen journals could be done in just a few minutes for the entire psychological abstracts database of more than 1,000 journals! We also discovered rather quickly that in the absence of any development of the case study method as a legitimate research methodology, the PsycINFO staff had designated a very wide variety of publications as clinical case studies. It seemed that any clinically oriented article that contained even a few paragraphs of a case vignette was labeled a "clinical case report." There were many essentially theoretical articles classified as clinical case reports that fit this description. Also, articles on new therapeutic techniques would contain a few clinical vignettes as illustration of the technique. We also discovered for ourselves what Bromley (1986) had reported in his book: The profession of medicine, whose scientific status clinical psychology yearned to emulate, had never stopped using the case study method, and psychiatry in particular published hundreds of psychopharmacology case studies a year demonstrating novel uses of or reactions to various drugs. These were generally only a page or two in length and provided almost no information about the person being treated, focusing instead on the history of the drug used and the immediate effects thereof.

Because Bromley (1986) proposed some well-thought-out quality standards for case studies in clinical psychology, using what he called the *quasi-judicial method* (see below), we decided as a first step to attempt to ascertain the number of currently published case studies in the journal literature that even approximated Bromley's standards. At that time, 1998, there were about 500,000 clinical citations in the PsycINFO database. Of these, there were 22,575 (4.5%) clinical case reports; 13,645 of these were treatment reports, and 9,462 were psychopathology reports. We then selected individual diagnostic categories—for example, depression or schizophrenia—and searched for cases by theoretical model. A team of four graduate students and myself examined the PsycINFO database for clinical case reports on schizophrenia (R. B. Miller, 1999). Initially, 386 clinical case reports were found. However, 326 were determined to be only brief, one- or two-page clinical vignettes used to support a theoretical or clinical argument. Of the remaining 60 clinical case reports, only 44 could legitimately be considered as attempting to be comprehensive case studies, and of these 44 only about

6 of the clinical case reports came close to meeting the standards Bromley set. The other 38 clinical case reports had key content areas missing, such as the patient's developmental history, socioeconomic background, description of the therapeutic context and the therapist's training, or frank discussion of the difficulties in the treatment. It is interesting that none of the 44 better clinical case reports were published in APA clinical or professionally oriented journals (*Journal of Abnormal Psychology*, *Journal of Consulting and Clinical Psychology*, and *Journal of Professional Psychology*, *Journal of Counseling Psychology*, or *Journal of Family Psychology*). In fact, this is true not only for the topic of schizophrenia but also across the board. Between the years 1967 and 1998, only 25 clinical case reports were published collectively in those five journals that might be reasonably considered to be attempts at a comprehensive narrative case study. (This survey of the PsycINFO database for 1967 to 1999 excluded psychopharmacology; neuropsychology; and $N = 1$ behavioral experimental case studies, which are often extremely brief and narrowly focused.)

We followed up this work with a similar study of the published case studies (clinical case reports) on depression. We found a similar pattern and then determined that given the relatively small number of reasonably good clinical case studies on any given clinical problem area, it would be feasible to create a clinical case study archive in which we attempted to collect copies of all the reasonably good published case studies relevant to clinical work. Currently, the Saint Michael's College Durrick Library has a collection of more than 350 clinical case reports and 125 books that are case collections. (See Appendix A for a listing of these publications.) These are the cases that were more than a one- or two-page clinical vignette, but most are far from meeting Bromley's (1986) standards for a quality comprehensive case study. The collection can be searched by age of client, sex, theoretical orientation of the therapy, and *Diagnostic and Statistical Manual of Mental Disorders* (American Psychiatric Association, 1994) diagnosis. The collection is still several years from being reasonably complete, and we expect that with the renewed interest in publishing case studies that has emerged in the last several years, it will be a continually growing collection. Nevertheless, it represents the beginning of a new research capability in clinical psychology and a base from which to work in creating higher standards for comprehensive clinical case studies in psychology. Eventually, students and practitioners will be able to go to the archive and find several cases that discuss working with a given particular (or at least a similar) problem from the clinical perspective of interest to the student (e.g., psychodynamic, family systems, cognitive, humanistic). If such cases are not there, it will indicate to the student a need to write up his or her own work with such a case, to fill a void in our literature. This dovetails nicely with one of the features of our graduate program in clinical psychology where students may do a case study as thesis research. In this way, the archive will become even more complete and useful to students and practitioners.

In addition to those cases for which copyright permission has been obtained for inclusion in the archive, we also list in the electronic library catalogue cases we selected that were already in the libraries' journal holdings. A separate list is kept of the cases that we selected but for which we were unable to obtain permission to copy from the publisher (these are included in Appendix A but listed with a double asterisk [**]). A second list of cases includes classic or well-known cases that have been recommended by experts from the various theoretical orientations to psychotherapy as exemplary illustrations of those approaches (e.g., in Corsini & Wedding, 1995, and Gurman & Messer, 1995). These cases may or may not be problem-solving focused and are not searchable through the library electronic catalogue as they are not part of the formal case study archive at this time (see Appendix B).

HISTORY AND PHILOSOPHY OF THE CASE STUDY

The case study has a long and venerable history extending back more than 2,000 years in medicine and 700 or 800 years in both the common-law and moral casuistry traditions of Europe. In fact, Bromley (1986) noted that in contrast to clinical psychology and other mental health professions in the latter half of the 20th century, medicine did not abandon the case study as a serious form of scientific investigation even as it adopted more experimental and quantitative research methods. Our own examination of the PsycINFO database confirms Bromley's observation. By far the greatest number of published case studies in the past 50 years involve psychotropic medications, neuropsychology, or other areas of medical–psychological interface.

Over the past 30 years, a series of articles and monographs written by distinguished psychologists from widely disparate theoretical orientations have developed a comprehensive and compelling albeit contrarian argument defending the traditional clinical case study (or newer improved versions of it) as a legitimate, even "scientific" research method for professional psychology (Bromley, 1977, 1986; Edelson, 1988; Edwards, 1996, 1998; R. Elliott, 2002; Fishman, 1999; Hilliard, 1993; Hoshmand, 1988, 1992; Klumpner & Frank, 1991; Levine, 1974, 1980; Messer & McCann, in press; Runyan, 1982; Schneider, 1998; Spence, 1992, 1993). Despite the fact that these authors had developed their views on the importance of case study research from diverse perspectives (including cognitive–behavioral, phenomenological, hermeneutic, psychoanalytic, life history, community/systems, and experimental–developmental psychology), they offered remarkably similar rationales for restoring the case study to its former prominence as a vehicle for reporting clinical observations, exploring theory, and documenting advances in professional effectiveness. Furthermore, their recommendations for improving the case study method were also quite similar and go a long way toward answering the most frequent complaints against it concerning sources of bias, generalizability of findings, and validity. Renewed interest in the case study method has come from three quite divergent quarters: the behavioral $N = 1$ case method of experimental research liberalized to accommodate cognitive–behavioral therapies (Edwards, 1996; M. B. Shapiro, 1966), practitioner-oriented training (Fishman, 1999; Peterson & Peterson, 1997; Schon, 1987, 1987/1992), and postmodern philosophy of science (Hoshmand & Polkinghorne, 1992; Manicus & Secord, 1983; Toulmin, 1990).

As practitioners began to design their own training programs in professional psychology, attention began to be paid to what clinicians actually did and how they thought and made decisions. Stripped of the requirements and expectations that they were doing "applied science," it became quite evident that the central feature of what they did was case-by-case problem solving. Professional work begins with cases and ends with cases. In between, one may find theory, generalizations, reviews of scientific research, discussion of moral or political dilemmas, or simply comparisons with other cases. One becomes a professional by learning to work with, analyze and understand, discuss, critique, supervise, and, ultimately, teach about cases. This is true whether the case is an individual, a family, an organization, or a community.

This being so, research that is based on group designs that uses statistical evaluations to express group data is conceivably as much as an impediment as a contributor to progress in the profession. No matter how conclusive the findings in a controlled study, it always remains an open question (i.e., a case-by-case judgment) as to how such data ought to be related to any given case. One must always evaluate whether the case is a sufficient match with the population studied and how the inevitable differences between the experimental conditions and the actual clinical situation will affect the applicability of the findings. The contextual complexity of a real case always carries with it the likelihood that in the final clinical decision of what to do, the factors found to be operative in the controlled study will be trumped by the many unique or distinct contextual elements in the real world (uncontrolled) case.

This factor of context was a natural link to the emerging postmodern philosophy of psychology and social science that began to make its presence felt in psychology during the last 20 years of the 20th century. As I discussed in chapter 4, this movement was grounded in both the analytical philosophy of J. L. Austin and Ludwig Wittgenstein and the existential–phenomenological and hermeneutic continental philosophy of Dilthey, Husserl, and Heidegger. It questioned the ultimate authority of the scientific method to yield universally valid, culturally value-free truth claims. Particularly in what they liked to call the *human sciences*, these philosophers encouraged us to pay attention to and be grounded in the everyday experiences of life and the pragmatic tasks of everyday living. Human social behavior was seen as always communicative of narrative meaning and resistant to all attempts to reduce it to mechanistic physicalist laws. The meaning of human behavior required that it be understood in its full historical and social context and not simply explained as though it were a phenomenon in the basic natural sciences. Their mantra is that the methods of a discipline must be suited to the subject matter and tasks of that discipline. The methods of the physical sciences had no automatic entitlement to hegemony in the social or psychological domains.

In this postmodern view, meaningful communicative behavior is a creative process for all the participants in a psychological investigation. Meanings are often ambiguous, concealed, and even at times ineffable. There is nothing comparable in psychology to what Charles Taylor (1973) called the "brute data" of the natural sciences (except, of course, in pure physiological psychology, in which one works with biochemical processes). Consequently, this new philosophy of science concludes that psychologists must develop their own methods of research suitable to the subject matter (i.e., meaningful communicative behavior). The renewed interest in narrative psychology, life history research, psychobiography, qualitative research, and the case study method in clinical psychology are all a reflection of this shift away from a logical positivist conception of psychological science.

The older, pre-1960s case study methodology owed much to Freud and his early followers (most of whom were trained in medicine), who relied heavily on case studies as a means of communicating their observations, theories, and principles of practice. The psychoanalytic case study became the primary vehicle for communicating advances in theory and practice, both within psychoanalysis and in competing schools of psychotherapy. Through the work of Henry Murray (1938) at the Harvard Psychological Clinic, the psychoanalytic case study approach found its way into academia and was blended with other forms of psychological assessment. Murray influenced a whole generation of personologists trained in life history research (McAdams, 1994; Runyan, 1982; White, 1975) before World War II and in the period immediately after the war.

It is perhaps more surprising to discover that currently even psychoanalytic journals publish relatively few case studies, preferring more theoretical articles. In fact, the journal *Modern Psychoanalysis* was founded in the early 1990s with the express purpose of publishing comprehensive case studies—which, the editors noted, had nearly disappeared from the psychoanalytic journal literature. The Committee on Scientific Activities of the American Psychoanalytic Association concurrently reported their recommendations for improving the quality of psychoanalytic case studies (Klumpner & Frank, 1991). Edelson (1988) and Meadow (1996) have both offered carefully considered philosophical arguments in support of the scientific legitimacy of some versions of the psychoanalytic case study method in response to Grunbaum's (1984) critique of the logic of psychoanalytic arguments. In 1988, the Washington School of Psychiatry's journal, *Psychiatry: Interpersonal and Biological Processes*, began offering a regular new section of the journal devoted to case studies.

The turn toward theoretical writing that uses only brief clinical vignettes to illustrate theoretical interpretations or to illustrate clinical technique was not restricted to the psychoanalytic approach to psychotherapy in the latter half of the 20th century. Despite Rogers's (1942) early use of verbatim transcripts in his case studies, and Yalom's (1989) success with the bestseller *Love's Executioner*, the humanistic psychology journal literature followed the same general trend away from case studies during the latter half of the 20th century. There have been recent calls, however, for more and better case studies from this quarter as well (Edwards, 1998; Schneider, 1998). A new *Journal of Case Studies*, edited by Michel Hersen, appeared in 2001, geared particularly toward case formulations from a cognitive–behavioral perspective. This follows on Persons's (1995) warning that students being trained particularly in Boulder model doctoral programs to do manualized psychotherapies seem to lack the ability to synthesize information on individual clients and formulate treatment plans suited to the needs of individual clients.

Individuals associated with calls for a more radical evaluation of the knowledge base of professional psychology (Hoshmand & Polkinghorne, 1992; Howard, 1993; Levine, 1980) have argued for the importance of developing a narrative approach to applied areas of psychology. Although these arguments go beyond simply encouraging the publication of case studies (by questioning the logical positivist philosophy of science so often espoused by mainstream psychology), they do in fact include this very recommendation, because case studies are by their very nature narrative accounts of psychological phenomena, processes, and interventions. Hoshmand (1992) argued that not only is the case study an excellent vehicle for communicating professional knowledge, but also the writing of case studies is an excellent pedagogical device in the training of professional psychologists. Comprehensive and systematic case studies prepare students to integrate and synthesize information and think critically and creatively about the work they do. This has been found to be true for not only students writing case studies but also those who read them. The transfer of practical know-how from the case study to the trainee is far greater than from the theoretical or research article, even when the theory or research is about practice itself. It did not take long for those interested in the promotion of professional training as distinct from scientific training in psychological research to link up with those in psychology wishing to promote a new philosophy of science and research methodology for the discipline (e.g., R. B. Miller, 2000; Peterson & Peterson, 1997; Trierweiler & Stricker, 1992).

STANDARDS FOR IMPROVING
THE CASE STUDY METHOD

Despite his status as an experimentally trained developmental psychologist, Bromley (1977, 1986) nevertheless has concluded that a well-conducted and argued traditional case study in clinical psychology was potentially as objective and valid as any form of scientific research in psychology. He recognized that for all its scientific emphasis, modern medicine had never abandoned the case study method and that Western jurisprudence rests on a foundation of 500 years of case law that could serve as a powerful model for improving the case study method in psychology. Thus inspired, Bromley formulated guidelines for what he called the "quasi-judicial" approach to clinical case studies. He saw the case study as a highly flexible instrument for the complexities of real-world psychosocial problems and systematic efforts to ameliorate such problems. His quasi-judicial method uses the Western legal system's long-standing traditions for establishing the truth about human events and interactions as a model for evaluating facts, explanatory hypotheses, and the outcomes of cases. Bromley argued for the development of a case law tradition in psychology that will permit the evaluation of new cases in the light of past ones, using generally accepted standards of evidence and argument. Over time, this model would expect that multiple case studies would be published in support of innovative or controversial methods of treatment, often from different sources and geographic areas. This echoes Levine's (1974) recommendations for modifying the scientific method with adversarial and evidentiary methods drawn from the legal system.

A central feature of such an approach will be what the philosopher Coady (1992) referred to as the criteria for the *coherence* and *cohesion* of testimonial evidence (see chap. 5 for a discussion of Coady's work on testimony). Although the standards for evaluating the comprehensive narrative case study have yet to be fully developed, a sufficient consensus has already emerged in the literature to suggest that such standards might be quite readily agreed on, as in R. Elliott et al.'s (1999) efforts to create consensus standards for qualitative research in general. At a 1999 invited symposium that I chaired (R. B. Miller, 1999), a consensus emerged among leading advocates for the case study (D. B. Bromley, D. Fishman, D. J. A. Edwards, D. P. Spence, and L. T. Hoshmand) that the field was nearing the point where it could generate consensus standards similar to those Bromley (1986) originally articulated. Bromley's (1986) method views the case study as first and foremost a report of an episode of real-life problem solving—an account of the circumstances in a person's life, what was done to change those circumstances, and the outcomes of those efforts. Only secondarily is the case study about the development or validation of theories. This is a critical step away from what makes case studies so objectionable to the scientific community. Although Bromley (1986) used the language of problem-solving, the quasi-judicial case study is ultimately about the development of what we have been calling *practitioner knowledge* or what Aristotle would call *phronesis*.

Bromley's (1986) approach calls for a comprehensive and systematic case study that is structured to consider 24 content areas drawn from multiple theoretical perspectives: developmental, biological, environmental, intrapersonal, and family systems (e.g., identifying information, present circumstances, life history, social and economic circumstances, family dynamics, interests, and abilities). Case studies are to be conducted following six basic rules and 10 procedural steps for evaluating the evidence and explanations (arguments) of the case.

The basic rules include the following:

1. The psychologist must demonstrate scrupulous honesty and accuracy in the reporting of details of the case.
2. The case report must include a clear statement of the aims and purposes of the case study.
3. The final report must include an assessment of the extent to which the aims and objectives have been reached.
4. The investigator must provide evidence of her or his competence and training in clinical interviewing of the sort that would promote a long-term personal relationship with the subject of the case study;
5. It is necessary to consider the individual in an *ecological*, or social systems context.
6. The report should be written up in good, clear, simple English that is free of jargon and yet interesting and compelling to read.

In his 10 procedural steps for evaluating case explanations, Bromley (1986) used the legal notion of a *prima facie* explanation to show how reasoning about cases proceeds. This *prima facie* explanation is developed after an initial review of the background information (evidence), and then evidence is collected and evaluated in support of the *prima facie* explanation and compared with evidence that might support a different explanation of the case. The internal coherence of each explanation is examined, as is its correspondence with known facts about the world that are relevant to the case. Following these steps, the most likely explanation serves as a basis for designing interventions, and follow-up evidence is sought to see how successful the intervention was in addressing the original problem.

Bromley's (1986) approach also emphasizes that case description must not be confounded with theoretical interpretations and that the case investigators and authors must clearly identify their theoretical orientation and social, political, or moral stake in the case. All important features of the case must be supported with evidence that meets the standard of the "best evidence" rules of civil courts. Actual excerpts from written records, case interviews, and the like are an important element here. Wherever possible, it is helpful to have multiple perspectives incorporated into the case report (e.g., another health care professional, a significant other to the client, a supervisor, perhaps even the client). Supervisors or professional colleagues familiar with the case can provide an important interrater reliability to the therapist's interpretation of the process.

Finally, it is hoped that as the field of psychology builds a body of quality comprehensive clinical case reports, multiple case research will be published and that it will be possible to begin seeing patterns of similarities and differences among cases that permit a kind of case law to be established in psychology on how various cases are to be most effectively understood and handled. These "laws" would not be regarded as fixed and universal but, as in the legal system, as providing guidance and instruction to professionals tackling new cases. Local conditions or unique features of a case are always possible and would require modification in the case law. In different jurisdictions (read: *communities*), different case law may be required.

Both Fishman (1999) and Edwards (1998) have noted that in a more hermeneutic or phenomenological case study the emphasis may be less on problem solving and more on problem description or the theoretical elaboration of psychological experiences and constructs. Although much of what Bromley (1986) suggested would hold as guidelines for these case studies, some changes would be necessitated. There might be greater attention to the assessment phase and less to the "solution" aspects of the quasi-judicial case study. Different kinds of case studies will have slightly different standards, but all would share, for example, the six basic rules cited above. In all cases, the reliability and validity of the evidence must be examined, but there will be different methods for determining reliability and validity in a phenomenological study than in a pragmatic one. Fishman (1999) conducted a comprehensive analysis of the different approaches to case studies and advocated for a "pragmatic case study" approach that, like Bromley's (1986), is focused on problem solving rather than theory building and incorporates systematic quantitative measures of outcome wherever possible. His approach is particularly useful in considering case studies in professional psychology involving group, organizational, or community interventions, as contrasted with individual or family psychotherapy cases. Fishman and Miller (2001) proposed an on-line case study database of both narrative and pragmatic case studies that would allow for the accumulation and dissemination of clinical knowledge on an international scale.

It is one of the virtues of Bromley's work that it has been cited favorably by psychodynamic, phenomenological, cognitive, and community/ systems psychology advocates as a basic framework for a return to case study research.

CASE STUDY GUIDELINES

Based on the early work of Menninger (1962) on the psychiatric assessment interview, and Bromley's recommendations, as interpreted by Hoshmand (1992) and Fishman (1999), the following outline is offered for the comprehensive narrative psychotherapy case study that is viewed as an endeavor that demonstrates and develops clinical (practitioner) knowledge.

Introduction

1. *Identifying Client Information.* The client should be described in a preliminary manner indicating age, gender, and other identifying information including schooling or work status, socioeconomic class, religious affiliation, marital status, racial or ethnic identity, and prior treatment. The process of obtaining informed consent for the publication of the case study should be indicated.
2. *Identifying Therapist Information.* Note should be made of the therapist's age, gender, remarkable physical characteristics, training, theoretical orientation guiding the work, experience with similar cases, personality characteristics that would influence the process of therapy, and moral values and political views that might influence therapeutic or interpersonal relationships.
3. *Treatment Setting.* The office or setting where the work takes place should be fully described to present the context of the relationship. How was the client referred, what information or records were available, and what other staff were involved in treatment or planning of treatment? The length of treatment, number of sessions, duration of sessions, auxiliary treatments, record keeping of sessions, and supervision of treatment are all important factors.
4. *Presenting Problem.* The presenting problem and recent life circumstances that figure into the emergence of the problem are discussed. This should lead to a consideration of the initial treatment problem focus and how it is connected to the presenting problem. What makes this an important case study? What does it demonstrate or elucidate?

Exploration of the Problem and Setting a Treatment Target or Goal

1. The problem focus must be explored in both a developmental and psychosocial context to see the fuller meaning of the problem and to understand how the problem fits into the picture

of the individual's life as a whole. This will generally mean examining the following areas:

a. Family history
b. Schooling/work history
c. Competencies/hobbies/skills and talents
d. Peer relationships/groups
e. Medical history
f. Primary conflicts/defenses/self-schemas/coping mechanisms
g. Relationship formed with therapist during exploratory phase of the work. Trust, openness, resistance to help, depth of rapport, and so on, are important indicators of personality and defensiveness.

2. The above information is gathered for the purpose of understanding the problem in preparation for promoting growth, change, or problem resolution. In most cases it will fall short of a comprehensive life history, because it is focused on a clinical intervention or problem episode. It is important for the therapist to draw this information together into interpretive themes or schema (consistent with the guiding theoretical conception of the work) that allows for identification of the important psychological and interpersonal patterns of functioning in the world that typify this individual and contribute to the existing problem. These interpretive summaries (as in White, 1975) are subject to criticism in terms of both the cohesion (internal consistency) and coherence (external consistency) with common sense and clinical knowledge as a whole.

3. The information should be presented descriptively before it is interpreted to allow readers who use a different theoretical framework to develop their own hypotheses about the case. For this reason, it is critical for authors to present detailed information in as many of the basic areas identified above as possible, even if such information is not considered germane to the particular theoretical model guiding the therapist's work. In this way, cases can inform practice by allowing practitioners to examine cases from multiple perspectives and consider the power of competing explanations in the real-world problems addressed by professional practice. Obviously, a classical analyst will provide more information on early childhood experiences and memories than will a cognitive–behaviorist or experiential therapist, but these latter therapists ought to provide at least some detailed developmental history. This is the meaning of a systematic or comprehensive case study. Similarly, because it is conceivable that family dynamics

might influence the outcome of any therapy case, all case studies ought to report family dynamics even if these were not the primary focus of intervention.

4. During the early years of the mental hygiene, child guidance, and community mental health clinics the use of interdisciplinary teams that brought together psychiatric, psychological, and social work expertise was a regular staffing pattern, and cases were often approached in this manner. Murray's (1938) approach at the Harvard Psychological Clinic also used a team approach to evaluating and writing case studies. Contemporary integrative and eclectic approaches to treatment (e.g., Lazarus, 1995; Prochaska, 1995) also capture this notion of considering multiple possible explanations in any individual case, followed by a strategic decision as to the best possible intervention to attempt given the case context. Practical demands of availability of resources, degree of resistance, and unique characteristics of the case may dictate treatment strategy as much or more than the therapist's initial theoretical framework.

Quality of Evidence

1. In general, there are four sources of information in a narrative case study. The first two are nearly always present:
   a. the client's self-reports
   b. the therapist's observations of the client in the therapeutic relationship

The second group is often present in varying degrees:
   c. information from interviewing significant others (through their self-report and/or observation of same)
   d. other professionals' opinions or documents

2. It is generally agreed that important claims in a case study should be backed up whenever possible by a process of *triangulation* (Sherwood, 1969) in which evidence is presented from multiple sources (e.g., client self-report, therapist observations, and reports from significant others).

3. In the U.S. legal system, witnesses must be qualified before they can testify. Their testimony may be challenged on a number of grounds, for example, their honesty, conflicts of interest, insufficient knowledge of the pertinent events, and inconsistency. Whenever a therapist takes a client's self-report as valid for critical information in the case study, the reasons for considering the client a dependable or reliable witness should be indicated. When self-report is interpreted as indicating information other than its apparent or face content, reasons should be given

in the report. This may include showing contradictions in the self-report, defensiveness during the interview, and conflicts between the self-report and other sources of information in the case study. Inferences drawn from the case information should be differentiated from the basic information itself, and the reasoning behind the inferences should be detailed.

4. Expert witnesses in legal proceedings are held to higher standards than general witnesses, as forensic psychologists are well aware. Therapists writing case studies are essentially acting as expert witnesses in reporting a case, and one should expect to find in the case study support for their claim to be an expert witness. In other words, the therapist's qualifications to be an expert witness (education, training, and experience) should be documented. The kinds and quality of the records kept during the time the work was undertaken, as well as the nature and extent of supervision available to the therapist, are also important factors in weighing the quality of the evidence. Many kinds of therapeutic work do not lend themselves to video or audio recording. It would be unwise to insist that all cases reported have such records, but certainly detailed case notes that indicate content and process of the interviews would be a minimal documentation requirement for most work to be published.

5. The case study consists of a variety of different kinds of claims:
   a. Factual—the straightforward description of the actions and events in the individual's life.
   b. Inferences (low-level inferences of likely case circumstances drawn from the information in (a).
   c. Interpretations (higher level inferences concerning the meaning, pattern, or structure of the facts and circumstances).
   d. Assumptions from everyday knowledge about the reasons for, intentions, and purposes of various actions are relevant to the case.
   e. Theoretical assumptions drawn from one's theory of personality or psychotherapy that are relevant to the case.
   f. Conjectures or speculations about the case circumstances or explanation.
   g. Missing information that could not be determined or areas of confusion that remain despite one's efforts to sort out the case.

6. Each of these sorts of claims requires a different sort of argumentation or proof (Bromley, 1986; based on Toulmin, 1958).

Factual claims require observations or documentation via testimony physical evidence, whereas interpretations require a demonstration of reasoning or logic.

7. It is critical that the author of a case study also show a keen sensitivity to the degree of certainty attached to various claims and that knowledge claims be sufficiently qualified. It is important to indicate the degree of confidence one has in various claims: *highly probable, probable, possible, improbable, highly improbable, impossible,* and so on. These terms reflect the uncertainties of working the real world, and authors must show an awareness that various sorts of claims not only require different methods of proof but may also be made with different degrees of certainty. Terms such as *probable, likely, impossible,* and so on, should be attached to the key statements in the case study. For example, under most circumstances claims made about the current life functioning of an individual can be made with far more certainty than claims about events or psychological phenomena in the distant past. Claims about specific unconscious contents generally involve a higher level of theoretical assumptions and inferences than do claims about conscious experience or behavioral coping mechanisms and so require a more complex argument as well as, other things being equal, a somewhat reduced level of certainty. This reduction in certainty might be countered in the event that the account of unconscious content leads to a startlingly accurate prediction or outcome not anticipated by the seemingly more certain conscious or behavioral observations.

Therapeutic Process

1. A detailed account is offered of what was actually done and said in the treatment. This should include a time line of the treatment and critical events that occurred in the client's life over the course of treatment. This section addresses the following sorts of questions: How did the treatment unfold? What difficulties were encountered, and how were they dealt with? What seemed to be the critical points or junctures in the treatment? What were the therapist's emotional and cognitive reactions to the work (countertransference), and how were these handled? Was supervision sought, and what sort of recommendations came out of the supervisory process?

2. Transcripts of therapeutic dialogue are very useful in illustrating and bringing to life the quality of the work. Although one cannot reproduce lengthy excerpts of dialogue, it would

be appropriate to represent the nature of the dialogue at key points in the therapeutic process.

Outcome and Follow-Up

1. Narrative case studies often conclude with a statement of improvement in symptoms or specific areas of life functioning. Rarely does one learn about how the individual is functioning in the broad areas of concern addressed by the comprehensive psychosocial discussion of the problem. Outcome should be related back to the interpretive themes identified by the initial assessment. Did these themes remain central to the case, or did they change? Often, a new set of goals replaces the original goals of the therapy, and extensive follow-up would be desirable to see how these various factors played themselves out. How do significant others view these changes, and what about other professionals involved in the case? Are there important clinical or ethical problems that were revealed by this work that remain unresolved?

2. The cohesion and coherence of the therapeutic process report ultimately must be considered, just as earlier in the case study the coherence and cohesiveness of the problem assessment were examined. How internally consistent is this section of the report, and does it match up well with one's understanding of the therapeutic process as previously described in the literature or one's own experience with other or similar cases?

Discussion

This section addresses the following questions:

1. What should be learned from this case professionally, and how applicable is it to other situations and contexts?
2. How would one provide differently services to a similar case in the future? What made some of the problems harder to resolve or intractable?
3. How does the case compare to other published cases in the case law literature, to similar cases in the therapist's experience, and to the findings in empirical studies?
4. Does the case suggest any revisions in the guiding conception or theoretical position that provided the original framework of the case?
5. Finally, what has been learned about the case study process itself from this report, and how might case studies be done more effectively in the future?

CONFIDENTIALITY AND ETHICAL CONCERNS ABOUT CASE STUDIES

Some people have suggested that the demise of published comprehensive case studies was in part due to concerns over psychologists or their publishing outlets being sued for breach of confidentiality. Whether this is in fact the historical explanation, it is imperative that the confidentiality question be addressed fully if the case study method is to be resuscitated. The publication of comprehensive case studies provides professional psychologists with the kind of detailed understanding of the context and process of psychological practices that is critical to the knowledge base of the profession, particularly for training and educational purposes. The potential benefit to the field is well articulated in the preceding discussion, and it should be noted that the ultimate beneficiary of such improved training is one's clients. It is because of this benefit that the APA *Ethical Principles of Psychologists and Code of Conduct* (APA, 2002) has long recognized that case material may be shared in scientific and professional presentations so long as either the client consented in writing to this disclosure or the identity of the client is protected (see Standards 4.04[b] and 4.07; APA, 2002). However, the more detailed the case report, the greater the number of case reports published, and the wider the audience for case reports (as in a Web-based archive), the greater the potential risk that one or more readers may be able to infer or deduce a client's identity from the disguised material presented in a given case. This, then, is a true ethical dilemma, for the pursuit of knowledge to assist in the amelioration of human problems for society as a whole runs the risk of harming individual members of that society. It would be unwise in trying to resolve these two conflicting moral goods to prematurely choose to sacrifice one for the other. Rather, one should choose a judicious exploration of the specific contexts in which the decision must be made and develop ethical guidelines that would be tailored or attuned to the situations that arise in publishing specific case studies (Jonsen & Toulmin, 1988). This should be one of the responsibilities of the editorial board of journals that regularly publish case studies, and what follows is an attempt to anticipate some of the critical issues and possible solutions that need to be considered. The field is not advanced by claiming either that case studies are so invaluable that psychologists just have to accept as inevitable certain sorts of harm inflicted on clients or that the potential harm to clients is so great that it requires discouraging the publication of all case studies.

Gavey and Braun (1997) examined the ethical dilemmas occasioned by the increase in reliance on case study materials in professional psychology and believe that there are two primary areas of ethical concern. The first is protecting privacy (confidentiality) and is covered in Standards 4.04(b) and 4.07 of the APA *Ethical Principles of Psychologists and Code of Conduct* (APA, 2002). They noted that disguising a client's identity by altering identifying information in the case study may not be a foolproof method and that it would seem wise to also consider asking for informed consent from the client. This, however, raises the second, and more thorny, issue of the *kind* of informed consent to obtain. Should it be consent to participate in research (Standard 8.02) or simply consent that a case report concerning oneself be published in a certain form (Standard 4.07)?

To answer this question, it is helpful to try to anticipate the sort of potential harm to clients who might be at risk through the publication of a case report and that any rules or precautions would be designed to prevent. Most obvious would be the emotional sense of betrayal and vulnerability that might be engendered by the client reading her or his life's problems detailed in print. This reaction might be obviated by a prior consent, or it might ensue despite the fact that he or she consented at an earlier time. This problem might be lessened by having the client read the report prior to publication and by providing the client with several sessions to work through any difficulties with the report. One might even allow for the client's views to be incorporated into the published article. (In fact, in a slightly different context, White, 1975, indicated that this sort of dialogue between research participants and investigators was a regular feature of the personality case studies done at the Harvard Psychological Clinic under the direction of Henry Murray.)

A second sort of potential harm is far more troubling. This is the possibility that someone who knows the client or situation will, despite the disguised information, recognize the client (or a third party) in such a case study, learn from it information that they had not heretofore known, and then use the information in a manner harmful to the client (or a third party). Perhaps the information can be used to pursue a civil or criminal legal action against the client or cause a financial hardship, loss of employment, or loss of reputation for the client. In Standard 8.05, "Dispensing with Informed Consent," the Code of Conduct lists the sort of potentially harmful consequences that might follow the disclosure of confidential information: "risk of criminal or civil liability or damage [to] their financial standing, employability or reputation" (APA, 2002, pp. 1069–1070). Should any of these consequences actually materialize, the author and publisher of the report could both be potentially found at fault.

It should be noted that although many cases do have such potentially explosive elements, some do not. There will be some cases where the precautions discussed below will not be necessary. Unfortunately, even where a case contains "dangerous information," the personal or relational patterns of behavior described are relatively common in contemporary society, and it is increasingly difficult for a reader of a case report to even begin to narrow the field of possible individuals who might be the subject of the case study. Secret affairs, hidden addictions, fraudulent business practices, physical and sexual abuse, and so on, have become commonplace. Indeed, in some instances clients may be happy to have their life written about and feel some sense of satisfaction in having contributed to helping others who have suffered similar difficulties.

Nevertheless, given the nature of the work psychologists do, there also will be many cases where the consequences of a client being identified are so severe that it would seem unwise to risk in any way the disclosure of confidential information, no matter how well disguised. Gavey and Braun (1997) made a strong case for the position that one can never fully guarantee that information is sufficiently disguised to protect the client from being identified by all possible readers.

Neither is informed consent to publish a case study a complete solution to this dilemma. Gavey and Braun (1997) further suggested that the meaning to the client of being asked to give informed consent for participation in a case study is problematic. When would one ask for this consent: before or after the service? Would a person feel free to withhold such consent while asking for help? Or would the treatment process be altered by having asked a new client for such consent? The answers to these questions seem to depend greatly on the nature of the case, the professional relationship, and other contextual factors that are very difficult to anticipate. The authors end with questions to be explored rather than answers.

Although there are many unanswered questions, there is little to be said for the position that the sort of comprehensive case studies being advocated for here would require informed consent to participate in research. These case reports are essentially systematic accounts of the critical elements in professional practice. Although they may in one sense serve the same purpose as traditional research in that they inform the profession, they do so in a manner that does not require that clients be asked to sign informed consent for participation in research. Practices in a profession evolve, and creativity in practice is a highly sought after, even necessary, professional attribute. Creative problem solving with clients must not be hamstrung by being categorized as experimental research. Practitioners are limited in their creative applications of accepted methods of treatment by malpractice liability and by the ethical standard to practice within their range of training and competency (APA Code of Conduct Standard 2.02; APA, 2002). It may often be prudent to require informed consent (in the sense of release of confidential, if disguised, information) for the publication of case material. It would appear that the most appropriate time to ask for such consent would be at the completion of service, and this will require clinical tact and diplomacy. Although it might seem preferable to request consent at the beginning of the clinical relationship, it is unlikely that such consent would be very effective in that it would come from a client who does not yet know the extent of what she or he will be disclosing and experiencing in the professional relationship. Furthermore, consent at the beginning of the professional relationship might distort the work to be done, or give the client a false sense of importance and leverage in that relationship. With some clients, it may not be possible to know how coercive such a request will feel to them, and therefore it might be exploitative of the professional relationship even to ask for permission to publish a report of the work. One might also risk a future professional relationship by asking for consent to publish at the completion of service, and so one will need to weigh this in the decision.

Gabbard (2000) and Gabbard & Williams (2001) have taken up this dilemma in the context of publishing psychoanalytic case studies. He discussed the pros and cons of using a "thick" disguise of a case versus requesting from the client informed consent to publish. He noted that psychoanalytic writers and publishers are about evenly split on the question of whether to require informed consent from the client prior to publication of a case study. He concurred with Gavey and Braun (1997) that it is difficult to know for sure whether sufficient identifying information has been removed from a case, especially as the range of potential readers increases from other psychotherapists to family, friends, neighbors, or other acquaintances of the client. He particularly cited the rise of the Internet as a profound new challenge to the writer's ability to disguise a case from all potential readers.

The use of the computers and searchable electronic databases to breach the confidentiality of a case study is well illustrated in the controversy created by Loftus and Guyer's (2002) investigation into the validity of a case of purported repressed memories published by Corwin and Olafson (1997). Corwin and Olafson wrote the case study with the intention of concealing the identity of the client and her family. However, at professional meetings Corwin showed videotapes of the case that inadvertently included the client's real first name and city of residence. Using these two scraps of information, and the fact that the written case narrative indicated that there had been a legal court case involving custody of the client as a child, Loftus and Guyer "searched a legal database with a handful of keywords, and found an appellate court case involving the client" (p. 32). These court records included the father's first name and the first initial of his last name. The narrative had also indicated that he was now deceased, and so Loftus and Guyer then searched Social Security death records and newspaper obituaries in the region of the country that had been identified on the videotape until they determined the father's full name. Using the father's name, they were able to find the mother's full name in the divorce records. This was all done in an attempt to determine the accuracy and validity of a case study on repressed memories and not with any intent to misuse the information in the case study to manipulate or harm the client. Yet if psychological researchers can breach the confidentiality of a case study for scholarly purposes, what is to prevent others with less lofty intentions from doing the same?

This being the case, it would seem to tip the scales back in the direction of requiring that authors of case studies obtain informed consent, so that in the event that harm results, the client was clearly informed of that possibility and agreed to take that risk. Gabbard, however, agreed with Gavey and Braun (1997) that such informed consent is itself fraught with difficulties and may not fully protect the client either. He noted that according to the psychoanalytic perspective everything that the client says during the psychoanalytic session is open to interpretation and analysis. Therefore, the client's conscious informed consent to have the case study published may be a reflection of the transference and/or the client's narcissism, which the therapist should analyze before accepting the informed consent at face value. In other words, the informed consent must include informing the client of the possible unconscious meaning of giving consent. Gabbard (2000) suggested that it would therefore be much better to ask for informed consent at the point of termination of treatment, when the client's unconscious conflicts are better understood by both the analyst and the client and when the meaning of the request is less likely to damage the treatment. He also recommended reducing the life history and contextual details revealed in the case study in favor of increased emphasis on the client's unconscious fantasies and dynamics as well as detailed examples of client–therapist dialogue to illustrate treatment techniques. Although the latter is certainly consistent with the publication of comprehensive quasi-judicial case studies, the former is not. The loss of context information would seriously limit the pragmatic usefulness of the case study to other clinicians from other perspectives. In the end, he concluded that there is no perfect solution that both completely protects client from all possible harm and allows the field to develop its knowledge base. Although the client's right to privacy and confidentiality must take precedence over scholarly advancement where harm is clearly foreseeable or severe, he also leaves open the possibility that, with the use of thick disguise, at least some cases could be published without requiring informed consent.

It is clear that not all professional work in psychology will be available for case reports; perhaps only a minority of clinical experiences will both warrant a case study (in terms of its value to the knowledge base of the profession) and safely and ethically permit of publication. Psychotherapists will have to find ways to communicate through the case reports they can write what they have learned in other cases as well but that they cannot, for ethical reasons, report in detail. As a profession, psychotherapists will have "unspeakable" truths (R. B. Miller, 1998) that they can pass along to their trainees in clinical wisdom and rubrics without being able to supply all the clinical data that warrant such claims. This is true of all professions and guilds. There *are* professional secrets.

Assuming that publication is not clearly untenable, the following steps should be considered in moving toward publication while reducing the risk of harm.

1. Obtain written consent for publication from the client after he or she has read the report and had the opportunity to ask

for changes. As discussed above, Gabbard (2000) noted this is not without potential negative consequences for the client and may compromise the long-term effectiveness of treatment even if it is requested after termination (were the client to return to treatment at a later time).

2. Submit the case study and a detailed list of the disguised material to a trusted clinical supervisor familiar with the community in which the work was done. The colleague would then evaluate (a) how well-disguised the material is and (b) whether the changes materially alter the integrity or logic of the case study. A statement from this reader would accompany the case study when it is submitted for publication. Published versions would indicate whether material has been altered and that such an independent review to protect confidentiality had been conducted.

3. One of the goals of the individuals advocating a return to case study research is to publish multiple case studies on a similar problem (Schneider, 1998), because of the greater utility in evaluating the generality or range of applicability of the methods discussed. Here it may be possible to discuss different aspects of each of the cases in a series in more or less detail so that no single case is given in all its details. This would limit the risk of any one client becoming recognized. For example, in a series of three cases involving a suicidal adolescent, one might describe the family background from the first case, the educational history and peer relationships from the second, and the immediate presenting clinical circumstances from the third. Although there is an obvious loss of information with this approach, it is still preferable to a common approach taken in textbooks of providing fictionalized accounts of cases based on combining information from several cases. Because one has no way of knowing in such instances what has been taken from a case and what stems from the creative imagination of the author, such cases should be differentiated from those with disguised elements or multiple cases presented in a coordinated manner. One should avoid fictionalized case reports, for they undermine the concept of case studies as reports of real-life problem solving.

4. Because the name of the author or therapist may be a critical piece of information to the reader of a case trying to identify a client, the publishing of cases under pseudonyms, anonymously, under the name of a research team, or as a panel of editors who reviewed the case (see below) might greatly reduce the risk of harm to the client in cases where other efforts are

insufficient. Although such reports would initially contribute less to the author's professional career advancement, it might be possible for the editors to affirm the identity of the author for certain purposes (e.g., tenure and promotion committees). Professional word-of-mouth communication would probably allow for a certain amount of recognition of such efforts without risking author identification in the wider reading public.

5. Should a case be published on-line, there is a need to take further precautions because of the likelihood of an increased readership and the ability to search electronic data for the specific information contained in cases. Limiting access to case studies on a Web site to persons with a professional or academic research interest would be one effective means of reducing risk. By reducing the access, one reduces the chance identifications of clients or searches of the Internet by people seeking to violate privacy rather than do serious psychological research. Users could also be asked to take a pledge of confidentiality not to use any information to harm another person, and the general public and undergraduates should have their access restricted to review articles, abstracts, cases published with explicit consent and little associated risk, or classic cases that have been republished.

6. Another alternative in cases where confidentiality issues are particularly thorny might be to pursue informed consent for a case to be published posthumously. Historical archives containing personal or government documents often have restrictions that certain papers cannot be opened for a specified number of years. One might have revealing case studies with important clinical knowledge that a therapist or client might consent to be published posthumously after a specified number of years. Although this is perhaps a fanciful idea, who knows what psychohistorians and professional practitioners of the future might be able to do with such data! As the years pass, chance identifications will certainly lessen, as will the likelihood of untoward consequences should identities be discovered.

THE LOGIC OF ARGUMENT IN THE CASE STUDY

Bromley (1986) relied heavily on Toulmin's (1958) work on the logic of informal argument (formal argument being mathematical or symbolic logic) to evaluate the validity of inferences made from the data of a case study. The inferences provide the explanation of the case: what is the critical problem to be solved, what needs to be done, and how to account for the outcome.

(It is remarkable how many different aspects of Toulmin's work in philosophy have emerged in the psychological literature that calls for a change in how psychologists conceptualize their field.) Toulmin (1958) devoted a book to explicating everyday argumentation, and Bromley (1986) devoted a chapter in his case study book to summarizing its applicability to the case study. These should be consulted by individuals writing case studies, as the process is only outlined here. Bromley (1986, p. 195) presented Toulmin's (1958) six-step logic of argumentation

1. The *Claim* is an assertion of a fact, an inference or an interpretation of the facts. Any component of the case may give rise to assertions that need to be established by evidence or argument: the current circumstances, symptom picture, family history, personality or behavior patterns, opportunities for growth, and so on. Most of the case presented will be noncontroversial or peripheral, and these assertions may be considered equivalent to those in court that are stipulated as true rather than requiring proof. Arguments need be made for the essential aspects of the case only where a debatable interpretation of events or behaviors is made. Where the approach is outside of the mainstream, or where there are clear theoretical differences about how to work with a particular problem, there is a particular need that an argument be put forth.

2. The *Data* are the evidence for a claim or assertion that may be any of the kinds of evidence outlined above. One looks for the "best evidence," so if a client reports a health- or school-related problem, one would prefer to actually see the documents from the health center or school. If the behavior of significant others figures critically in the case formulation, one is encouraged to interview these individuals directly wherever this does not interfere with the clinical relationship.

3. The *Warrant* for the evidence is what makes the evidence legitimate to use to back up the Claim made in the case. Thus, one might say, for example, that the assertion of a learning disability was made on the basis of the individual having been assessed by a qualified school psychologist who used the appropriate tests that yielded a given score or, similarly, that the history of psychiatric hospitalizations, psychotropic drug prescriptions, and active hallucinations in the interview are all consistent with a diagnosis of schizophrenia.

4. The *Qualifier* of the Claim assesses the degree of confidence in the initial assertion given the evidence and its warrant. Thus, one might say the claim is possible, probable, highly probable, and so on.

5. The *Rebuttal* of the Claim or reservations involve introducing evidence that limits or contradicts the assertion, questioning whether the evidence offered initially is actually warranted or interpreting the evidence to have a different meaning.
6. The *Backing* provides further evidence for the Claim that shows that the Rebuttal is incorrect and defends the original assertion by critiquing the rebuttal.

In a case study, as in a legal case, only the central or controversial aspects of the case can receive the complete logical argumentation just outlined; otherwise, every case would have to be a book-length report. Perhaps some very important cases may deserve such careful argumentation, but often many fact patterns in a case are uncontroversial, and the case connects to one's everyday or clinical experience sufficiently that all of the warrants for the assertions need not be explicitly argued.

USING BROMLEY'S (1986) CRITERIA
TO CRITIQUE NARRATIVE CASE STUDIES

The critiques of three cases (Boyer, 1977; Chessick, 1982; Goldman & Greenberg, 1995) that have been evaluated using Bromley's quasi-judicial method are presented below; each is preceded by a brief abstract of the case. The cases are all authored by distinguished psychotherapists who publish widely and who are recognized as outstanding representatives of the particular approaches to psychotherapy are discussed in the cases. The discussions below are meant to be illustrative, not exhaustive, of the application of Bromley's quasi-judicial method of case study analysis. They also are not intended as a critique of the contribution of the cases to our current literature. In fact, the cases were selected because they have been recognized as of considerable value already, and yet the application of the quasi-judicial method provides a comprehensive structure for considering how similar case studies might be improved substantially in the future.

Chessick (1982): Intensive Psychotherapy of a Borderline Patient

Richard Chessick (1982) is a psychiatrist widely published in both intensive psychotherapy and the philosophy of psychiatry. His theoretical orientation is rooted in the interpersonal school of psychiatry associated historically with Harry Stack Sullivan and Frieda Fromm-Reichman (although they are not mentioned specifically in the article) and more generally with contemporary psychodynamic approaches to psychotherapy, such as object relations theory and self-psychology. In this case, Chessick worked with a young woman experiencing serious interpersonal problems in her marriage that included sexual frigidity and frequent rages. She was seen several times per week in face-to-face psychotherapy for most of the 11-year period of the psychotherapy, although there were times she cut back to once per week. The account includes the process of her working through an extreme negative transference, in which she voiced fantasies of kidnapping Chessick's children and holding them hostage so that he would have sex with her, or murdering them outright. As these issues are explored and related to her childhood, it is discovered that she was raised in an apartment above the family business—a mortuary, where she frequently played as her parents embalmed bodies. The father is described as both playful and sadistic and the mother as distant and highly moralistic. After several years of intensive psychotherapy, the patient begins to be sexually responsive; gives birth to a child, whom she loves dearly; and develops new career opportunities that would permit her to be financially independent of her husband, should he leave. Chessick considered the case highly successful, untreatable by any other less time-consuming method, and wondered (in 1982) how such cases will ever be permitted to be treated under the managed-care health insurance programs that at the time were just emerging.

Confidentiality

Chessick (1982) indicated that a fictitious name is used in this case, but there is no other discussion of issues that relate to confidentiality and informed consent. Given the level of detailed life history information, there is considerable risk that the patient's true identity could be deduced from the case study should it be read by someone acquainted with her. Perhaps other information in the case (e.g. patient's age, husband's occupation, parents' nationality, or years in treatment) was altered to prevent the disclosure of her identity, but this was not stated and would be important for the reader to know if it had been done. In the absence of information that would allay such fears, it appears that this patient should have been asked for her written consent for this case to be published in its present form.

Quality of Evidence

Chessick (1982) does a fine job of providing descriptions of the patient's self-reports about her life experience and history that are theoretically neutral. At times, he slips into a psychoanalytic manner of writing where it is unclear whether he is trying to give summary descriptions or interpretations of the patient's behavior. An example of this is the following: "The father's penis was described repeatedly by this patient not as a sexual object but as a bad breast that could destroy her" (p. 416). It would have been helpful to see a verbatim account of what exactly the patient said that led to this statement in the report.

Chessick (1982) gives a great deal of credence to the client's self-reports of both her past and current life circumstances in her marriage, at work, and in her family of origin. Obviously, he believes her to be trustworthy and reasonably accurate, but he does not say what about her led him to trust these self-reports. Furthermore, he gives the reader very little information about himself that would establish himself as an "expert witness" and lead the reader to trust his report of the case. In fact, he was at the time of this report a widely respected authority on interpersonal psychotherapy with borderline patients, which is one of the reasons the report was selected for inclusion here. Despite this absence of information about the therapist's background and training, Chessick does build the reader's confidence in the integrity of the report by openly acknowledging interpretive errors he made during the first year of treatment and reflecting in the report on the theoretical disputes in the field concerning how to work with patients who have these "borderline" problems. He qualifies his own claims about the relationship between the improvement he witnessed and the theory of "soothing self-objects" that he uses to explain that improvement, again raising readers' confidence that he understands the limitations of clinical knowledge in such a difficult area of investigation and treatment.

Given the length and difficulty of the treatment, one would have expected that the therapist might have consulted colleagues or supervisors to discuss the case. Reporting their input would have been useful to the reader.

Content Areas

Although Chessick (1982) gave a quite detailed family and developmental history, there are two areas that might have been developed further. It is mentioned that the patient had difficulty making friends throughout her life, with the exception of a few girlfriends during the grade school years. Because these were so rare in her history, it would have been interesting to know more about how those relationships developed and what became of the friendships. Also, the report indicates that she was a teacher by training and career choice, and yet nothing is said about her feelings about her work or her success on the job. Finally, although the therapy was lengthy, there are virtually no follow-up data. Given the unusual length of the treatment, it might be said that the follow-up period was in a sense included in the treatment because of the tapering off of sessions. However, the concluding paragraph leaves the status of the patient's marriage in doubt, and one wonders whether, if she divorced, she was able to maintain the gains that had clearly occurred in the psychotherapy.

Rebuttal of Alternative Theoretical Approaches

As would be predicted from a family systems and even an object relations point of view, in the 4th year of the therapy the patient's husband became symptomatic just as she began to make important changes in her style of interacting with him and significant others in her life. Yet Chessick (1982) did not ask or agree to see the husband until the 9th year of treatment. Because the case ends with the husband threatening daily to leave the marriage, one wonders why Chessick did not address the couple's problems more aggressively. Was it simply his individual psychotherapy training, or did he feel that his clinical responsibility was only to the client whom he has contracted to serve? He is to be credited for reporting details of the case that would invite such criticism, but it would have been even better if he had anticipated and answered such criticism.

Moral Engagement

A psychotherapeutic relationship such as this one invites much moral reflection. The patient's confusion of violence and sexuality at the level of fantasy raises concerns about what exactly happened to her as a child as she played in the mortuary as her father embalmed bodies. At the very least, the father showed an utter lack of awareness as to how a young child would feel in the presence of such activities, and the mother also seems oblivious. As with most such traumas from parental insensitivity, where the parents in other ways clearly were responsible and caring, the child is left in a tremendous dilemma with her or his rage and sense of injustice.

One should not, however, assume that moral engagement in this case requires moral condemnation of either the parents for their insensitivity or the patient for her own violent fantasies toward the therapist. In terms of the moral dimension of therapy, what this woman needed and received from Chessick was a morally reparative relationship that did not demand more of her than she could give and gave her unconditional empathic support. He extended to her a higher level of moral care than she could return at the time but one that anyone would hope would be extended to them had they experienced the childhood traumas of this patient. This is, of course, typical of most psychotherapy clients. They are offered care that is attuned to their developmental issues, not the kind of care therapists themselves require. Clients cannot develop moral reciprocity unless they first receive more than they can give.

Many who read this case are troubled by the fact that about halfway through the therapy, while the patient is still raging against Chessick, but is now sexually more alive and active with her husband, her abhorrence of motherhood drops away, and she very much wishes to have a child. Here is a decision that will affect not only the client, but also her husband and the unborn child. Should a morally engaged therapist raise the question with her of whether it is fair to the child to be cared for by a mother who is still suffering with emotional upheavals from her own childhood? On the other hand, wanting to be a mother is a common experience of women in her age group, and she is showing developmental progress toward a greater emotional connectedness and love for others as well as more autonomy and responsibility. Respecting the client as a moral agent, who must develop her own decision-making ability in the area of critical life questions, is also a way of being morally engaged. This is perhaps one of the ways that a morally engaged psychotherapy differs from the moral treatment of such issues within various religious traditions. In many religious contexts, the idea of moral engagement tends to focus on instructing the other person in right and wrong even when that person is admitting his or her own wrongdoing and asking for help with it.

By treating another person with respect, fairness, and compassion, the psychologist or psychotherapist performs a reparative moral function that helps the client not only to "feel better" but also, by promoting moral development, to do better. This is, of course, nothing more than what morally engaged and reasonably attuned parents do for their children on a daily basis.

Boyer (1977): Working With a Borderline Patient

Boyer (1977) is a highly regarded psychoanalyst with a reputation for specializing in working with the most severely disturbed patients who can be seen on an outpatient basis. This certainly applies in this case, in which he works psychoanalytically with a middle-aged woman from an upper-class social registry background who has a life long history of psychiatric hospitalizations for depression, serious suicide attempts, sadomasochistic sexual relationships, alcoholism, and an adult son whose recent hospitalization for psychosis motivated her to try to become a good mother to him. She was seen several times per week over a course of many years, during which time Boyer discovered that she had been sexually abused as a child separately by both of her parents and the family chauffeur. She had come to believe as an adolescent that the only way her sister would survive was if she (the client) gave up her own life—thus the pattern of self-destructiveness and suicidal behavior. After several years of negative transference in which she almost dies, the client begins to rid herself of destructive relationships, goes back to college, develops a career, and reconciles with her son.

Confidentiality

Again the only obvious expression of author concern about confidentiality is the fictitious name of the client. Unless other information has been substantially altered, the level of detail in this report and the social status of the client (aristocratic family in the Northeast) would lead one to wonder whether informed consent to publish the case study should have been obtained.

Unlike the Chessick (1982) case, the patient here begins therapy in a deteriorated, intoxicated, and "impulse driven" state. Yet Boyer (1977) begins the case report with extensive and detailed life history information. Readers are not told exactly how this information on life history was obtained, from whom, and how certain he is of its accuracy. Is this because of the psychoanalytic tradition's emphasis on the importance of "psychic reality" as the critical element in therapy? One cannot tell from the report. Neither does the reader know how much of this information Boyer had at the start of treatment, or whether this information, which appears first in the report, was actually pieced together over many years. Furthermore, Boyer has a tendency, common among psychoanalytic authors, of combining in one statement straightforward description of the patient's actions, consciously expressed thoughts and feelings, interpretations of unconscious fantasies, defenses, and the fantasized or real impact these psychodynamic processes (within the patient) have on the therapist. It would greatly clarify the case study to have these different claims separated and the evidence for each component specified.

Boyer (1977) reveals a good deal about himself and his practice, although he does not discuss his particular training as a psychoanalyst or what his primary orientation is within psychoanalysis. These, too, would have been helpful for readers to know. One's trust that he is giving a fair account of what transpired in the sessions is increased by two features of this report. First, he describes the patient's actions during the sessions in great detail, and his own countertransference (boredom, irritation) reactions as well, even when these do not put him in the best light. Furthermore, he acknowledges a serious mistake (not inquiring more about the patient's relationship with her beloved grandfather) that almost resulted in the patient's suicide. Boyer also gives considerable detail about the patient's daily functioning in the world over the course of the treatment, and we learn how she is changing not only in the sessions (e.g., not coming to therapy intoxicated) but in her relationships with her sisters, mother, children, sexual relationships with men, and her enrollment in college courses. These client-reported changes correspond generally with therapist-observed changes in the patient's interactional patterns during the therapy hours, thus giving a greater weight to both forms of evidence.

Given the difficulty of the case, one would have thought it might have been the subject for some consultation with other colleagues, supervisors, and so forth. Such input would have been very useful to the reader.

Content Areas

The patient entered therapy because she had been told by her psychotic son's therapist that her son could not improve further unless she got help for her own problems. Boyer (1977) realizes in the middle of the treatment that this was one of the primary reasons he agreed to treat her, even though many other therapists had turned her down as unsuitable for psychodynamically oriented treatment. Yet one reads only a few lines in the case study about the changes in her relationship with her son; readers would be entitled to know more about the realization of this goal. Her daughters are also mentioned only in passing, and it would be interesting to know how this rapprochement occurred.

During the therapist's first extended absence, the patient nearly killed herself, and yet when he next went away he did not seem to take necessary precautions, and she ended up hospitalized for psychiatric reasons. Is this an unavoidable risk in doing outpatient treatment with such a difficult client, or might there have been ways to bridge the therapist's absence with other supportive services in the community? It would have been useful to have this addressed in the case study.

Rebuttal of Alternative Theoretical Approaches

During the first year of the treatment, Boyer (1977) allowed the patient to attend sessions intoxicated, and on one such occasion she threw herself at his feet and reached up to his crotch to fondle him. He describes this all in a matter-of-fact manner, yet we know that most approaches to therapy would have not permitted either to happen. He saw these situations as her test of his disgust with her, and so he allowed these forms of acting out in the sessions. A more thorough discussion of that subject was in order. Do severely traumatized individuals need to be given this much leeway to become engaged in therapy? Boyer does not seem concerned about the ethical or legal ramifications of having allowed the patient to act out sexually on a number of occasions during the early years of treatment. (He never engaged in any sexual contact with her, but one wonders how a state ethics board would view this.) The remarkable degree of improvement in what most therapists would have considered a "hopeless middle-aged borderline schizophrenic" suggests that we should be careful not to criticize what we do not understand, but a discussion of these unorthodox methods would have been helpful.

Moral Engagement

It is clear that this is a woman who had been morally abused as well as sexually. Her wealthy, socialite parents failed miserably in providing the most basic and rudimentary social and emotional care. Her own self-destructive, high-risk behaviors merely mimic those of her parents in their actions toward her or each other, and she has been no more available to her own children than her parents were to her. She is the most difficult kind of victim of abuse to help: one who has become abusive toward herself and others. Yet she is asking for help precisely because she has been told that her adult schizophrenic son will never improve unless she does, and so she enters therapy again despite many previously failed treatments. The goal of therapy is explicitly moral, although Boyer (1977) does not explicitly note it—she wishes to become a *good mother*.

The patient does not need to be told how morally objectionable she has been behaving (because her presence in therapy indicates that she already knows this). She needs instead a reason to believe she belongs in the moral universe and that her own attempts to be a good person will be met by reciprocal rather than punitive responses. As in the Chessick (1982) case, Boyer (1977) attempts to create a relationship that will offer the kind of self-awareness that will permit her to take control of these self-destructive patterns and choose a different life for herself. She keeps testing him to find out if he is not really going to turn out like her parents (self-absorbed), and she obliterates memories of him between sessions to protect herself from abandonment. It would have been easy for a less experienced or less morally engaged therapist to view this patient as a lost cause, or "bad client" not worthy of more effort from the therapist.

This is the critical point of moral engagement in the case, the point of caring about her as another human being, despite the grossness of her actions and appearance. Boyer (1977) set limits without being punitive, and treated her the way he would have wanted to be treated had he himself had such an abusive childhood. (In fact, Boyer comments that one of the reasons he came to specialize in treating these kinds of severe cases was because of his exposure to such a person in his own household growing up.)

Goldman and Greenberg (1995):
A Process–Experiential Approach to Case Formulation

Goldman and Greenberg (1995) presented a case to illustrate the process of case formulation in contemporary short-term humanistic–experiential psychotherapy. It owes much to the Gestalt therapy tradition of Fritz Perls. As such, it is focused on the here and now, with little or no history or background of the individual presented. One knows at the beginning that this woman (i.e., the client) is moderately depressed and experiencing marital problems, having left her husband several times, only to return when he promises to quit gambling. As the case unfolds, one also learns that the client's brother is diagnosed as "schizophrenic" and has threatened his mother with violence.

Confidentiality

As an example of short-term experiential psychotherapy in a moderately depressed individual, there is much less disclosure of highly charged life history or current life circumstance information in this case. It is arguable that informed consent to publish this case study would *not* need to have been obtained.

Quality of Evidence

This client was assessed both before and after treatment using a battery of self-report checklists and rating scales that provide another view of the client in addition to that of the therapist. In addition, many excerpts of the session transcripts are quoted verbatim (in keeping with the tradition of reporting case studies initiated by Carl Rogers in the 1940s). The excerpts are each followed by a commentary that places the interactions in the conceptual framework used by the therapist. Although it is stated that the client improved her ability to stand up for herself in her marriage, there is little specific detail given about the changes in her interactions with her husband. Whether this is because of the purpose of the case study write-up (to show case formulation) or because of the short-term nature of the therapy (15 sessions) is difficult to say.

Content Areas

As noted above, the short-term nature of this case study leaves underdocumented a good deal of the client's developmental life history, current functioning, and life circumstances. To some extent this is compensated for by extensive excerpts of dialogue at critical junctures in the therapy, something that is missing from the other two cases reviewed. The dialogue demonstrates the process of shifting emotional awareness by use of the two-chair technique.

In principle, there is no reason why life history information could not have also been included, or be required of those wishing to publish case studies. Even if the authors believe the information of no direct relevance to their work, a comprehensive case report might require it to increase the usefulness of the case to readers from different orientations.

Although it is evident from the case study that the authors are well published in experiential psychotherapy, there is no discussion of the therapist's experience of forming a relationship with this client, even though the development of an empathic relationship is emphasized. Readers do not get much of a sense of who this client is as a person. Again, this may be because of the purpose of the case study as an example of case formulation from a particular theoretical viewpoint. As such, it illustrates the difference between a case study written to describe a clinical situation and one such as this, which was written more to illustrate a clinical theoretical position.

Rebuttal of Alternative Theoretical Approaches

This was a case in treating major depressive disorder by process–experiential means. Given that the more common approach to this disorder is medication with or without some form of cognitive psychotherapy, it would have been helpful to the reader to understand why the authors prefer this mode of treatment over the other more commonly prescribed ones. This falls under Bromley's (1986) guideline that requires case studies to not only defend the conceptualization employed but also rebut alternative conceptualizations that might be used in the specific case. Also, one is struck in the limited family history by the statement that the client is "married to a compulsive gambler" and expected to "endure" his gambling the way her mother tolerated her father's gambling. This certainly suggests that the problem may have its roots in early developmental processes, which might lead some practitioners to think that longer term therapy would be necessary. It also raises questions as to whether the model being used is equipped to tackle the complexities of such a problem as compared with, for example, a structural family therapy or developmental psychodynamic approach. Such a discussion focused on an individual case would both clarify the thinking that went into the case and further the reader's understanding of the implications of different theories in the field.

Moral Engagement

Anyone looking for the moral dimension in psychotherapy should see a red flag when the term *gambling* or *compulsive gambling* appears in a case history. This is of course a quintessential issue in conventional religious morality, for it suggests engaging voluntarily in a practice that is fraught with personal risks and hardship that is potentially ruinous for the entire family. As is true in many such families, this woman is highly conflicted about her marriage, and although she wants to be with her husband when he is not gambling, she wants to leave him when he resumes the pattern. Also typical is her own sense of shame and guilt, that she holds herself responsible for not doing more to stop her father and husband from gambling. What does it mean about the moral universe of the client that she reports that her mother believes that she must endure this sort of treatment from the men in her life? What other ways must she endure harmful actions on their part, and to what extent is her depression the result of the suppressed righteous indignation or rage she feels being so victimized? The experiential therapist works with her to take responsibility for her own life rather than her husband's or her father's. When offered an empathic relationship that continually focuses on what she may be feeling that she cannot express or acknowledge to herself or others, she discovers that she feels a great deal of anger. She is angry with her father for his gambling and for emotionally abandoning her mother to raise the children without him, with her mother for her passivity in the face of her father's gambling, and with her husband for his own gambling addiction. After the anger she also finds a reservoir of sadness for the opportunities missed in her relationships to feel real closeness and love. The case is described as a successful treatment of depression, which of course it is, but it is also the successful righting of the client's moral universe. The people who are harming others are held responsible, and those who are caring for others are permitted to feel self-respect and not be punished.

Given Bromley's (1986) extensive criteria for a comprehensive narrative case study, it would of course be possible to critique each of these cases more fully. As noted above, the intent here is to illustrate the power of the conceptual framework that Bromley brought to bear on the problem of evaluating case studies. It is always difficult to know how stringent one should be in applying these criteria to cases given the limitations of both the clinical situation and the publication process. One simply cannot provide evidence, warrants, qualifiers, rebuttals, and backup for every claim made in a comprehensive case account. The art and critical judgment come in deciding which claims are the most central, which evidence the most sound, which rebuttals the most cogent, and what qualifications to place on the conclusions. The use of quasi-judicial review panels of the type I describe shortly would certainly make those decisions easier in the future.

WRITING ABOUT CASES:
TYPES OF PUBLICATIONS NEEDED IN THE FIELD

For the case study method to be resuscitated in psychology, there is a need for three kinds of scholarly endeavors to be encouraged by journal editors in the discipline. Once the publication of case study reports is again encouraged, we will have to develop criteria for deciding which of the hundreds of thousands of psychotherapy and clinical psychology cases that are worked with each year should be recorded in the literature. We should be encouraging mainstream journals to publish the following kinds of articles:

- Case study reports, including assessment or diagnostic problems, treatment, consultation; and individual, couples, families, and systems cases. All theoretical perspectives should be encouraged so long as the elements of a comprehensive case report are added to the typical protocol. Cases will be selected that (a) provide a model for work with a particular type of case where none others have been published, (b) provide support for a particular theoretical issue or controversy of importance, (c) provide a refutation of previously published case claims, (d) illustrate the social, political, and moral dimensions of professional work.
- Critical analytical literature reviews of previously published cases or commentaries on previously published case studies. As indicated above in the brief overview of my PsycINFO search

for case studies on schizophrenia, one can eventually find outstanding comprehensive case studies in the clinical literature, but locating the studies and separating the wheat from the chaff is no easy task. Case studies are rarely published, and when they are, it is often by journals that have not published a case study in years. It would be a great service to help the professional community identify the case studies that have already been published but are not widely accessible and to show their strengths, weaknesses, and findings.

- Philosophical/methodological articles on the nature of case reasoning, the logic of reliability and validity in a case study; the interplay of psychological, social, political, and moral issues in the case study; technical improvements in actual methods of collecting or evaluating information; and confidentiality dilemmas.

QUASI-JUDICIAL REVIEW BY PANELS OF PSYCHOLOGICAL INQUIRY

Over the last 500 years, as the sciences have been developing a method for teasing the truth out of nature, the judicial system has been developing a method for teasing the truth out of human beings who are embroiled in one sort of a conflict or another. Paralleling the development of the empirical natural sciences, the law has evolved a sophisticated concern with the fair and objective evaluation of testimonial and physical evidence relating to the actions and behaviors of human beings and rules and procedures for obtaining such evidence (Loevinger, 1967). We are used to thinking of the law primarily in terms of meting out retributive justice: punishment. Although the criminal law might provide significant guidance for investigating clinical situations where egregious transgressions of social norms and moral behavior are involved, it is only a part of the story. It is in the civil law that one finds a set of principles or rules for dealing with the more garden variety interpersonal conflicts: betrayal, abandonment, family strife, dishonesty in business dealings, disregard for the well-being of others, malevolent intentions, malfeasance in the conduct of business or maintenance of property, and so on. The civil law regulates a vast array of the critical relationships in people's lives, and in the process it has developed a method of investigating the circumstances surrounding such conflicts and for determining, to the extent possible, the truth of the claims and inferences made by the conflicted parties. The judicial process ultimately ends in a judgment that may result in serious penalties for one or more of the participants in the conflict. The courts decide not only the facts but also who is responsible for those conditions and what, if anything, should be done to rectify the damage.

For all our criticisms of lawyers and the courts, our society as a whole still places much more faith in the judicial method of arriving at the truth than it does in the scientific method. Although the opinion of the scientific community is sought, for example, on the question of whether smoking cigarettes causes cancer, a legal judge and jury of citizens will ultimately decide this question after a trial. Can one imagine our society ever giving the authority to levy $200 billion in damages against the tobacco companies to a panel of scientists from the National Academy of Sciences? On matters of great social and human consequence, we have put our trust in the legal system to tell us who did what to whom. Certainly a system that is trusted to find the truth about human conflicts when so much is at stake (life, liberty, one's good name, material wealth, etc.) might be trusted to investigate interpersonal conflicts of the more garden variety. By no means am I suggesting that we seek to replace psychological services with prosecution and retribution. My point is not how the legal system attempts to solve problems or control behavior but rather how the legal system attempts to investigate behavior to determine who did what to whom. It is a sophisticated system of investigation that sets out to determine the facts of a case; the reasonable inferences or interpretations that can be placed on the facts; and, at times, also who is responsible for a particular set of circumstances taking place.

Granted, the judicial system is far from perfect, and its powers to intervene, although great, are limited to very few options (do nothing, punish, or prohibit certain actions). Yet considering the tremendous overlap with psychology in the kinds of problems being dealt with (interpersonal conflicts), it is astonishing that we have not sooner thought to look to legal methodology for help. We tend to focus on the results of the legal process in terms of dramatic cases where justice is not served, or where the influence of politics and wealth leads to a miscarriage of justice, and fail to see the methodology for evaluating evidence that has evolved and the many successes of that system of investigation. Our infatuation with the methodology of the physical sciences has further diverted our attention away from a natural ally in the search for reliable and valid observations and inferences about human behavior.

PANELS OF PSYCHOLOGICAL INQUIRY

Although what follows is partially inspired by the work of others cited above, particularly Bromley (1986) and Levine (1974), the particular form of quasi-judicial process that I recommend is my own. I propose that what are currently being published as case studies in psychology should be seen as arguments for a particular interpretation of events, much like a legal brief argues in support of a certain conclusion in matters before a court. Such a case study should be presented to an independent panel of professional psychologists acting as judges (a "Panel of Psychological Inquiry") for a decision as to its merits. The panel would decide the validity of the data presented and the strength of the inferences being drawn from that data. The panel members would not have any authority over the practice of psychology or in determining malpractice; they would only try the truth of a factual or theoretical claim. Their power would be more like a thesis committee than a civil court of law. They would certify knowledge claims only.

Such panels of psychological inquiry would be available at the local, regional, national, and perhaps international levels, allowing for important and controversial cases to work their way up to wider audiences and more seasoned psychological judges. It would also allow for appeals of decisions to a higher panel. The psychologist–judges hearing a case would be aided in their decisions by arguments put forth by one or more psychologists who would advocate for a different interpretation of the case or who might challenge the credibility of the facts of the case itself. The authors of the case study might be cross-examined by opposing psychologists, and some witnesses might be called, or documentary evidence presented. Concerns for confidentiality will have to be paramount, and many of these hearings, or parts of them, would probably not be open to the public, as is true today in courts and congressional hearings dealing with sensitive topics. Such hearings could be held in private where necessary, maintaining confidentiality as well as any case conference in a clinical setting. The opinions issued by the panel as to the nature of a problem, the interventions attempted, and the outcomes could be made in a manner that would make the tracking of the identity of the client almost impossible. Readers would know that the panel had heard all the evidence to back up the findings in the case, even if all of the evidence could not be presented to the reader. Indeed, there are some well-known cases in the federal court system where even the identity of the complainant was protected for reasons of privacy (*Roe v. Wade* is perhaps the most famous contemporary case of this kind).

The findings, and any dissenting opinions, will be published for the profession by the panel's organizational structure and will permit the development of a body of widely available case law in psychology. Over time, other psychologists may choose to write articles reviewing the conflicting opinions of different Panels of Psychological Inquiry and recommend how future cases should be decided. Such reviews would be published in more traditional journals, not with the findings of the panels. It will obviously be very important who is appointed as judges on these panels and that the appointed individuals have a record of professional experience relevant to the cases that will be heard. Equally important is that they have a reputation for being fair and open-minded in their work. Some collaboration among psychological associations, institutions of higher learning, and clinical training institutes would be desirable in setting up such a system. It is interesting that from the 1200s forward, the development of the common law in Europe was closely linked to the development of the university faculties of law. This was well illustrated in Germany in the 1400s, when local judges, whose jurisdictions often conflicted, submitted their disputes to the law faculties at the universities, whose decisions based on the common law were final (Stein, 1973).

One of the advantages of such a system is the opportunity to bridge the gap between clinical practitioners and academic psychology. Academic clinical psychologists might serve as panel judges, advocates for or against various case presentations, authors of psychological briefs (the preliminary case studies), or opinions and dissenting opinions of the panels, and review articles of prior opinions. Their analysis of the evidentiary and theoretical claims of the case studies presented to them would be of such direct relevance to practitioners that we would no longer have to worry about the question of why clinicians do not read the clinical psychology journals. Although the clinicians would gain much in terms of legitimacy for their knowledge claims, and systematized principles of practice, those in the academy stand to gain an entire new avenue of professional involvement. Busy clinicians may have the case material that warrants presentation but not the time or skill to present it well to a panel. An academician who has studied the rulings of the panels and knows the psychological case law, and therefore may be an articulate advocate for a case finding, would be a great asset to a clinician wishing to have her or his work recognized. This academician may not practice enough to have a great deal of her or his own case material to present or to have a case that is relevant to a research question of interest. Collaboration would benefit both the clinician and the researcher in the pursuit of their career goals in psychology. These panels would also be a tremendous opportunity for clinicians who wish to curtail their direct service but would like to continue to contribute to the profession without necessarily having to go into administration or retirement. Most important, the clients and communities benefit as psychologists put less energy into undermining the validity of each others' research and work and more energy into solving the real problems of living that surround us.

THE QUASI-JUDICIAL AS AN EXTENSION OF THE CLINICAL METHOD OF INVESTIGATION

By suggesting that the legal method of assessing truth claims be explored as a model of case study psychological research, I do not mean to suggest that the traditional clinical case study report is currently without any claim to validity. In fact, I believe that in a certain kind of clinical setting—which, for lack of a better term, I call a *democratic* one—clinical case work is already subjected informally to many of the same processes that the Panel of Psychological Inquiry would more formally put into place. Much of the professional work psychologists do takes place within a social context that has the potential for producing observations, inferences, and interpretations that have been carefully examined and scrutinized by a team of people. Both the clinicians who have claimed that their knowledge was primarily intuitive and the scientists who have demanded that clinical work be validated by experimental investigation have missed this feature of the clinical landscape and have thus contributed to the scientist–practitioner impasse.

My clinical experience has been that in a democratic clinical setting there are multiple checks on the subjectivity of the clinician. The most obvious, of course, is supervision, although this is rightly criticized as offering only a limited check on the influence of theoretical biases. However, there are many other checks that come into play—the most important being the regular participation in clinical case conferences by staff. Here, the clinical staff rotates the responsibility for presenting cases that they find problematic or intriguing and solicit input from the other clinical staff as to how to proceed. Particularly where these case conferences are attended by staff from varied training and professional backgrounds, such conferences provide a real opportunity to sort out treatment biases and expectations and the theoretical blinders that all clinicians bring to our work. I worked for several years at a community mental health center in which the staff had trained in cognitive, psychoanalytic, family systems, biological, and humanistic graduate programs and represented five different professions and five different degrees. Managed by an open-minded doctoral-level psychologist, our case conferences were intellectually and clinically challenging. Often, weeks after presenting an initial case, the staff member would present a follow-up that would allow us to see if our ideas had been helpful. Particularly where such a staff has time for regular case conferences, informal peer supervision, cotherapy, or work with different members of the same family or neighborhood, multiple perspectives and views can be brought to bear on a case.

Critical here is the intellectual and interpersonal atmosphere of a clinic. In an environment where intellectual exploration and curiosity are allowed to flourish, where there is no ideological or theoretical orthodoxy governing practice, and the views of individual staff members are respected, staff members are free to question each others' decisions, assessments, and biases. The weekly clinical case conference in such a treatment setting has the potential to function as an informal panel of inquiry. The clinical case conferences I described above share many features with "the diagnostic council" used by Murray at the Harvard Psychological Clinic.

In such a setting one does not rely totally on another clinician's view of a client to assess the case report. One sees other clinicians' clients in the waiting room, hallways, sometimes out in the community or in the newspaper. One hears about other clinician's clients from one's own clients who may live with or near them. In an open environment these observations can be brought into the case conferences and enter into the clinical understanding of the case. Even when confidentiality limits what one can share with another clinician, it does not limit one from forming a judgment of the quality of the case report or clinical work. In such a community clinic one often has contact with other community human service providers or educational institutions that provide information on the client's life experiences and adaptation. Here the entire institution's perspective on a client may be altered by the perceptions of the staff situated differently in the community. When clients pit one institution against another, this can be an eye-opening experience.

THE MORAL CONTEXT
OF CLINICAL KNOWLEDGE

I am reminded, as I think about how clinical knowledge is validated in everyday clinical practice, of Richard Rorty's (1979) discussion of how members of a knowledge-community come to their common understandings of the truth in a postmodern world where we have given up on Descartes's goal of absolute truth. Rorty's account is a socio–moral–political account of knowledge. Knowledge is possible when a community of knowledge seekers have the intellectual interests and social–political freedom to explore together the questions that interest them. Knowledge is dependent on certain moral conditions being present in the community: intellectual and personal freedom, mutual respect, freedom of speech and assembly, and so forth. The end result are dialogue, discussion, and debate that lead to the development of a consensus of belief—the closest we can ever get to knowing the truth. Whether one accepts Rorty's epistemology or not, one can take from his observations an awareness that the quality of the intellectual work of a community is not independent of the social, moral, and political structures and rules of that community.

Being fair to ideas is derivative of being fair to people. Psychologists' clinical knowledge is embedded in moral institutions and frameworks in another sense as well. As I discussed in chapter 3, there are excellent grounds for believing that clinical work in psychology is fundamentally a moral undertaking, guided by one's moral assumptions of justice, fairness, human rights, and responsibilities and one's concept of the good life. No one was more aware of the implicit moral agenda of clinical work than Erik Erikson. Psychology textbooks often leave out that for each of his eight stages of development he regarded a specific moral virtue as indicative of ego development (for example, "fidelity" was the virtue congruent with identity in adolescence.) Erikson (1963) observed that the goal of psychoanalysis to reduce neurotic anxiety was insufficient to the interpersonal problems of the Nuclear Age. Erikson argued that if human kind is to survive, psychoanalytic insight must be coupled with the virtue of judiciousness. He defined "judiciousness" in the following manner: "Judiciousness in its widest sense is a frame of mind which is tolerant of differences, cautious and methodical in evaluation, just in judgment, circumspect in action, and—in spite of all this apparent relativism—capable of faith and indignation" (p. 416).

It is interesting that Erikson (1963) repeatedly returned in his work to the twin themes of the nature of clinical evidence and how clinical work is guided by moral concerns. The proposed Panels of Psychological Inquiry open the door not only to method of evaluating evidence and inference but also for the frank and open discussion of the moral context of clinical practice and the morally laden nature of many observations of psychological health or dysfunction. In the courts it is clear that to find a human being to be the cause of another's suffering is to assign responsibility for that pain and suffering. Responsibility is clearly a moral concept, and the law as an institution that enforces central social norms and moral values is comfortable with this mission. It brings to bear moral reasoning on the empirical evidence presented and decides the case using the facts, the law, and moral principles of fairness and equity.

It is my view that whether we acknowledge this or not, psychologists must be doing the same thing when they draw conclusions from their research on, for example, the causes of child abuse, alcoholism, depression, and antisocial behavior. They are looking for the cause, not in the reductionistic or naturalistic sense but in the human quasi-legal sense of whom or what to hold responsible for these abhorrent human conditions. Moral judgment (not moralizing) must be implicit in one's conclusions. However, because psychologists' scientific framework forbids them from overtly entering the moral realm, they find ways to conceal their moral judgments in "diagnoses," outcome measures, and in their interpretation of the data by announcing we have found a "causal factor" rather than a "responsible party."

In the concept of judiciousness one finds theory and method inexorably combined. It is fair to say that in doing psychotherapy clinicians try to bring some justice into the world for people who have been victimized (wittingly or unwittingly) by family and other social institutions. By giving the kind of support and understanding of which they have otherwise been deprived, clinicians hope to redress a wrong done and alleviate some of their pain and suffering. To properly understand another human being requires a judicious manner of investigation and thinking by the clinician, and in understanding the case studies written by others, one must be judicious oneself. Panels of Psychological Inquiry would formalize a judicious process of review for case studies and at a symbolic level signal that professional psychology is prepared to allow its role in maintaining that the moral standards of society see the light of day.

7

THE MORALLY ENGAGED CLINICAL PSYCHOLOGIST: RECOMMENDATIONS ON EDUCATION AND TRAINING

Both in terms of historical development and current social function, psychology is by its very nature a morally engaged discipline. The problem has been that our moral engagement both as scientists and as practitioners has been concealed behind an ideology of moral neutrality. Human beings cannot avoid having interests and values that influence, for good or ill, every decision they make. The French existentialist Jean Paul Sartre's often-quoted aphorism bears repeating here: "not to decide, is to decide," and so not to decide to have moral values as a clinical psychologist is to decide to have moral values as a clinical psychologist. The difference between having implicit, assumptive, nonconscious, moral values and having explicit, clear, and examined moral values is a large part of what this book is about. We can deny or avoid the moral dimension of psychology only at our own, and our clients', peril.

Thus, the current student, professor, or practitioner of psychology need not change anything about his or her manner of engaging in psychology to make it moral, because it already is just that. What needs to change is *the way* it is moral, and that of course means to change our own self-definition, how we present what we do to the public, and how we teach our students and learn to become clinical psychologists (or other mental health professionals). In so doing, we would in one sense change very little about the framework of clinical services, but in another, very real sense, we would be changing a great deal.

It is imperative that we recognize that moral values are not just another set of attitudes or beliefs that can be funneled through the scientific method to be dissected, number crunched, and teased apart. One can do this if one chooses, and psychologists certainly have in the past; however, such research does very little that would help us decide what our values *should be*. For these moral "beliefs and attitudes" are the very reasons for which people live and die: the hopes, dreams, aspirations, passions, terrors, agonies, and abominations of human existence. They make life meaningful or dreadful. These moral issues must be decided by the exercise of human judgment and wisdom (phronesis), and the solutions to moral dilemmas will not be found through the collection and analysis of data alone. Better information about the patterns of behavior in the population may provide us with a clearer picture of some of the choices before us, but it can never make those choices for us in a mechanical way. We have to decide, given the circumstances and facts of a situation, what we wish to make of our lives. Life, no matter how regimented in modern bureaucracies, tightly structured organizations, and institutions, always remains open to creative decisions. By *creative decisions* I do not mean decisions by a few creative, artistic, individuals, but rather, as Scarry (1985) pointed out, the creative use of human imagination that can lead to productive work for all members of the community.

The vocabulary of suffering, compassion, caring, purpose, and choice is critical to moral engagement, community, and sanity. We lose much of our humanity when we objectify these concepts in a language of etiology, diagnosis, treatment, prognosis, and relative efficacy. The morally engaged clinical psychologist is a bulwark against the demoralizing (and de-moralizing) forces in contemporary life, which often bring students to our classes and clients to our clinics.

For the reader, having reached this concluding chapter is evidence of having made a serious step in the direction of becoming a morally engaged psychologist. It is only the first of what I hope will be many steps of self-reflection and reflection in practice and it may take some time for a moral orientation to clinical psychology to become integrated into the way one practices psychology. Here are some recommended means to this end. The first three recommendations apply equally to all members of the discipline: clinical researchers, practitioners, faculty, and student trainees. Because chapters 5 and 6 contain a number of recommendations on how to be a morally engaged clinical researcher, the remainder of the recommendations in this chapter focus on clinical practice and training for clinical practice.

RECOMMENDATIONS FOR CLINICAL PSYCHOLOGISTS

1. To make decisions on moral values in an informed and deliberate manner, it is imperative that psychologists, and aspiring psychologists, take seriously the study of philosophical or theological ethics. A course on ethics, moral philosophy, or contemporary ethical issues is a good first step. Another approach, self-education, might include reading of one's own classic works such as Plato's *Republic* (1941), Aristotle's *Nichomachean Ethics* and *Politics* (McKeon, 1941), Kant's *Groundwork of the Metaphysic of Morals* (1785/1964), Mill's *Utilitarianism* (1963), or Rawls's *A Theory of Justice* (1971). The Shakow report (Committee on Training in Clinical Psychology, 1948) encouraged graduate programs in clinical psychology to admit students who had been broadly and liberally educated in the humanities. Although this is no longer what most graduate departments require, students would be well advised for their own benefit to pursue these sorts of courses in their undergraduate education in addition to the psychology major. There are a number of excellent resources for examining the way in which philosophical issues play out in clinical psychology itself: Rychlak's (1981) *Introduction to Personality and Psychotherapy*; R. B. Miller's (1992b) *The Restoration of Dialogue: Readings in the Philosophy of Clinical Psychology*; and Messer, Saas, and Woolfolk's (1988) *Hermeneutics and Psychological Theory: Interpretive Perspectives on Personality, Psychotherapy, and Psychopathology*.

2. Armed with the conceptual framework from such a course of study, one must do the difficult internal work of identifying and evaluating the grounds of, or reasons for, her or his own moral standards, principles, and direction in life. I try to stimulate this kind of self-examination in my Theories of Psychotherapy graduate course by having students prioritize the six moral and ethical values orientations to mental health and psychotherapy that I have identified as inherent in at least one of the major theoretical approaches to psychotherapy. The list is presented in an order that represents my perception of the degree of popularity of the various views in our culture.

    a. Relief from distressing feelings, thoughts, bodily sensations, movements, and so on and their replacement with calm, relaxed, comforting internal feelings and bodily experiences are emphasized. These goals are often associated with the medical model in that it emphasizes the kind of subjective complaints that blend mental and physical descriptions of the problem and therefore invite a disease or medical interpretation.

b. Competence, adaptability, productivity, rationality, self-sufficiency, and so on, are emphasized. This cluster of goals emphasizes adjustment to contemporary societal expectations, particularly insofar as the person is able to work and earn a living. These values tend to invite a kind of behavioral or cognitive–behavioral approach in psychology in that they emphasize adaptation to the environment and keeping one's emotions in check.

c. Positive social relationships, connectedness, and loyalty to the family or local community and responsibility to others, compassion, and a balance of autonomy and dependency are sought. These are values often found in interpersonal, object relations, or family therapies. The emphasis is on loving and caring for others.

d. Personal growth or integration of the self, authenticity, wisdom, personal meaning making, and spirituality are most valued. These are values often associated with humanistic–existential perspectives on psychotherapy and some Jungian or religiously affiliated therapies (pastoral counseling, Buddhist therapy, etc).

e. Exploring and being open to the heights or depths of the human experience of being, including joy and despair, freedom, mortality, creativity, alienation, changes and risk, are emphasized. These are values often associated with some of the more radical humanistic–existential therapies.

f. Building social communities that support people in their struggles to overcome repressive social–economic and political circumstances and to actively work for cultural change is most valued. These are values more likely to be supported by community psychologists, social workers, radical and feminist therapists, and some systems-oriented family therapists.

One of the things that can happen in considering these value orientations is that a person may discover that his or her values conflict with an orientation to therapy he or she had been attracted to learning. Because these value positions are rarely noted by theorists, and as a culture we often leave our values unexpressed and not articulated, it is not difficult for this to occur. Consequently, a critical source of tension in the profession has been denied and not dealt with in an open manner that might yield to some new consensus or understanding.

In general, individuals can identify two or three values that they would want to promote in their work and one or two that they would never have even thought would pertain to doing psychotherapy. Next, I ask the participants in this exercise to try to develop a justification or reasons for why they selected the values they did and why they prioritized those values higher than some of the others. The purpose, of course, is to show (a) that we do have reasons for our values but that (b) the basis for these value choices are often not very well worked out or rely on intuition or a felt sense that certain positions are more emotionally compelling than others. Lewis's (1990, 2000) six orientations (chap. 3) to moral thinking can be of assistance here in finding the justification for one's moral principles.

From this exercise participants often discover that it would be hard to create a psychotherapy that was morally right for everyone and that psychologists will need to learn to tolerate diverse psychotherapies. The dream of a universal psychotherapy technique or approach recedes into the shadows. Nevertheless, the list of moral values that have been found to be implicit in various approaches to clinical interventions is not infinite, and not all are mutually exclusive. So, although a universal psychotherapy is beyond our reach, it is not the case that anything goes, or that values are completely individualistic.

3. As one identifies the most important moral ends that one hopes one's clinical work will serve, and looks for a cogent justification of those ends, an additional but related task presents itself for moral consideration: What are the moral values of the institution or supervisors for which, or for whom, I am working? Are their values consistent with my own, or am I headed for conflicts in the clinical workplace as a result of implicit or explicit moral differences? Because the institution or supervisor may not have undertaken such a process of moral introspection, one has to infer from their clinical decision making, or directly probe their moral beliefs, to resolve this potential source of conflict. Although it is true that sometimes moral differences are clearly captured by statements of theoretical orientations to treatment, this is not always the case, and on the basis of different moral values two psychoanalysts might disagree more about clinical matters than expected. Whether one wishes to air these differences and attempt to promote moral dialogue is itself a moral decision. As indicated in chapter 3, it is my hope that psychology will become a

discipline and profession in which moral views are automatically seen as relative, even central, to what psychologists are about and where there is a rule of truth in moral advertising. However, the trainee or recent graduate of a clinical training or research program may not be in a position to challenge the de-moralized clinical atmosphere of an entire institution. It is better to recognize the problem and look for a position in which the moral values that underpin one's clinical or research orientation are more consonant with those of the institution or of one's supervisor.

SPECIFIC RECOMMENDATIONS
FOR CLINICAL PRACTICE

4. In addition to the usual recommendations on starting clinical work with a client, the morally engaged clinician must always begin by tending to the client's *suffering*, in the full sense of that term as discussed in chapter 2. We must attempt to understand the emotional anguish in terms of the physical pain, cognitive confusion, social isolation, and moral disengagement from the individual's own community. This must take precedence over making a diagnosis, defining a treatment plan, or any attempts to change behavior, although ultimately, over time, it may lead to all of these. Once the moral nature of the problem has begun to be identified in terms of the interpersonal hurt, betrayal, abandonment, humiliation, or assault that the client has experienced or perpetrated, we must examine the compatibility of the moral values that are implicitly guiding his or her life and those we ourselves have identified. This may seem a laborious procedure, but many a therapeutic relationship that got off to a good start flounders on the rocks of a moral disjuncture where it becomes clear that what the "good life" therapist is working for with the client is not the "good life" that the client actually seeks. We often mislabel these as simply *cultural differences*, but these are the moral differences in cultures, and it is best to examine them at the beginning of a clinical relationship.

5. Doing justice to the client's problem is more than a manner of speech because, once having recognized the moral dimension in the clinical problem, the morally engaged clinician must also respond in a morally supportive way, not just an emotionally supportive way. One has to be prepared to bring one's own moral values to the table to affirm the sense of wrong done to or by an individual. This gives a sense of urgency and

importance to the work, no matter how seemingly mundane the symptoms of anxiety or depression first appear to be. Do not hide behind the façade of professional or scientific moral neutrality, but clearly side with the possibility of a life in which one deserves to be treated fairly, even if it is not possible in reality. Call the good things that have been done "good" and, when necessary, the terrible, unspeakable, acts also what they are: "bad," "heinous"—even, if you will, "evil." This applies across the board in clinical work; whether one is dealing with a minor adjustment disorder or severe psychosis, morally good and morally despicable things have happened in clients' lives that have profoundly affected them and may be the reason they have asked to be seen.

As with any interpretation or confrontation in a clinical relationship, such interventions must be made with tact, diplomacy, kindness, and at a point in time when the client is more likely to be receptive. Try to avoid using, at least with clients, terms such as *healthy, illness, disorder, dysfunction, appropriate* or *inappropriate, unproductive,* and all the *Diagnostic and Statistical Manual of Mental Disorders* (American Psychiatric Association, 1994) category names, for they tend to conceal or hide the moral dimension of the problem and our work.

6. When you looks at a client you should try, no matter how disturbingly the person is behaving, to see her or him as a moral agent—as a person who has the ultimate capacity to be responsible for her or his own behavior, and not as a human billiard ball ricocheting through space controlled entirely by external forces (whether these be physiological or social psychological). Moral agents, because they can be self-consciously concerned with good and evil, develop responsibility and control over their own lives.

7. The work of therapy is largely about making suffering that feels meaningless become meaningful. Suffering can be a great motivational and creative force, if the moral import of the suffering is recognized. Suffering is about how I should not be treated, or treat others, and what I am going to do to see to it that I am not treated, or will not treat others, that way ever again. It brings with it a sense of purpose and direction to life that must be reflected in the community of the sufferer or it is lost to the individual as well. When the community responds in a de-moralized manner, then the clinician must be morally engaged, or the situation turns hopeless, in that even the people who are saying they wish to help add to the sense of isolation and suffering.

8. When in clinical meetings, case conferences, and supervision, consider the possibility that the differences being expressed about proper clinical diagnosis or treatment are as much differences in moral values regarding psychotherapy as they are about a different clinical perspective on the case. If one approaches such differences with the tolerance that moral differences demand of those who have examined the reasons for ethical positions, one will be surprised how the differences become clearer and, often, less contentious. What is being presented as a theoretical difference, or an awareness of different research results, may well reflect different value orientations that have never been examined by the clinicians involved.

RECOMMENDATIONS TO STUDENTS AND TRAINEES

9. Students should take the initiative to seek out faculty members in psychology or the other mental health professions who have an interest in practice models that have evolved out of clinical practice itself: psychodynamic, interpersonal, existential–humanistic, family systems, Ericksonian (Milton Erickson) hypnosis, and so on. One should not be limited by departmental or disciplinary boundaries. There may be faculty in counseling, social work, psychiatry, nursing, rehabilitation, or other departments in the humanities who are committed to a clinical knowledge approach to psychological issues or who have adopted a human sciences perspective on that work. There are more faculty out there who are like this than one might think, but for survival reasons in academia they may keep a low profile. Their courses can be taken as electives outside the major, or the psychology department may permit an "independent study in psychology" type of course with a faculty member from one of these departments, especially if the faculty member has a doctoral degree in psychology.

10. As a student, do not be afraid to let the more traditional faculty in psychology know of your interest in a morally grounded narrative approach to studying clinical work. Although some will be defensive or critical, at most colleges and universities undergraduates who actually care enough about the field of psychology to do independent reading or thinking are in such short supply that faculty will be impressed and intrigued that someone has actually been exploring the philosophical issues in psychology. This will

probably be truer at small colleges than large universities, but it is worth a try in either case. Do not expect that faculty will change their orientation to the field on the basis of a few conversations (they may have spent years committed to the viewpoint you are challenging), but if you are respectful in how you approach these issues, conversations can evolve and deepen over time. At the very least, you will be challenged each time to make the case for a morally engaged clinical psychology with sharper and clearer logical arguments.

11. One can also seek out mental health practitioners in the community outside of academia who might like to discuss their work with students. Practitioners outside of the academic world tend to be far more oriented to developing and communicating clinical knowledge than their academic brethren. Find out what they read to help them with their work. Most surveys of practitioners in psychology indicate that practitioners do not think they can learn much about practice from reading traditional empirical research published in psychology journals. In what is now a familiar pattern, readers can rightly expect that the scientific community respond to such practitioners by claiming that this lack of interest in the scientific approach is a sign of intellectual laziness or inferiority. I hope that readers are now prepared to see such criticisms for what they are—defensiveness and dissociation—and can move forward to learn from the practice community how they have developed clinical knowledge.

    One will have to bring the critical-thinking skills discussed in chapter 5 to this task, for all clinical knowledge claims must be evaluated using the indigenous methodology drawn from assessing testimony in everyday life and the consensual knowledge-building processes of democratic learning communities. One has to keep an open mind and draw on as many different perspectives and resources as one can early in one's career, to develop one's own orientation to clinical work. Look for clinical knowledge that grows out of "diagnostic council" kinds of settings.

12. There is a large and dynamic practice-oriented scholarly literature that exists outside of the mainstream psychological literature that offers great rewards to those who explore it. The choices are too numerous to mention, and many have been cited throughout this volume. Look for the work of experienced clinical practitioners who write first and foremost about their practices and clinical experiences and relate practice to theory in plain English. Read across various

theoretical orientations, and look for points of convergence in clinical descriptions and techniques. This is a form of convergent validation of theory and practice. Sometimes a highly abstract theory is necessary, but as a practitioner discipline, unless a psychology theory can be directly translated into specific strategies and actions to take in working with people, it is of little value.

13. Read case studies, all that you can get your hands on, on whatever topics interest you in clinical psychology (see Appendix A). Look for opportunities in your classes, or work, to write case studies for papers, theses, independent studies, and so on. Focus on pragmatic or narrative case studies that are problem-solving or phenomenologically oriented, and not one's attempting to resolve theoretical discord. Case studies are an acceptable research method in mainstream psychology, and so it will be hard for a psychology professor to entirely rule out such a project. Assume that a case study can be more than simply an exploratory study developing hypotheses for experimental exploration or disconfirmation, and work to solve the case. Some traditional university psychology graduate programs, and many PsyD programs, have permitted case studies as doctoral dissertations in psychology, and so there are precedents even in the mainstream for making such a request. Even if you have not had clinical experiences about which to write, by reading multiple autobiographies and biographies of the same person one can often extract sufficient information to construct a good case study on a particular episode of problem solving in the person's life. There are in fact many parallels between good biographical writing and narrative life history research in psychology (M. C. Bateson, 1989).

Graduate students are strongly urged to try doing a case study based on clinical work in the practicum or internship experience. We have had this option for 5 years now at Saint Michael's College Graduate Program in Clinical Psychology, and the students uniformly report that it is a very meaningful and instructive way to do a final thesis or major project. First, it forces one to think long and hard and in detail about the clinical work one is doing (reflective practice), and second, it allows for a full discussion of your own experience as a moral agent in a clinical setting. No other research method offers those opportunities.

14. In choosing undergraduate or graduate practicum sites, look for a democratic training and supervision environment in

which professionals encourage critical thinking in students and each other and in which multiple theoretical perspectives to clinical work are encouraged.

15. The process of developing clinical knowledge depends on consensual or convergent validation in open intellectual environments. In entering the world of clinical reality, look for points of agreement on diagnosis and treatment across disciplines, theoretical perspectives, individuals, even cultures or generations. When one hears, for example, from a psychoanalyst, a cognitive–behaviorist, and a family therapist that "depression is usually about suppressed anger and hostility," it has more consensual validity than if three psychoanalysts had all said the same thing. The validity grows further if one sees a client who demonstrates this same dynamic of beginning to discuss depressed or sad feelings and then moves into frustration and anger. If, after this happens, one shares the experience with a fellow trainee, who chimes in that they also had such a case working with a recently arrived immigrant from eastern Europe, then the validity of the *heuristic generalization* that "depression is about suppressed anger" now has substantial weight. This is a piece of practitioner knowledge, not a scientific hypothesis. It is meant to direct clinical practice—to help us know what to do with a person who is depressed to alleviate their depression.

16. One can learn a great deal about clinical reality by being on the other side of the equation—that is, as a client. Psychoanalytic training institutes require personal analysis, but very few psychology training programs do. Required psychotherapy is, to my mind, a contradiction in terms, but voluntary psychotherapy is highly recommended as a means of preparing one for the work of a psychologist and to develop one's clinical knowledge.

17. Subscribe to psychology journals that encourage independent thinking about the discipline: *Journal of Mind and Behavior*; *Journal of Theoretical and Philosophical Psychology*; *Journal of Phenomenological Psychology*; *Journal of New Ideas in Psychology*; *Journal of Psychotherapy Integration*; *Psychotherapy: Theory and Practice*; *Psychiatry: Interpersonal and Biological Processes*; *Journal of Orthopsychiatry*; *Journal of Humanistic Psychology*; and *Family Process,* to name some of the more prominent ones.

18. Graduate programs should be, but rarely are, open democratic learning and intellectual environments. If we really cared about the validity of knowledge being taught and learned in

our graduate schools, this would not be true. Clinical faculty have a critical responsibility to work to promote such an environment, and students should seek out graduate training from a program that is receptive to viewing clinical work as based on clinical knowledge with all its social and moral implications. Several are listed in chapter 4, but there are likely to be many supporters of this approach among the faculty of professional schools of psychology (many of whom offer the PsyD degree). Mainstream psychologists disparage these practitioner programs and routinely advise undergraduates that their professional lives will be ruined by pursuing such a course of study. They neglect to identify their own interest in keeping psychology scientific when offering such advice.

19. All clinical knowledge, as Aristotle noted, is a form of *phronesis* and is provisional and contingent on circumstances (time, place, culture, individual participants, etc.). One has to have a very high tolerance for uncertainty, ambiguity, and ambivalence—for one's own and other people's human fallibility—to become a good clinician. One has to always be learning, growing, and changing, because it is an enormous responsibility to join other people in their effort to make a life worth living. What works for one clinician in a particular clinical setting may not work for the same clinician working with a very different population or setting. Each of us brings ourselves as the primary therapeutic tool in any therapeutic encounter. Because we are each unique human beings, how we integrate and synthesize clinical knowledge from others will also be somewhat unique and idiosyncratic. A wise clinician once told me that before a piece of clinical knowledge can be really useful to anyone, we have to take it into ourselves and make it our own. I thought at the time that that was just some humanistic "mumbo jumbo" and could not possibly be true. It is.

It's frustrating for new students to hear this, because it means that it will be a long and difficult path to becoming a good clinician. This is unfortunately true as well, but it is also a great gift to have such an opportunity to make our own lives meaningful by such a vocation. Those who have to have certain answers to life's mysteries would do best to look elsewhere for a career.

Human suffering demands a moral response from those who are witness to it. Technical, standardized, mechanical responses, although temporarily helpful, are never enough to alleviate human suffering. These must be accompanied by a compassionate, caring response that extends a sense of community to people who are isolated in their misery and pain. Professional psychologists cannot wrap themselves in the mantel of scientific objectivity and respectability and at the same time provide real comfort and assistance to those who are suffering. One has to choose whether to be helpful as a morally engaged psychologist at the level of individual persons, families, or local organizations or whether to work for some component of the nation–state and adopt the moral values of power and control over others. This is not an easy choice, because there are contexts in which the exercise of power and control, with restraint, is a genuine good for the community and society; this is often associated with the role of scientific expert and is consequently a more lucrative approach to clinical psychology. Unfortunately, the trade-off on working for some aspects of bureaucratically controlled psychological services or mental health care facilities is that it often involves simulating a concern for the suffering of one's clients. Given how individualistic and self-absorbed we are as a culture, and how concealed the moral agenda of professional science remains, it is not surprising that we have come to expect no more of our mental health professionals than that they simply simulate being helpful rather than truly help those who suffer. So the choice is one of conscience and personal discretion, and it is not an easy decision to make. What better place to start one's career as a morally engaged clinical psychologist than with an emotionally difficult moral decision?

APPENDIX A

THE SAINT MICHAEL'S COLLEGE CLINICAL CASE STUDY COLLECTION AT DURRICK LIBRARY

The Saint Michael's College Clinical Case Study Collection is a project I created in conjunction with my responsibilities as director of the Graduate Program in Clinical Psychology at the college. The purpose of the project is to make readily available to psychology students, faculty, and practitioners comprehensive, problem-solving, clinical case studies that would otherwise be inaccessible. The plan of the archive is to accumulate case studies that document the successes and failures of the differing approaches to clinical treatment across the full spectrum of psychological problems (diagnoses). At present few published cases meet the standards for problem-solving case studies specified by Bromley (1986), so I have undertaken to collect case studies that are reasonable approximations to this standard. In general, this means that the case description is more than a few paragraphs and that there is some detailed description of the nature of the problem (beyond a mere *Diagnostic and Statistical Manual of Mental Disorders* [American Psychiatric Association, 1994] diagnosis), the client's family situation and history, the actual clinical interactions with the client, and the outcome.

Our initial focus has been on two sources: (a) articles from peer-reviewed journals and (b) casebooks that are a compendium of cases around a theme. These were generally located via the Advanced Search mode in

PsycINFO, indicating *clinical case report* as the first keyword, or previously in PsycLIT by searching for type of publication, TY = CLINICAL-CASE-REPORT, as discussed in chapter 6. Monographs occasionally contain case material, and we have included these wherever possible, but because of the difficulty identifying and locating such cases, this remains an underdeveloped feature of the collection. Once case studies are identified, we check to see if they are in the library's general collection of journals or monographs; if not, we contact the publisher or its representative to obtain copyright permission to place a copy of the case study in our collection. Case studies for which the copyright permission was denied or proved too costly appear in the list below preceded by a single asterisk (*). These are obviously not available in the collection, but we list them as potentially useful case studies for research or training purposes, and of course, individual students and practitioners may be able to obtain them from their libraries or order them through interlibrary loan.

This collection contains more than 350 individual case studies and more than 125 casebooks and is being developed on a continuing basis. Cases can be searched through the college library's electronic catalogue (accessible via the Web at http://voyager.smcvt.edu/cgi-bin/Pwebrecon.cgi?DB=local&PAGE =First). Once at this Web address, one chooses the "Guided Search" option, which presents the user with three "Search for" boxes. Next, one types in the first box, "SMC Clinical Case Study Collection" and then two other descriptors, one in each of the two remaining boxes. One can search for author and title, and one can also sort the cases by four other criteria: gender of the client, age of the client, diagnosis, and therapeutic orientation. Keyword search terms for use with this collection are listed below:

- Diagnostic categories: *childhood disorders* (specify), *delirium/ dementia, substance related, mood disorders, somatoform, dissociative, eating disorders, impulse control, due to medical condition, schizophrenia/psychotic, anxiety disorders, factitious, sexual/gender, sleep, adjustment disorders, personality disorders, relational* (specify), *abuse and neglect,* other
- Type of therapy categories: *psychoanalytic* (includes *Freudian, object relations, ego psychology, Jungian, Adlerian,* and *Sullivanian*), *biological treatments, humanistic,* CBT (cognitive–behavioral), *family therapy, play therapy, group therapy, integrative* or *eclectic,* other (specify)
- Gender: *male/female*
- Age: *toddler, preschool, primary school age, pre-adolescent, adolescent, young adult, adult, middle-age, elderly* (60 years +)

More than one diagnosis or therapeutic orientation may be indicated for a given case study. In the listing that follows, the case studies are already sorted by diagnosis or problem type and then listed alphabetically by author.

Where a case is listed electronically with more than one diagnosis, we have placed it under the first diagnosis for this listing.

Knowing, for example, that there are more than 60 cases on anxiety disorders, the user could then sort this subgroup further by theoretical orientation (medical, cognitive–behavioral, psychodynamic, family systems, humanistic), and age of client, or gender. Eventually, a clinical practitioner or student knowing that she or he is beginning to do, for example, humanistic therapeutic work with an adult female with major depression could consult the collection and come away with three or four case studies that match the client on all four characteristics (age, gender, diagnosis, therapy orientation). We expect this to be a major contribution to clinical training in the future.

This case study collection is still in an early stage of development. Although our ultimate goal is to be able to have a relatively complete collection of the most comprehensive and well-argued problem-solving, quasi-judicial cases in the literature, we are still a very long way from being able to make that claim. We welcome suggestions of cases to be included in the collection from authors, readers, students, faculty, and practitioners. Please send us references, or, if possible, a photocopy of the case study that you would like to see included, and we will evaluate it the way we have the cases already in the collection. Correspondence should be addressed to Case Study Collection, c/o Professor Ronald B. Miller, Department of Psychology, Saint Michael's College, One Winooski Park, Colchester, VT 05439. E-mail: rmiller@smcvt.edu

Below are listed the case studies contained in the Saint Michael's College Collection as well as cases that were found to be of academic interest but that we were not able to include in the collection because of our inability to obtain copyright permission, although they may be obtained through other libraries or interlibrary loan. These latter cases are indicated in the listing below preceded by a single asterisk (*). Cases preceded by a double asterisk (**), are cases within the St. Michael's College library journal holdings but are not part of the case study *reserve* collection. These latter cases (double asterisks) are listed as part of the Case Study Collection in the Durrick Library electronic catalogue and can be searched by diagnosis, treatment, gender, and age. Cases marked with a dagger (†) were classified according to the second edition of the *Diagnostic and Statistical Manual of Mental Disorders* (American Psychiatric Association, 1980). Casebooks are listed separately here, but they are integrated into the collection and can be sorted electronically only for author and title.

ADJUSTMENT DISORDERS

Bemak, F., & Timm, J. (1994). Case study of an adolescent Cambodian refugee: A clinical, developmental and cultural perspective. *International Journal for the Advancement of Counseling, 17,* 47–58.

**Brems, C. (1989). Projective identification as a self-psychological change agent in the psychotherapy of a child. *American Journal of Psychotherapy*, 43, 598–607.

Campion, J. (1985). The contribution of Kleinian psychotherapy to the treatment of a disturbed five-year-old girl and her family. *Journal of Family Therapy*, 7, 341–356.

Daya, R. (1985). Buddhist psychology, a theory of change processes: Implications for counselors. *International Journal for the Advancement of Counseling*, 2, 114–124.

Kast, V. (1991). Imploring eyes: Grief, dream, and fairytale. *Quadrant*, 24, 25–33.

Mishne, J. M. (1984). Trauma of parent loss through divorce, death and illness. *Child and Adolescent Social Work*, 1, 74–88.

Rao, S. P. N. V. S. (2002). Adjustment reaction of childhood. *Child Psychiatry Quarterly*, 10, 8–22.

ANXIETY DISORDERS

Adams-Silvan, A., & Silvan, M. (1994). Paradise lost: A case of hysteria illustrating a specific dynamic of seduction trauma. *International Journal of Psycho-Analysis*, 75, 499–510.

*Alfonso, V. (1992). Brief morita intervention with a socially anxious child: A case study. *International Bulletin of Morita Therapy*, 5, 26–34.

**Allers, C., Mullis, F., & White, J. (1997). The treatment of dissociation in an HIV-infected, sexually abused adolescent male. *Psychotherapy*, 34, 201–205.

Alvin, P. (1994). Agoraphobia: The interface between anxiety and personality disorder. *Bulletin of the Menninger Clinic*, 58, 242–261.

Anderson, K., Taylor, S., & McLean, P. (1996). Panic disorder associated with blood injury reactivity: The necessity of establishing functional relationships among maladaptive behaviors. *Behavior Therapy*, 27, 463–472.

Baptiste, D. A. (1990). Night terrors as a defense against homosexual panic: A case report. *Journal of Gay and Lesbian Psychotherapy*, 1, 121–131.

*Bar-Yoseph, T., & Wiztum, E. (1992). Using strategic psychotherapy: A case study of chronic PTSD after a terrorist attack. *Journal of Contemporary Psychology*, 22, 263–276.

Bennett, G. (1998). Clinical diagnosis and management of anxiety in the elderly. *Journal of Geriatric Psychiatry*, 33, 155–164.

**Biran, M. (1987). Two-stage therapy for agoraphobia. *American Journal of Psychotherapy*, 41, 127–136.

Black, B., & Uhde, T. (1992). Elective mutism as a variant of social phobia. *Journal of the American Academy of Child and Adolescents*, 31, 1090–1094.

Bowler, J. (1996). An attachment theory approach to the treatment of separation anxiety beyond infancy. *Psychotherapy in Private Practice*, 15, 71–79.

Campbell, D. (1999). Family therapy and beyond: Where is the Milan systemic approach today? *Child Psychology & Psychiatry Review*, 4, 76–84.

Cela, J. A. (1995). A classical case of a severe obsessive–compulsive defense. *Modern Psychoanalysis, 20,* 271–277.

Chertoff, J. (1998). Psychodynamic assessment and treatment of traumatized patients. *Journal of Psychotherapy Practice and Research, 7,* 35–46.

Chhabra, S., & Fielding, D. (1985). The treatment of scriptophobia by *in vivo* exposure and cognitive restructuring. *Journal of Behavior and Experimental Psychiatry, 16,* 265–269.

Cohen, I. H., & Lichtenberg, J. D. (1967). Alopecia areata. *Archives of General Psychiatry, 17,* 608–614.

**Coleman, D. (1982–1983). Prestructural determinants in a case of phobia. *International Journal of Psychoanalytic Psychotherapy, 9,* 537–551.

Conrad, P. (1985). The hypnotic treatment of a case of intention tremor and muscle spasm. *Australian Journal of Experimental Hypnosis, 13,* 121–128.

**Ellis, P., Piersma, H., & Grayson, C. (1990). Interrupting the reenactment cycle: Psychotherapy of a sexually traumatized boy. *American Journal of Psychotherapy, 44,* 525–535.

Delmonte, M. (1996). The use of hypnotic regression with panic disorder. *Australian Journal of Clinical and Experimental Hypnosis, 17,* 1–5.

Desland, M. (1997). Post-traumatic stress disorder. *Australian Journal of Clinical and Experimental Hypnosis, 25,* 61–75.

**De Voge, J., Minor, T., & Karoly, P. (1981). Effects of behavioral intervention and interpersonal feedback on fear and avoidance components of severe agoraphobia: A case analysis. *Psychological Reports, 49,* 595–605.

**Flannery, R. (1972). Covert conditioning in the behavioral treatment of an agoraphobic. *Psychotherapy: Theory, Research and Practice, 9,* 217–220.

**Frame, C., Turner, S., Jacob, R., & Szekely, B. (1984). Self-exposure treatment of agoraphobia. *Behavior Modification, 8,* 115–122.

Frances, A., & Petit, T. (1984). Boy with seriously ill mother manifests somatic complaints, withdrawal, disabling fears. *Hospital and Community Psychiatry, 35,* 439–440.

French, C. (1995). The meaning of trauma: Hypnosis and PTSD. *Australian Journal of Clinical and Experimental Hypnosis, 23,* 113–123.

Gammelgaard, J. (1992). They suffer mainly from reminiscences. *Scandinavian Psychoanalytic Review, 15,* 104–121.

Gordon-Cohen, N. (1987). Vietnam and reality: The story of Mr. D. *American Journal of Dance Therapy, 10,* 95–109.

**Gorham, E. (1997). Sixteen-step strategic family therapy for the treatment of child sexual abuse: A treatment adaptation and case example. *Psychotherapy in Private Practice, 16,* 21–37.

Grant, J. (1997). When one model is not good enough therapy. *Psychodynamic Counseling, 3,* 49–62.

Grassick, P. (1991). The fear behind the fear: A case study of apparent simple injection phobia. *Journal of Behavior Therapy and Experimental Psychiatry, 21,* 281–287.

**Greer, J. (1994). Return of the repressed in the analysis of an adult incest survivor: A case study and some tentative generalizations. *Psychoanalytic Psychology, 11*, 545–561.

Hare-Mustin, R. T. (1979). Family therapy following the death of a child. *Journal of Marital and Family Therapy, 5*, 51–58.

Hingley, S. (2001). Psychodynamic theory and narcissistically related personality problems: Support from case study research. *British Journal of Medical Psychology, 74*(Pt. 1), 57–72.

Hyer, L., Jacob, M., & Pattison, M. (1987). Later-life struggle: Psychological and spiritual convergence. *Journal of Pastoral Care, 41*, 141–148.

Ireland, S., & Ireland, M. (1994). A case history of family and cult abuse. *Journal of Psychohistory, 21*, 417–428.

Kay, J. (1996). Is psychoanalytic psychotherapy relevant to the treatment of OCD? *Journal of Psychotherapy Practice and Research, 5*, 341–354.

Kellett, S., & Beail, N. (1997). The treatment of chronic post-traumatic nightmares using psychodynamic interpersonal therapy. *British Journal of Medical Psychology, 70*, 35–49.

*Khawaja, N., & Oei, T. (1998). Catastrophic cognitions and the clinical outcome: Two case studies. *Behavioral and Cognitive Psychotherapy, 26*, 271–282.

King, M., & Stanley, G. (1986). The treatment of hyperhidrosis. *Australian Journal of Clinical and Experimental Hypnosis, 14*, 61–64.

**Laguna, L., Healey, C., & Hope, D. (1998). Successful interdisciplinary intervention with an initially treatment-resistant social phobic. *Behavior Modification, 22*, 358–371.

**Lane, R., & Foehrenbach, L. (1994). Psychotherapy of a man with panic, somatization, and traumatic anxiety: A psychoanalytic case study. *Journal of Contemporary Psychotherapy, 24*, 107–123.

**Last, C., Barlow, D., & O'Brien, G. (1984). Cognitive changes during *in vivo* exposure in an agoraphobic. *Behavior Modification, 8*, 93–113.

Lipsett, L. (1998). Hypnosis in the treatment of social phobia. *Australian Journal of Clinical and Experimental Hypnosis, 26*, 57–64.

Meyer, W. S. (1985). The Oedipus complex: A reminder of its clinical import. *Clinical Social Work Journal, 13*, 234–245.

**Milrod, B. (1998). Unconscious pregnancy as an underlying dynamism in panic disorder. *Journal of the American Psychiatric Association, 46*, 673–690.

Moore, B. (1988). A young child's use of a physical–psychological metaphor. *Metaphor and Symbolic Activity, 3*, 223–232.

*Moylans, A., & Dadds, M. (1992). Hyperhidrosis: A case study and theoretical formulation. *Behavior Change, 9*, 87–95.

O'Brien, J. (1979). A modified thought stopping procedure for the treatment of agoraphobia. *Journal of Behavior Therapy and Experimental Psychiatry, 10*, 121–124.

**Osofsky, J., Cohen, G., & Drell, M. (1995). The effects of trauma on young children: A case study of two-year-old twins. *International Journal of Psychoanalysis, 76*, 595–607.

Owens, E., & Piacentini, J. (1998). Behavioral treatment of obsessive compulsive disorder in a boy with comorbid disruptive behavior problems. *Journal of the American Academy of Child and Adolescent Psychiatry, 37*, 443–446.

Pam, A., Inghiltera, K., & Munson, C. (1994). Agoraphobia: The interface between anxiety and personality disorder. *Bulletin of the Menninger Clinic, 58*, 242–261.

**Schwartz, C., Houlihan, D., Krueger, K. F., & Simon, D. A. (1997). The behavioral treatment of a young adult with post traumatic stress disorder and a fear of children. *Child and Family Behavior Therapy, 19*, 37–49.

Sidoli, M. (1984). Analysis: A space for separation. *Journal of Analytical Psychology, 29*, 139–154.

**Sohn, L. (1995). Unspoken assaults. *International Journal of Psychoanalysis, 76*, 565–575.

Stamm, J. (1972). Infantile trauma, narcissistic injury and agoraphobia. *Psychiatric Quarterly, 46*, 254–272.

Stravynski, A. (1983). Behavioral treatment of psychogenic vomiting in the context of social phobia. *Journal of Nervous and Mental Disease, 171*, 448–451.

Tracey, N., Blake, P., Warren, B., Hardy, H., Enfield, S., & Shein, P. (1996). Will I be to my son as my father was to me?: Narrative of a father of a premature baby. *Journal of Psychotherapy, 22*, 168–194.

**Trad, P., & Pfeffer, C. (1988). Treatment of an abused preadolescent and the role of parental self-reporting. *American Journal of Psychotherapy, 42*, 124–134.

Viederman, M. (1993). A countertransference cure evoked by enactment. *Journal of Psychotherapy Practice and Research, 2*, 334–341.

**Waldman, M. (1992). The therapeutic alliance, Kundalini, and spirituality/religious issues in counseling: The case of Julia. *Journal of Transpersonal Psychology, 24*, 115–149.

Willshire, D. (1996). Trauma and treatment with hypnosis. *Australian Journal of Clinical and Experimental Hypnosis, 24*, 125–136.

Wolpe, J., & Abrams, J. (1991). Posttraumatic stress disorder overcome by eye-movement desensitization: A case report. *Journal of Behavior Therapy and Experimental Psychiatry, 22*, 39–43.

Woltmann, A. G. (1971). The riddle of the Amazon. *Psychoanalytic Review, 58*, 135–148.

Yusin, A. (1973). Attempted suicide in an adolescent—The resolution of an anxiety state. *Adolescence, 8*(29), 17–28.

CHILDHOOD AND ADOLESCENT DISORDERS

*Ascher, M. (1985–1986). Conjoint treatment of mother and her 16-month-old toddler. *International Journal of Psychoanalytic Psychotherapy, 11*, 315–330.

Bembray, J., & Ericson, C. (1999). Therapeutic termination with the early adolescent who has experienced multiple losses. *Child and Adolescent Social Work Journal, 16*, 177–189.

Berse, P. (1980). Psychotherapy with severely deprived children: Keith. *Journal of Child Psychotherapy*, 6, 49–55.

Bowler, J. (1996). An attachment theory approach to the treatment of separation anxiety beyond infancy. *Psychotherapy in Private Practice*, 15, 71–79.

Caracushansky, S., Giampeitro, A., & Marechal, R. (1987). The use of myths and fairy tales in a Bernian approach to psychotherapy. *Transactional Analysis Journal*, 17, 277–285.

Carey, L. (1990). Sandplay therapy with a troubled child. *Arts in Psychotherapy*, 17, 197–209.

*Cath, S. H., & Cohen, H. (1967). Elbow rubbing and the wish to be beaten: A study of a case and the possible genesis of perversion. *Israel Annals of Psychiatry and Related Disciplines*, 5, 185–197.

Diamond, G. M., Diamond, G. S., & Liddle, H. (2000). The therapist–parent alliance in family-based therapy for adolescents. *Journal of Clinical Psychology*, 56, 1037–1058.

Durand, M., & Mindell, J. (1990). Behavioral treatment of multiple childhood sleep disorders: Effects on child and family. *Behavior Modification*, 14, 37–49.

Emanuel, L. (1997). Facing the damage together: Some reflections arising from the treatment in psychotherapy of a severely mentally handicapped child. *Journal of Child Psychotherapy*, 23, 279–302.

Erdreich, M., Soliman, P., & Shihor (1985). The disidentification syndrome of youth and its treatment. *Dynamic Psychiatry*, 18, 371–381.

Furman, E. (1981). Treatment via the parent: A case of bereavement. *Journal of Child Psychotherapy*, 7, 89–101.

Garber, B. (1991). The analysis of a learning-disabled child. *Annual of Psychoanalysis*, 19, 127–150.

Klein, J., Feinstein, J., & Feinstein, S. (1986). The role of the pediatrician in manic–depressive disorder in childhood and adolescence. *International Journal of Adolescent Medicine and Health*, 2, 119–128.

Langlands, S. (1995). A process of mourning in the life and in the analysis of an adolescent. *International Forum on Psychoanalysis*, 4, 185–195.

Lebovici, S. (1974). Observations on children who have witnessed the violent death of one of their parents: A contribution to the study of traumatization. *International Review of Psychoanalysis*, 1, 117–123.

Muir, E. (1984). On asking what you are not supposed to ask: The use of transference in the integration of individual and family therapy. *Journal of Child Psychotherapy*, 10, 239–249.

Owens, E., & Piancentini, J. (1998). Behavioral treatment of obsessive–compulsive disorder in a boy with comorbid disruptive behavior problems. *Journal of the American Academy of Child and Adolescent Psychiatry*, 37, 443–446.

Pumariega, A., & Snow, S. (1984). Multilevel intervention on behalf of a catastrophically ill child. *Family Systems Medicine*, 3, 326–333.

**Rabenu, P., & Rabenu, T. (1995). The role of free movement in separation–individuation. *Psychoanalytic Study of the Child*, 50, 150–167.

Ravagli, B. M. (1999). The rehabilitation of primary object relations in the first year of intensive therapy with a severely deprived child. *Journal of Child Psychotherapy*, 23, 447–472.

Sherman, J., & Formanek, R. (1985). School phobia in a multiphobic family: The family that phobes together. *Child and Adolescent Social Work*, 2, 114–124.

*Sikelianos, M. (1975). The use of symbolic drawing, metaphor, and illusion in the therapeutic–creative process. *Israel Annals of Psychiatry and Related Disciplines*, 13, 142–161.

Smith, J. (1993). Working close to the edge: The use of dual paradigms in psychotherapy with an adolescent. *Australian Journal of Psychotherapy*, 12, 152–165.

Stiles, K., & Kottman, T. (1990). Mutual storytelling: An intervention for depressed and suicidal children. *School Counselor*, 37, 337–342.

Sugarman, A. (1999). The boy in the iron mask: Superego issues in the analysis of a two-year-old encopretic. *Psychoanalytic Quarterly*, 68, 497–517.

Taichert, L. (1979). Two adolescents at risk for schizophrenia: A family case study. *International Journal of Family Therapy*, 7, 138–148.

*Tonelli, G. (1986). Issues in the differential diagnosis: A case study of a latency age borderline child. *Smith College Studies in Social Work*, 56, 206–223.

Trevatt, D. (1999). An account of a little boy's attempt to recover from the trauma of abuse. *Journal of Child Psychotherapy*, 25, 267–287.

Wetchler, J. (1990). Family treatment of a fifteen-year-old social isolate. *Journal of Family Psychotherapy*, 1, 29–38.

*Williams, D., Nover, R., Castellan, J., Greenspan, S., & Lieberman, A. (1987). A case of double vulnerability for mother and child: Louise and Robbie. *Clinical Infant Reports*, 3, 39–79.

*Williams, D., Nover, R. A., Ward, D. B., Castellan, J. M., Greenspan, S. I., Lieberman, & A. F. (1987). Two infants, a family, and the service system: The Lake family. *Clinical Infant Reports*, 3, 81–124.

DISORDERS DUE TO A MEDICAL CONDITION OR INJURY

Buskirk, J. R. (1992). Headlock: Psychotherapy of a patient with multiple neurological and psychiatric problems. *Bulletin of the Menninger Clinic*, 56, 361–378.

Daigneault, S., Braum, C., & Montes, J. (1997). Pseudodepressive personality and mental inertia in a child with a focal left-frontal lesion. *Developmental Neuropsychology*, 13, 1–22.

Debimpe, V. (1977). Complex partial seizures simulating schizophrenia. *Journal of the American Medical Association*, 237, 1339–1341.

DISSOCIATIVE DISORDERS

**Appelbaum, S. (1996). Multiple personality disorder and the choice of self: Change factors in a brief therapy case. *Journal of Contemporary Psychotherapy*, 26, 103–116.

**Davis, P., & Osherson, A. (1977). The concurrent treatment of a multiple personality woman and her son. *American Journal of Psychotherapy, 31*, 505–515.

Fink, D. (1992). The psychotherapy of multiple personality disorder: A case study. *Psychoanalytic Inquiry, 12*, 49–70.

Goldman, J. (1995). A mutual story-telling technique as an aid to integration after abreaction in the treatment of MPD. *Dissociation: Progress in the Dissociative Disorders, 8*, 53–60.

Hine, J. (1997). Dissociation: A case study. *Transactional Analysis Journal, 27*, 207–219.

Kirsch, I., & Barton, R. (1988). Hypnosis in the treatment of multiple personality: A cognitive–behavioral approach. *British Journal of Experimental and Clinical Hypnosis, 5*, 131–137.

Levenson, J., & Berry, S. (1983). Family intervention in a case of multiple personality. *Journal of Marital and Family Therapy, 9*, 73–80.

**Loewenstein, R., Hamilton, J., Alagna, S., Reid, A., & deVries, M. (1987). Experimental sampling in a study of multiple personality disorder. *American Journal of Psychiatry, 144*, 19–24.

Schnabel, J. (1994). Chronic claims of alien abduction and some other traumas as self-victimization syndromes. *Dissociation, 7*, 51–62.

Smith, D., Titus, E., & Carr, M. (1989). An integrative treatment technique in multiple personality disorder. *Medical Psychotherapy, 2*, 1–10.

Snow, M., White, J., Pilkington, L., & Beckman, D. (1995). Dissociative identity disorder revealed through play therapy: A case study of a four-year-old. *Dissociation, 8*, 120–123.

Somer, L., & Somer, E. (1997). Phenomenological and psychoanalytic perspectives on a spontaneous artistic process during psychotherapy for dissociative identity disorder. *Arts in Psychotherapy, 24*, 419–429.

Witztum, E., Buchbinder, J., & van der Hart, O. (1990). Summoning a punishing angel: Treatment of a depressed patient with dissociative features. *Bulletin of the Menninger Clinic, 54*, 524–537.

Wurmser, L. (2000). Magic transformation and tragic transformation-splitting of ego and superego in severely traumatized patients. *Clinical Social Work Journal, 28*, 385–402.

EATING DISORDERS

Achimovich. (1985). Suicidal scripting in the families of anorectics. *Transactional Analysis Journal, 15*, 21–29.

**Adelson, M. (1996). Aura: A case history. *Journal of Clinical Psychoanalysis, 5*, 529–551.

Anonymous. (1998). Clinical commentary XXIII. *British Journal of Psychotherapy, 15*, 105–122.

Bergner, R. (1997). The use of a recent formulation of bulimia nervosa in the successful treatment of a bulimic woman. *Family Therapy, 24*, 71–79.

Bridges, N. (1999). Psychodynamic perspective on therapeutic boundaries: Creative clinical possibilities. *Journal of Psychotherapy Practice and Research, 8,* 292–300.

Chatoor, I., Conley, C., & Dickson, L. (1988). Food refusal after an incident of choking: A posttraumatic eating disorder. *Journal of the American Academy of Child and Adolescent Psychiatry, 2,* 105–110.

*Emmett, S. (1989). Rebecca B., control artist: Case study of a bulimic collegian. *Journal of College Student Psychotherapy, 2,* 205–220.

Giles, T. (1988). Distortion of body image as an effect of conditioned fear. *Journal of Behavior Therapy and Experimental Psychiatry, 19,* 143–146.

Miller, L. (1997). Mother–daughter and absent father: Oedipal issues in the therapy of an 11-year-old girl with an eating disorder. *Journal of Child Psychotherapy, 23,* 81–102.

Mirkin, M. (1983). The Peter Pan syndrome: Inpatient treatment of adolescent anorexia nervosa. *International Journal of Family Therapy, 5,* 179–189.

Parsons, M. (1982). Imposed termination of psychotherapy and its relation to death and mourning. *British Journal of Medical Psychology, 55,* 35–40.

Rusbridger, R. (1986). Observations on a case of bulimia. *Journal of Child Psychotherapy, 12*(2), 5–28.

Singer, L., Ambuel, B., Wade, S., & Jaffe, A. (1992). Cognitive–behavioral treatment of health-impairing food phobias in children. *Journal of the American Academy of Child and Adolescent Psychiatry, 31,* 847–852.

Smeijsters, H., & van den Hurk, J. (1993). Research in practice in the music therapeutic treatment of a client with symptoms of anorexia nervosa. In M. H. Heal & T. Wigram (Eds.), *Music therapy in health and education.* London: Jessica Kingsley.

Theissen, I. (1983). Using fairy tales during hypnotherapy in bulimerexia and other psychological problems. *Medical Hypnoanalysis, 4,* 139–144.

Walters, E. (1997). Anorexia nervosa in a young boy with gender identity disorder of childhood: A case report. *Clinical Child Psychology and Psychiatry, 2,* 463–467.

White, J. (1984). Bulimia utilizing individual and family therapy. *Journal of Psychosocial Nursing, 22*(4), 22–28.

Woods, P., & Grieger, R. (1993). Bulimia: A case study with mediating cognitions and notes on a cognitive–behavioral analysis of eating disorders. *Journal of Rational-Emotive & Cognitive-Behavioral Therapy, 11,* 159–172.

FACTITIOUS DISORDERS

Stone, M. H. (1977). Factitious illness: Psychological findings and treatment recommendations. *Bulletin of the Menninger Clinic, 41,* 239–254.

IMPULSE CONTROL DISORDERS

Johnson, B., Franklin, L., Hall, K., & Prieto, L. (2000). Parent training through play: Parent–child interaction therapy with a hyperactive child. *Family Journal, 8,* 180–186.

Schmidt, K., & Friedson, S. (1990). Atypical outcome in ADHD. *Journal of the American Academy of Child and Adolescent Psychiatry, 29,* 556–570.

MOOD DISORDERS

Arieti, S. (1976). Psychoanalysis of severe depression: Theory and therapy. *Journal of the American Academy of Psychoanalysis, 4,* 327–345.

Barash, D. (1986). Deflecting suicide: A clinical case report. *Bulletin of the Menninger Clinic, 50,* 367–378.

Barth, R. (1985). Beating the blues: Cognitive–behavioral treatment for depression in child-maltreating young mothers. *Clinical Social Work Journal, 13,* 317–328.

Betchen, S. J. (1992). Short-term psychodynamic therapy with a divorced single mother. *Families in Society, 73,* 116–121.

Birner, L. (1983). Depression and the edge of violence. *Modern Psychoanalysis, 8,* 191–205.

**Bose, J. (1995). Trauma, depression, and mourning. *Contemporary Psychoanalysis, 31,* 399–407.

Bush, C. A. (1988). Dreams, mandalas, and music imagery: Therapeutic uses in a case study. *Arts in Psychotherapy, 15,* 219–225.

Chessick, R. (1983). Mental health and the care of the soul in mid-life. *Journal of Pastoral Care, 37,* 5–12.

Curtis, H. C. (1990). The patient as existential victim: A classical view. *Psychoanalytic Inquiry, 10,* 498–508.

Close, R. (2000). Logotherapy and adult major depression: Psychotheological dimensions in diagnosing the disorder. *Journal of Religious Gerontology, 11,* 119–140.

Dahl, A. (1988). Aspects of the analysis of a patient with severe depression. *Scandinavian Psychoanalytic Review, 11,* 3–23.

**Downey, T. (1988). The disavowal of authority in a child of divorce. *Psychoanalytic Study of the Child, 43,* 279–289.

Dye, N., & Fine, H. (1977). Concept of character revisited: An ego-psychological view with some thoughts on the depressive character. *Psychological Reports, 41,* 763–776.

Edward, J. (1987). The dream as a vehicle for the recovery of childhood trauma. *Clinical Social Work Journal, 15,* 356–360.

Evans, D., Jeckel, L., & Slott, N. (1982). Erotomania: A variant of pathological mourning. *Bulletin of the Menninger Clinic, 46,* 507–520.

*Feuchtwanger, D. (1985). Creative inter-personal experience of mourning in psychotherapy. *Israel Journal of Psychiatry and Related Science, 22,* 105–112.

Fosshage, J. (1990). The analyst's response. *Psychoanalytic Inquiry, 10,* 601–622.

Fosshage, J. (1990). Clinical protocol. *Psychoanalytic Inquiry, 10,* 461–477.

Fox, B., & Scipio, W. (1968). An exploratory study in the treatment of homosexuality by combining principles from psychoanalytical theory and conditioning: Theoretical and methodological considerations. *British Journal of Medical Psychology, 41*, 273–282.

Freudenthal, G. (1995). Major depression: A case study. *Modern Psychoanalysis, 20*, 251–262.

Fulmer, R. (1983). A structural approach to unresolved mourning in single parent family systems. *Journal of Marital and Family Therapy, 9*, 259–269.

**Gavshon, A. (1990). The analysis of a latency boy: The developmental impact of separation, divorce and remarriage. *Psychoanalytic Study of the Child, 45*, 217–233.

Gizynski, M. N. (1985). The effects of maternal depression on children. *Clinical Social Work Journal, 13*, 103–116.

Gootnick, I. (1982). The problem of treating an intensely suffering patient: To gratify or frustrate. *Psychoanalytic Review, 69*, 487–496.

Gorkin, M. (1985). On the suicide of one's patient. *Bulletin of the Menninger Clinic, 49*, 1–9.

Gottlieb, A. R. (1996). John: Some thoughts on mourning. *Clinical Social Work Journal, 24*, 271–276.

Gurian, B. (1998). Clinical diagnosis and management of anxiety in the elderly. *Journal of Geriatric Psychiatry, 33*, 155–164.

Hetherington, A. (1999). A psychodynamic perspective on early childhood trauma in an adult: A case study. *Psychodynamic Counseling, 5*, 73–85.

Hyer, L., Jacob, M., & Pattison, E. (1987). Later-life struggle: Psychological/spiritual convergence. *Journal of Pastoral Care, 41*, 141–148.

**Imber, R. (1995). Clinical notes on masochism. *Contemporary Psychoanalysis, 31*, 581–589.

Koetting, M. G. (2001). Therapeutic metaphor as a barrier to the self: A case of an older adult. *Journal of Clinical Geropsychology, 7*, 245–250.

Langlands, S. N. (1995). A process of mourning in the life and in the analysis of an adolescent. *International Forum of Psychoanalysis, 4*, 185–195.

Larsen, J., Hein, L., & Stromgren, L. (1998). Ventricular tachycardia with ECT. *Journal of ECT, 14*, 109–114.

Lipchik, E., & Vega, D. (1985). A case study from two perspectives. *Journal of Strategic and Systemic Therapies, 4*, 27–41.

Maltsberger, J. (1996). In conscience's talons: The suicide of a Vietnam veteran. *Suicide and Life-Threatening Behavior, 26*, 424–430.

Mammen, O., Shear, K., Jennings, K., & Popper, S. (1997) Case study: Ego-systonic anger attacks in mothers of young children. *Journal of the American Academy of Child and Adolescent Psychiatry, 36*, 1374–1377.

Milbrath, C., Bauknight, R., Horowitz, M., Amaro, R., & Sugahara, C. (1995). Sequential analysis of topics in psychotherapy discourse: A single-case study. *Psychotherapy Research, 5*, 199–217.

Miller, J. & Miller, A. (1990). Reflections on the commentaries. *Psychoanalytic Inquiry*, *10*, 585–591.

Miller, J., & Sonnenberg, S. (1973). Depression following psychotic episodes: A response to the challenge of change. *Journal of the American Academy of Psychoanalysis*, *1*, 253–270.

Minty, B. (1986). Staying with a client. *Journal of Social Work Practice*, *2*, 15–30.

Moses, I. (1995). The "happy childhood" of a depressed boy. *International Forum of Psychoanalysis*, *4*, 196–198.

Muller, J. (1981). The analyst's mythology of needs: A Lacanian view. *Psychoanalytic Inquiry*, *10*, 567–584.

Nezu, A., & Nezu, C. (2001). Problem solving therapy. *Journal of Psychotherapy Integration*, *11*, 187–205.

Nilman, I., & Lewin, C. (1989). Inhibited mourning in a latency age child. *British Journal of Psychotherapy*, *5*, 523–531.

Ornstein, P. (1990). How to enter a psychoanalytic process conducted by another analyst: A self-psychology view. *Psychoanalytic Inquiry*, *10*, 478–497.

**Ortmeyer, D. (1995). Interpersonal psychoanalysis with a masochistic patient. *Contemporary Psychoanalysis*, *31*, 591–601.

Parsons, M. (1982). Imposed termination of psychotherapy and its relation to death and mourning. *British Journal of Medical Psychology*, *55*, 35–40.

Rapmund, V. (1999). A story around the role of relationships in the world of a depressed woman and the healing process. *Contemporary Family Therapy*, *21*, 239–266.

Richman, J. (1997). Being suicidal and elderly in changing times: A case history. *Suicide and Life-Threatening Behavior*, *27*, 34–40.

Roshni, D. (2000). Buddhist psychology, a theory of change processes: Implications for counselors. *International Journal for the Advancement of Counseling*, *22*, 257–271.

Selekman, M. D. (1993). Turning out the light on a seasonal affective disorder. *Journal of Systemic Therapies*, *15*, 40–51.

Siegel, B. (1982). Penis envy. *Bulletin of the Menninger Clinic*, *46*, 363–376.

Silven, D., & Gallagher, D. (1986). Resistance in cognitive–behavioral therapy: A case study. *Clinical Gerontologist*, *6*, 75–78.

Silverman, M. J. (1987). Clinical material. *Psychoanalytic Inquiry*, *7*, 147–165.

Small, J. (1988). The rediscovery of the lost twin: An account of therapy for a child and his parents. *British Journal of Psychotherapy*, *5*, 19–28.

Solomon, I. (1985). On feeling hopeless. *Psychoanalytic Review*, *72*, 55–69.

Stiles, K., & Kottman, T. (1990). Mutual storytelling: An intervention for depressed and suicidal children. *School Counselor*, *37*, 337–342.

Swartz, H. A., Markowitz, J. C., & Spinelli, M. G. (1997). Interpersonal psychotherapy of a depressed, pregnant, HIV-positive woman. *Journal of Psychotherapy Practice and Research*, *6*, 166–178.

Trop, J., & Stolorow, R. (1991). A developmental perspective on analytic empathy: A case study. *Journal of the American Academy of Psychoanalysis, 19*, 31–46.

Viederman, M. (1993). A countertransference cure evoked by enactment. *Clinical and Research Reports, 2*, 334–341.

Viederman, M. (1999). Presence and enactment as a vehicle of psychotherapeutic change. *Journal of Psychotherapy Practice & Research, 8*, 274–283.

**Wheelock, I. (1997). Psychodynamic psychotherapy with the older adult: Challenges facing the patient and the therapist. *American Journal of Psychotherapy, 51*, 431–444.

Weimer, S. (1978). Using fairy tales in psychotherapy: Rapunzel. *Bulletin of the Menninger Clinic, 42*, 25–34.

Wexler, D. A., & Butler, J. M. (1976). Therapist modification of client expressiveness in client-centered therapy. *Journal of Consulting and Clinical Psychology, 44*, 261–265.

OTHER CONDITIONS THAT MAY BE A FOCUS OF CLINICAL ATTENTION

Disorders Due to Abuse and Neglect

Abrahams, J., & Hoey, H. (1994). Sibling incest in a clergy family: A case study. *Child Abuse and Neglect, 18*, 1029–1035.

Aldridge, D., Brandt, G., & Wohler, D. (1990). Toward a common language among the creative art therapies. *Arts in Psychotherapy, 17*, 189–195.

Beech, S. (2000). My mother messed with me: The legacy of abuse by his mother for a 10-year-old boy. *Journal of Child Psychotherapy, 26*, 259–280.

Bernstein, A. E. (1989). Analysis of two adult female patients who had been victims of incest in childhood. *Journal of the American Academy of Psychoanalysis, 17*, 207–221.

Close, H. (1970). Forgiveness and responsibility: A case study. *Pastoral Psychology, 21*(205), 19–25.

Cole, E. (1982). Sibling incest: The myth of benign sibling incest. *Women & Therapy, 1*, 79–89.

Delmonte, M. (1996). The use of hypnotic regression with panic disorder: A case report. *Australian Journal of Clinical Hypnotherapy and Hypnosis, 17*, 1–5.

Emde, R., Boyd, C., & Mayo, G. (1968). Family treatment of *folie à deux*. *Psychiatric Quarterly, 42*, 698–711.

Hall, C. A., & Henderson, C. (1996). Cognitive processing therapy for chronic PTSD from childhood sexual abuse: A case study. *Counseling Psychology Quarterly, 9*, 359–371.

Lyon, K. (1992). Beth: A case history. *Psychoanalytic Inquiry, 12*, 71–94.

Ney, P., & Mulvihill, D. (1982). Case report on parent abuse. *Victimology: An International Journal, 7*, 194–198.

Parens, H. (1987). Cruelty begins at home. *Child Abuse & Neglect, 11*, 331–338.

Parker, R. (1997). Sarah's story: Using ritual therapy to address psychospiritual issues in treating survivors of childhood sexual abuse. *Counseling and Values, 42*(1), 41–54.

Ratigan, B. (1995). Inner world, outer world: Exploring the tension of race, sexual orientation and class and the internal world. *Psychodynamic Counseling, 1*, 173–186.

Smith, P. (1997). Secret friends: Borderline symptomatology and post-traumatic stress disorder in a case of reported sexual abuse. *British Journal of Psychotherapy, 14*, 18–32.

Whelan, M. (1995). The loss of the sense of reality in incest and child sexual abuse: A psychoanalytic perspective. *Australian & New Zealand Journal of Psychiatry, 29*, 415–423.

Relational Disorders

Focht-Birkerts, L., & Beardslee, W. (2000). A child's experience of parental depression: Encouraging relational resilience in families with affective illness. *Family Process, 39*, 417–434.

Wetchler, J. (1990). Family treatment of a fifteen-year-old social isolate. *Journal of Family Psychotherapy, 1*, 29–38.

PERSONALITY DISORDERS

Barlow, S. (1996). Origins of BPD: Cronus eating his children—A case report. *Journal of the American Academy of Psychoanalysis, 24*, 499–513.

Becker, C. B. (2002). Integrated behavioral treatment of comorbid OCD, PTSD, and borderline personality disorder: A case report. *Cognitive and Behavioral Practice, 9*, 100–110.

Bennett, A. (1997). A view of the violence contained in chronic fatigue syndrome. *Journal of Analytical Psychology, 42*, 237–251.

Berry, S. & Roath, M. (1982). Family treatment of a borderline personality. *Clinical Social Work Journal, 10*, 3–14.

Biancoli, R. (2000). On impediments to the process of individuation. *International Forum on Psychoanalysis, 9*, 227–238.

Chessick, R. (1982). Intensive psychotherapy of a borderline patient. *Archives of General Psychiatry, 39*, 413–419.

*Conn, J. (1955). Treatment of symptomatic psychopathy. *Archives of Criminal Psychodynamics, 1*, 111–136.

Davison, G. (2000). A cognitive–behavioral analysis of a patient with borderline personality disorder. *Cognitive and Behavioral Practice, 7*, 497–500.

Dublin, P. (1992). Severe borderlines and self psychology. *Clinical Social Work Journal, 20*, 285–294.

Gabbard, G. O., & Nemiah, J. C. (1985). Multiple determinants of anxiety in a patient with borderline personality disorder. *Bulletin of the Menninger Clinic, 49,* 161–172.

Greenberg, R. P., & Pies, R. (1983). Is paradoxical intention risk-free: A review and case report. *Journal of Clinical Psychiatry, 44,* 62–69.

Hingley, S. (2001). Psychodynamic theory and narcissistically related personality problems: Support from case study research. *British Psychological society, 74,* 57–72.

Hurtig, A. (1985). Case presentation: Adolescent borderline patient with severe cardiac involvement: Diagnosis and treatment from a psychoanalytic–developmental perspective. *Psychoanalytic Psychology, 2,* 67–77.

*Orne, M., Dinges, D., & Orne, E. (1984). On the differential diagnosis of multiple personality in the forensic context. *International Journal of Clinical & Experimental Hypnosis, 32,* 118–169.

Preodor, D., & Wolpert, E. (1979). Manic–depressive illness in adolescence. *Journal of Youth and Adolescence, 8,* 111–130.

Valenti, S. A. M. (2002). Use of object relations and self-psychology as treatment for sex addiction with a female borderline patient. *Sexual Addiction and Compulsivity, 9,* 249–262.

*Watkins, J. (1984). The Bianchi case (L.A. Hillside Strangler): Sociopath or multiple personality? *International Journal of Clinical & Experimental Hypnosis, 32,* 67–101.

**Wheelis, J., & Gunderson, J. (1998). A little cream and sugar: Psychotherapy with a borderline patient. *American Journal of Psychiatry, 155,* 114–122.

SCHIZOPHRENIA/PSYCHOTIC DISORDERS

Boyer, L. (1975). Meanings of a bizarre suicidal attempt by an adolescent. *Adolescent Psychiatry, 4,* 371–381.

Bradshaw, W. (1998). Cognitive–behavioral treatment of schizophrenia: A case study. *Journal of Cognitive Psychotherapy, 12,* 13–25.

Cerney, M. (1984). Unraveling the symbiotic bond: Psychotherapeutic change in a schizophrenic patient. *Bulletin of the Menninger Clinic, 48,* 479–497.

Ekstein, R., & Friedman, S. (1971). Do you have faith that I'll make it? *Reiss Davis Clinic Bulletin, 8,* 94–105.

Juni, S. (1980). The stigma of mental illness as a cultural phenomenon: A study of schizophrenia in the orthodox Jewish family. *Family Therapy, 7,* 223–235.

**Khantizian, E., Dalsimer, J., & Semrad, E. (1969). The use of the interpretation in the psychotherapy of schizophrenia. *American Journal of Psychotherapy, 23,* 182–197.

Kjellqvist, E. (1995). The regeneration of a soul's history. *Scandinavian Psychoanalytic Review, 18,* 160–175.

**Klein, B. (1990). Survival dilemmas: Case study of an adult child of a schizophrenic parent. *Clinical Social Work Journal, 18,* 43–56.

**McGlashan, T., & Hayfack, B. (1988). Psychotherapeutic models and the treatment of schizophrenia: The records of three successful psychotherapists with one patient at Chestnut Lodge over 18 years. *Psychiatry, 51,* 340–362.

*Pontalti, C., & Menarini, R. (1997). Group-analytic family psychotherapy: A transcultural perspective (L. Hyde, Trans.). *Group Analysis, 30,* 349–359.

*Schmiedeck, R. (1973). Letters from a schizophrenic patient: Their role in psychotherapy. *International Journal of Psychoanalytic Psychotherapy, 2,* 221–239.

*Searles, H. (1972). Intensive psychotherapy chronic schizophrenia. *International Journal of Psychoanalytic Psychotherapy, 1,* 30–51.

Searles, H. (1972). The function of the patient's realistic perceptions of the analyst in delusional transference. *British Journal of Medical Psychology, 45,* 1–18.

**Sheiner, S. (1969). Investigative learning in a schizophrenic. *American Journal of Psychoanalysis, 29,* 205–211.

**Silver, A. (1997). Chestnut Lodge, then and now: Work with schizophrenia and obsessive compulsive disorder. *Contemporary Psychoanalysis, 55,* 227–249.

**Smith, J. (1975). Life and death of a schizophrenic. *Psychotherapy, 12,* 2–7.

**Umbarger, C., & Hare, R. (1973). A structural approach to patient and therapist disengagement from a schizophrenic family. *American Journal of Psychotherapy, 27,* 274–284.

White, J. (1985). The chemistry of a psychoanalysis. *Modern Psychoanalysis, 10,* 199–215.

Wundheiler, L. (1976). Liberty boy: The play of a schizophrenic child. *Journal of the American Academy of Child Psychiatry, 15,* 475–490.

SEXUAL AND GENDER IDENTITY DISORDERS/ISSUES

*Allison, J. (1975). Choosing a therapeutic system for treating sexual dysfunction: A traditional approach. *Psychotherapy: Theory, Research and Practice, 12,* 320–323.

Barnett, I. (1972). The successful treatment of an exhibitionist: A case report. *International Journal of Offender Therapy and Comparative Criminology, 16,* 125–129.

Bass, B. (1996). Short-term cognitive–behavioral treatment of hypoactive sexual desire in an individual with a history of childhood sexual abuse. *Journal of Sex and Marital Therapy, 22,* 284–289.

*Bemporad, J., Dunton, H. D., & Spady, F. H. (1976). The treatment of a child foot fetish. *American Journal of Psychotherapy, 30,* 303–316.

Berent, I. (1973). Original sin: I didn't mean to hurt you, Mother: A basic fantasy epitomized by a male homosexual. *Journal of the American Psychoanalytic Association, 21,* 262–284.

*Brinkley-Birk, A., & Birk, L. (1975). Sex therapy for vaginismus, primary impotence, and ejaculatory incompetence in an unconsummated marriage. *Psychiatric Opinion, 12*, 38–42.

Chopin-Marce, M. (2001). Exhibitionism and psychotherapy: A case study. *International Journal of Offender Therapy and Comparative Criminology, 45*, 626–633.

*Denko, J. D. (1973). Klismaphilia: Enema as a sexual preference. *American Journal of Psychotherapy, 27*, 232–250.

Eagle, M. (1993). Enactments, transference, and symptomatic cure: A case history. *Psychoanalytic Dialogues, 3*, 93–110.

Ellis, M. (1997). Who speaks? Who listens? Different voices and different sexualities. *British Journal of Psychotherapy, 13*, 369–383.

†**Freedman, A. (1978). Psychoanalytic study of an unusual perversion. *Journal of the American Psychoanalytic Association, 26*, 749–777.

Fox, B., & Scipio, W. (1968). An exploratory study in the treatment of homosexuality by combining principles from psychoanalytical theory and conditioning: Theoretical and methodological considerations. *British Journal of Medical Psychology, 41*, 273–282.

*Gagliardi, F. A. (1976). Ejaculation retardata: Conventional psychotherapy and se therapy in a severe obsessive–compulsive disorder. *American Journal of Psychotherapy, 30*, 85–94.

Garippa, P. A., & Sanders, N. (1997). Resolution of erectile dysfunction and inhibited male orgasm in a single homosexual male and transfer of inhibited male orgasm cure to his partner: A case report. *Journal of Sex & Marital Therapy, 23*, 126–130.

Gottesfeld, M. (1978). Treatment of vaginismus by psychotherapy with adjunctive hypnosis. *American Journal of Clinical Hypnosis, 20*, 272–277.

**Haber, C. H. (1991). The psychoanalytic treatment of a preschool boy with a gender identity disorder. *Journal of the American Psychoanalytic Association, 39*, 107–129.

Hopkins, J. (1984). The probable role of trauma in a case of foot and shoe fetishism: Aspects of the psychotherapy of a 6-year-old girl. *International Review of Psychoanalysis, 11*, 79–91.

Meyenburg, B. (1999). Gender identity disorder in adolescence: Outcomes of psychotherapy. *Adolescence, 34*, 305–313.

†**Miller, M., & Monroe, J. (1973). Psychoanalytic therapy of homosexuality. *Psychiatric Forum, 3*, 15–21.

Mitchell, S. (1981). The psychoanalytic treatment of homosexuality: Some technical considerations. *International Review of Psychoanalysis, 8*, 63–80.

Moergen, S., Merkel, W., & Brown, S. (1991). The use of covert sensitization and social skills training in the treatment of an obscene telephone caller. *Behavior Therapy and Experimental Psychiatry, 21*, 269–275.

Money, J. (1981). Paraphilia and abuse–martyrdom: Exhibitionism as a paradigm for reciprocal couple counseling combined with antiandrogen. *Journal of Sex and Marital Therapy, 7*, 115–123.

Myers, M. (1982). Homosexuality, sexual dysfunction, and incest in male identical twins. *Canadian Journal of Psychiatry, 27*, 144–147.

†**Olesker, W. (1995). Unconscious fantasy and compromise formation in a case of an adolescent female homosexual. *Journal of Clinical Psychoanalysis, 4*, 361–381.

Paul, R., Marx, B., & Orsillo, S. (1999). Acceptance-based psychotherapy in the treatment of an adjudicated exhibitionist: A case example. *Behavior Therapy, 30*, 149–162.

Pietsch, U. K. (2001). Strategic treatment of female hypoactive sexual desire disorder. *Journal of Family Psychotherapy, 12*(4), 31–44.

Ratigan, B. (1995). Inner world, outer world: Exploring the tension of race, sexual orientation and class and the internal world. *Psychodynamic Counseling, 1*, 173–186.

**Ruiz, P., Lile, B., & Matorin, A. (2002). Treatment of a dually diagnosed gay male patient: A psychotherapy perspective. *American Journal of Psychiatry, 159*, 209–215.

†**Segal, B., & Sims, J. (1972). Covert sensitization with a homosexual. *Journal of Consulting and Clinical Psychology, 39*, 259–263.

†**Serban, G. (1967). The existential therapeutic approach to homosexuality. *American Journal of Psychotherapy, 23*, 491–501.

Skene, R. (1973). Construct shift in the treatment of a case of homosexuality. *British Journal of Medical Psychology, 46*, 287–292.

Snyker, E. (1992). Treatment of exhibitionism in intensive short-term dynamic psychotherapy. *International Journal of Short-Term Psychotherapy, 7*, 13–30.

†*Socarides, C. (1969). Psychoanalytic therapy of a male homosexual. *Psychoanalytic Quarterly, 38*, 173–190.

*Socarides, C. (1973). Sexual perversion and the fear of engulfment. *International Journal of Psychoanalytic Psychotherapy, 2*, 432–448.

Trop, J. (1991). A developmental perspective on analytic empathy: A case study. *Journal of the American Academy of Psychoanalysis, 19*, 31–46.

Veenhuizen, A., Van Strien, D., & Cohen-Kettenis, P. (1992). The combined psychotherapeutic and lithium carbonate treatment of an adolescent with exhibitionism and indecent assault. *Journal of Psychology & Human Sexuality, 5*(3), 53–64.

Wallace, L. (1969). Psychotherapy of a male homosexual. *Psychoanalytic Review, 56*, 346–364.

*Wickramasekera, I. (1968). The application of learning theory to the treatment of a case of sexual exhibitionism. *Psychotherapy: Theory, Research and Practice, 5*, 108–112.

SLEEP DISORDERS

Brylowski, A. (1990). Nightmares in crisis: Clinical applications of lucid dreaming techniques. *Psychiatric Journal of the University of Ottawa, 15*, 79–84.

Connell, H., Persley, G., & Sturgess, J. (1987). Sleep phobia in middle childhood: A review of six cases. *Journal of the American Academy of Child and Adolescent Psychiatry, 26,* 449–452.

*Contos, A. (1999). The case of how the boogie man disappeared. *Australian Journal of Clinical and Experimental Hypnosis, 27,* 125–135.

Durand, M., & Mindell, J. (1990). Behavioral treatment of multiple childhood sleep disorders: Effects on child and family. *Behavior Modification, 14,* 37–49.

Eccles, A., Wilde, A., & Marshall, W. (1988). *In vivo* desensitization in the treatment of recurrent nightmares. *Journal of Behavior Therapy and Experimental Psychiatry, 19,* 285–288.

Ford, R. (1995). Hypnotic treatment of a sleeping problem in an 11-year-old boy. *Contemporary Hypnosis, 12,* 201–206.

**Gorton, G. E. (1988). Life-long nightmares: An eclectic treatment approach. *American Journal of Psychotherapy, 42,* 610–618.

*Howsam, D. G. (1999). Hypnosis in the treatment of insomnia, nightmares, and night terrors. *Australian Journal of Clinical and Experimental Hypnosis, 27,* 32–39.

*Johnsgard, K. W. (1969). Symbol confrontation in a recurrent nightmare. *Psychotherapy: Theory, Research & Practice, 6,* 177–182.

Kellett, S., & Beail, N. (1997). The treatment of chronic post-traumatic nightmares using psychodynamic–interpersonal psychotherapy: A single-case study. *British Journal of Medical Psychology, 70,* 35–49.

Kraft, T. (1986). The successful treatment of a case of night terrors (*pavor nocturnus*). *British Journal of Experimental & Clinical Hypnosis, 3,* 113–119.

*Stevenson, D. V. (1991). The analysis of an adult with night terror. *Psychoanalytic Quarterly, 60,* 607–627.

*Menaglio, D. (1993). The case of Mr. C. *Australian Journal of Clinical and Experimental Hypnosis, 21,* 95–107.

SOMATOFORM DISORDERS

Cardone, L., Marengo, J., & Calisch, A. (1984). Conjoint use of art and verbal techniques for the intensification of the psychotherapeutic group experience. *Arts in Psychotherapy, 9,* 263–268.

Conrad, P. (1985). The hypnotic treatment of a case of intention tremor and muscle spasm. *Australian Journal of Clinical and Experimental Hypnosis, 13,* 121–128.

Frances, A., & Petti, T. (1984). Boy with seriously ill mother manifests somatic complaints, withdrawal, disabling fears. *Hospital and Community Psychiatry, 35,* 439–440.

Gottlieb, A. (1996). John: Some thoughts on mourning. *Clinical Social Work Journal, 24,* 271–276.

Jenkins, J., & Cofresi, N. (1998). The sociosomatic course of depression and trauma: A cultural analysis of suffering and resilience in the life of a Puerto Rican woman. *Psychosomatic Medicine, 60,* 439–447.

King, M., & Stanley, G. (1986). The treatment of hyperhidrosis: A case report. *Australian Journal of Clinical and Experimental Hypnosis, 14,* 61–64.

Small, J., & Greenway, M. (1988). The rediscovery of the lost twin: An account of therapy for a child and his parents. *British Journal of Psychotherapy, 5,* 19–28.

SUBSTANCE-RELATED DISORDERS

Carvalho, E. R., & Brito, V. C. A. (1995). Sociometric intervention in family therapy: A case study. *Journal of Group Psychotherapy, Psychodrama & Sociometry, 47,* 147–164.

Crouppen, G. A. (1990). The treatment of substance abuse as a symptom of pathological mourning in intensive short-term dynamic psychotherapy. *International Journal of Short-Term Psychotherapy, 5,* 59–74.

Dattilio, F. (1990). Cognitive marital therapy: A case report. *Journal of Family Psychotherapy, 1,* 15–31.

Diana, D. A. (2002). Harm reduction: From substance abuse to healthy choices. *Journal of College Student Psychotherapy, 16,* 255–268.

Forrest, G. (1975). The problems of dependency and the value of art therapy as a means of treating alcoholism. *Art Psychotherapy, 2,* 15–43.

*Hasenbush, L. L. (1977). Successful brief therapy of a retired elderly man with intractable pain, depression, and drug and alcohol dependence. *Journal of Geriatric Psychiatry, 10,* 71–88.

Ionedes, N. S. (1979). Adlerian psychotherapy in practice: The case of Mr. and Mrs. T. *Journal of Individual Psychotherapy, 35,* 70–78.

Koch, P. M. (1987). Reparenting in the therapeutic relationship with a birth parent: A case. *Child & Adolescent Social Work Journal, 4,* 237–244.

Nelson, M. (1988). Imagery, self-containment, and the PSI. *Psychotherapy Patient, 4,* 345–360.

Todd, T., & Selekman, M. (1989). Principles of family therapy for adolescent substance abuse. *Journal of Psychotherapy & the Family, 6*(3–4), 49–70.

Wilson, J., & Steiner, H. (2002). Conduct problems, substance use and social anxiety: A developmental study of recovery and adaptation. *Clinical Child Psychology & Psychiatry, 7,* 235–247.

CASEBOOKS

Adams, J. (1974). *The Christian counselor's casebook.* Grand Rapids, MI: Zondervan.

Akeret, R. (1995). *Tales from a traveling couch: A psychotherapist revisits his most memorable patients.* New York: Norton.

Alvarez, A. (1992). *Live company: Psychoanalytic psychotherapy with autistic, border-line, deprived, and abused children.* New York: Tavistock/Routledge.

Axline, V. (1964). *Dibs: In search of self.* Boston: Houghton Mifflin.

Bader, D. (1994). *Jodie's story.* New York: Columbia University Press.

Barlow, D. (Ed.). (1983). *Clinical handbook of psychological disorders.* New York: Guilford Press.

Barrett, D. (1998). *The pregnant man: Cases from a hypnotherapist's couch.* New York: Times Books.

Basch, M. (1992). *Practicing psychotherapy: A casebook.* New York: Basic Books.

Berenstein, F. (1995). *Lost boys: Reflections on psychoanalysis and countertransference.* New York: Norton.

Berg, C. (1947). *Deep analysis: The clinical study of an individual case.* New York: Norton.

Bernheimer, C., & Kahane, C. (Eds.). (1985). *In Dora's case: Freud–hysteria–feminism.* New York: Columbia University Press.

Bettelheim, B. (1961). *Paul and Mary: Two case histories from "truants from life."* Garden City, NY: Anchor Books.

Bohart, A., & Tallman, K. (1999). *How clients make therapy work: The process of active self-healing.* Washington, DC: American Psychological Association.

Bollas, C. (1989). *Forces of destiny: Psychoanalysis and human idiom.* Northvale, NJ: Jason Aronson.

Boscolo, L. (1987). *Milan systemic family therapy: Conversations in theory and practice.* New York: Basic Books.

Brussel, J. (1968). *Casebook of a crime psychiatrist.* New York: Bernard Geis Associates.

Burton, A., & Harris, R. E. (Eds.). (1947). *Case histories in clinical and abnormal psychology.* New York: Harper.

Byock, I. (Ed.). (1997). *Dying well: Peace and possibility.* New York: Riverbend Books.

Callis, R., Polmantier, P., & Roeber, E. (1955). *A casebook of counseling.* New York: Appleton-Century-Crofts.

Chapman, A. (1975). *Gromchik, and other tales from a psychiatrist's casebook.* New York: Putnam.

Chernin, K. (1995). *A different kind of listening: My psychoanalysis and its shadow.* New York: HarperCollins.

Chesser, E. (1952). *Unquiet minds; leaves from a psychologist's casebook.* New York: Rich & Cowan.

Cleckley, H. (1982). *The mask of sanity.* St. Louis, MO: Mosby.

Cohen, J., & Cohler, B. (Eds.). (2000). *The psychoanalytic study of lives over time: Clinical and research perspectives on children who return to treatment in adulthood.* San Diego, CA: Academic Press.

Confer, W., & Ables, B. (Eds.). (1983). *Multiple personality disorder: Etiology, diagnosis and treatment.* New York: Human Sciences Press.

Cooper, S., & Wannerman, L. (1977). *Children in treatment: A primer for beginning psychotherapists.* New York: Brunner/Mazel.

Cooper, S., & Wannerman, L. (1993). *A casebook of child psychotherapy: Strategies and technique.* Northvale, NJ: Jason Aronson.

Cummings, N., & Sayama, M. (1995). *Focused psychotherapy: A casebook of brief, intermittent psychotherapy throughout the life cycle.* New York: Brunner/Mazel.

Dattilio, F. (Ed.). (1998). *Case studies in couple and family therapy: Systemic and cognitive perspectives.* New York: Guilford Press.

Daugherty, W. (1958). *A psychological warfare casebook.* New York: Arno Press.

Davanloo, H. (Ed.). (1980). *Short-term dynamic psychotherapy.* New York: Jason Aronson.

Dewald, P. (1994). *The psychoanalytic process: A case illustration.* Northvale, NJ: Jason Aronson.

Dryden, W., & Bannister, D. (Eds.). (1987). *Key cases in psychotherapy.* New York: New York University Press.

Eigen, M. (1995). *Reshaping the self: Reflections on renewal through therapy.* Madison, CT: Psychosocial Press.

Emery, G., Hollon, S., & Bedrosian, R. (1981). *New directions in cognitive therapy: A casebook.* New York: Guilford Press.

Erickson, M., & Rossi, E. (1979). *Hypnotherapy, an exploratory casebook.* New York: Irvington.

Farber, S. (1993). *Madness, heresy, and the rumor of angels: The revolt against the mental health system.* Chicago: Open Court.

Feindler, E., & Kalfus, G. (Eds.). (1990). *Adolescent behavior therapy handbook.* New York: Springer.

Fensterheim, H., & Glazer, H. (Eds.). (1983). *Behavioral psychotherapy: Basic principals and case studies.* New York: Brunner/Mazel.

Finnel, J. (Ed.). (1983). *Mind and body problems.* Northvale, NJ: Jason Aronson.

Frankiel, R. (Ed.). (1994). *Essential papers in object loss.* New York: New York University Press.

Freeman, A., & Dattilio, F. (Eds.). (1992). *Comprehensive casebook of cognitive therapy.* New York: Plenum.

Friedrich, W. (Ed.). (1991). *Casebook of sexual abuse treatment.* New York: Norton.

Furman, E. (1974). *A child's parent dies: Studies in childhood bereavement.* New Haven, CT: Yale University Press.

Gedo, J. (1979). *Beyond interpretation: Toward a revised theory for psychoanalysis.* New York: International Universities Press.

Glenmullen, J. (1993). *The pornographer's grief: And other tales of human sexuality.* New York: HarperCollins.

Golan, S., Pomerantz, J., & Baker, J. (1974). *The Bethlehem diaries: Student–mental patient encounters*. San Francisco: Canfield Press.

Goldberg, A. (1999). *Being of two minds: The vertical split in psychoanalysis and psychotherapy*. Hillsdale, NJ: Analytic Press.

Goldberg, A. (Ed.). (1978). *The psychology of the self: A casebook/written with the collaboration of Heinz Kohut*. New York: International Universities Press.

Goldberg, A. (Ed.). (2000). *Errant selves: A casebook of misbehavior*. Hillsdale, NJ: Analytic Press.

Golden, L. (1998). *Case studies in child and adolescent counseling* (2nd ed.). Upper Saddle River, NJ: Merrill.

Goldstein, E., & Farmer, K. (1992). *Confabulations: Creating false memories, destroying families*. Boca Raton, FL: SirS.

Greenwald, H. (Ed.). (1973). *Great cases in psychoanalysis*. Northvale, NJ: Jason Aronson.

Gurman, A. (Ed.). (1985). *Casebook of marital therapy*. New York: Guilford Press.

Hacking, I. (1998). *Mad travelers: Reflections on the reality of transient mental illnesses*. Charlottesville: University Press of Virginia.

Haley, J., & Hoffman, L. (1967). *Techniques of family therapy*. New York: Basic Books.

Hedges, L. (1994). *In search of the lost mother of infancy*. Northvale, NJ: Jason Aronson.

Heller, P., & Freud, A. (1990). *A child analysis with Anna Freud* (S. Burkhardt & M. Weigand, Trans.). Madison, CT: International Universities Press.

Hersen, M., & Last, C. (Eds.). (1985). *Behavioral therapy handbook*. New York: Springer.

Hexum, A., & O'Hanlon, W. (1990). *The complete clinical work of Milton H. Erickson*. New York: Norton.

Janis, I. (1958). *Psychological stress: Psychoanalytic and behavioral studies of surgical patients*. New York: Wiley.

Kanzer, M., & Glenn, J. (Eds.). (1980). *Freud and his patients*. New York: Jason Aronson.

Kaplan, H. (1979). *Disorders of sexual desire and other new concepts and techniques in sex therapy*. New York: Brunner/Mazel.

Kaufman, B., & Kaufman, S. (1982). *A land beyond tears: A liberating approach to death and dying*. Garden City, NY: Doubleday.

Kirch, I., & Rhue, J. (Eds.). (1986). *Casebook of clinical hypnosis*. Washington, DC: American Psychological Association.

Klein, M. (1961). *Narrative of a child analysis: The conduct of the psycho-analysis of children as seen in the treatment of a ten-year old boy*. New York: Delacorte Press/S. Lawrence.

Knight, B. (1992). *Older adults in psychotherapy: Case histories*. Newbury Park, CA: Sage.

Laing, R. (1969). *The divided self: An existential study in sanity and madness*. Baltimore: Penguin Books.

Lasky, R. (1993). *Dynamics of development and the therapeutic process*. Northvale, NJ: Jason Aronson.

Last, G., & Hersen, M. (Eds.). (1994). *Adult behavior casebook*. New York: Plenum.

Lazarus, A. (1985). *Casebook of multimodal therapy*. New York: Guilford Press.

Lewis, C. (1985). *Listening to children*. New York: Jason Aronson.

Lindner, R. (1973). *The fifty-minute hour: A collection of true psychoanalytic tales*. New York: Bantam Books.

Little, M. I. (1990). *Psychotic anxieties and containment: A personal record of an analysis with Winnicott*. Northvale, NJ: Jason Aronson.

Luborsky, L., & Crits-Christoph, P. (1990). *Understanding transference: The core conflictual relationship theme model*. New York: Basic Books.

Lynn, S., Kirsch, I., & Rhue, J. (Eds.). (1996). *Casebook of clinical hypnosis*. Washington, DC: American Psychological Association.

Madanes, C. (1984). *Behind the one-way mirror: Advances in the practice of strategic therapy*. San Francisco: Jossey-Bass.

Mahony, P. (1986). *Freud and the rat man*. New Haven, CT: Yale University Press.

Malan, D. (1976). *Toward the validation of dynamic psychotherapy: A replication*. New York: Plenum.

Malan, D. (2001). *Individual psychotherapy and the science of psychodynamics* (2nd ed.). London: Arnold.

Malan, D., & Osimo, F. (1992). *Psychodynamics, training, and outcome in brief psychotherapy*. Boston: Butterworth-Heinemann.

Manfield, P. (Ed.). (1998). *Extending EMDR: A casebook of innovative applications*. New York: Norton.

Mann, J. (1973). *Time-limited psychotherapy*. Cambridge, MA: Harvard University Press.

Mann, J., & Goldman, R. (1982). *A casebook in time-limited psychotherapy*. New York: McGraw-Hill.

Masterson, J. (1972). *Treatment of the borderline adolescent: A developmental approach*. New York: Wiley Interscience.

Masterson, J., Sifneos, P., & Toplin, M. (1991). *Comparing psychoanalytic psychotherapies: Developmental, self, and object relations*. New York: Brunner/Mazel.

Mathelin, C. (1999). *Lacanian psychotherapy with children: The broken piano* (S. Fairfield, Trans.). New York: Other Press.

McDaniel, S., Lusterman, D., & Philpot, C. (Eds.). (2001). *Casebook for integrating family therapy: An ecosystemic approach*. Washington, DC: American Psychological Association.

McDougall, J., & Lebovici, S. (1989). *Dialogue with Sammy: A psychoanalytic contribution to the understanding of child psychosis*. London: Free Association Books.

Miller, M. (1982). *Psychiatry: A personal view*. New York: Scribner.

Moustakas, C. (1977). *Turning points*. Englewood Cliffs, NJ: Prentice Hall.

Moustakas, C. (1992). *Psychotherapy with children: The living relationship*. Greeley, CO: Carron.

Mueser, K. (1997). *Sexual abuse in the lives of women*. Amsterdam: Harwood Academic.

Myers, W. (1984). *Dynamic therapy of the older patient*. New York: Jason Aronson.

Napier, A., & Whitaker, C. (1978). *The family crucible*. New York: Harper & Row.

Nichols, M. (1998). *The power of the family: Mastering the hidden dance of family relationships*. New York: Fireside.

Norcross, J. (Ed.). (1987). *Casebook of eclectic psychotherapy*. New York: Brunner/Mazel.

Norcross, J., & Saltzman, N. (Eds.). (1990). *Therapy wars: Contention and convergence in differing clinical approaches*. San Francisco: Jossey-Bass.

Oltmanns, T., Neale, J., & Davison, G. (1991). *Case studies in abnormal psychology* (3rd ed.). New York: Wiley.

Orcutt, C. (1995). *Integration of multiple personality disorder in the context of the Masterson approach*. New York: Masterson & Klein.

Osbourne, R., Lafuze, J., & Perkins, D. (2000). *Case analyses for abnormal psychology: Learning to look beyond the symptoms*. Philadelphia: Psychology Press.

Ostow, M. (Ed.). (1979). *The psychodynamic approach to drug therapy*. New York: Van Nostrand Reinhold.

Palef, S. (1995). *A self-psychological perspective on multiple personality disorder*. Hillsdale, NJ: Analytic Press.

Pankejeff, S., Brunswick, R., Gardiner, M., & Freud, S. (1971). *The wolf man*. New York: Basic Books.

Papajohn, J. (1982). *Intensive behavior therapy*. New York: Allyn & Bacon.

Papp, P. (Ed.). (1977). *Family therapy: Full length case studies*. New York: Gardner Press.

Parker, B. (1962). *My language is me: Psychotherapy with a disturbed adolescent*. New York: Basic Books.

Perez, J. (1979). *Family counseling*. New York: Van Nostrand Reinhold.

Perry, S., Frances, A., & Clarkin, J. (1990). *A DSM–III–R casebook of treatment selection*. New York: Brunner/Mazel.

Piontelli, A. (1992). *From fetus to child: An observational and psychoanalytic study*. New York: Tavistock/Routledge.

Pipher, M. (1994). *Reviving Ophelia: Saving the selves of adolescent girls*. New York: Ballantine Books.

Ponton, L. (1997). *The romance of risk: Why teenagers do the things they do*. New York: Basic Books.

Roberts, M., & Walker, C. (Eds.). (1989). *Casebook of child and pediatric psychology*. New York: Guilford Press.

Rogers, A. (1995). *A shining affliction: A story of harm and healing in psychotherapy.* New York: Viking.

Rosen, R., & Leiblum, S. (Eds.). (1995). *Case studies in sex therapy.* New York: Guilford Press.

Ross, C. (1994). *The Osiris complex.* Toronto, Ontario, Canada: University of Toronto Press.

Rothstein, A., Glenn, J., & Barrett, D. (1999). *Learning disabilities and psychic conflict: A psychoanalytic casebook.* Madison, CT: International Universities Press.

Rule, A. (1999). *A rage to kill and other true cases.* New York: Pocket Books.

Schneiderman, S. (1986). *Rat man.* New York: New York University Press.

Schoenewolf, G. (1990). *Turning points in analytic therapy: From Winnicott to Kernberg.* Northvale, NJ: Jason Aronson.

Schwartz, H. (Ed.). (1988). *Bulimia: Psychoanalytic treatment and theory.* Madison, CT: International Universities Press.

Schwartz, H., Bleiberg, E., & Weissman, S. (Eds.). (1995). *Psychodynamic concepts in general psychiatry.* Washington, DC: American Psychiatric Press.

Schwartz, R. (Ed.). (1995). *Internal family systems therapy.* New York: Guilford Press.

Sharpe, S. (2000). *The ways we love: A developmental approach to treating couples.* New York: Guilford Press.

Sholevar, G., & Glenn, J. (Eds.). (1991). *Psychoanalytic case studies.* Madison, CT: International Universities Press.

Silverstein, C. (Ed.). (1991). *Gays, lesbians, and their therapists: Studies in psychotherapy.* New York: Norton.

Siskind, D. (1992). *The child patient and the therapeutic process: A psychoanalytic, developmental, object relations approach.* Northvale, NJ: Jason Aronson.

Spanos, W. (1966). *A casebook on existentialism.* New York: Crowell.

Spitzer, T., & Spitzer, R. (1980). *Psychobattery: A chronicle of psychotherapeutic abuse.* Clifton, NJ: Humana Press.

Stevenson, I. (1974). *Twenty cases suggestive of reincarnation* (2nd ed.). Charlottesville: University Press of Virginia.

Tashman, H. (1959). *The marriage bed: An analyst's casebook.* New York: University Publishers.

Vitkus, J. (1988). *Multiple personality disorder: Psychotherapy with hypnosis.* New York: McGraw-Hill.

Wallerstein, R. S. (1986). *Forty-two lives in treatment: A study of psychoanalysis and psychotherapy.* New York: Guilford Press.

Webb, N. (Ed.). (1991). *Playtherapy with children in crisis: A casebook for practitioners.* New York: Guilford Press.

Webb, N. (Ed.). (1993). *Helping bereaved children: A handbook for practitioners.* New York: Guilford Press.

Wedding, D., Corsini, R. J., & Stewart, A. W. (Eds.). (1989). *Case studies in psychotherapy*. Itasca, IL: F. E. Peacock.

Whitaker, C., & Bumberry, W. (1988). *Dancing with the family: A symbolic–experiential approach*. New York: Brunner/Mazel.

White, R., Riggs, M., & Gilbert, D. (1982). *Case workbook in personality*. Prospect Heights, IL: Waveland Press.

Wilson, C. (Ed.). (1995). *Fear of being fat*. Northvale, NJ: Jason Aronson.

Wilson, C., Hogan, C., & Mintz, I. (1992). *Psychodynamic technique in the treatment of the eating disorders*. Northvale, NJ: Jason Aronson.

Winnicott, D. (1987). *Holding and interpretation*. New York: Grove Press.

Winnicott, D. (1990). *Therapeutic consultations in child psychiatry*. New York: Basic Books.

Yalom, I. (1989). *Love's executioner*. New York: HarperCollins.

Yalom, I. (2000). *Momma and the meaning of life: Tales of psychotherapy*. New York: Perennial.

Yalom, I., & Elkin, G. (1974). *Every day gets a little closer: A twice told therapy*. New York: Basic Books.

Zax, M., & Stricker, G. (1963). *Patterns of psychopathology*. New York: Macmillan.

APPENDIX B

RECOMMENDED CLASSIC CASE STUDIES IN PSYCHOTHERAPY

Some case studies have, over time, come to be considered classics in the field. Sometimes this is because the case communicates a client problem, treatment process, and definitive outcome that would qualify the case as an excellent quasi-judicial case study. Other times, the appellation "*classic*" indicates that the case was important in establishing a particular theoretical position, had particular historical significance, or demonstrated convincingly a specific technique of psychotherapy. Regardless, it is help-ful in evaluating current case studies to compare them to those that have already been recognized as contributing significantly to the mental health disciplines.

The cases in this list were selected on the basis of the recommendations appearing in Wedding and Corsini (2001) and Gurman and Messer (1995), as well as from colleagues in the field.

Abrams, J. L. (1983). Cognitive–behavioral strategies to induce and enhance a col-laborative set in distressed couples. In A. Freeman (Ed.), *Cognitive therapy with couples and groups* (pp. 125–155). New York: Plenum.

Ackerman, N. (1966). Rescuing the scapegoat. In N. Ackerman (Ed.), *Treating the troubled family* (pp. 210–236). Northvale, NJ: Jason Aronson, Inc. (original work published 1966).

Ard, B. N. (1971). The case of the black and silver masochist. In A. Ellis (Ed.), *Growth through reason: Verbatim cases in rational–emotive therapy* (pp. 15–45). Hollywood, CA: Wilshire Books.

Arlow, J. A. (1976). Communication and character: A clinical study of a man raised by deaf–mute parents. *Psychoanalytic Study of the Child, 31,* 139–163.

Beck, A. T., Rush, J., Shaw, B., & Emery, G. (1979). Interview with a depressed and suicidal patient. In *Cognitive therapy of depression* (pp. 225–243). New York: Guilford Press.

Binswanger, L. (1958). The case of Ellen West. In R. May, E. Angel, & H. Ellenberger (Eds.), *Existence: A new dimension in psychology and psychiatry* (pp. 237–364). New York: Basic Books.

Bornstein, B. (1949). The analysis of the phobic child, some problems of theory and technique in child analysis. *Psychoanalytic Study of the Child, 4,* 181–226.

Boyer, L. B. (1977). Working with a borderline patient. *Psychoanalytic Quarterly, 46,* 389–420.

Chessick, R. D. (1977). *Intensive psychotherapy of the borderline patient.* New York: Jason Aronson.

Ellis, A. (1971). A twenty-three-year-old woman, guilty about not following her parents' rules. In A. Ellis (Ed.), *Growth through reason: Verbatim cases in rational emotive therapy* (pp. 223–286). Hollywood, CA: Wilshire Books.

Farber, S. (1993). *Madness, heresy, and the rumor of angles.* Chicago: Open Court.

Frank, I. (1981). My flight toward a new life. *Journal of Individual Psychology, 37,* 15–30.

Freud, S. (1955). Notes upon a case of obsessional neurosis. In J. Strachey (Ed. and Trans.), *The Standard Edition of the Complete Works of Sigmund Freud.* (Vol. 10, pp. 155–257). New York: W.W. Norton. (original work published 1909).

Good, E. P. (1980). Be my friend. In N. Glasser (Ed.), *What are you doing?* (pp. 18–33). New York: HarperCollins.

Holt, H. (1966). The case of Father M: A segment of an existential analysis. *Journal of Existentialism, 6,* 369–495.

Jackson, D. (1967). The eternal triangle. In J. Haley & L. Hoffman (Eds.), *Techniques of family therapy* (pp. 176–264). New York: Basic Books.

Karon, B. P., & Rosberg, J. (1981). The mother–child relationship in a case of paranoid schizophrenia. In *Psychotherapy of schizophrenia: The treatment of choice* (pp. 337–353). New York: Jason Aronson.

Klein, B. C. (1986). A piece of the world: Some thoughts about Ruth. *Women and Therapy, 5,* 33–40.

Laing, R. D., & Esterson, A. (1964). *Sanity, madness, and the family.* Baltimore: Penguin Books.

Linder, R. M. (1982). *The fifty-minute hour: A collection of true psychoanalytic tales.* New York: Jason Aronson.

Lockart, R. A. (1975). Mary's dog is an ear mother: Listening to the voices of psychosis. *Psychological Perspectives, 6,* 144–160.

Maultsby, M. C. Jr. (1971). A relapsed client with severe phobic reactions. In A. Ellis (Ed.), *Growth through reason: Verbatim cases in rational emotive therapy* (pp. 179–222). Hollywood, CA: Wilshire Books.

May, R. (1973). Black and impotent: The life of Mercedes. In *Power and innocence* (pp. 81–97). New York: Norton.

Melamed, B., & Siegel, L. (1975). Self-directed *in vivo* treatment of an obsessive–compulsive checking ritual. *Journal of Behavior Therapy and Experimental Psychiatry, 6,* 31–35.

Mosak, H. H., & Maniacci, M. (1994). The case of Roger. In D. Wedding & R. J. Corsini (Eds.), *Case studies in psychotherapy*. Itasca, IL: F. E. Peacock.

Napier, A. Y., & Whitaker, C. A. (1978). *The family crucible*. New York: Harper & Row.

Papp, P. (1983). The daughter who said no. In *The process of change* (pp. 67–120). New York: Guilford Press

Penn, P. (1977). *Family therapy: Case studies*. New York: Gardner Press.

Rogers, C. R. (1942). The case of Herbert Bryan. In C. R. Rogers, *Counseling and psychotherapy* (pp. 261–437). Boston: Houghton Mifflin.

Rogers, C. R. (1961). Some of the directions evident in therapy. In C. R. Rogers, (Ed.), *On becoming a person* (pp. 73–106). Boston: Houghton Mifflin.

Rogers, C. R. (1967). A silent young man. In C. R. Rogers, G. T. Gendlin, D. V. Kiesler, & C. Truax (Eds.), *The therapeutic relationship and its impact: A study of psychotherapy with schizophrenics* (pp. 401–406). Madison: University of Wisconsin Press.

Rosberg, J., & Karon, B. P. (1981). The Oedipus complex in an apparently deteriorated case of schizophrenia. In *Psychotherapy of schizophrenia: The treatment of choice* (pp. 353–362). New York: Jason Aronson.

Savitz, C. (1986). Healing and wounding. *Journal of Analytical Psychology, 31,* 319–340.

Spielvogel, A. (1988). The case of Chris. *Journal of Transpersonal Psychology, 20,* 21–28.

Sullivan, B. S. (1989). Christina. In *Psychotherapy grounded in the feminine principle* (pp. 164–172). Wilmette, IL: Chiron.

Umbarger, C., & Hare, R. (1973). Disengagement from a schizophrenic family. *American Journal of Psychiatry, 27,* 274–284.

Winnicott, D. W. (1972). Fragment of an analysis. In P. L. Giovacchini (Ed.), *Tactics and technique in psychoanalytic therapy* (pp. 455–493). New York: Science House.

Wolf, M. M., Risley, T., & Mees, H. (1965). Application of operant conditioning procedures of an autistic child. In L. P. Ullmann & L. Krasner (Eds.), *Case studies in behavior modification* (pp. 138–145). New York: Holt.

Wubbolding, R. (1980). Teenage loneliness. In N. Glasser (Ed.), *What are you doing?* (pp. 120–129). New York: HarperCollins.

Yalom, I. D. (1989). *Love's executioner*. New York: HarperCollins.

Yalom, I. D., & Elkin, G. (1990). *Every day gets a little closer: A twice-told therapy*. New York: Basic Books.

Young, J. E. (1981). Cognitive therapy and loneliness. In G. Emery, S. Hollon, & R. C. Bedrosian (Eds.), *New directions in cognitive therapy* (pp. 139–159). New York: Guilford Press.

REFERENCES

Adorno, T. W., Frenkel-Brunswick, E., Levinson, D. J., & Sanford, R. N. (1950). *The authoritarian personality*. New York: Harper & Row.

Allport, G. (1937). *Personality: A psychological interpretation*. New York: Holt.

Allport, G. (1942). *The use of personal documents in psychological research*. New York: Social Science Research Council.

Amato, J. A. (1990). *Victims and values: A history and a theory of suffering*. New York: Praeger.

American Psychiatric Association. (1980). *Diagnostic and statistical manual of mental disorders* (2nd ed.). Washington, DC: Author.

American Psychiatric Association. (1994). *Diagnostic and statistical manual of mental disorders* (4th ed.). Washington, DC: Author.

American Psychological Association. (2002). Ethical principles of psychologists and code of conduct. *American Psychologist, 57*, 1060–1073.

Ansbacher, H. L., & Ansbacher, R. R. (Eds.). (1970). *The individual psychology of Alfred Adler*. New York: Basic Books.

Argyris, C., & Schon, D. A. (1974). *Theory in practice: Increasing professional effectiveness*. San Francisco: Jossey-Bass.

Austin, J. L. (1964). A plea for excuses. In D. F. Gustafson (Ed.), *Essays in philosophical psychology*. New York: Anchor/Doubleday.

Baier, K. (1965). *The moral point of view*. New York: Random House.

Bakan, D. (1968). *Disease, pain and sacrifice: Towards a psychology of suffering*. Chicago: University of Chicago Press.

Bakan, D. (1971). *Slaughter of the innocents: A study of the battered child phenomenon*. Boston: Beacon Press.

Bandura, A. (1986). *Social foundations of thought and action: A social cognitive theory*. Englewood Cliffs, NJ: Prentice Hall.

Barrett, W. (1958). *Irrational man: A study in existential philosophy*. Garden City, NY: Doubleday/Anchor.

Bateson, G. (1971). The cybernetics of "self": A theory of alcoholism. *Psychiatry, 34*, 1–18.

Bateson, M. C. (1989). *Composing a life*. New York: Atlantic Monthly Press.

Belar, C. D., & Perry, N. W. (1992). National conference on scientific–practitioner education and training for the professional psychologist. *American Psychologist, 47*, 71–75.

Bennett, W. J. (Ed.). (1995). *The moral compass: Stories for a life's journey*. New York: Simon & Schuster.

Berger, P. L., & Luckman, T. (1966). *The social construction of reality*. Garden City, NY: Doubleday/Anchor.

Bergin, A. (1980). Psychotherapy and religious values. *Journal of Consulting and Clinical Psychology*, 48, 95–105.

Bernstein, R. (1983). *Beyond objectivism and relativism*. Philadelphia: University of Pennsylvania Press.

Bertalanffy, L. von (1969). *General system theory*. New York: G. Braziller.

Bhaskar, R. (1994). *Plato, etc.* London: Verso.

Bourg, E. F., Bent, R. J., McHolland, J., & Stricker, G. (1989). Standards and evaluation in the education and training of professional psychologists: The National Council of Schools of Professional Psychology Mission Bay Conference. *American Psychologist*, 44, 66–72.

Bowen, M. (1978). *Family therapy in clinical practice*. Northvale, NJ: Jason Aronson.

Boyer, L. B. (1977). Working with a borderline patient. *Psychoanalytic Quarterly*, 46, 389–420.

Brazier, D. (1995). *Zen therapy: Transcending the sorrows of the human mind*. New York: Wiley.

Breggin, P. (1991). *Toxic psychiatry*. New York: St. Martin's Press.

Breggin, P. (1997). *The heart of being helpful*. New York: Springer.

Breuer, J., & Freud, S. (1982). *Studies in hysteria* (J. Strachey, Ed. & Trans.). New York: Basic Books. (Original work published 1895)

Bridgman, P. (1928). *The logic of modern physics*. New York: Macmillan.

Bromley, D. B. (1977). *Personality description in ordinary language*. Chichester, England: Wiley.

Bromley, D. B. (1986). *The case study method in psychology and related disciplines*. Chichester, England: Wiley.

Bruner, J. (1976). *On knowing: Essays for the left hand (expanded ed.)*. Cambridge, MA: Harvard University Press.

Buber, M. (1958). *I and thou* (2nd ed.). New York: Scribner's.

Bugental, J. (1987). *The art of the psychotherapist*. New York: Norton.

Cahan, E. D., & White, S. H. (1992). Proposals for a second psychology. *American Psychologist*, 47, 224–235.

Campbell, D. T. (1975). "Degrees of freedom" and the case study. *Comparative Political Studies*, 8, 178–193.

Caplan, P. (1995). *They say you are crazy*. Reading, MA: Addison-Wesley.

Care, N. (2000). *Decent people*. Lanham, MD: Rowman & Littlefield.

Chaplin, J. P., & Krawiec, T. S. (1979). *Systems and theories of psychology* (4th ed.). New York: Holt.

Chesler, P. (1972). *Women and madness*. New York: Harcourt Brace Jovanovich.

Chessick, R. (1982). Intensive psychotherapy of a borderline patient. *Archives of General Psychiatry*, 39, 413–419.

Chessick, R. (1987). *Great ideas in psychotherapy*. Northvale, NJ: Jason Aronson. (Original work published 1970)

Christie, D. J., Wagner, R. V., & Winter, D. D. N. (Eds.). (2001). *Peace, conflict, and violence: Peace psychology for the 21st century.* Upper Saddle River, NJ: Prentice Hall.

Churchill, S. (2000). Phenomenological psychology. *Encyclopedia of Psychology, 6,* 162–168.

Coady, C. A. J. (1992). *Testimony: A philosophical study.* New York: Oxford University Press.

Comer, R. J. (1998). *Abnormal psychology* (3rd ed.). New York: Freeman.

Committee on Training in Clinical Psychology. (1948). Recommended graduate training program in clinical psychology. *American Psychologist, 3,* 539–558.

Compact edition of the Oxford English dictionary (Vol. 2). (1971). Glasgow, Scotland: Oxford University Press.

Connor, W. R. (1999). Moral knowledge in the modern university. *Ideas, 6,* 1–7.

Conze, E. (1959). *Buddhism: Its essence and development.* New York: Harper.

Corsini, R. J., & Wedding, D. (1995). *Current psychotherapies* (5th ed.). Itasca, IL: F. E. Peacock.

Corwin, D. L., & Olafson, X. (1997). Videotaped discovery of a reportedly unrecallable memory of child sexual abuse: Comparison with a childhood interview videotaped 11 years before. *Child Maltreatment, 2,* 91–112.

Cowen, E. L., Gardner, E. A., & Zax, M (1967). *Emergent approaches to mental health problems.* New York: Appleton-Century-Crofts.

Dahl, N. (1984). *Practical reason, Aristotle and weakness of the will.* Minneapolis: University of Minnesota Press.

Danto, A. (1971). *What philosophy is: A guide to the elements.* New York: Harper & Row.

Daubert v. Merrill Dow Pharmaceuticals, 509 US 579 (1993).

Davidson, D. (1979). Mental events. In T. Honderich & M. Burnyeat (Eds.), *Philosophy as it is.* London: Penguin.

Davidson, D. (1984). *Inquiries into truth and interpretation.* Oxford, England: Oxford University Press.

de la Rey, C. (2001). Peace and reconciliation. In D. J. Christie, R. V. Wagner, & D. D. N. Winter (Eds.), *Peace, conflict, and violence: Peace psychology for the 21st century.* Upper Saddle River, NJ: Prentice Hall.

de Sousa, R. (1999). Moral emotions. Retrieved December 9, 1999, from http://www.chass.utoronto.ca/~sousa/moralemotions.html

Diamond, L. (2001). *The peace book.* San Francisco: Conari.

Edelson, M. (1988). *Psychoanalysis: A theory in crisis.* Chicago: University of Chicago Press.

Edwards, D. J. A. (1996). Case study research method: The cornerstone of theory and practice. In M. Reinecke, F. Dattilio, & A. Freeman (Eds.), *Cognitive therapy with children and adolescents: A casebook for clinical practice* (pp. 10–37). New York: Guilford Press.

Edwards, D. J. A. (1998). Types of case study work: A conceptual framework for case-based research. *Journal of Humanistic Psychology, 38,* 36–70.

Elliott, M., Browne, K., & Kilcoyne, J. (1995). Child sexual abuse prevention. *Child Abuse & Neglect, 19,* 579–594.

Elliott, R. (2002). Hermeneutic single case efficacy design. *Psychotherapy Research, 12,* 1–20.

Elliott, R., Fischer, C. T., & Rennie, D. L. (1999). Evolving guidelines for publication of qualitative research studies in psychology and related fields. *British Journal of Clinical Psychology, 38,* 215–229.

Ellis, A. (1962). *Reason and emotion in psychotherapy.* New York: Lyle Stuart.

Engel, G. L. (1980). The clinical application of the biopsychosocial model. *American Journal of Psychiatry, 137,* 535–544.

Epstein, M. (1995). *Thoughts without a thinker: Psychotherapy from a Buddhist perspective.* New York: Basic Books.

Erickson, M. (1992). *Healing in hypnosis.* New York: Irvington.

Erikson, E. (1963). *Childhood and society* (2nd ed.). New York: Norton.

Faberow, N. L. (Ed.). (1963). *Taboo topics.* New York: Atherton Press.

Fisher, S., & Greenberg, R. (1985). *The scientific credibility of Freud's theories and therapy.* New York: Columbia University Press.

Fishman, D. B. (1999). *The case for pragmatic psychology.* New York: New York University Press.

Fishman, D. B., & Miller, R. B. (2001). *Systematic case studies in psychotherapy: Method and database.* Unpublished manuscript.

Fogelman, E. (1994). *Conscience and courage: Rescuers of Jews during the Holocaust.* New York: Doubleday.

Frankl, V. (1959). *Man's search for meaning.* New York: Pocket Books.

Freud, S. (1959). The question of lay analysis. In J. Strachey (Ed. and Trans.). *The standard edition e of the complete psychological works of Sigmund Freud* (Vol. 20, pp. 183–258) New York: Norton. (Original work published 1926)

Freud, S. (1959). Further recommendations in the technique of psychoanalysis: Observations on the transference-love. In J. Riviere (Trans.), *Collected papers of Sigmund Freud* (Vol. 2, pp. 377–391). New York: Basic Books. (Original work published 1915)

Freud, S. (1965). *The new introductory lectures on psychoanalysis.* New York: Norton. (Original work published 1933)

Freud, S. (1966). *Introductory lectures on psycho-analysis* (J. Strachey, Ed. & Trans.). New York: Norton. (Original work published 1920)

Fromm, E. (1941). *Escape from freedom.* New York: Holt.

Fromm, E. (1973). *The anatomy of human destructiveness.* New York: Holt.

Fromm-Reichmann, F. (1950). *Principles of intensive psychotherapy.* Chicago: University of Chicago Press.

Gabbard, G. O. (2000). Disguise or consent: Problems and recommendations concerning the publication and presentation of clinical material. *International Journal of Psychoanalysis, 81,* 1071–1086.

Gabbard, G., & Williams, P. (2001). Editorial: Preserving confidentiality in the writing of case reports. *International Journal of Psychoanalysis, 82,* 1067–1068.

Gadamer, H. G. (1976). *Philosophical hermeneutics* (D. Linge, Trans.). Berkeley: University of California Press.

Gavey, N., & Braun, V. (1997). Ethics and the publication of clinical case material. *Professional Psychology: Research and Practice, 28,* 399–404.

Gay, P. (1988). *Freud: A life for our time.* New York: Norton.

Gazzaniga, M. S., & Heatherton, T. F. (2003). *Psychological science: Mind, brain and behavior.* New York: Norton.

Geertz, C. (1973). *The interpretation of cultures.* New York: Basic Books

Gergen, K. J. (1985). The social constructionist movement in modern psychology. *American Psychologist, 40,* 255–265.

Gergen, K. (1991). *The saturated self: Dilemmas of identity in contemporary life.* New York: Basic Books.

Giorgi, A. (1970). *Psychology as a human science: A phenomenology based approach.* New York: Harper & Row.

Glasser, W. (1975). *Reality therapy, a new approach to psychiatry.* New York: Harper & Row.

Goffman, E. (1961). *Assylums: Essays on the social situation of mental patients and other inmates.* New York: Doubleday.

Goldfried, M. R. (1980). Toward the delineation of therapeutic change principles. *American Psychologist, 35,* 991–999.

Goldfried, M. (1995). Toward a common language for case formulation. *Journal of psychotherapy Integration, 5,* 221–224.

Goldman, R., & Greenberg, L. S. (1995). A process–experiential approach to case formulation. *In Session: Psychotherapy in Practice, 1,* 35–36, 42–51.

Goodstein, L. (1988). Report of the Executive Vice-President: 1987. The growth of the APA. *American Psychologist, 43,* 491–498.

Gotkin, J., & Gotkin, P. (1991). *Too much anger, too many tears.* New York: HarperCollins. (Original work published 1975)

Greenwood, L. H. G. (1909). *Aristotle, Nicomachean Ethics Bk, VI.* Cambridge, England: Cambridge University Press.

Grunbaum, A. (1984). *The foundations of psychoanalysis: A philosophical critique.* Berkeley: University of California Press.

Gurman, A. S., & Messer, S. B. (1995). *Essential psychotherapies: Theory and practice.* New York: Guilford Press.

Habermas, J. (1971). *Knowledge and human interests* (J. Shapiro, Trans.). Boston: Beacon Press.

Habermas, J. (1973). *Theory and practice* (J. Vertel, Trans.). Boston: Beacon Press.

Hare, R. (1963). *Freedom and reason*. London: Oxford University Press.

Harre, R. (1972). *Philosophies of science*. Oxford, England: Oxford University Press.

Havel, V. (1990). *Disturbing the peace: A conversation with Karel Hvizdala* (P. Wilson, Trans.). New York: Vintage Books.

Haveliwala, Y., Scheflin, A. E., & Ashcroft, N. (1979). *Common sense in therapy*. New York: Brunner/Mazel.

Hegel, G. W. F. (1969). *Science of logic*. London: Allen & Unwin. (Original work published 1832)

Heidegger, M. (1962). *Being and time* (J. Macquarrie & E. Robinson, Trans.). London: SCM Press.

Heider, F. (1958). *The psychology of interpersonal relations*. New York: Wiley.

Heisenberg, W. (1958). *Physics and philosophy: The revolution in modern science*. New York: Harper Torchbooks, Harper & Bros.

Hempel, C. G. (1963). *Aspects of scientific explanation*. New York: Free Press.

Herman, E. (1995). *The romance of American psychology: Political culture in the age of experts*. Berkeley: University of California Press.

Hilliard, R. B. (1993). Single-case methodology in psychotherapy research process and outcome research. *Journal of Consulting and Clinical Psychology, 61*, 373–379.

Holt, R. (1962). Individuality and generalization in the psychology of personality. *Journal of Personality, 30*, 377–404.

Horney, K. (1966). *New ways in psychoanalysis*. New York: Norton. (Original work published 1939)

Hoshmand, L. T. (1988). Alternate research paradigms: A review and teaching proposal. *The Counseling Psychologist, 17*, 3–79.

Hoshmand, L. T. (1992). *Orientation to inquiry in a reflective professional psychology*. Albany: State University of New York Press.

Hoshmand, L. T., & Polkinghorne, D. E. (1992). Redefining the science–practice relationship and professional training. *American Psychologist, 47*, 55–66.

Howard, G. (1986). *Dare we develop a human science?* Notre Dame, IN: Academic Publications.

Howard, G. (1991). Culture tales: A narrative approach to thinking, cross cultural psychology, and psychotherapy. *American Psychologist, 3*, 187–197.

Howard, G. S. (1993). I think I can! I think I can! Reconsidering the place for practice methodologies in psychological research. *Professional Psychology: Research and Practice, 24*, 237–244.

Hunter, K. M. (1996). Narrative, literature, and the clinical exercise of practical reason. *Journal of Medicine and Philosophy, 21*, 321–340.

Imber-Black, E. (Ed.). (1993). *Secrets in families and family therapy*. New York: Norton.

James, W. (1907). *Pragmatism*. New York: Longman.

James, W. (1962). *Essays on faith and morals*. New York: New American Library. (Original work published 1899)

James, W. (1966). *Is life worth living? Essays on faith and morals*. New York: New American Library. (Original work published 1896)

James, W. (1983a). *Essays in psychology*. Cambridge, MA: Harvard University Press. (Original work published 1892)

James, W. (1983b). *Talks to teachers on psychology*. Cambridge, MA: Harvard University Press. (Original work published 1892)

Jervis, G. (1975). *Manuale critico di psichiatria* [The critical handbook of psychiatry]. Milan: Feltrinelli.

Johnson, W. R. (1981). Basic interviewing skills. In C. E. Walker (Ed.), *Clinical practice of psychology* (83–122). New York: Pergamon Press.

Jonsen, A. R., & Toulmin, S. (1988). *The abuse of casuistry*. Berkeley: University of California Press.

Jourard, S. (1964). *The transparent self*. New York: Van Nostrand.

Jung, C. (1963). *Memories, dreams, and reflections*. New York: Pantheon.

Kant, I. (1929). *The critique of pure reason* (N. Kemp-Smith, Trans.). London: Macmillan. (Original work published 1781)

Kant, I. (1964). *Groundwork of the metaphysic of morals* (H. J. Paton, Trans.). New York: Harper & Row. (Original work published 1785)

Karon, B. P., & VandenBos, G. R. (1981). *Psychotherapy of schizophrenia: Treatment of choice*. New York: Jason Aronson.

Kazdin, A. E. (1981). Drawing valid inferences from case studies. *Journal of Consulting and Clinical Psychology, 49*, 183–192.

Kelly, H. (1992). Common sense psychology and scientific psychology. *Annual Review of Psychology, 43*, 1–23.

Kiesler, C., & Morton, T. (1988). Psychology and public policy in the "health care revolution." *American Psychologist, 43*, 993–1003.

Kirk, S., & Kutchins, H. (1992). *The selling of DSM: The rhetoric of science in psychiatry*. New York: Aldine de Gruyter.

Kirschner, S. (1996). *The religious and romantic origins of psychoanalysis: Indivuation and integration in post-Freudian theory*. New York: Cambridge University.

Kleinman, A. (1988). *The illness narratives: Suffering, healing and the human condition*. New York: Basic Books.

Kleinman, A., Das, V., & Lock, M. (1997). (Eds.). *Social suffering*. Berkeley: University of California Press.

Kleinman, A., & Kleinman, I. (1997). The appeal of experience; The dismay of images: Cultural appropriations of suffering in our times. In A. Klienman, V. Das & M. Lock (Eds.). *Social suffering*. Berkeley: University of California Press.

Klumpner, G. H., & Frank, A. (1991). On methods of reporting clinical material. *Journal of the American Psychoanalytic Association*, 537–551.

Kobor, P., Silver, H., & Wurtz, S. (2002). *Behavioral and sciences research budget in the FY 2003 budget*. Washington, DC: American Association for the Advancement of Science.

Koch, S. (1981). The nature and limits of psychological knowledge: Lessons from a century of psychology as science. *American Psychologist, 36,* 257–269.

Korchin, S. (1976). *Modern clinical psychology*. New York: Basic Books.

Kramer, P. (1993). *Listening to Prozac*. New York: Penguin Books.

Kuhn, T. S. (1970). *The structure of scientific revolutions* (2nd ed.). Chicago: University of Chicago Press.

Laing, R. D. (1965). *The divided self*. London: Penguin Books.

Landesman, C., & Care, N. S. (Eds.). (1968). *Readings in the theory of action*. Bloomington: Indiana University Press.

Lazarus, A. (1995). Multimodal therapy. In R. Corsini & D. Wedding (Eds.), *Current psychotherapies* (5th ed., pp. 322–355). Itasca, IL: F. E. Peacock.

Leahey, T. H. (1997). *A history of psychology: Main currents in psychological thought*. Upper Saddle River, NJ: Prentice Hall.

Levinas, E. (1989). Ethics as first philosophy. In S. Hand (Ed.), *The Levinas reader* (pp. 75–87). Oxford, England: Blackwell.

Levine, M. (1974). Scientific method and adversary method: Some preliminary thoughts. *American Psychologist, 29,* 661–677.

Levine, M. (1980). Investigative reporting as a research method: An analysis of Bernstein and Woodward's *All the President's Men*. *American Psychologist, 35,* 626–638.

Levine, M. (1982). Method or madness: On the alienation of the professional. *Journal of Community Psychology, 10,* 3–14.

Levinson, D. J., Darrow, C. N., Klein, E. B., Levinson, M. H., & McKee, B. (1978). *The seasons of a man's life*. New York: Ballantine.

Lewis, H. (1990). *A question of values: Six ways we make the personal choices that shape our lives*. New York: Harper & Row.

Lewis, H. (2000). *Question of values: Six ways we make the personal choices that shape our lives* (Rev. and updated ed.). Crozet, VA: Axios Press.

Lifton, R. J. (1986). *The Nazi doctors: Medical killing and the psychology of genocide*. New York: Basic Books.

Lilly, G. C. (1987). *An introduction to the laws of evidence* (2nd ed.). St. Paul, MN: West.

Loevinger, L. (1967). Law and science as rival systems. *University of Florida Law Review, 19,* 530.

Loftus, E., & Guyer, M. (2002). Who abused Jane Doe: The hazards of the single case history: Part I. *Skeptical Inquirer, 26*(3), 24–32.

London, P. (1964). *The modes and morals of psychotherapy*. New York: Holt.

MacIntyre, A. (1984). *After virtue* (2nd ed.). Notre Dame, IN: University of Notre Dame Press.

MacKenzie, N., & MacKenzie, J. (1977). *The Fabians*. New York: Simon & Schuster.

MacKinnon, R. A., & Michaels, R. (1971). *The psychiatric interview in clinical practice*. Philadelphia: W. B. Saunders.

Mahrer, A. (1978). *Experiencing: A humanistic theory of psychology and psychiatry*. New York: Brunner/Mazel.

Mahrer, A. (1988). Discovery oriented psychotherapy research: Rationale, aims and methods. *American Psychologist, 43*, 694–702.

Mahrer, A. (2002). *Becoming the person you can become: The complete guide to self-transformation*. Boulder, CO: Bull.

Malan, D. (1979). *Individual psychotherapy and the science of psychodynamics*. Oxford, England: Butterworth Heinemann.

Manicus, P., & Secord, P. (1983). Implications for psychology of the new philosophy of science. *American Psychologist, 38*, 399–413.

Marcuse, H. (1964). *One dimensional man: Studies in the ideology of advanced industrial society*. Boston: Beacon Press.

Margolis, J. (1966). *Psychotherapy and morality*. New York: Random House.

Martin, J., & Sugarman, J. (2000). Between the modern and the post-modern. *American Psychologist, 55*, 397–406.

May, R. (1969). *Love and will*. New York: Dell.

May, R. (1982). The problem of evil: An open letter to Carl Rogers. *Journal of Humanistic Psychology, 22*, 10–21.

McAdams, D. P. (1994). *The person: An introduction to personality psychology*. Fort Worth, TX: Harcourt Brace.

McFall, R. M. (1991). Manifesto for a science of clinical psychology. *Clinical Psychology Review, 44*, 75–88.

McFall, R. M. (2000). Elaborate reflections on a simple manifesto. *Applied and Preventive Psychology, 9*, 5–21.

McKeon, R. (1941). *The basic works of Aristotle*. New York: Random House.

Meadow, P. (1996). Psychoanalysis: An open system of research. *Modern Psychoanalysis, 21*, 359–380.

Meehl, P. (1954). *Clinical vs. statistical prediction: A theoretical analysis and review of the evidence*. Minneapolis: University of Minnesota Press.

Meehl, P. (1967). What can the clinician do well. In D. Jackson & S. Messick (Eds.), *Problems in human assessment* (pp. 594–599). New York: McGraw-Hill.

Meehl, P. (1970). Psychology and the criminal law. *University of Richmond Law Review, 5*, 1–30.

Meehl, P. (1973a). *Psychodiagnosis: Selected papers*. Minneapolis: University of Minneapolis Press.

Meehl, P. (1973b). Why I do not attend case conferences. In *Psychodiagnosis: Selected papers* (pp. 225–302). Minneapolis: University of Minneapolis Press.

Meehl, P. (1978). Theoretical risks and tabular asterisks: Sir Karl, Sir Ronald, and the slow progress of soft psychology. *Journal of Consulting and Clinical Psychology, 46*, 806–834.

Meehl, P. (1983). Subjectivity in psychoanalytic inference: The nagging persistence of Wilhelm Fliess's *achensee* question. In J. Earman (Ed.), *Testing scientific theories: Minnesota studies in the philosophy of science* (pp. 349–411). Minneapolis: University of Minnesota Press.

Meehl, P. (1997). Credentialed persons, credentialed knowledge. *Clinical Psychology: Science and Practice, 4*, 91–98.

Menninger, K. A. (1962). *A manual for psychiatric care* (2nd ed.). New York: Grune & Stratton.

Messer, S. & McCann (in press). Research perspectives on the single case study: Single-case method. In J. S. Auerbach, K. N. Levy, & C. E. Schaffer (Eds.), *Relatedness, self-definition, and mental representation: Essays in honor of Sidney J. Blatt*. London: Routledge.

Messer, S. B., Saas, L. A., & Woolfolk, R. L. (Eds.). (1988). *Hermeneutics and psychological theory: Interpretive perspectives on personality, psychotherapy, and psychopathology*. New Brunswick, NJ: Rutgers University Press.

Mill, J. S. (1963). Utilitarianism. In J. M. Robson (Ed.), *The collected works of John Stuart Mill: Vol. 10*. Toronto: University of Toronto Press.

Mill, J. S. (1974). *A system of logic ratiocinative and inductive: Being a connected view of the principles of evidence and the methods of scientific investigation*. Toronto, Ontario, Canada: University of Toronto Press. (Original work published 1840)

Miller, G. A. (1956). The magical number seven plus or minus two: Some limits on our capacity for processing information. *Psychological Review, 63*, 81–97.

Miller, G. A., Galanter, E., & Pribram, K. (1960). *Plans and the structure of behavior*. New York: Holt, Rinehart and Winston.

Miller, I. J. (1996). Time-limited brief therapy has gone too far: The result is invisible rationing. *Professional Psychology: Research & Practice, 27*, 567–576.

Miller, R. B. (1982). A call to armchairs. *Psychotherapy: Theory, Research, and Practice, 20*, 208–219.

Miller, R. B. (1992a, August). Nature and limits of clinical knowledge. In A. Mahrer (Chair), *How can the philosophy of science significantly advance clinical practice?* Symposium conducted at the 100th Annual Convention of the American Psychological Association, Washington, DC.

Miller, R. B. (Ed.) (1992b). *The restoration of dialogue: Readings in the philosophy of clinical psychology*. Washington, DC: American Psychological Association.

Miller, R. B. (1998). Epistemology and psychotherapy: The unspeakable, unbearable, horrible truth. *Clinical Psychology: Science and Practice, 5*, 242–250.

Miller, R. B. (1999, August). Doing justice to the case study method. In R. Miller (Chair), *Case study standards and the knowledge base of professional psychology*. Symposium conducted at the 107th Annual Convention of the American Psychological Association, Boston.

Miller, R. B. (2000). Epistemology of practice. In A. Kazdin (Ed), *The Encyclopedia of psychology* (Vol. 3, pp. 232–234).

Miller, R. B. (2001). Scientific vs. clinical-based knowledge in psychology: A concealed moral conflict. *American Journal of Psychotherapy, 55,* 344–356.

Miller, R. B. (in press). Suffering in psychology: The demoralization of psychotherapeutic practice. *Journal of Psychotherapy Integration.*

Minuchin, S. (1974). *Families and family therapy.* Cambridge, MA: Harvard University Press.

Mitroff, I. (1974). *The subjective side of science.* Amsterdam: Elsevier.

Moore, G. E. (1903). *Principia ethica.* Cambridge, England: Cambridge University Press.

Mosher, L., & Burti, L. (1994). *Community mental health: A practical guide.* New York: Norton. (Original work published 1988)

Moustakas, C. (1994). *Phenomenological research methods.* Thousand Oaks, CA: Sage

Murray, H. (1938). *Explorations in personality.* New York: Oxford University Press.

Myers, D. (1998). *Psychology* (5th ed.). New York: Worth.

Nisbett, R. E., & Ross, L. (1981). *Human inference: Strategies and shortcomings of social judgments.* Englewood Cliffs, NJ: Prentice Hall.

Nozick, R. (1981). *Philosophical explanations.* Cambridge, MA: Belknap Press.

Nussbaum, M. (1990). *Love's knowledge: Essays on philosophy and literature.* New York: Oxford University Press.

Nussbaum, M. (1994). *The therapy of desire: Theory and practice in Hellenistic ethics.* Princeton, NJ: Princeton University Press.

Nussbaum, M. (2001). *Upheavals of thought: The intelligence of emotions.* New York: Cambridge University Press.

O'Donohue, W. (1989). The (even) Bolder Model: The clinical psychologist as metaphysician–scientist–practitioner. *American Psychologist, 44,* 1460–1468.

Patterson, J., & Kim, P. (1991). *The day America told the truth.* New York: Prentice Hall.

Pedersen, P. B. (2001). The cultural context of peacemaking. In D. J. Christie, R. V. Wagner, & D. D. Winter (Eds.), *Peace conflict and violence: Peace psychology for the 21st century.* Upper Saddle, NJ: Prentice Hall.

Persons, J. B. (1995). Introduction: The lost art and science of case formulation. *In Session: Psychotherapy in Practice, 1,* 1–2.

Peterson, D. R. (1985). Twenty years of practitioner training in psychology. *American Psychologist, 40,* 441–451.

Peterson, D. R., & Peterson, R. L. (1997). Ways of knowing in a profession: Towards an epistemology for the education of professional psychologists. In D. R. Peterson (Ed.), *Educating professional psychologists: History and guiding conception* (pp. 191–228). Washington, DC: American Psychological Association.

Piaget, J. (1952). *The origins of intelligence in children* (M. Cook, Trans.). New York: International Universities Press.

Plato. (1941). *Plato's Republic*. (E. B. Jowett, Trans.). New York: Modern Library.

Polanyi, M. (1962). *Personal knowledge: Towards a post-critical philosophy*. Chicago: University of Chicago Press.

Polkinghorne, D. E. (1983). *Methodology for the human sciences*. Albany: State University of New York Press.

Polkinghorne, D. E. (1988). *Narrative knowing and the human sciences*. Albany: State University of New York Press.

Polkinghorne, D. E. (1999). Traditional research and psychotherapy practice. *The Journal of Clinical Psychology, 55*(2), 1425–1440.

Popper, K. (1959). *The logic of scientific discovery*. New York: Basic Books.

Pribram, K. (1986). The cognitive revolution and mind/brain issues. *American Psychologist, 41*, 507–520.

Prilleltensky, I. (1994). *The morals and politics of psychology: Psychological discourse and the status quo*. Albany: State University of New York Press.

Prochaska, J. O. (1995). An eclectic and integrative transtheoretical approach. In A. S. Gurman & S. B. Messer (Eds.), *Essential psychotherapies: Theories and practice* (pp. 403–440). New York: Guilford Press.

Putnam, H. (1978). *Meaning and the moral sciences*. London: Routledge & Kegan Paul.

Quine, W. O. (1980). *From a logical point of view: Logico–philosophical essays* (2nd ed., rev.). Cambridge, MA: Harvard University Press.

Rachels, J. (1993). *The elements of moral philosophy* (2nd ed.). New York: McGraw-Hill.

Raimy, V. (Ed.). (1950). *Training in clinical psychology*. New York: Prentice Hall.

Rawls, J. (1971). *A theory of justice*. Cambridge, MA: Harvard University Press.

Reik, T. (1948). *Listening with the third ear: The inner experience of a psychoanalyst*. New York: Grove Press.

Remnick, D. (1996). *King of the world*. New York: Vintage Books.

Richardson, F. C., Guignon, C. B., & Fowers, B. J. (1999). *Re-envisioning psychology: Moral dimensions of theory and practice*. San Francisco: Jossey-Bass.

Ricoeur, P. (1977). The question of proof in Freud's psychoanalytic writings. *Journal of the American Psychoanalytic Association, 25*, 835–871.

Robinson, D. (1989). *An intellectual history of psychology* (3rd ed.). Madison: University of Wisconsin Press.

Roe v. Wade. 410 U.S. 113 (1973).

Rogers, C. R. (1942). *Counseling and psychotherapy*. Boston: Houghton Mifflin.

Rogers, C. R. (1955). Persons or science: A philosophical question. *American Psychologist, 10*, 267–278.

Rogers, C. R. (1960). *On becoming a person*. Boston: Houghton Mifflin.

Rogers, C. R. (1985). Towards a more human science of the person. *Journal of Humanistic Psychology, 25*, 7–24.

Rorty, R. (1979). *Philosophy and the mirror of nature*. Princeton, NJ: Princeton University Press.

Runyan, W. M. (1982). *Life histories and psychobiography*. New York: Oxford University Press.

Russell, B. (1959). *Problems of philosophy*. New York: Oxford University Press.

Rychlak, J. F. (1968). *A philosophy of science for personality theory*. Boston: Houghton Mifflin.

Rychlak, J. F. (1969). Lockean vs. Kantian theoretical models and the cause of therapeutic change. *Psychotherapy Theory, Research and Practice, 6*, 214–222.

Rychlak, J. F. (1981). *Introduction to personality and psychotherapy*. Boston: Houghton Mifflin.

Rychlak, J. F. (1988). *The psychology of rigorous humanism* (2nd ed.). New York: New York University Press.

Rychlak, J. (1994). *Logical learning theory: A human teleology and its empirical support*. Lincoln: University of Nebraska Press.

Rychlak, J. F. (1997). *In defense of human consciousness*. Washington, DC: American Psychological Association.

Rychlak, J. F. (2002). *The human image in post-modern America*. Washington, DC: American Psychological Association.

Ryle, D. (1949). *Concept of mind*. London: Hutchinson.

Sabine, G. (1960). *A history of political theory* (3rd ed.). New York: Holt.

Sacks, O. (1987). *The man who mistook his wife for a hat*. New York: Harper Perennial.

Sadler, J. Z. (1997). Recognizing values: A descriptive-causal method for medical/scientific discourses. *Journal of Medicine and Philosophy, 22*, 541–565.

Sarason, S. B., Levine, M., Goldenberg, I. I., Cherline, D. L., & Bennett, E. M. (1966). *Psychology in community settings: Clinical, educational, vocational, and social aspects*. New York: Wiley.

Satir, V. (1972). *Peoplemaking*. Palo Alto, CA: Science and Behavior Books.

Scarry, E. (1985). *The body in pain*. New York: Oxford University Press.

Schneider, K. (1998). Toward a science of the heart: Romanticism and the revival of psychology. *American Psychologist, 53*, 277–289.

Schon, D. A. (1987). *Educating the reflective-practitioner*. San Francisco: Jossey-Bass.

Schon, D. A. (1992). The crisis of professional knowledge and the pursuit of an epistemology of practice. *Journal of Interprofessional Care, 6*, 49–63. (Original work published 1987)

Schultz, A. (1962). *Collected papers* (Vol. 1). The Hague, The Netherlands: Martinus Nijhoff.

Schutz, A. (1970). *On phenomenology and social relations*. Chicago: University of Chicago Press.

Searles, J. (2003). Contemporary philosophy in the United States. In N. Bunnan & E. P. Tsui-James (Eds.), *The Blackwell companion to philosophy* (pp. 2–22). Malden, MA: Blackwell.

Seyle, H. (1974). *Stress without distress*. New York: Harper & Row.

Shanteau, J. (1992). The psychology of experts: An alternative view. In G. Wright & F. Bolger (Eds.), *Expertise and decision support* (pp. 11–23). New York: Plenum.

Shapiro, D. (1966). *Neurotic styles*. New York: Basic Books.

Shapiro, M. B. (1966). The single case in clinical–psychological research. *Journal of General Psychology, 74*, 3–23.

Sherwood, M. (1969). Logic of explanation in psychoanalysis. New York: Academic Press.

Siegel, B. (1986). *Love, medicine, and miracles*. New York: Harper & Row.

Singer, S. I. (1988). The fear of reprisal and the failure of victims to report a personal crime. *Journal of Quantitative Criminology, 4*, 289–302.

Skinner, B. F. (1953). *Science and human behavior*. New York: Free Press.

Skinner, B. F. (1971). *Beyond freedom and dignity*. New York: Bantam/Vintage.

Slife, B. D. (2000). The practice of theoretical psychology. *Journal of Theoretical and Philosophical Psychology, 20*, 97–115.

Slife, B. D., & Williams, R. N. (1997). Toward a theoretical psychology: Should a subdiscipline be formally recognized? *American Psychologist, 52*, 117–129.

Soelle, D. (1975). *Suffering*. Philadelphia: Fortress.

Spence, D. P. (1992). *Narrative and historical truth: Meaning and interpretation in psychoanalysis*. New York: Norton.

Spence, D. P. (1993). Traditional case studies and prescriptions for improving them. In N. E. Wilson (Ed.), *Psychodynamic treatment research: A handbook for clinical practice* (pp. 37–52). New York: Basic Books.

Spitzer, R., Gibbon, M., Skodol, A. E., Williams, J. B., & First, M. B. (1994). *Learning companion to the DSM–IV casebook*. Washington, DC: American Psychiatric Press.

Stace, W. T. (1960). *Mysticism and philosophy*. Philadelphia: Lippincott.

Stein, P. (1973). The common law. In P. P. Weiner (Ed.), *Dictionary of the history of ideas* (Vol. 2, pp. 691–696). New York: Scribner's.

Sterba, J. P. (1989). Justifying morality: The right and the wrong ways. In J. P. Sterba (Ed.), *Contemporary ethics: Selected readings* (pp. 138–154). Englewood Cliffs, NJ: Prentice Hall.

Stevenson, C. L. (1944). *Ethics and language*. New Haven, CT: Yale University Press.

Strupp, H. H. (1980). Humanism and psychotherapy: A personal statement of the therapist's essential values. *Psychotherapy: Theory, Research and Practice, 17*, 396–400.

Strupp, H. H. (1981). Clinical research, clinical practice, and the crisis of confidence. *Journal of Consulting and Clinical Psychology, 49*, 216–219.

Strupp, H. H. (1989). The Vanderbilt Psychotherapy Research Project: Past, present, and future. In L. Simek-Downing (Ed.), *International psychotherapy: Theories, research, and cross-cultural implications* (pp. 191–209). New York: Praeger.

Suarez-Orozco, M. M. (1991). The heritage of enduring a "dirty war": Psychosocial aspects of terror in Argentina, 1976–1988. *Journal of Psychohistory, 18,* 469–505.

Sullivan, H. S. (1954). *The psychiatric interview.* New York: Norton.

Szasz, T. (1965). *The ethics of psychoanalysis: The theory and method of autonomous psychotherapy.* New York: Dell.

Szasz, T. (1974). *The myth of mental illness: Foundations for a theory of personal conduct* (Rev. ed.). New York: Harper & Row. (Original work published 1960)

Szasz, T. (1988). *Pain and pleasure (2nd expanded ed.).* Syracuse, NY: Syracuse University Press. (Original work published 1957)

Take a stand on Mideast. (2001, May 16). *Burlington Free Press,* p. A10.

Taylor, C. (1973). Peaceful co-existence in psychology. *Social Research, 40,* 55–82.

Tjeltveit, A. (1999). *Ethics and values in psychotherapy.* London: Routledge.

Toulmin, S. (1958). *The uses of argument.* Cambridge, England: Cambridge University Press.

Toulmin, S. (1963). *Foresight and understanding: An enquiry into the aims of science.* New York: Harper Torchbooks.

Toulmin, S. (1972). *Human understanding: The collective use and evolution of human concepts.* Princeton, NJ: Princeton University Press.

Toulmin, S. (1990). *Cosmopolis.* Chicago: University of Chicago Press.

Toulmin, S. (2000). *Return to reason.* Cambridge, MA: Harvard University Press.

Trierweiler, S. J., & Stricker, G. (1992). Research and evaluation competency: Training the local clinical scientist. In R. L Peterson, J. D. McHolland, R. J. Bent, E. Davis-Russell, G. E. Edward, E. Magidson, et al. (Eds.), *The core curriculum in professional psychology* (pp. 103–113). Washington, DC: American Psychological Association and the National Council of Schools of Professional Psychology.

Trierweiler, S. J., & Stricker, G. (1998). *The scientific practice of professional psychology.* New York: Plenum.

Tversky, A., & Kahneman, D. (1974). Judgment under uncertainty: Heuristic and biases. *Science, 185,* 1124–1131.

Urmson, J. (1956). *Philosophical analysis.* London: Oxford University Press.

Valenstein, E. (1998). *Blaming the brain.* New York: Free Press.

Wachtel, P. L. (1972). *Psychoanalysis and behavior therapy: Towards an integration.* New York: Basic Books.

Wann, K. T. (Ed.). (1960). *Behaviorism and phenomenology: Contrasting bases for modern psychology.* Chicago: University of Chicago Press.

Warnke, G. (1987). *Gadamer: Hermeneutics, tradition and reason.* Stanford, CA: Stanford University Press.

Watson, J. B. (1919). *Psychology from the standpoint of a behaviorist*. Philadelphia: Lippincott.

Watzlawick, P. (Ed.). (1984). *The invented reality: How do we know what we believe we know? Contributions to constructivism*. New York: Norton.

Wedding, D., & Corsini, R. J. (2001). *Case studies in psychotherapy*. Itasca, IL: F. E. Peacock.

Weil, S. (1951). *Waiting for God*. (E. Crawford, Trans., With an introduction by L. A. Fielder). New York: G. P. Putnam's Sons.

Welch, B. (1994). Managed care: The basic fault. *Psychoanalysis & Psychotherapy, 11,* 166–176.

Wetzel, L., & Ross, M. A. (1983). Psychological and social ramifications of battering: Observations leading to counseling methodology for victims of domestic abuse. *Personnel and Guidance Journal, 61,* 423–428.

Whitaker, C. A., & Bumberry, W. M. (1988). *Dancing with the family: A symbolic–experiential approach*. New York: Brunner/Mazel.

Whitaker, R. (2002). *Mad in America*. Cambridge, MA: Perseus.

White, R. (1964). *The study of lives*. New York: Atherton.

White, R. (1975). *Lives in progress* (3rd ed.). New York: Holt.

Wiggins, J. (1973). *Personality and prediction: Principles of personality assessment*. Reading, MA: Addison-Wesley

Witmer, L. (1996). Clinical psychology. *American Psychologist, 51,* 248–251. (Original work published 1907)

Wittgenstein, L. (1958). *Philosophical investigations*. New York: Macmillan.

Woolfolk, R. (1998). *The cure of souls: Science, values, and psychotherapy*. San Francisco: Jossey-Bass.

Woolfolk, R., & Richardson, F. (1984). Behavior therapy and the ideology of modernity. *American Psychologist, 39,* 777–786.

Yalom, I. (1981). *Existential psychotherapy*. New York: Basic Books.

Yalom, I. (1989). *Love's executioner*. New York: HarperCollins.

Yalom, I., & Elkins, G. (1977). *Every day gets a little closer: A twice told therapy*. New York: Basic Books.

Young-Eisendrath, P. (2000). *The resilient spirit: Transforming suffering into insight and renewal*. Reading, MA: Addison-Wesley Longman.

Young-Eisendrath, P., & Miramato, S. (2002). *Awakening and insight: Zen Buddhism and psychotherapy*. New York: Brunner-Routledge.

Zimbardo, P. G., Haney, C., Banks, W. C., & Jaffe, D. (1974). The psychology of imprisonment: Privation, power, and pathology. In Z. Rubin (Ed.), *Doing unto others: Explorations in social behavior* (pp. 61–73). Englewood Cliffs, NJ: Prentice-Hall.

AUTHOR INDEX

Adorno, T. W., 153
Allport, G., 171
Amato, J. A., 55, 56, 58
American Psychiatric Association, 26,
    27, 49, 88, 165, 200, 203, 257,
    259
American Psychological Association, 20,
    217, 218, 219
Ansbacher, H. L., 93, 109
Ansbacher, R. R., 93, 109
Argyris, C., 136, 189
Ashcroft, N., 172
Austin, J. L., 173

Baier, K., 85
Bakan, D., 25, 26, 58
Bandura, A., 194
Banks, W. C., 140
Barrett, W., 108
Bateson, G., 109
Bateson, M. C., 252
Belar, C. D., 10
Bennett, E. M., 4
Bennett, W. J., 96
Bent, R. J., 11
Berger, P. L., 154
Bergin, A., 95, 104
Bernstein, R., 176, 182
Bertalanffy, L. von, 109
Bhaskar, R., 119
Bourg, E. F., 11
Bowen, M., 109
Boyer, L. B., 225, 229, 230, 231, 232
Braun, V., 217, 219, 220, 221
Brazier, D., 55
Breggin, P., 41, 42, 45, 141, 142
Breuer, J., 44
Bridgman, P., 125
Bromley, D. B., *xii*, *xiv*, 36, 201, 202, 203,
    204, 208, 209, 210, 214, 223,
    224, 234, 235, 237, 257
Browne, K., 187
Bruner, J., 171
Buber, M., 35, 108
Bugental, J., 33, 172

Bumberry, W. M., 108, 109
Burti, L., 41

Cahan, E. D., 148, 152
Campbell, D. T., 200
Caplan, P., 19, 89
Care, N., 86
Chaplin, J. P., 147
Cherline, D. L., 4
Chesler, P., 19
Chessick, R., 94, 119, 225, 226, 227, 228,
    230, 232
Christie, D. J., 47
Churchill, S., 149, 155
Coady, C. A. J., 176, 177, 178, 208
Comer, R. J., 14, 15
Committee on Training in Clinical
    Psychology, 11, 18, 172, 173, 245
The Compact Oxford English Dictionary,
    28, 133
Concise Oxford English Dictionary, 191
Conze, E., 55
Corsini, R. J., 204, 287
Corwin, D. L., 220
Cowen, E. L., 170

Dahl, N., 90
Darrow, C. N., 150
Daubert v. Merrill Dow Pharmaceuticals,
    116
Davidson, D., 130, 177
de la Rey, C., 58
de Sousa, R., 86
Diamond, L., 97

Edelson, M., 204, 206
Edwards, D. J. A., 154, 204, 207, 210
Edwards, M. B., 205
Elliott, M., 187
Elliott, R., 153, 154, 192, 204, 208
Ellis, A., 108
Engel, G. L., 68
Epstein, M., 55

307

SUBJECT INDEX

quality standards, 202–203, 208–210
quasi-judicial approach, 208–210, 236–239
research link, 196
theoretical interpretation issue, 208–210
as true knowledge source, *xii–xii*
Casebooks, 279–285
Casuistry method, 35–36, 91
Categorical imperative, 97
Causality, 132–136
  assumption in science, 126
  and clinical knowledge, 34–35
  definition, 132–133
  prediction relationship, 132–136
  in psychology, critique, 132–136
Character traits, in morality systems, 81–82
Childhood disorders, case studies, 263–265
Childhood history, case study guidelines, 212
Christian theology, suffering in, 55–59
The Church, and science, history, 30–32
Civil law tradition, 236–237
The Claim, 224
Classic case studies, 287–290
Client-centered psychotherapy, 94
Clinical case conferences, 239–241
Clinical interview
  actuarial method comparison, 165–166
  common sense knowledge in, 172
Clinical intuition. *See* Intuition
Clinical knowledge, 159–197. *See also* Phronesis
  anecdotal data in, 176–179
  bias vulnerability, 152–153
  Carl Rogers' perspective, 161–162
  case study approach, 35–38
  concept of, 32–35
  confidentiality factor, 184–188
  development of, 189–192
  epistemology, 189–192
  everyday knowledge link, 170–173, 191–192
  illustrative examples, 183–188
  limits of, 192–194
  moral context, 241–242
  Paul Meehl's perspective, 163–166
  practical wisdom link, 160
  research link, 195–197
  scientific psychology boundary, 192–194

Clinical psychology, 9–22
  Boulder model influence, 10–12
  medical model influence on, 27
  moral dimension, 17–22
  scientific model disconnect, 9–17
Clinical reality
  moral dimension, 17–20, 186
  scientific training disconnect, 15–17
Clinicians, attitude toward researchers, 12–13
Coady, C. A. J., 176–178
Cognitive-behavioral theory
  DSM–IV Casebook vignette, 76
  implicit morality, 103, 105–106, 246
  moral neutrality claim, 67–68
  psychology textbook emphasis, 14
  suffering de-emphasis, 43
Coherence criterion
  case study method, 208–209, 216
  in testimony evaluation, 178
Cohesion criterion, case studies, 178, 208, 216
Collaborative research, 153–154
Common law tradition, 239
Common sense knowledge
  clinical knowledge relationship, 167–173, 191–192
  conceptual analysis, 174–176
  legitimacy, 170–173
Compulsive gambling, case formulation, 234–235
Confidentiality, 217–223
  case studies, 217–223
  and clinical knowledge, 184–186
  and dangerous data pervasiveness, 187–188
  illustrative case formulations, 226, 229–230, 233
  research participation versus case studies, 219
Constitutive means (Aristotle), 90
Control needs, prediction link, 135–136
Controlled studies, 205
Corporate-sponsored clinical psychology, 197
"Cosmetic psychopharmacology," 41–42
Cosmopolis (Toulmin), 30, 120
Countertransference, 107
Covering Law, 125
Creativity, and pain and suffering, 47–48
Critical realist perspective, 128, 141
Critical-theory approach, 153

Informal logic, 138
Informed consent, 218–223
  and case report publication,
      218–223
  illustrative case studies, 226,
      229–230, 233
  timing of request for, 219–221
Insight. See Clinical intuition
Intensive psychotherapy, case
      formulation, 225–229
Intentional realm, 129
Interdisciplinary teams, 213
Internal means (Aristotle), 90
Internal validity, 12
Internet, and confidentiality, 220, 223
Interpretation (psychotherapeutic), 67,
      212, 214–215
Intimacy, as moral value, 99
Introduction to psychology courses,
      6–7
Introduction to psychology textbooks,
      7, 13–15
Intuition
  versus actuarial prediction, 164–165
  in anecdotal data evaluation,
      178–179
  and clinical knowledge
      development, 33, 167–170
  and The Good definition, 99–100
  in humanistic therapies, 107–109
  in psychoanalytic approach, 107
  versus rational morality, 97–98

James, William, 17–18, 79–80
Jewish theology, 55–56, 58–59
Job's suffering, 58–59
Judeo-Christian theology
  and deontological moral systems, 82
  in implicit therapeutic values, 103
  suffering in, 55–57, 58–59
Judgmentalism prohibition, 20, 67
Judicial method, 236–237. See also
      Quasi-judicial method
Judiciousness concept, 242
Jung, Carl, 68, 93–94

Kant, Immanuel, 80, 82
Kleinman, Arthur, 26–27, 45
Knowledge by acquaintance, 179
Kramer, Peter, 41, 75

Laws of behavior, 123
Legal methodology, 236–237. See also
      Quasi-judicial method
Legislation, scientific basis, history,
      122–123
Liability issue, case reports, 218
Life history research
  Henry Murray's contribution, 154
  renewed interest in, 206
Local science, 166, 173, 192
Logic of argument, 223–225
Logical-learning theory, 80
Logical positivism
  disastrous effects of, 157
  history, 29–30
  moral relativism link, 84–85
Love, in contemporary morality, 99
Love thy neighbor as thyself maxim, 103

Mahrer, Alvin, 59–60
Malpractice. See Liability issue
Managed care, 40
Martyrdom, 56, 61
Masochism
  and Christianity, 56
  spiritual status aspect, 62
Materialism
  in contemporary morality, 98
  practical psychology distinction,
      149–151
  reductionism link, 142
Meaning
  human sciences approach, 153–154
  universal sense of, 63
Means and ends relationship
  in Aristotelian ethics, 89–91
  in psychotherapy, 103
Measurement, critique of, 136–137
Medical model
  in academic psychology, 7–8
  denial of suffering in, 46–47, 157
  DSM–IV Casebook vignette, 75
  implicit morality in, 104–105
    case illustration, 111–112
  moral neutrality claim, 67–68
  reductionism, 142
  and suffering, 27, 39–43
Medication use, implicit morality in,
      104–105, 111–112
Meditation, 68
Meehl, Paul, 163–166, 194

Religion. *See* Theology
The Renaissance
    humanism in, 31–32
    moral values in, 111
Repression (defense mechanism), 43–49
Research. *See* Science
Research participation, informed consent,
    219
Research *subjects*, 122, 139–140
Research training
    clinical practice confrontation, 15–17
    professional practitioners, history, 11–12
    psychology textbooks emphasis, 13–15
Researchers, attitudes toward clinicians,
    12–13
Rhetorical tradition, 33
Rogers, Carl, 94, 161–162, 154
Rules of argument, 138
Rychlak, J. F., 80

Sacrifice, religious context, 56, 61
Saint Michael's College case study
    collection, 257–278
Scarry, Elaine, 45–48
Schizophrenia, case studies, 202–203,
    273–274
Schon, D. A., 189–192
Science. *See also* Academic psychology
    academic psychology framework, 6–8
    Carl Rogers' perspective, 161–162
    clinical psychology disconnect, 9–10,
        192–194
        history, 11–15
    clinical psychology intersection,
        195–197
    clinical reality confrontation, 15–17
    critical assumptions, 126–127
        critique of, 127–143
    current meaning in psychology,
        147–151
    hegemony of, history, 28–32
    implicit morality in, 104–110
    magisterial view of, history, 119–125
    moral neutrality position, 24–25
    Paul Meehl's perspective, 162–166
    political order link, 120, 123–125,
        143–148
    popular psychology disconnect, 7–9
    versus practical wisdom, 89–92
    pragmatism link, 17–18
    received/mainstream view, 125–127

Scientific method, 101, 127, 137–140
Scientism
    in contemporary Western morality,
        100–102
    definition, 118–119
    origins, 101, 119–125
    as replacement for religion, 86
Secularization of morality, 86
Self-actualization, 108
Self-induced suffering, 62
Self-report
    illustrative case reports, 227
    quality of evidence in, 213–215
Sexual abuse, 187, 266–267
Sexual identity disorders, 274–277
Sexual love, 31–32
Shakow report, 172, 245
Shame, 65, 74
Short-term therapy, case report, 232–235
Sickness
    concept of, 26–27
    denial of suffering in, 45–46
Sin, suffering association, 56
Skinnerian psychology, 122, 135–136,
    145
Sleep disorders, case studies, 277
Social constructionism, 5
Social control, 151
    clinical psychology implicit morality,
        106–107
    mental health professions function,
        88–89
    and US Government influence,
        143–146
Social engineering, 123
Social isolation, and suffering, 57–58
Social justice, 197
Social practices, 117–118
Sociology, qualitative research, 154–155
Socratic Agolden mean," 82
Soelle, Dorothy, 56–58
Somatoform disorders, case studies,
    277–278
Soviet psychiatry, 145–146
Spiritual approaches, 68
SSRIs, 75, 111
State-sponsored clinical psychology, 197
Statistical evaluations, 100–101, 205
Structural violence, 47
Subjects in experiments, 122, 139–140
Substance-related disorders, case studies,
    278

Suffering, 39–69
    and biomedical model, 39–43
    definition, 25–28
    denial of, 43–49, 157
    and imagination, 47–48
    moral dimension, 23–25
    objectification problem, 47, 62
    theology, 55–57
    as totalizing experience, 58, 60
Sullivan, H. S., 185
Superego, 93
Support groups, 57
Survey research, superficiality, 87
Symptom approach
    DSM–IV approach, 27
    implicit morality in, 104–105
    in psychiatry, 42
    and suffering, 39–43
Symptom substitution argument, 112
Szasz, Thomas, 59

Tacit knowledge, 189
Team approach, in case studies, 213
Technology, hegemony of, 28–29
Technology of behavior, 122
Ten Commandments, 82–83
Testimony, 176–179. *See also* Anecdotal data
Textbooks in psychology, 7, 13–15
Theology
    and divine punishment, 62
    moral systems influence of, 82
    Newtonian theory parallels, 120–122
    topic of suffering in, 55–59
Theories-facts distinction, 126, 131–132
Theoretical knowledge, 92
Therapeutic relationship
    clinical knowledge factor in, 169–170, 184–186
    implicit morality in, 95
    moral dimension centrality, 64–65, 95
Thirty Years War, 30, 97, 120
Torture perpetrators, denial in, 45–47
Toulmin, Stephen, 29–31, 119–125
Training programs. *See* Education and training

Transference, 107
Treatment goals, case study guidelines, 211–213
Triangulation, 213
Truth in moral packaging rule, 113–114

Unconditional positive regard, 94, 108
Unconscious conflicts
    case report standards, 215
    therapeutic moral dialogue in, 67
Understanding
    versus causal explanations, 152
    in clinical knowledge, 33–34, 152
    concept of, 133–135
Universality principle, 126, 129–130
Unspeakable truths, 221
US Government, influence of, 143–148
Utilitarianism, 81–95
    advantages of, 83–84
    versus deontological moral systems, 82
    flaws, 83–84
    influence on psychology, 81–95
    moral relativism link, 84–85
    psychotherapeutic values influence, 95
    scientific morality influence of, 81–86

Validity standard, in case studies, 210
Value-free claim
    versus Aristotle's *phronesis*, 89–92
    challenges to, 71–73
    existential psychotherapy incompatibility, 61
    practice implications, 20–22, 49
    in scientific and clinical psychology, 49
    trends, 67–68

The Warrant, 224
Weltanschauung, 29
Witmer, Lightner, 72

Zimbardo prison study, 140

ABOUT THE AUTHOR

Ronald B. Miller, PhD, received his bachelor of arts degree from Oberlin College in 1970 and his doctorate in clinical psychology from the University of Vermont in 1976. He was a Woodrow Wilson Fellow in the Department of Moral Philosophy in 1970–1971 at the University of Saint Andrews, Scotland. Dr. Miller has been on the faculty of Saint Michael's College in Colchester, Vermont, since 1983 and is a professor of psychology there. Dr. Miller is also director of the master's program in clinical psychology at the college, a program that he helped found in 1983. He is the editor of *The Restoration of Dialogue: Readings in the Philosophy of Clinical Psychology* (American Psychological Association [APA], 1992) and served as both a consulting and associate editor for the *Encyclopedia of Psychology* (APA & Oxford University Press, 2000) with responsibility for the coverage of the history and philosophy of psychology. For this and related work, Dr. Miller was awarded in 2001 the Distinguished Service Award of the Division 24 (Theoretical and Philosophical Psychology) of the APA. Dr. Miller has maintained a private practice for over 25 years specializing in individual and couples therapy and school consultation. He is married to Naomi P. Shapiro, LCSW, who is a play therapist and a partner in the practice. They live in Shelburne, Vermont, with their two children, Ari and Maya Shapiro-Miller.